THREE NIGERIAN EMIRATES

THREE NIGERIAN EMIRATES

A STUDY IN ORAL HISTORY

Victor N. Low

Northwestern University Press
Evanston, Illinois 1972

LIBRARY OF CONGRESS CATALOG CARD NUMBER: 74–176163
ISBN 0–8101–0371–0
PRINTED IN THE UNITED STATES OF AMERICA

VICTOR N. LOW is Assistant Professor of History at Michigan State University and Visiting Lecturer at The Hebrew University of Jerusalem

To Helga

CONTENTS

Preface		xi
Notes on Terminology		xv
CHAPTER 1 INTRODUCTION: THE BORDER STATES		3
The Border States	3	
Physiography	4	
Ethnic Stratification	6	
Territorial Organization	9	
Emirate Administration	11	
Political Clientage	19	
Occupational Ranking	20	
PART I		
CHAPTER 2 STATE AND SOCIETY IN ISLAM		25
The Muslim State	25	
Jihad and Conquered Land	27	
Judicial/Religious Authority	31	
Slavery	33	
CHAPTER 3 THE USES OF ORAL TESTIMONY		39
Sources Used in this Study	39	
The Problem of Entree	40	
Field Methodology	42	
The Verification of Oral Census Data	46	

The Value of Oral Census Data 51
The Verification and Value of Other Oral Data 54

CHAPTER 4 THE NIGERIAN SUDAN TO 1800 59

Kanem-Bornu 59
The Hausa States and the Origins of the Sokoto Jihad 63
Shaikh Usuman dan Fodio 65
The Fulani of Northeast Nigeria until the Jihad 66
A Classification of Northeast Nigerian Fulani 73
Barebari of the Border States 75

PART II

CHAPTER 5 GOMBE: CA. 1800–41 81

Kwararafa States of the Gongola Basin 81
The Fulanin Kitaku of Southwest Bornu 86
Modibbo Buba Yero (?–ca. 1841) 90
Early Emirate Government in Gombe 98

CHAPTER 6 KATAGUM: CA. 1805–46 103

The Habe Kingdoms of Shira, Teshena, and Auyo 103
The Jihad in Bornu 107
Mallam Zaki: The Foundation of Katagum Emirate 114
Suleimanu, or Liman Adandaya (ca. 1814–16) 117
Al-Kanemi and the Border States 118
Dan Kauwa (1827–ca. 1846) 123
Central Government in Katagum under Dan Kauwa 126

CHAPTER 7 HADEJIA: CA. 1805–63 133

Sambo Digimsa (ca. 1805–48):
The Foundation of Hadejia Emirate 133
Buhari (ca. 1848–63) 136

PART III

CHAPTER 8 GOMBE: CA. 1841–1900 149

Gombe Emirate at the Death of Buba Yero 149
Suleimanu (ca. 1841–44) 152
Muhammadu Kwairanga (ca. 1844–82) 153
Demographic Change in Kwairanga's Reign 155
Central Administration under Kwairanga 157
Abdulkadir Zailani (ca. 1882–88) 159
Mallam Jibril 161
Hassan (ca. 1888–95) 164
The Sudanese Mahdiya and the Sokoto Caliphate 167
Mallam Hayatu bn. Sa'idu 170
Rabeh 171
Tukur (1895–98) 175
Umaru (1898–1922) 176

CHAPTER 9 KATAGUM: CA. 1846–1900 179

Abdurrahman (ca. 1846–51) 179
Kadr (ca. 1851–68) 182
Haji (ca. 1868–96) 185
Katagum-Misau Hostilities 190
Abdulkadir (1896–1905) 193
The Katagum Civil War 195

CHAPTER 10 HADEJIA: CA. 1863–1900 199

Hadejia at the Death of Buhari (ca. 1863) 199
Umaru II (ca. 1863–65) 200
Haru (ca. 1865–85) 203
Muhammadu (ca. 1885–1906) 207
Hadejia and the Kano Civil War 208
Central Government in Late-Nineteenth-Century Hadejia 211

APPENDIXES 215

I. Gombe Emirate: Major *'Yan Sarki* Appointments 217
II. Katagum Emirate: Major *'Yan Sarki* Appointments 218
III. Descendants of Ardo Abdua 219
IV. Gombe Abba ca. 1900 220
V. Katagum City ca. 1900 224
VI. Hadejia City ca. 1900 228

REFERENCES 233

Bibliography 235
Informants 249

INDEX 271

MAPS AND FIGURES

Gombe ca. 1800–1841 83
Katagum-Hadejia ca. 1800–1850 105
Gombe ca. 1841–1900 151
Katagum-Hadejia ca. 1850–1900 181
Gombe Abba ca. 1900 220
Katagum City ca. 1900 224
Hadejia City ca. 1900 228

Ethnic and Subethnic Groups ca. 1900 envelope
The Border States of Northeast Nigeria ca. 1900 envelope
Gombe ca. 1900 envelope
Katagum ca. 1900 envelope
Hadejia ca. 1900 envelope

PREFACE

The present work has been prepared with several kinds of reader in view: the Nigerian who seeks to learn something more of his precolonial background to nationhood; the specialist or apprentice in oral history, for whom another methodological perspective may prove useful; the Africanist concerned to broaden his knowledge of Sudanic polities; and the student of Islamic history and institutions.

The work is divided into three main sections of text, and a fourth of appendixes. An Introduction (Chapter 1) and Part I (Chapters 2–4) are prefatory, designed to provide essential points of reference on the natural, ethnic, social, administrative, political, and religious environment, as well as to adumbrate a few of the more evident themes encountered beyond. Thus Chapter 1 offers a short account of the area's physical setting; its multiethnic character; probable patterns of demographic change in the nineteenth century; and differences in sociopolitical status and religious affiliation associated with agnatic descent from one ethnic group or another. The basic authority structure of each emirate is then summarized, with due stress on the grant of landed estates and commercial privileges to titled officials at each level of government, on the four social groupings (or classes) engaged in civic affairs, and on the position of royals. Although variations among the several political systems are noted and briefly analyzed, an underlying similitude of administrative mode is apparent. A key societal institution, political clientage, is considered here, as well as the role of a man's chief occupation as a determinant of social placement.

Chapter 2 is concerned with Islamic doctrine as it seems to have guided the rulers of Gombe, Katagum, and Hadejia in their establishment and observance of legal norms for the conduct of public life (e.g., war, diplomacy, the ordering of justice) and also as it influenced the disposal of these polities' main source of wealth, annexed land and captured slaves or their descendants.

Chapter 3 considers at length what source material is available for a history of this genre; how documents of an oral nature have been gathered, weighed, and deployed; several of the more significant problems encountered while in the field; and a few potential avenues of future exploration by students of precolonial African societies. Much of the data assembled and mentioned has not been presented here, a fact which owes more to limitations of space than it does to the seeming irrelevance, imprecision, or doubtful reliableness of collateral lines of inquiry. The chapters that follow are intended to serve as a prelude to further publications, of greater depth and breadth, on particular features of these and neighboring polities, as well as a guide to some of the uses of oral documents of the kind employed in this book.

Chapter 4 surveys the major states and communities of the Nigerian savanna to 1800, or the eve of the Sokoto jihad, with special reference to Kanem-Bornu, Hausaland, and the nomadic Fulani of the northeast.

Part II (Chapters 5–7) consists largely of historical narratives which set forth and analyze the core political events and institutions of Gombe, Katagum, and Hadejia from their establishment as Fulani emirates after 1800 until the mid-century, when they had assumed a character that endured, with some elaboration though minor basic change, through 1900. Part III (Chapters 8–10) brings the historical narrative to ca. 1900, or the eve of British colonial rule. The chronicles, analyses, and commentaries have been grouped according to successive reign, partly because so high a measure of traditional and remembered history treats of throne-centered activity, partly because the oral archives normally date an occurrence by this expedient. The emirates are themselves grouped under separate chapter heads, but the frequency of cross-reference to shared historical episodes and to corresponding administrative forms again suggests an essential resemblance in political ethos amid superficial divergences in styles of government, foreign policy, devotion to Islamic precepts, and other central themes defined in Part I.

Appendixes I–VI present data on major appointments to office until 1900 and metropolitan ward, palace, and market divisions in that period, with explanatory notes. An end-pocket envelope contains a map for each emirate showing detailed ethnic, demographic, administrative, and other data ca. 1900, as well as a table of ethnic and subethnic proportions and a map of northeast Nigeria.

At least two kindred though separate questions may fairly be asked of such a book. Why is its focus predominantly on *political* events and institutions—still more, on administrative and military affairs at the state level? And what does it furnish historians of other African or Islamic areas?

In a time when surveys of the premodern African experience have begun to declare the manifold virtues of socioeconomic research, we might heed the balancing perception that "ever since Thucydides the writing of history, at least that writing which has vitality and significance, has tended to dwell largely on politics, and in particular on politics as it extended into war."[1] Although Chapter 3 urges and illustrates a number of means whereby our recovery of the more recent African past may be quickened, and its range expanded to embrace a much wider field of cultural and demographic evidence, if the paramount subject of an investigator is that geopolitical unit the state, his dominant concern will perforce be with politics, domestic and foreign. While ethnic, religious, trade, and ancillary desiderata may often light up the more latent features of a political action or process, they cannot illumine these fully without a clear view of the manifest.

An adequate response to the second of these dual queries might well depend on which other African or Islamic area is in question. A summary account and analysis of how Muslim Fulani dominion was won and sustained in this region may be of some value to scholars of other traditional polities, even where these were non-Muslim in their basic ideological design. Observers of Islamic statecraft will, it is hoped, remark useful comparative points of reference. When so little is known of so heterogeneous a part of the human landscape before 1900, an interpretative outline of what proceeded along this terrain in that period should further our comprehension of what has occurred within cognate fields, whether areal or thematic. And though students of more physically or institutionally remote historical zones may find little or nothing familiar to note here, they might wish to consider a new approach in the use of oral documents.

In a deeply authentic sense, this work has been a collaborative venture of its author and of the several hundred Nigerian citizens whose names are given at the end of this work. I must acknowledge not only their contribution, spacious and indispensable during 14 months of intensive field research, but also their kindness, patience, and encouragement, often in difficult circumstances. My gratitude is proportional.

To the emirs, councilors, and district heads of Gombe, Katagum, and Hadejia I owe an equal debt. Without their unfailing consideration for my daily and more special needs little would have been accomplished in the field. So too Mallams

1. M. I. Finley, *New York Review of Books*, March 23, 1967, p. 25.

Muhammadu Yuguda Gombe, Muhammad Bello Katagum, and Amar Muhammadu Hadejia were essential partners, as well as good friends.

Of others who gave generously of their time and knowledge, I would mention first Leonard M. Thompson of Yale University, always an incisive, thoughtful critic. Gustave E. von Grunebaum, Director of the Near Eastern Center, University of California at Los Angeles, guided me firmly across the shoals and riptides of introductory Islamic studies, making a rough passage buoyant. I have also been fortunate over the past decade in having access to the counsel and reflections of a number of West Africanist scholars, among them Abdullahi Smith, Murray Last, John Lavers, and Muhammad al-Hajj of Ahmadu Bello University; Jacob F. Ade Ajayi, Emmanuel Ayandele, Roland Adeleye, and Khalil Mahmoud of the University of Ibadan; John Hunwick of the University of Ghana; A. D. H. Bivar, Mervyn Hiskett, M. G. Smith, Phyllis Kaberry, and Edith Chilvers of the University of London; Thomas Hodgkin and Anthony H. M. Kirk-Greene of Oxford University; and John Paden and Ronald Cohen of Northwestern University. To each the present work, though none of its deficiencies, is due in some part.

The eighteen months of field and archival research, with an initial six months of composition, were made possible through an award from the Foreign Area Fellowship Program of the Social Science Research Council and American Council of Learned Societies under a grant by the Ford Foundation. The cost of preparing the maps and other illustrative material was met by Ralph H. Smuckler, Dean of International Studies and Programs at Michigan State University, and Alfred Opubor, Director of the African Studies Center, MSU. I am indeed grateful for their assistance.

Ann Paden of Northwestern University Press has been throughout a model of the concerned but patient editor. Sherman Hollander's cartographic work does both him and the Department of Geography, MSU, full credit.

Finally, this book has profited in ways both great and small from the companionship of seven persons, each endowed with rare gifts of sympathy and psychic grace: The Honorable Alhaji A. Dafua Gadau, Consul-General of the Federal Republic of Nigeria, New York City; Arthur and Josephine Pearse of West Bexington, Dorset; the late Mallam Salihu Atiku Kumo, whose tragically premature death by illness in his mid-twenties deprived the Nigerian community of scholars of an uncommonly auspicious member; Michael and Brigit Onwuejeogwu of the University of Ibadan; and above all my wife, to whom the book is fittingly dedicated.

NOTES ON TERMINOLOGY

In view of the linguistic diversity in these emirates and of the advantage of using a common nomenclature, all non-English terms, unless otherwise indicated, are given here in the most proximate Hausa form. Exceptions are shown thus: A. = Arabic; F. = Fulfulde (Fula, Fulani); K. = Kanuri; and B. = Bolewa.

Sarki, pl. *sarakuna*, is Hausa for "chief, man in charge" of something, whether a state, province, town, group of craftsmen, marketplace, or modern rest-house.

In Hausa, *-n* is the genitival suffix of masculine nouns; e.g., Sarkin Katagum, "(the) chief, man in charge of, Katagum," and Sarkin Pawa, "(the) chief, man in charge of, butchers." The feminine form is *-r*. The suffix *-awa* denotes "people of"; e.g., Auyakawa, "(the) people of Auyo."

In Hausa, *dan* ("son of") is put between one's given name(s) and the name(s) of one's father; e.g., Musa dan Ibrahim. The feminine form is *'yar* ("daughter of") and the plural, *'yan* ("children of").

The choice of an areal nomenclature to describe the savanna/sahilian regions of western Africa is always arbitrary. A useful distinction, one adopted here, is that made by J. S. Trimingham. He defines the Central Sudan as the zone between Songhay, on the middle Niger, and Wadai, east of Lake Chad; all the savanna/sahil west of Songhay to the Atlantic is termed the Western Sudan.

By "eastern emirates" we mean those of the Border States (Gombe, Katagum, Hadejia, Misau, Jema'are) together with Bauchi and Adamawa.

The names of the three main Border States are pronounced GAHM-bay, Kah-TAH-gum, and Hah-DAY-jah.

For textual citations footnoted as "Informants," see References, pp. 249–70.

THREE NIGERIAN EMIRATES

CHAPTER 1: INTRODUCTION

THE BORDER STATES

THE BORDER STATES

Between ca. 1805 and 1835 six Islamic polities emerged on the western edge of the Bornu Empire in north-central Africa. Each polity, or *emirate*, was founded and centrally governed by Fulani immigrants of pastoral nomadic background. In approximate order of territorial size, these new emirates were Gombe, Katagum, Hadejia, Misau, Jema'are, and Marma. During some 70–95 years, or until the British occupation of northern Nigeria in 1900–1903, the rulers of all but one acknowledged the political and religious primacy of the Fulani house of Shaikh Usuman dan Fodio, rendering him and his successor sultans of the Sokoto Caliphate periodic tribute, martial aid, and other, less tangible marks of fealty. The sultans for their part held certain unchallenged rights over these and all other constituent provinces of the empire centered on Sokoto, most significantly perhaps with regard to the appointment or dismissal of their provincial surrogates (*emirs*) and to the mediation of inter-emirate disputes. The emirs in turn were delegated entire authority over domestic political and religious affairs, selecting from their own followers men to staff high government office, whether civil, clerical, or military.

Throughout most of the nineteenth century this area—in particular Gombe, Katagum, and Hadejia—constituted that geopolitical unit referred to by Heinrich Barth as "The Border States." Forming a 200-mile deep, often contested eastern hinterland of the Sokoto Caliphate, these emirates divided the Kanuri Empire of Bornu from the remainder of the sultan's domain—from which they were separated as well by major historical and ethnic differences. Unlike the Hausa-Fulani emirates farther west (e.g., Kano, Zaria, Katsina), each of the main Border States arose in an almost wholly non-Muslim, non-Hausa cultural context; each was created by leaders of pastoral or semisedentary Fulani bands lately resident in Bornu, and each incorporated, through conquest or peaceful submission, several ancient kingdoms of which little beyond their antiquity is yet known to modern historians. Indeed, the genesis and growth of these precolonial Islamic polities have themselves gone unexamined thus far by students of West African history; their combined size (14,000 square miles), population (two to two-and-a-half million today), and ethnic diversity, as well as the common socio-political heritage of their founding groups, would suggest a notable lacuna in our knowledge of the Nigerian past.

The respective origins and development of Gombe, Katagum, and Hadejia reveal enough points of divergence—ethnic, administrative, demographic—to indicate that local more than external circumstance varied sharply with each. Although sharing a common ethos, in pursuit of a single, unifying ideal—the permanent holy war (A. *jihād*)—and confronted by cognate challenges to their survival, the Fulani governments of each evolved on often separate lines. For close to one hundred years each strove with mixed success to stabilize its heterogenous components, and by 1900 each had experienced a number of civil shocks and human relocations. If a general theme is discoverable in their collective history before the colonial era, it may lie in how the rulers of each went about the job of building a new state from the givens of a cultural mosaic, and why the maintenance of secure Islamic government proved so difficult to realize.

PHYSIOGRAPHY

Gombe, Katagum, and Hadejia emirates together constitute a cross section of the Sudan (northern) Savanna zone. Situated within 10° to 13° north and 9½° to 11½° east, the political boundaries of each have remained essentially unaltered since the imposition of British colonial rule in 1902–3. The Sudan Savanna, a broad expanse of terrain which extends from the Senegambia eastward as far as the Red Sea, has been defined as a "very distinct geographical region typified as much by its climate and vegetation as by its people and ways of life."[1]

1. R. W. J. Keay, *An Outline of Nigerian Vegetation* (Lagos: The Government Printer, 1959), p. 25.

The Nigerian Sudan is typified in turn by an annual rainfall of 30 to 44 inches concentrated in the main agricultural season of June through September, followed by eight dry months when crops (chiefly cereals, peanuts, and cotton) are harvested and resown; a variety of craft occupations are pursued; and cattle are moved southward to find better pasturage. Throughout the year both petty and long-distance trade are conducted as part- or full-time careers, and regular market days are observed in most of the more settled areas.

Vegetation patterns in Gombe, Katagum, and Hadejia exhibit many of the blendings and permutations typical as well of other orchard-bush lands of the Western and Central Sudan, ranging from "a light, closed canopy, with a sprinkling of under-shrubs and a sparse growth of grass" to "a more open growth of less height, more spreading and lower branched, with no canopy, and many stunted shrubs and a dense growth of grasses."[2] Annual rainfall, and thus luxuriance of vegetation, lessens with increasing latitude; southern Gombe shades off into the Guinea (southern) Savanna, while the far north of Hadejia lies on the verge of the Sahil.

In relief, the emirates are characterized by undulating plains broken at five major watercourses, numerous wood-fringed streams, and three upland ranges. Topographically, Gombe is separable on a line drawn to approximate the modern Bauchi–Gombe–Dadin Kowa motor road. Above this imaginary divide, a broad sandstone plateau rolls away to the north, toward the right bank of the Gongola River, where rising elevation alternates with shallow ravines. South of this line hilly outcrops, averaging 500 feet in height, increasingly predominate as the landscape merges with the foothills of the Tangale-Waja Highland. The most prominent natural feature of Gombe is the Gongola itself, which served in the nineteenth century as an effective political boundary with Bornu and Bauchi. Entering the emirate from Bauchi on the west, the river flows in a gentle arc northeasterly to a point just beyond Nafada, bends sharply southward until it reaches Dadin Kowa, and then continues with a single detour in the same general direction to its confluence with the Benue in Adamawa. A fertile belt of alluvial swamp, thick dark loam with clay infusions (*fadama*) four to fifteen miles wide, accompanies the Gongola on either bank as far south as Dadin Kowa, and was for some one hundred years the main locus of human residence in Gombe State. Elsewhere the prevailing soil-type is light and sandy (*jigawa*), often unsuited to intensive cultivation, but

2. H. V. Lely, *The Useful Trees of Northern Nigeria* (London: Crown Agents for the Colonies, 1925), ix.

in the center and the southwest quadrant of the emirate *fadama* is occasionally as common as *jigawa,* and here settlement occurred on a considerable scale.[3]

Katagum and Hadejia are similar to Gombe in their land-configuration and soil-formation patterns.[4] Three rivers, the Misau (Dingaya), the Katagum, and the latter's major tributary, the Jema'are, wind through Katagum from the southwest diagonally into Bornu, while the Hadejia River bisects that emirate in a like direction. As with the Gongola, the basin areas of these four watercourses have been the chief sites of *fadama* and thus of permanent habitation. And as in Gombe, large tracts of thinly peopled bush have existed wherever *jigawa* prevails, in central and northeast Katagum, for example, and in the far north and southeast of Hadejia. From July through October much of the land in each emirate is under flood, hence in areas drained by the several main rivers many towns and villages were situated on riverain bluffs or on hillocks.

ETHNIC STRATIFICATION

Although official Nigerian population figures have been of doubtful reliability,[5] the present-day total for all three emirates probably is on the order of two-and-a-half million persons, almost all of whom are native born. For several decades the lingua franca in most urban and many rural communities has been Hausa. In the nineteenth century, however, few Hausa-speakers are said to have resided in Gombe, while in Katagum and Hadejia the number of people using Hausa as a first or second language, though reportedly much higher, was still, it seems, far less than today.[6]

3. See J. D. Falconer, *The Geology and Geography of Northern Nigeria* (London: Macmillan, 1911), pp. 46–47; T. F. Carlyle, Appendix 1 to "Gombe Division Intelligence Report," in "Annual Report, Bauchi Province," NAK SNP 10/4 873 737p/1916; and A. M. Krzywon, "Agricultural Notebook for Gombe Emirate," mimeographed (Gombe, 1959), pp. 1–6.

4. See J. M. Smith, "Agricultural Notebook for Southern Katagum Division," mimeographed (Azare, 1960), pp. 1–3.

5. See S. A. Aluko, "How Many Nigerians? An Analysis of Nigeria's Census Problems, 1901–63," *The Journal of Modern African Studies,* III (1965), 371–92.

6. Informants IA: 1–6; IG: 1–2, 5–8; IIA: 1–5; IIB: 1, 3–6, 8–9; IIIA: 1–17. The 1952 Nigerian census gave no administrative district of Gombe as high as a 25 per

Ethnic differentiation in the Border States has historically been conditioned more by patrilineal than by linguistic or other cultural referents (although these may, and often do, overlap).[7] A man or woman is generally distinguished ethnically, by himself and his neighbors, according to the ethnic designation (*kabila,* pl. *kabilu*) of his father, who in turn is described in this way. Thus a man who speaks Hausa on most occasions, and whose mother was a Kanuri, is considered to be a Fulani if his father was of that *kabila.* Since *kabilu* are popularly assigned in so uniform a manner and since ethnic derivation has been an important determinant of social, political, and economic status in all these emirates, some knowledge of the ethnic composition of each before 1900 should further appreciably our understanding of their development as centralized Islamic kingdoms.

From the early decades of the nineteenth century there has existed a three-fold division of *kabilu*: persons have in the first instance been classified ethnically as either Habe, Fulani, or Barebari.[8] According to the best available evidence, of the free adult-male population in Gombe Emirate ca. 1900–10 about 33 per cent were Habe, 60 per cent Fulani, and 7 per cent Barebari. The respective figures for Katagum were 33, 38, and 29; and for Hadejia 37, 15, and 48. Thus while

cent Hausa component. It reported only four such districts (out of ten) in Katagum. And though a majority of respondents in Hadejia were listed as Hausa, it is evident that canvassers or the government subsumed all Auyakawa who speak Hausa today under the general head of this latter, convenient category. See R. Mansell Prothero, "African Ethnographic Maps, with a New Example from Northern Nigeria," *Africa,* XXXII, no. 1 (1962), 65.

7. For example, the Tera community of a major Bolewa town, Kafarati (in Gombe), while they adopted the Bolewa language after settling there in the mid-nineteenth century, remain identified, by themselves and others, as Tera. The term *ethnic group* is employed here in the current sense of "a social group which, within a larger cultural and social system, claims or is accorded a special status in terms of a complex of traits (*ethnic traits*) which it exhibits or is believed to exhibit. Such traits are diverse. . . . Prominent among them are those drawn from the religious and linguistic characteristics of the social group, the distinctive skin-pigmentation of its members, their national or geographical origins or those of their forebears" (Melvin M. Tumin, "Ethnic Group," in *A Dictionary of the Social Sciences,* ed. J. Gould and W. L. Kolb [Glencoe: The Free Press, 1964], p. 243). To varying degrees some or all of these criteria of ethnic differentiation have been found in the Border States, including shade of color and ancestral ties with outside political or geographic units, e.g., Bornu.

8. The correct singular forms of these in the Border States region are *Kado, Bafilace,* and *Barbarbare.* Kado has come generally to be employed far less than Habe in the singular, however. *Fulani* is often pronounced *Filani,* or replaced by its Kanuri (Bornu) cognate, *Fellata.* And *Barebari* is found written by most European authors in the transliterated form, *Beriberi.*

the proportion of free Habe men in this period is said to have been around one-third of the total for each emirate, the ratios of Fulani and Barebari appear to have differed markedly by emirate.[9]

Within these three basic ethnic groupings several subcategories, also referred to as *kabilu,* were found; examples include the Bolewa, Tera, and Auyakawa (Habe); Fulanin Shira, Fulanin Kitaku, and Fulanin Sambo (Fulani); and Kanuri, Mangawa, and Lerewa (Barebari).[10] And one major Fulani segment in Gombe contained its own (historically significant) *kabila* divisions. But it was by the primary ethnic unit to which a free man belonged that his position in emirate society at large was in good part decided. Of the three, that of Fulani has been at once the most prestigious and easily defined. Its members shared until the jihad a common language (Fulfulde, or Fula), history, and social customs and institutions.[11] With the Fulani conquest of the Border States region ca. 1805–35 an ever-increasing portion of northeast Nigerian Fulani exchanged their nomadic pastoralism for a village or town environment, although many have remained, at least in Katagum and Hadejia, transhumants. The newly settled, or Town, Fulani (*Fulanin Gida*—literally, "House Fulani") were and still are acknowledged by the generality of Habe and Barebari of this area to be of a higher ascriptive sociopolitical status and they have traditionally claimed—and been accorded—special deference in the conduct of public affairs.

A Barebari is definable as anyone, other than a Habe or Fulani, whose patriline can be identified with a *kabila* formerly resident in Bornu and whose forefather(s) came from there, either by choice or through enslavement. Barebari as a whole in these emirates have been ranked on the sociopolitical scale midway between the Fulani and Habe, seemingly by virtue of their putative conversion to Islam before the jihad.

Conventionally lowest in sociopolitical status are those *kabilu* known collectively as Habe. Often non-Muslim until (or even well after) the Fulani conquest, they were a prime object of exploitation during the 1800s by Fulani and Barebari slaveraiders. Because of the widespread practice of concubinage in the Border States (particularly by Town Fulani), continuous immigration of Fulani and

9. For an explanation of how these rough estimates have been arrived at, see pp. 48–49 below.

10. All major categories and their subdivisions of *kabilu* ca. 1900 are given by emirate on an end-pocket chart together with rough percentages of each per total emirate free adult male population in that period.

11. These are summarized below, pp. 66–72. The Fulani tongue is called *Fillanci* or *Fillatanci* in Hausa, *Fellata* or *Felatafelata* in Kanuri.

Barebari settlers, and the absence of any cultural onus or legal disability attaching to descent from a Habe mother, the relative numbers of Habe in each emirate probably have undergone a sharp decline over the past 150 years. All five of the major Habe groups—Bolewa, Tera, Shirawa, Teshenawa, and Auyakawa—appear to have lived in their present habitat for close to a millennium.[12]

TERRITORIAL ORGANIZATION

The precolonial systems of territorial organization in all three emirates were analogous to those described by Ronald Cohen for Bornu and M. G. Smith for the Hausa-Fulani emirates of northwest Nigeria in that period.[13] At the political

12. According to the classification of African languages devised by Professor Joseph Greenberg, the several ethnic groups referred to here and below are arranged linguistically as follows:

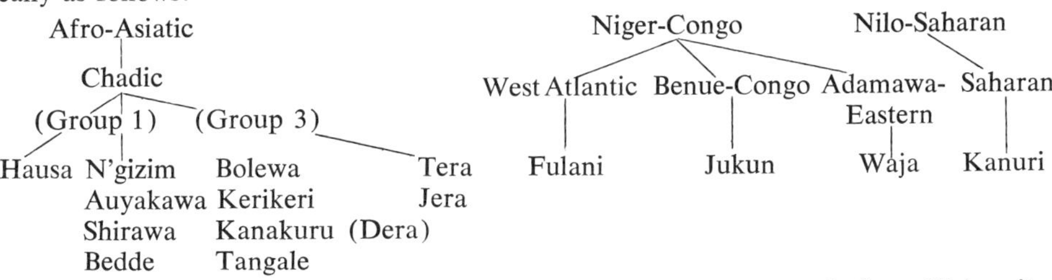

See Joseph H. Greenberg, *The Languages of Africa* (Bloomington: Indiana University Press, 1966), pp. 8–9, 46, 130. In this book I have attempted to heed "the risks in uncritically drawing historical inferences about common origin and migrations from present linguistic relationships." Paul Newman continues, "the weakness of linguistic classification for historical reconstruction stems from the fact that such classifications do not take into account language shifting [adoption by a group of another's language]. On the basis of linguistic evidence alone there is no way to distinguish relationships due to common ancestry from those resulting from an historically distinct population shifting its language." Newman instances the case of Kafarati (Gombe Emirate), partially composed of former Tera speakers who changed their language to that of the Bolewa after the latter founded the town ca. 1850 and absorbed the nearby Tera settlement of Kwamu ("Linguistic Relationship, Language Shifting, and Historical Inference," *Afrika und Übersee* LIII [1967], 221).

13. Ronald Cohen, *The Kanuri of Bornu* (New York: Holt, Rinehart and Winston, 1967), pp. 20–30, 92–108; "From Empire to Colony: Bornu in the Nineteenth and Twentieth Centuries," in *Profiles of Change: African Society and Colonial Rule,* ed. Victor Turner, *Colonialism in Africa, 1870–1960,* vol. 3 (Cambridge: At the University

and commercial apex of each was the royal capital—a new, strongly fortified walled city (*birni, gari*) founded in the earlier phase of the jihad on the banks of the largest river within the state. As lineages, clans, or clan groups moved into the metropolitan precincts they were given land by the emir on which to farm and build compounds. If the new settlers were of sufficient number, or if political exigencies so warranted, they were administered as a separate ward (*unguwa*) directly under a titled ward head (*mai-unguwa*), and the site received its own name (e.g., *Unguwar* ["ward of the"] *Rakumanani*).

From the time of its establishment, each capital contained a Friday mosque, open to urban and nearby rural congregants for the weekly joint service; a communal prayer ground used on the two annual Muslim festivals of *'Id al-fitr* and *'Id al-kabīr*; a mudbrick royal palace; and the emirate central market.[14] In time, and from political, as much as population, pressures, the city walls became extended, other but lesser mosques and market areas were added, and the number of compounds roofed with mud instead of thatch greatly increased as the ranks of titled officials, wealthy traders, and royal progeny were multiplied. Yet much of the ground enclosed by the outer city walls remained unoccupied; when the metropolitan area was threatened by war such vacant plots were used to accommodate villagers who sought refuge, and to raise crops until the danger abated. Although significant variations occurred in scale and pace of population growth at each nineteenth-century capital—Gombe Abba, Katagum, and Hadejia—the general pattern of urban development in all three was fairly constant.

Walled towns elsewhere in the emirates were similar in physical design, whether established after the onset of the jihad or at an earlier date. Each had a specially assigned compound for the local chief—often, like the emir, referred to by the Hausa title of *sarki* (pl. *sarakuna*) or by an equivalent ethno-linguistic variant.[15]

Press, 1971), pp. 81–93; and M. G. Smith, "The Hausa of Northern Nigeria," in *Peoples of Africa*, ed. James L. Gibbs (New York: Holt, Rinehart and Winston, 1965), pp. 129–32; "Hausa Inheritance and Succession," in *Studies in the Laws of Succession in Nigeria*, ed. J. D. M. Derrett (London: Oxford University Press, 1965), pp. 233–34; and *The Economy of Hausa Communities of Zaria* (London: H.M.S.O., 1955), pp. 4–5. The account that follows is based on data supplied by a wide variety of informants in Gombe, Katagum, and Hadejia emirates.

14. See maps of Gombe Abba, Katagum, and Hadejia ca. 1900, appendixes IV–VI.

15. The most common title of a Fulani townhead in the late 1800s was *lamido*, or *lamda* (pl. *lamibe*); it is still widely used in the Border States. Less common but often found was (and is) the title of *ardo* (pl. *ardo'en*). Since among settled Fulani the official designation of lamido was highly prized on grounds of prestige, an ardo might prevail on his emir—with the aid of gifts—to confer upon him the title of

Many during the 1800s acquired Friday mosques, communal prayer grounds, and markets of their own. Unwalled towns of comparable or somewhat lesser magnitude might also have these traditional attributes of urban Muslim culture, even when situated near a walled town which had them as well.[16] A town was often (like the capital) administratively divided by wards, and it always had one or several ancillary villages and hamlets (*kauyuka,* sing. *kauye*) in the immediate neighborhood (and sometimes as far distant as 15–20 miles). The resident administrator of a village normally was appointed by and responsible to the sarki of the parent town.[17] As in Hausaland and Bornu, the local community—now designated a Village Area—consisted of a walled or unwalled town with its satellite hamlets and was held as an estate by one or another of the higher emirate officials. Just as the local community usually was comprised of several different *kabilu,* so too its political center often had a multiethnic character, as did (less often) certain outlying settlements.[18] The border of such an ensemble frequently was marked by some topographical feature, for example, a stream, line of trees, rock pile, or rising ground.

EMIRATE ADMINISTRATION

Integrally associated with the territorial organization outlined above were those systems of local, provincial, and central government which developed in

lamido. The many Bolewa townheads in Gombe were called by the Bolewa title of *moi,* an apparent variant on the Kanuri *mai,* leader (or possibly on the Hausa *mai,* owner of).

16. Such towns frequently were fortified by a stockade (*kafi*), built of branches four to six feet in length set close together in the ground and without ligatures or sharpened tops. A *kafi* had several entrances, each formed by two short plump sticks forked to hold a chest-high crosspiece laid over them at night. A ditch, eight to ten feet deep, surrounded the stockade on its outer side.

17. In Hausa, the headmen of *kauyuka* are called *dagatai* (sing. *dagaci*). This term, of Kanuri provenance, was rarely used in precolonial Gombe and Katagum and infrequently in Hadejia. Rather, a Fulani *kauye* was governed directly by a *jauro* (pl. *jaurube*) or *ardo,* a Barebari by a *bulama,* and a Habe by an official whose title varied with the *kabila* of its people. The Fulani referred to all Habe villageheads as *ardidai* (sing. *ardido*).

18. See maps of Gombe, Katagum, and Hadejia emirates ca. 1900 in end-pocket envelope.

Gombe, Katagum, and Hadejia over the last century. Again, the systems prevailing there by 1900 were essentially cognate with Hausa and Kanuri behavior, as summarized by Smith and by Ronald Cohen.

> Traditional and modern government proceeds through a system of titled offices (*sarautu*, singular, *sarauta*), each of which is in theory a unique indissoluble legal corporation having definite rights, powers and duties, special relations to the throne and to other offices, special lands, farms, compounds, and formerly, slaves.[19]
>
> The full range of Hausa governmental functions are articulated through *sarautu*.[20]
>
> All titled officials, or even untitled royal followers, could be given fiefs or rights of revenue collection for their own support in one or more settlements spread throughout the state. The rights to revenue collection were granted by the Shehu, nominal owner of all land within the political boundaries of Bornu, in return for services rendered to the throne.[21]

The centrality and omnipresence of this web of titled offices in the operations of precolonial government will be evidenced in several chapters that follow. Here we may indicate briefly how the system was organized and how it functioned within the much fuller matrix of sociopolitical relations.

While ultimate sovereignty in the caliphate over all lands and their administration lay with the sultan, Shaikh Usuman's deputation of local authority in the provincial seats was respected by later sultans, so long as the emirs and their successors continued periodically to furnish Sokoto with martial aid and a share of state revenue and attended on the sultan whenever summoned.[22] Failure to meet one or another of these conditions normally was adjudged an act of grave disobedience and adequate grounds for deposition of the offending emir.[23] If in good health and free of serious threat of invasion from unbelievers, an emir was also expected to appear, after the autumn harvest, at a conference of all the

19. Smith, "Hausa of Northern Nigeria," p. 132.

20. M. G. Smith, "Field Histories among the Hausa," *Journal of African History*, II (1961), 90.

21. Cohen, "From Empire to Colony," p. 188.

22. Denis Murray Last, *The Sokoto Caliphate* (London: Longmans, 1967), *passim*.

23. For instances of this imperial recourse in the Border States, see pp. 153, 191, and 196 below.

emirs held annually in the Sokoto area, accompanied by his own chief warrior-administrators. It was on this occasion that he brought the required gifts and took part, with his entourage, in whatever campaigns the sultan had projected that year. Such imperial assemblies provided the emirs a chance for renewal in person of their religious/political vows of homage (*chaffa*) to the sultan, who then conferred on them a much-coveted blessing in his capacity as imam and Commander of the Faithful.[24]

During the remainder of the year each emir continued, through correspondence and emissaries, in close touch with Sokoto. The vizier (waziri) of the sultan had general supervisory authority over the Border States and was his lord's vehicle of communication with them. He might tour the administrative centers every three or four years (and a severe political upheaval could bring him at once), but his main roles were those of advising the emirs and of mediation when disputes broke out among them, especially in the realm of boundary adjustment. The appointment of a new emir was announced or confirmed, and the installation conducted, either by the waziri or his own titled representative to the emirate. The latter was on call to help resolve intra-emirate disputes among high state officials.[25]

Military, fiscal, and ceremonial relations between the sultan and his provincial deputies were to a striking degree replicated at successive levels of government within the Border States. Each titled office below the emirship was delegated a broad measure of local autonomy by its immediate overlord (*uban daki*). Retention of this authority by a given official presupposed that he supply the emir (directly or through his *uban daki*) with troops and matériel levied from those men, of titled position, who served him, in turn, as clients or slaves; that he act as a conduit for the conveyance of tax receipts from his subordinates to his superior, without keeping more than an alloted amount; and that he respond

24. Informants IA: 1–6; IG: 1–8; IIA: 1–5; IIB: 1–9; IIIA: 1–17. Beginning in the reign of Sultan Umaru dan Ali (1881–91), these visits by the eastern emirs were reduced to bi- or triennial events, but the emirs then sent additional gifts each year to Sokoto (*ibid.*; and Last, *The Sokoto Caliphate,* p. 124). Such presents were dispatched as well on the grand Muslim festivals of *'Id al-fitr* and *'Id al-kabīr.*

25. *Ibid.*, pp. 201–4. For examples of the waziri's role in resolving Border States political crises and conflict, see below, pp. 136, 139–42, 185, 192, 194, and 196. Nineteenth-century political relations between the Sokoto establishment and the caliphate's provincial *sarakuna* are well summarized in Roland A. Adeleye, *Power and Diplomacy in Northern Nigeria 1804–1906* (London: Longman Group, 1971), pp. 37–38, 40, 45–51.

whenever called to join the *uban daki* as well as render him *chaffa* at regular intervals.[26]

These obligations of an official to his *uban daki* were, in a sense, the logical outgrowth of certain imperatives dictated by canon law, in particular the divine charge on Islamic rulers to preserve the Community of Believers from all menace to its continued observance of Muslim practice and to wage Holy War against unbelievers. In the geopolitical ambit of northeast Nigeria until 1900 a proper response to this injunction implied the establishment and successful maintenance of a garrison state, able to marshal both men and supplies on short notice. Hence the premium conferred on those qualities of valor and skill at arms which figured so largely in appointments to titled office that were chiefly administrative; and hence too the need for reliable sources of revenue, used in good part by the emirs and other officials to purchase horses, weapons, and military stores.

Unlike Zaria (Zazzau), none of the Border States employed descriptive words to distinguish the several gradations of emirate officialdom.[27] But four separate administrative rank orders were found, and these were based on five clearly definable orders of social status or rank (*daraja*) in local society. The body politic was divided firstly between men of free (*da*, pl. *'ya'ya*) and men of slave (*bawa*, pl. *bayi*) parentage. Freemen were in turn classified under one or another of four distinct social-class rubrics: 1) those of royal blood (*dengin sarki*), of whom princes (*'yan sarki*, sing. *dan sarki*) were the most honored;[28] 2) servants or clients (*barori*, sing. *bara*); 3) Muslim clerics or teachers (*mallamai*, sing. *mallam*); and 4) commoners (*talakawa,* sing. *talaka*), that is, free men who lacked a patron and had no office or religious calling.[29] It was possible for a man to ascend from one *daraja* to a higher one, either (for a slave) by manumission or some other means of enfranchisement, or through an agreement between a commoner and a noncommoner to enter upon a client-patron relationship (thus raising the commoner to the condition of a client), or by training (of a *talaka* or *bara*) as a cleric (*mallam*). We shall see however that several additional determinants of social placement were present.

26. For a much fuller discussion of the *uban daki,* or patron, in the precolonial political systems of these emirates, see below, pp. 128–30, 158–59, and 212–13.

27. For the nomenclature used at Zaria, see p. 131, n. 91 below. Other differentia of official rank were present as well in each emirate.

28. All kin of *sarakuna,* at whatever administrative level, were (and are) referred to as *dengin sarki,* and the sons of *sarakuna* as *'yan sarki*. In the present context and hereafter we are concerned only with royal *dengin sarki,* especially princes.

29. A *talaka* in Hadejia Emirate is, for example, also called *maizaman kansa* (one who lives on his own).

As the early emirs introduced and refined their organs of central government, possession of higher state office came to devolve upon members of four of these five primary social aggregates, namely royals, clients, clerics, and slaves.[30] Commoners, who constituted far the most numerous free community in each Border State, were denied direct access to all such offices, although a few were appointed in the second half of the century to newly created occupational titles. But since a commoner could gain clerical or client status he might thereby qualify to compete for those titled offices that had greater political rewards and significance.

Any free titleholder not of royal or clerical status was considered a client of the man who appointed him. If his title had been conferred by the emir it is probable that he was counted among the highest state officers, the *manya-sarakuna,* a group which also included the leading throne-appointed titleholders of other social orders. Succession to office, and especially to free titles, was often hereditary, passing down a single lineage or confined to a certain lineage group (that is, to a brother, uncle, nephew, or cousin of the erstwhile official). The incidence of highest offices (*manya-sarautu*) being reserved for particular descent groups varied by emirate (and within each emirate by reign), as did the proportion of such offices traditionally awarded each of the four social aggregates eligible to fill titled positions. Thus at Gombe Abba in the late 1800s, of the thirteen *manya-sarautu* of central emirate government, all but two were hereditary, while four had always been occupied by royals, five by clients (here, Fulani clan chieftains), one by clerics, and three by slaves. At Katagum, of the eight precolonial *manya-sarautu,* seven were always, and the eighth became, hereditary, while the respective figures by social group were zero, six, one, and one. But at Hadejia, of twelve such offices, only two were always, and two more became, hereditary; one was held by royals, two by clients, one by clerics, and eight by slaves. These variations in the allocation of high office reflected and expressed related differences in the historical development of each emirate; their significance emerges when they are viewed with reference to major political events, in particular those associated with the founding of these states and with the several constitutional crises which followed.

In Gombe and Katagum, it is useful to speak of provincial government as

30. Although eunuchs filled a number of titled offices in Hausaland, they had no political role in these emirates. Imported as children in small numbers from Bornu and Damagaram, eunuchs were found only at court, as messengers and attendants of royal wives and concubines. They served a similar function in Bornu, especially in the nineteenth century (see Ronald Cohen, "Slavery among the Kanuri," *Trans-action,* IV [January–February, 1967], 49).

contrasted with both central and local government before 1900, since (unlike Hadejia) most land outside the capital environs was divided into fairly compact estates, or fief areas, each having either—as in Katagum—its own provincial capital where the fiefholder (*hakimi,* pl. *hakimai*) lived, or—as in Gombe—a like arrangement *and* a complementary system of absentee ownership, the fiefholder residing at Gombe Abba.[31] (In Hadejia, as in Zaria, estates held by a given official were generally more scattered about the emirate, and the fiefholder lived at the emirate capital.)[32] Katagum was peculiar not only in the fact that all major enfeoffed officials were stationed on their fief land, but also in that most of them were *'yan sarki*—princes of the realm—and thus had prospects (however variable) of inheriting the crown.[33]

The system of titled offices which obtained for central government in the Border States was found also at provincial and community levels of administration, alike in form and process. The chief of a town appointed his own subordinate officials, who lived near his compound, as well as the chiefs or headmen of villages under him. The latter in turn were assisted by an official staff of their

31. The undefined use by historians of Africa of such terms as *fief* and *estate, owner* and *landlord,* is beset with semantic snares and should, in the interest of clarity, be eschewed. Yet historians are, like all students of human life, compelled to draw on a common (and often limited) fund of locutions available from their own language—even if these can be misleading when found outside the context they were devised for.

By *fief* and *estate* we mean land and its inhabitants in the Sokoto Caliphate over which an official (the sultan, an emir, or a subject of the emir) assigned general administrative duties to one of his titled agents, whose recompense was derived chiefly in the form of gifts, *corvée* labor, and a share of the proceeds from taxes or tribute received from the people he governed (either directly, or through his own titled subordinate). A *fiefholder* was, accordingly, an official at whatever stratum of emirate government authorized in this manner to administer a fief.

32. For Zaria in the nineteenth century, see M. G. Smith, *Government in Zazzau, 1800–1950* (London: Oxford University Press, 1960), Map B facing p. 84. For precolonial Bornu, see Ronald Cohen, "Social Stratification in Bornu," *Social Stratification in Africa,* ed. Arthur Tuden and Leonard Plotnicov (New York: The Free Press, 1970), p. 232. For the placement of particular fief areas in Gombe and Katagum, see maps of these emirates ca. 1900 in end-pocket envelope.

33. *Crown* and *throne* are terms which, it may be argued, are inapplicable to the Border States. They are admitted here for reasons of convenience, and their presence can be justified on grounds that an emir's regalia included a special (white) turban (*rawani*), the placing of which on his head by the sultan's representative was an essential and solemn feature of his investiture, while he always gave audience seated on a mud platform, or dais (*gadon sarki*). In Hausa, *rawani* is also used metaphorically to mean "titled office"; e.g., *Sarki ya kwace rawaninsu* ("the chief dismissed him from office"—literally, "the chief took away his turban").

own choosing. So too each of the highest officials at all three basic levels of territorial administration, and many lesser officeholders, had a number of titled staff. There existed in short a clearly defined hierarchical edifice, built of successively articulated clientage relations between men of government rank, with all free officials (but the meanest and the emir) at once patrons and clients, and hence a chain of command along which orders, requests, and intelligence could move in culturally familiar ways. Cementing the layers of this pyramid were messengers (*jekadu,* sing. *jekada*), themselves either clients or slaves and often bearing a title, who lived much of the year in the settlements they were assigned to as agents of their superior. The local position of a *jekada* had evolved by 1900 into one of great influence and was liable to numerous forms of abuse. He "was supposed to be paid by the fiefholders, but he also lived on the people, and his extortions proved the ruin of the country. His power was unlimited for he alone had the ear of the Chief, and all taxes passed through his hands."[34]

At the summit was the emir, himself a client of the sultan of Sokoto, who appointed him. Subject, like every titled official in the emirate, to dismissal at the pleasure of his immediate superior and patron, the manner of his selection was exceptional only in that it involved the deliberations of a nominating council, made up of certain of the highest state officeholders, both slave and free, and titled clerics (but never royals), which referred the names of one or several candidates to Sokoto. Competition for the crown, as for other offices, was often keen and prolonged. In some of the Hausa-Fulani states more than one dynastic patrilineage took part,[35] but in Katagum succession rivalries were confined to agnates of two royal houses linked by descent from a common ancester, while in Gombe and Hadejia they engaged the princes of a single house. To help insure political stability in Katagum its nominating council appears to have favored the principle of rotation in office of leading representatives of both lineage segments, but, as at Gombe Abba and Hadejia, other criteria usually received equal or greater weight; these included the relative size of a candidate's entourage, his political and administrative experience, martial prowess, and demonstrated commitment to Islamic precepts.[36]

34. F. D. Lugard, quoted in C. K. Meek, *Land Tenure and Land Administration in Nigeria and the Cameroons* (London: H.M.S.O., 1957), p. 160. See pp. 129 and 212–13 for a fuller consideration of the role of *jekadu.*

35. Smith, "The Hausa of Northern Nigeria," p. 133.

36. Such yardsticks were applied as well to other candidates for titled office. The last-mentioned, religious commitment, has been reported from Bornu: "Informants often told me that whether or not a man was a good Muslim, or whether he could

Wherever an office was hereditary, the contest which ensued between aspirants to it upon, if not before, the death, retirement, or deposition of the incumbent sharply divided kin against kin. At installation, the new official appointed his close relations, clients, and favorite slaves to those titled offices within his control which by custom were nonheritable. A man's popularity among the body politic was on the whole a function of the size of his following, which depended in turn on those qualities (apart from lineage ties) that made for effectual leadership in these societies, qualities that are seen best in the requisite attributes of a candidate for the throne. It is thus apparent that a medley of political and personal characteristics of those eligible to fill a particular vacancy figured in the decision on whom to appoint. The official responsible for making a given appointment had to evaluate each of these qualities, advised by his councilors and often by his superior. In the case of royal titles, a further, normally decisive, criterion was the kinship relation of aspirants to men disposing of such positions: the latter strongly inclined to prefer their own sons over brothers, uncles, or nephews, and their full brothers over those born of different mothers. The importance to Border State history of this habitual preference was greatest, of course, as it affected appointments to royal positions, and its influence will appear often in passages below, most readily with regard to nineteenth-century Katagum.

The number, titles, delegated functions and authority, and financial rewards of political office varied by emirate and within each emirate by geographic and rank placement. Of the thousands of titled positions that would have existed before 1900,[37] many carried names drawn from Kanuri and Hausa nomenclature; for example, *galadima, chiroma,* or *madaki.* (A subordinate official in one vertical section of government could be known, for example, as *Galadiman Madakin Gombe,* and countless variations on this pattern were found.) The work of an officeholder was not always implicit in his title, unless he was the head of a town or village or had specialized duties of an essentially military, religious, or occupational kind. Most of the highest officials in each emirate combined administrative with conciliar and military functions, and all had estates attached to their offices

---

be considered a better Muslim than the rivals with whom he was competing for a political position, was an important criterion in the selection for succession to office" (Ronald Cohen, "Power, Authority and Personal Success in Islam and Bornu," in *Political Anthropology,* ed. Marc Schwartz, Arthur Tuden, and Victor Turner [Chicago: Aldine Publishing Company, 1966], p. 130).

37. At least 2,500 name-bearing settlements (including wards of larger units) have been identified in these emirates by present-day informants as having five or more free adult males ca. 1900–10.

which descended to successive occupants (as, on a lower scale, did lesser officials at court and in local government). Through titled staff, in particular the *jekadu,* they assessed and collected taxes, requisitioned labor and supplies as needed, and levied troops, all in their fief areas. The emoluments of office lay chiefly in the shares of tax and other revenue retained by them when these were channeled upward to the throne, in the spoil of successful campaigns, and in gifts provided by those men who sought their favor or continued loyalty.

POLITICAL CLIENTAGE

As in Hausaland and Bornu, several institutions of clientage informed a wide range of social and political behavior in the Border States area.[38] Each of these had in common a status-inequality between client and patron; the premise of a voluntary, dissoluble consociation entered upon to the mutual benefit of the contracting parties; and certain enjoined obligations incumbent on each for the period of this connection.[39] Political clientage always involved a titled official as patron, and either a dependent official or an untitled servant as client. The first of these client types offered his patron political support (together with that of his own titled and untitled clients); he received back the protection and mediating

38. For the Hausa-Fulani emirates, see M. G. Smith, Introduction to Mary Smith, *Baba of Karo: A Woman of the Muslim Hausa* (London: Faber & Faber, 1954), pp. 31–33; for Bornu, Cohen, "Social Stratification," p. 247. This paragraph is based on replies of a wide range of informants in the old and new emirate capitals to a checklist of questions drawn from M. G. Smith's published work on political clientage in Hausaland.

39. Although we are concerned here only with clientage in its political aspect, three other types of clientage relation were and are prevalent as well: domestic, commercial, and female. M. G. Smith defines domestic clientage as a form of "substitute kinship," that is, "an association in which men not originally linked by ties of consanguinity of affinity adopt the relative statuses and roles of senior and junior kinsmen" (Introduction to Mary Smith, *Baba of Karo,* pp. 32–33). The commercial variety engages as patron and client a wealthy trader and his agent, and also a trader and the official with jurisdiction over his commercial activity. Female clientage occurs between women of dissimilar age or generation and of different kin groups, the older woman (patroness) having one or several such clients at the same period. A nonclientage but common and related institution is that of bond-friendship, whereby two men or two women of similar age but separate kin groups share "gifts, secrets, advice and labour" (Smith, "The Hausa of Northern Nigeria," pp. 134–35, 149–50).

service of his superior, as well as such gifts as a horse, weapons, and garments appropriate to his office. The second type included untitled messengers and compound servants or courtiers who might also work on their patron's farm. In exchange for general sustenance (clothes, food, lodgings, a small farm plot), provision of bridewealth on marriage, and security of person, the untitled client performed a number of menial tasks. This clientage relation tended strongly to be perpetuated through several generations of servant and master, as did that kind between occupants of two vertically juxtaposed offices (thus enhancing the hereditary nature of titled offices). We have said that it was to an official's advantage to acquire more followers than his rivals had when competing for higher rank, and it is obvious that a man who sought to maintain or advance his position in life would seek out the patron most able to aid him in this endeavor. Just as the system of political clientage worked symbiotically to sustain and improve the lot of those who participated on either side, so its pervasive, enduring presence in the conduct of emirate affairs can be viewed as eloquent evidence that it worked well.

OCCUPATIONAL RANKING

Social placement of individual male adults in the Border States was affected by several, often overlapping elements, of which the divisions into royals/clients/commoners/slaves, and Fulani/Barebari/Habe, already have been reviewed. Another, based on religious differences, is considered below. A fourth element, of comparable significance to the sociopolitical structure and processes of each Border State, was that of occupational ranking. As in most precolonial Sudanic polities, agriculture was here the universally essential productive activity, but all adults had other gainful occupations as well; for example, they worked as craftsmen and traders or served as clerics and officeholders. Many occupations were hereditary, and these as a rule had more prestige (*girma*) than did occupations open to free choice. (In the case of titled offices, this distinction applied to those in the keeping of a single descent-group.) Once again there were close analogies with Kanuri and Hausa custom, where

> Occupation is a major status distinction. . . . Bornu life is complex, and one of the major indications of this is its multitude of economic, political, and religious specializations. These may be full-time spe-

> cialties, and often are in the urban areas, or they may only be part-time in which a man works his farm during the short growing season and looks after his trade or craft during the dry months.[40]
>
> During the last century craftsmen were organized in units under local craft leaders, who received official recognition and were responsible for collecting tax or organizing such services or supplies as the chief required. To a lesser extent, these senior craftsmen were also responsible for controlling the quality and price of the goods marketed locally. An occupational structure reminiscent of guilds resulted, and, if membership were hereditary, apprenticeship began in childhood.[41]

The popular ranking of gainful occupations (*sana'o'i,* sing. *sana'a*) by their respective degrees of status or prestige was the sole element of social placement which differed by emirate, while the occupations practiced by 1900 within each state varied appreciably. Of some 50 occupations followed in each capital area, the highest status was accorded to officeholding. The ranking of other occupations among the first 25 at Gombe Abba, Katagum, and Hadejia affords a revealing index of late nineteenth-century cultural and economic heterogeneity in these emirates.[42]

As in Hausaland, where today "the most appropriate model of . . . [social] stratification" for men "is that based on occupational class,"[43] the list in the table (p. 22) can serve also to indicate the relative status of particular male citizens in that period, although the important role of ethnic, religious, and other cultural determinants must be borne in mind. A few of the occupations given here were practiced by women as well as men, but females had on the whole their own occupational groupings, and accordingly ranked themselves in different sequences. (The average woman, who is said to have married several times during her lifetime, did not share the status of her husband.)

Because all commoners and slaves, and most clients, worked on farms in the wet season, a number of these occupations were less than full time, but they all

40. Cohen, "Social Stratification," p. 247.

41. M. G. Smith, "Exchange and Marketing among the Hausa," in *Markets in Africa,* ed. Paul Bohannan and George Dalton (Evanston, Ill.: Northwestern University Press, 1962), p. 305.

42. Informants IA: 1–6; IG: 1–8; IIA: 1–5; IIB: 1–6; IIIA: 1–17. See Table on p. 22 of occupational rankings in each emirate ca. 1900.

43. Smith, "The Hausa of Northern Nigeria," p. 139.

Occupational Ranking

	Gombe	*Katagum*	*Hadejia*
2.	*blacksmiths	*blacksmiths	long-distance traders
3.	cattlemen	sewers (clothing)	petty traders
4.	*butchers	weavers (clothing)	cattlemen
5.	weavers (clothing)	spinners (cotton)	*butchers
6.	*dyers (cotton)	builders (house)	sewers (clothing)
7.	sewers (clothing)	*barber/doctors	spinners (cotton)
8.	*barber/doctors	*Koranic clerics	*blacksmiths
9.	dry-season farmers	*Islamic scholars	builders
10.	long-distance traders	long-distance traders	*dyers
11.	builders (house)	cattlemen	brokers
12.	cloth-beaters	*leather workers	food sellers
13.	*leather workers	*ferrymen	*barber/doctors
14.	*goldsmiths	*well-diggers	cloth-beaters
15.	carpenters	*dyers (cotton)	Muslim necromancers
16.	peddlers	fishermen	*goldsmiths
17.	*Islamic scholars	*butchers	*leather workers
18.	*Koranic clerics	brokers	*praise-singers
19.	*praise-singers	shepherds	potters
20.	hunters	carpenters	*Islamic scholars
21.	brokers	goat-keepers	*Koranic clerics
22.	Muslim necromancers	cloth-beaters	fishermen
23.	*ferrymen	*goldsmiths	*ferrymen
24.	food-sellers	petty traders	weavers (clothing)
25.	fishermen	potters	hunters

*occupations that were always or usually hereditary

were significant sources of household income, and the level of remuneration for an occupation was in fact a major criterion in adjudging its status. Two other touchstones were the value of one's product or service to the general public and the extent of popular awareness (*sananne*) of the activity.

PART I

CHAPTER 2

STATE AND SOCIETY IN ISLAM

THE MUSLIM STATE

It has long been a commonplace of social and political thought about Islam that religion throughout the Muslim world is inseparably interfused with most public, economic, and cultural affairs. For a Believer, "Life is one and indivisible; religion pervades and determines all its aspects. The whole of life is ordered by the religious, all-embracing divine law."[1] For traditional polities established in the name of Allah and His Prophet Muhammad, such an attitude is unrhetorical, and no sound portrayal of their genesis and development would neglect the Islamic factor, in either its pure or its applied configurations. To comprehend even the manifest bearing of personal behavior and sociopolitical institutions in Gombe, Katagum, and Hadejia requires some familiarity with the nature of the Muslim faith, its codified expression in canon law, and the broader human setting in which these have been enacted.

The founders of Muslim political science were at one in their presupposition that man is innately a social animal, destined by human nature to live with his fellows in some kind of organized community. The Qur'an identifies the Islamic body politic as a nation or brotherhood (A. *umma*), under the eternal sovereignty of Allah, "in whose membership alone the believer obtains prosperity in this world and salvation in the next."[2] The Prophet Muhammad described his followers

1. Erwin I. J. Rosenthal, *Political Thought in Medieval Islam* (Cambridge: At the University Press, 1962), p. 23.

2. Majid Khadduri, *War and Peace in the Law of Islam* (Baltimore: Johns Hopkins Press, 1955), pp. 3–4.

as "an *umma* in distinction from the rest of the people," and directed that a Believer's allegiance to it must take precedence over all previous group loyalties, whether lineage or ethnic, social or political. Hence the permanent legal and theological separation in Islam between the servants of God (the *umma Muhammadiyya*) and all other persons (A. *kāfirūn, kuffār,* sing. *kāfir*). Allah for His part will safeguard each Muslim irrespective of station in life and distinguish him from his brethren in faith only according to his relative degree of "piety" and "godfearing."

The classical (orthodox) formulation of proper Islamic government has been summarized in a few basic postulates. A Muslim's chief role in the world is the service of Allah (A. *'ibāda*).[3] The right performance of this role demands that he participate in a commonwealth of his co-religionists, and this implies the existence of a government, whose main function in turn is to make possible the regular fulfillment of *'ibāda.* The Muslim state has thus an essentially moral foundation and task, which is further revealed alike in the "foremost civic-religious duty"[4] of its leadership—to command the good and forbid the evil—and in the rulers' acknowledgment of canon law (the *Sharī'a*) as qualifying their executive and jural powers. Within such an ideal state all legally responsible Muslims are equal before the law, although social and political circumstances may often impose disabilities on certain groups of the Faithful (slaves, women, oppressed free classes, for example). A significant correlate of this egalitarian dogma is that individuals who fail to accept Islam cannot be awarded full citizenship in the properly defined Muslim state. Such people when residing inside its borders have traditionally been "neutralized in largely self-governing religious communities of their own whose relations to the ruling *umma Muhammadiyya* are settled by treaties that tend to degenerate into unilateral contracts."[5]

To secure Muslim citizens in their capacity for serving Allah, the Islamic state must protect them against neighboring infidels as well as from schismatics and heretics within. The first of these corporate obligations generally has been construed in terms of Holy War (A. *jihād*), a device which came to have two further warrants in Islam: that of propagating the Faith when other means failed (thus

3. This paragraph and the next two are drawn from Gustave E. von Grunebaum, *Islam, Essays in the Nature and Growth of a Cultural Tradition* (New York: Barnes and Noble, 1961), pp. 127–40. By "orthodox" is meant Sunni doctrine, followed historically by the great preponderance of Muslims (including almost all those in West Africa).

4. *Ibid.,* p. 127.

5. *Ibid.,* p. 128.

insuring converts the benefit of correct guidance) and the conviction that only servants of Allah are entitled to the highest political rewards. To actualize the preconditions for *'ibāda*, the state should also compel obedience to canon law (the medium of *'ibāda's* maintenance) by its Muslim citizenry and provide a suitable environment for compliance with its injunctions.

The Qur'an ordains that ultimate authority over the *umma* resides with Allah, Who delegated its exercise to His Messenger (Prophet), Muhammad. Allah remains the titular head of the total Islamic community, and His vicegerant on earth is to govern in strict conformance with divinely inspired commandments set down in the Qur'an. But since shortly after Muhammad's death (A.D. 632) the question of who should occupy the office of successor (A. *khalīfa*) to the Prophet has divided the *umma*.[6] While growing rapidly in size and political influence, the Islamic world soon fragmented, with rival claimants to that position controlling separate states and empires. By the fourteenth century A.D., Ibn Khaldun could draw from 700 years of Islamic history the distinction between a theocratic government, based on the *Sharī'a* alone, and one based largely upon reason and human law. The former, embodied in the caliphate (A. *khilāfa*), expressed—in its purest form—the prophetic conception of a Muslim community; the latter, established through force of arms and exemplified in the power-state (A. *mulk*), was regulated more by rational than by revealed legislation.[7]

JIHAD AND CONQUERED LAND

If it was by conquest that most Islamic polities were founded and the territorial frontiers of the *umma* enlarged, there has been a firm doctrinal sanction for recourse to violence. By enjoining the Muslim ruler to safeguard his people from non-Believers outside the community, the *Sharī'a* effectively partitions the

6. T. W. Arnold, "Khalifa," in *Encyclopaedia of Islam* (Leiden: E. J. Brill, 1936), II, pp. 882–84; and *The Caliphate* (New York: Barnes & Noble, 1966), *passim*. The Caliph traditionally bore two other titles as well, both of them having a dual political/religious significance: *Amīr al-Muminīn* (Commander of the Believers, or Armies of Islam), which emphasized his secular responsibilities, and *imām*, which "had special reference to his religious function as leader of the faithful in public worship" (*ibid.*, pp. 14–15, 33–34, 201). Each title has at times been used alone by, or applied to, persons of sharply diverse occupations and offices.

7. Ibn Khaldun, *The Muqaddimah*, trans. Franz Rosenthal, 3 vols. (Princeton: Princeton University Press, 1967), 2d ed., II, 138–39.

world into already Islamized areas (*dār al-Islām*) and those which continue beyond the pale (*dār al-harb*, the realm of war). As originally conceived, *dār al-Islām* comprehended only those parts of the world under Muslim governors, but in time this definition gave way to more flexible constructions, ranging from any region where *'ibāda* is allowed to wherever "at least one Muslim custom is still observed."[8] In its most general sense, however, *dār al-Islām* signified the territory of Islam, the inhabitants of which may include scriptuaries—adherents (especially Christians and Jews) of other faiths who by virtue of their belief in one God, possession of a written religious code, and payment of the Qur'anic poll tax (A. *jizya*), are "protected persons" (A. *dhimmis*)—and polytheists (A. *mushrikūn*), whose enduring presence and unbelief are tolerated as a matter of convenience, and who normally have paid *jizya* as well.

The Islamic world's relation to *dār al-harb* has been a primary concern of Muslim legists. Because of the divine charge on Believers to universalize obedience to Allah and His commandments, the *umma* shares a perpetual mandate and calling to diffuse Islam outside its borders until the earth has been cleansed of all disbelief. Whenever possible this should be accomplished through peaceful inducement, but, if necessary, other, coercive methods can be employed. On campaign against unbelievers the Muslim captain is authorized to allow scriptuaries a choice between group conversion, acceptance of the legal condition of "protected persons," or combat; polythesists are offered (at least in theory) the first and last of these options only. Hence the jihad is both a major instrument of state policy and an ultimate weapon in the transformation of land in the status of *dār al-harb* to that of *dār al-Islām*. While prudence may often dictate a momentary suspension of hostilities, the period of truce must not be of more than ten years' duration.

In its most inclusive meaning, a Muslim is defined by orthodox jurists as any person who avows belief in Allah and the Apostleship of Muhammad; gives the annual mandatory alms (A. *zakāt*); observes the five daily ritual prayers; fasts in the daylight hours of the holy month of Ramadan; and strives to perform at least once the pilgrimage to Mecca and Medina. These "pillars of Islam" are duties incumbent on each Muslim as an individual. Pursuance of the jihad is, rather, a collective responsibility of the *umma* as a whole (or of each political segment thereof), and if discharged by a part of that community no longer binds

8. Gustave E. von Grunebaum, *Medieval Islam* (Chicago: University of Chicago Press, 1961), p. 9.

the remainder of it—although if not pursued at all, the entire *umma* is at fault. The collective nature of this prescription has several significant aspects. It derives from necessity, as indicated by the requirements of eligibility for service in a jihad. It offers the Islamic state a permanent legal warrant to make war on foreign unbelievers who refuse to submit to Allah and His lieutenants, even when an invasion of *dār al-harb* is otherwise unprovoked. Conversely, it imposes on all qualified Muslims the burden of periodic, often hazardous tours of military service and on all Muslim rulers of calling, outfitting, and (perhaps) leading jihads at frequent intervals. Since no other kind of war is lawful in Islamic jurisprudence, it also denies legal sanction to armed conflicts between pretenders to the mantle of successor to Muhammad, except in the guise of opposing schismatics and heretics.

The personal rewards, both heavenly and mundane, of engagement in a jihad may be thought by the Faithful to outweigh its privations and perils. The Muslim who dies in the struggle with infidels is a martyr of Islam and assured of a station in paradise. It has been said that "one drop of blood spilled on the battlefield, one night spent under arms, will count for more than two months of fasting or prayer" in the reckoning up of a man's accounts on his death.[9] According to the *Sharī'a*, property can legitimately be procured in Islam either by "taking possession of things in a state of nature, which may be called original acquisition";[10] by its contractual transfer from one owner to another; or by inheritance. The appropriation of property by jihadists, whether forcible or otherwise, bestows on them corporately full title to it under the right of original acquisition, on the ground that its ownership is automatically alienated when they resist a jihad instead of accepting Islam or the status of protected or tolerated peoples. Such property taken in a jihad belongs to all who fought in the Muslim ranks and includes not only movables and immovables in the usual sense but persons as well, both prisoners of war and their dependents. Adult male captives may be killed, held to ransom, exchanged for Muslim prisoners, freed, or enslaved, while captive dependents are liable to enslavement alone. The division of spoil begins with a Qur'anic allotment of one-fifth of the total "to Allah and to the Apostle, and to the near kin, and to orphans, and to the poor, and to the wayfarer";[11] in time this share came to be considered that portion legally reserved to the state.

9. *Ibid.*
10. Khadduri, *War and Peace*, p. 119.
11. Q. VIII, 42.

The remaining four-fifths is divisible among the surviving warriors, as varyingly determined by the four main orthodox schools of law.[12]

The Fulani conquest of Hausaland and the Border States had, therefore, a coherent, intellectually tenable rationale, one anchored firmly in classical Islamic thought. The subsequent disposal by various emirs of *dār al-harb* taken by force or by suasion from its Habe rulers can be viewed in a similar sense, although—as with the Fulani jihad—other, sometimes less honorable, motives would seem to have been present as well, especially with the passing of the first generation of more devout militants who established the Sokoto Caliphate.[13]

Basic to the arrangements for ownership and administration of these conquered lands was the Muslim distinction in law between three kinds of territory within *dār al-Islām*. First are those areas accounted "dead" (or, in the African English term, "bush"), that is, which have not been cultivated or built upon and whose title is held by the state and may be assigned by its ruler. Next are "living" or "vivified" land, the rights in which are usufructory and lapse when their tenants allow them to go fallow or otherwise unemployed a set number of years. This second kind is in turn divided into tithe or *zakāt* land, on which the user (a Muslim) pays a tax devoted by state authorities to some pious object, and tribute or *kharāj* land, namely those occupied by defeated or otherwise subjected people who, in exchange for regular payment of *kharāj*, may continue in their possession. A third kind, dedicated or *wakf* land, usually bears the meaning of ground reserved by the state for a spiritual purpose (the construction and maintenance of a mosque, for example), but it can also be applied, as it was by the victorious Fulani, to all *dār al-harb* brought under Islamic dominion. In practice, however,

12. All Sunni Muslims adhere to one or another of four surviving orthodox codes of Islamic jurisprudence that were founded in the eighth and ninth centuries: the Mālikī, Hanafi, Shāfi'i, and Hanbali. While differing in a number of their doctrinal positions on finer points of canon law, they do not form sectarian categories within the Sunni world. Each school or "way" (A. *madhhab*) draws upon the same fundamental sources of Muslim ritual and dogma, and all are mutually acknowledged by their followers to be of commensurate orthodoxy. In West and Northwest Africa and Upper Egypt the Maliki *madhhab* is far the most widely observed.

13. The Fulani mallams (A. *'ulamā*), especially Usuman dan Fodio with his nearest kin Abdullahi and Muhammad Bello, drew in their many legal works mainly upon Maliki authors of the late Abbasid period, who were guided in turn by surviving traditions of Muslim behavior in the first two decades after the Prophet's death (see Mervyn Hiskett, "An Islamic Tradition of Reform in the Western Sudan from the 16th to the 18th Century," *Bulletin of the School of Oriental and African Studies*, XXV [1962], 592).

outside the environs of Sokoto the sultan and his emirs treated conquered inhabited areas as *kharāj,* a legal term which has traditionally been translated as "land-tax" (H. *kurdin kasa*) but that appears to have become widely used in the caliphate to denote most kinds of revenue secured from Muslim as well as unconverted Habe. The latter, who paid tribute in the form of a poll tax, were, it seems, at least in the Border States, left in effective possession of their pre-jihad settlements, farms, orchards, and grazing fields.[14]

The Fulani warrior-chiefs thus had two separate though related grounds on which to justify their imposed suzerainty over the Habe of northern Nigeria: the right of conquest as defined by the laws of jihad, and the wider of two possible interpretations of what constitutes *wakf*. In the Border States today both grounds are advanced to explain the nineteenth-century employment of force against Habe communities of that region and the virtual exclusion of Habe from the major free offices of precolonial government. Barebari towns and petty kingdoms in Katagum and Hadejia are said to have submitted without hesitation to the emirate founders, because they were already well-Islamized and/or in order to escape the charge of polytheism leveled by the Fulani at the Kanuri of Bornu.[15]

JUDICIAL/RELIGIOUS AUTHORITY

Just as there is no separation acknowledged in orthodox Islam between things "temporal" and things "spiritual" (the terms themselves are unknown to Muslim theologians), so the *Sharī'a* recognizes no legal distinction within *dār al-Islām* between authority and power. Both are incarnate in the person of the rightly-guided caliph or imam (*amīr al-muminīn*), who must rule according to God-centered commandments. To this end he may appoint agents—councilors, judges, leaders at prayer, emirs, generals—to exercise on his behalf any portion

14. C. K. Meek, *Land Tenure and Land Administration in Nigeria and the Cameroons* (London: H.M.S.O., 1957), pp. 163–66; *Land Law and Custom in the Colonies* (London: Oxford University Press, 1949), pp. 230–42; and J. N. D. Anderson, *Islamic Law in Africa* (1954; London: Frank Cass, 1970), pp. 184–87.

15. Informants IIA: 1–5; IIB: 1–9; IIE: 1, 4, 8–9, 13–15, 18; IIG: 5–9, 11–13; IIJ: 14–15; IIIA: 1–17; IIID: 2, 4–5; IIIE: 2–7, 10; IIIF: 1, 3–7; IIIH: 1, 4–6; III I: 1–5, 7.

of his prerogatives, but he remains the final arbiter on earth of every human affair.[16]

The more specific duties of a caliph (or of his local vicegerent, an emir) have been summarily described as "judgment, taxation, the Friday service and the *jihād*."[17] To discharge the first of these duties Shaikh Usuman assigned judicial authority in the various emirates to the head of each state and the heirs to his throne. The emir then appointed a distinguished scholar as chief justice (*babban alkali*) in the capital to hear the most difficult, serious, or politically resonant cases. Major fief areas in Katagum and Gombe had their own judges (*alkalai,* sing. *alkali*) appointed by the fiefholders; their decisions could be appealed, through the chief justice or emir, as far as the sultan. Alkalis were assisted by staffs which included one or more canon lawyers (A. *muftū*) able to render formal legal opinions at their request and who generally served them as scribes as well. (The official medium of court documents, as for correspondence with other emirates and Sokoto, was Arabic.)[18]

The first imam, or leader of public ritual prayer in Islam, had been the Prophet. With his death the office was inherited by the caliphs or, increasingly, their representatives. It "became thus one of the chief attributes of the rulers and the transference of power to the governors of the provinces was seen in a form visible to all when the Caliph's deputy placed himself at the head of the community assembled for prayer."[19] Like previous caliphs, Shaikh Usuman deputized his local governors to exercise the function of imam (H. *liman*) or to appoint other qualified men to do so. Emirs of the Border States are said to have often led Friday prayers in the metropolitan central mosques, but since every mosque, however modest in size and congregation, must have its imam, the number of

16. Thus Shaikh Usuman declared in writing that an *imām* was required of his community (A. D. H. Bivar, "The *Wathiqāt ahl al-Sudān*: A Manifesto of the Fulani Jihad," *Journal of African History,* II [1961], 240). Roland A. Adeleye has noted that "The appointment of the Shaikh as *Amīr al-Muminīn* [imam] was the central act in the foundation of the Caliphate" (*Power and Diplomacy in Northern Nigeria 1804–1906* [London: Longman Group, 1971], p. 44).

17. Reuben Levy, *The Social Structure of Islam* (Cambridge: At the University Press, 1957), pp. 293–94.

18. Informants IA: 1–6; IG: 1–8; IIA: 1–5; IIB: 1–9; IIIA: 1–17. It has been reported that "all letters [preserved] in the Sokoto Chancery are in Arabic" (Denis Murray Last, *The Sokoto Caliphate* [London: Longmans, 1967], pp. 191–92).

19. Cl. Huart, "Imām," in *Encyclopaedia of Islam* (Leiden: E. J. Brill, 1927), II, 473.

persons who filled this most purely religious of emirate offices was legion by the late nineteenth century.[20]

The chief imam of each Border State, together with the chief alkali, chief palace scribe (*magatakarda*), and the emir's waziri, constituted an informal royal advisory council, available whenever he was in doubt regarding the Islamic propriety of a contemplated course of action. Its members appear to have been consulted more often in some reigns than others, yet it seems that most precolonial emirs relied on the council's opinion not only to justify through legal precedent a controversial deed or procedure but also to help guide the crown in paths of righteousness.[21]

As traditional as the role of an imam in Islamic society has been that of the untitled man who delivers a sermon (A. *khutba*) during the main Friday prayer service and on the two major festival days. In the course of his sermon a potentially significant "political" rite is enacted when the assembled worshippers pray that Allah may bless their sovereign.[22] While the *Sharī'a* does not prescribe this attribute of the *khutba*, and Shaikh Usuman is reported to have discouraged its use,[23] emirs of Gombe, Katagum, and Hadejia are said to have generally permitted (if not approved) the mention of their name and that of the sultan. On at least one occasion public reluctance to pray for an emir is cited in evidence of widespread popular disaffection provoked by his refusal to make the annual gift offerings to Sokoto.[24]

SLAVERY

Slavery as a social institution probably was a common feature of Habe and Barebari polities of the Border States region well before 1800.[25] If so, those

20. Informants IA: 1–6; IG: 1–8; IIA: 1–5; IIB: 1–9; IIIA: 1–17.
21. *Ibid.*
22. A modern scholar of Islam has described the latter custom as "the public manifestation by means of which the people not only publicly recognized an individual to be their immediate ruler, but also acknowledged, together with him, the sovereignty of a higher chief, a caliph" (Maurice Gaudefroy-Demombynes, *Muslim Institutions* [London: George Allen & Unwin, 1961], pp. 75–76).
23. Joseph Schacht, "Islam in Northern Nigeria," *Studia Islamica,* VII (1957), 135.
24. See p. 153 below.
25. The Fulani pastoral nomads from whose ranks the founding clans of the Border States emerged do not seem to have become slaveowners until the onset of the jihad

cultural and other changes wrought in it by the Fulani conquest would have been more in the realm of new legal sanctions and safeguards than in the habitual existence of the practice of human bondage. Wherever Islam was accepted or imposed the relationships of a slave to his master, and to the wider community of freemen and slaves, were regulated henceforth by jural codes based on the Qur'an and the relevant Muslim Traditions (A. *Hadīth*) as interpreted under Maliki law. Qur'anic passages can be cited to demonstrate that enslavement of certain unbelievers is "in accordance with the divinely established order of things."[26] The Prophet commended those who dealt humanely with their slaves and made it an act of piety, indemnified in heaven, for a Muslim owner to emancipate his own, but nowhere in the canon of Islamic law or theology is the abandonment of institutionalized slavery encouraged on Muslim communities.

West African Islam, while conforming to the Maliki school of jurisprudence, has often been successful in its incorporation of local slavery customs whenever these did not clash too painfully with orthodox opinion. Where other schools permit the slave half the civil rights of a free Muslim, Maliki doctrine leans toward the recognition of his full rights in law. He can serve as the leader of communal prayer, own some property, have up to four wives (instead of the usual two), and be enfranchised if his master abuses him unduly. The legal disabilities which remain, however, are numerous and burdensome enough to suggest that involuntary servitude was a less than desirable condition for the mass of precolonial slaves in the Sokoto Caliphate.

Under the *Sharī'a* slaves are classified as chattels, that is, domestic animals, but they normally are accorded the legal status of quasi-children. They are procurable by gift, purchase, inheritance, or as prizes of war, and property rights in captured slaves can be transferred at the master's will. Slaves may not themselves inherit property nor conduct trade except on their master's behalf, and they are forbidden to marry without his leave, while the master can dissolve such unions if he sees fit. Yet without violence being done to Islamic law or tradition, a number of high government offices in Bornu and the Sokoto Empire were held by slaves, and daughters of the emirs were frequently married to leading slave

---

(Derrick J. Stenning, *Savannah Nomads: A Study of the Wodaabe Pastoral Fulani of Western Bornu Province, Northern Region, Nigeria* [London: Oxford University Press, 1959], pp. 65, 131–32). For slavery in a Barebari society of Bornu prior to 1800, see Ronald Cohen, "Slavery among the Kanuri," *Trans-action,* IV (January–February, 1967), 48–49.

26. R. Brunschvig, "'Abd," in *Encyclopaedia of Islam* (Leiden: E. J. Brill, 1927), I, 25; and Q. XVI, 71, 75; XXX, 28.

titled officials.[27] Neither was descent from a slave girl by a freeman any bar to social or political eminence in the Border States: female slaves often served their masters as concubines, and since in Islam the issue of this kind of union are free at birth it is unremarkable that, for example, the last four nineteenth-century emirs of Gombe had slave mothers (several of whom had been captured in war).[28] Smith has noted that prominent slave officials in the Hausa-Fulani emirates had more wealth, status, and power than many freeman, including some royals; that they kept their own slaves and clients; and that "when they committed abuses these had to be borne in patience," as they represented the emir or one of his nobles.[29] This phenomenon was true equally of the Border States, as was the fact that "the position and privileges of other slaves also corresponded with those of their owners."[30] Hence the absence throughout the caliphate of evidence of slave insurrections during the century of Fulani rule. It seems fair to conclude, with Smith, that slaves were "often freer than the free," not only in Hausaland but in the eastern emirates as well.[31]

This conclusion applies with particular strength to the more affluent of those persons born into captivity, the *dimajai* (sing. *dimajo*). A *dimajo* could not be sold by his master, whose relation to him was more paternalistic than domineering. Trained from childhood to observe the societal norms of his emirate, and accepted by his master's family and their free attendants as a familiar though subordinate associate in household activities, the domestic *dimajo* was, in fact, treated much as a ward by his owner, who arranged for his Qur'anic education, his first marriage, and a separate compound. As a Muslim at birth and a well-integrated member of the local community in his adult years, he was often indistinguishable from the generality of freemen around him. He spoke their language, shared their social, economic, and political concerns, and followed one or another of their occupational pursuits. Many of these advantages accrued in like measure to captured slaves, especially if they had been taken and converted at a young age.[32]

27. M. G. Smith, "Slavery and Emancipation in Two Societies," *Social and Economic Studies,* III (1954), 251–54; and "The Hausa System of Social Status," *Africa,* XXIX (July, 1959), 242. For the case of Bornu, see Cohen, "Slavery among the Kanuri," p. 49.

28. Informants IA: 1–6; IG: 1–8. The mother herself (A. *'umm walād*) is enfranchised on the death of her master if she has borne him a child.

29. Smith, "The Hausa System of Social Status," p. 242.

30. *Ibid.*

31. *Ibid.* The statement appears to have applied no less to Bornu (see Cohen, "Slavery among the Kanuri," p. 49).

32. These widely reported conditions were paralleled in Hausaland (Smith, "Slavery and Emancipation," pp. 250–51, 267, 269–72).

In the second half of the nineteenth century Gombe, Katagum, and Hadejia all saw the rise to positions of great wealth and influence of several slave officials. Indeed by 1900 the political ascendance of throne-slave officials had reached a point where they often are said to have been the peers, if not the actual superiors, of even the highest free officeholders. At Hadejia this condition can be dated from the mid-century and was the product of a successful revolt against Sokoto by an emir who sought to provide himself with dependable generals by appointing several of his favorite slaves to what soon were among the chief titled offices of central government. At Gombe Abba, the evolution of eminent slave titles was encouraged mainly by an ever-increasing royal need to balance the power of Fulani provincial governors whose fiefdoms contained large immigrant populations of their own clan descent-lines with an effective counterweight, the loyalty of which could more easily be assured. At Katagum, where the political and demographic equations had assumed yet another form, the crown was less inclined to give precedence at court to slave officials. That none of these emirates experienced slave uprisings would suggest again that even if most slaves were far more confined by law and tradition than most freemen, they still enjoyed (as in Hausaland and Bornu) a large number of codified safeguards and enough social mobility to have made their existence endurable.

The ratio of slave to free persons in late-nineteenth-century Zaria has been reckoned at one-to-one, in Daura at "considerably less" than one-to-three.[33] Similar variations were found in this period in Gombe and Katagum emirates as a whole, and over different sections of each. Slaves obtained in war, raids, or as tribute were a common article of local and long-distance trade throughout northern Nigeria, and they served as a frequent medium of exchange. But such persons, and their privileged *dimajai* descendants, had an equally important function in the urban and rural economies as both agricultural and domestic laborers. All men of sufficient means, including high slave officials, owned one or more slave-farm settlements (*rinji, rindawa*; sing. *barinje, rindi*; F. *rumada,* sing. *rumde*)—fief lands on which some of their slaves lived in the wet season or the year round, supervised by the masters' agents. As the number of slaves increased in each emirate, so did the number of *rinji.* Most of these were sited within several miles of the capital or of an outlying administrative seat, that is, close to the permanent residence of an overlord or that of his provincial subordinate staff. Sons and grandsons of deposed or dead officials and failed contenders for titled office might transfer their establishments from an urban to rural setting and found

33. Smith, "The Hausa System," p. 242.

new *rinji* there on which they resided themselves. Near each emirate capital was the royal slave-farm (*gandun sarki*), while corresponding settlements grew up outside each local government center, worked by slaves of the resident chief.[34]

34. Informant groups I, II, and III. For the Hausa-Fulani emirates, see M. G. Smith, Introduction to Mary Smith, *Baba of Karo: A Woman of the Muslim Hausa* (London: Faber & Faber, 1954), p. 22, and the description of slave-farmed estates, pp. 40–43.

CHAPTER 3

THE USES OF ORAL TESTIMONY

SOURCES USED IN THIS STUDY

Two major kinds of evidence have been examined in the composition of this book: oral and written.[1] Oral evidence is of the kind preserved in "field histories," conveyed in 1964–65 by persons having specialized knowledge of the Border States area until ca. 1900. Written evidence can be grouped into (1) unpublished, either official archives or unofficial manuscripts, and (2) published material, again either official or unofficial. Unpublished and published sources may each in turn be subdivided into primary and secondary. Apart from the circumstance of publication, no one of these paired categories is absolute.

Archival matter used here is found mainly in field reports, often termed "district notebooks," prepared by colonial officers in the first three decades (ca. 1905–1935) of British administration of northeast Nigeria. Available at the National Archives, Kaduna, such reports frequently contain helpful ethnographic and historical sections, the latter based wholly on oral data. Other archival holdings include several hundred letters exchanged between the eastern emirates, especially Gombe, and Sokoto. A number of manuscripts of Nigerian provenance, in Arabic or Hausa, round out the unpublished documentation. All this material can be rich in suggestive references to both diplomatic and domestic affairs, ranging

1. The period of full-time research extended from January, 1964, through September, 1965. Of these twenty-one months, three were spent in British and Nigerian archives and libraries; two surveying Arabic and Hausa documents at Ibadan, Kaduna, and Jos; fourteen in field interviews in Gombe, Katagum, and Hadejia; and two reading source material en route.

as it does from correspondence with the caliphal chancery through full-dress narratives to chronicles of important dynasties and nonroyal lineages.

Published evidence of an official and primary nature consists largely of some dozen works, in the original Arabic and/or English translation, by leading figures of the Sokoto establishment (e.g., Shaikh Usuman dan Fodio, his brother Abdullahi and his son Muhammad Bello). Primary, unofficial publications are in the form either of nineteenth- and early twentieth-century traveler accounts or of oral testimony transcribed in a Western language. Though deficient in bulk and depth for much of the precolonial Border State period, travelogues may provide significant detail about key events, in particular those of the 1820s, 1850s, and 1890s; examples are Hugh Clapperton on the city of Katagum (1824), Heinrich Barth on the campaigns of Sarkin Hadejia Buhari (1851, 1854). Secondary published sources, whether official or unofficial, are too varied for clear-cut definition, but it is worth noting that several of the books, including provincial gazetteers, draw heavily upon field material now gathered in archival records, material which is itself in good part oral documentation.

Finally, it seems that for Gombe, Katagum, and Hadejia proper there are no fixed recitational texts, but one professional monograph,[2] and a very few articles.

THE PROBLEM OF ENTREE

In the relative absence of written sources for this region and period, as well as of linguistic or archaeological evidence, oral field histories—in the sense referred to below—have normally proven far the most plentiful and rewarding avenue of approach. The potential of oral testimony for reconstructing the shape and content of traditional societies has been demonstrated by such pioneers of African historiography as M. G. Smith and Jan Vansina.[3] I began the selection

2. Paul Newman, *A Grammar of Tera* (Berkeley and Los Angeles: University of California Press, 1970).

3. See M. G. Smith, "Field Histories among the Hausa," *Journal of African History,* II (1961), 87–101; and Jan Vansina, *Oral Tradition: A Study in Historical Methodology,* trans. H. M. Wright (Chicago: Aldine, 1965), and "Once Upon a Time: Oral Traditions as History in Africa," *Daedalus* (Spring, 1971), pp. 442–67. The latter includes a partial revision by Vansina of his typology.

of suitable field methods with Smith's work on Hausa-Fulani government as a primary guide. Smith pivots his research and analysis of Zaria, 1800–1950, on the perceptive thesis that emirate politics and administration in northwest Nigeria proceed through a network of titled offices, and that hence "a study of the *sarauta* [officeholding] system promised the fullest and most precise information regarding Zaria government and history; and precisely because such data were in some sense ubiquitous, this expectation was fulfilled."[4]

The value of this mode of historical inquiry in the eastern emirates was apparent. Officeholding continues to be the most prestigeful occupation for men and, after agriculture, the most common. It has surely been the most influential upon the whole matrix of public affairs. On each of these grounds it has remained a topic of enduring significance to local historians and to the generality of elders alike. Even more, because of its pervasively manifest character in Border State government, the system of titled offices provided a natural access route into neighboring fields of concern, both political and administrative. I was fortunate to have a methodological point of departure immediately at hand.

I had a second advantage during the formative stages of field research, one seldom conferred upon the American apprentice in African studies until the Peace Corps arrived: a 20-month tour, 1960–61, as education officer at the only high school then serving the Border States area. While there I directed the Bauchi Province Historical Project, and was enabled to know a wide range of elders and government officials in Gombe, Katagum, Misau, and Jema'are. A number of these men were to become essential contributors to the later work.

When I returned in 1964 to northeast Nigeria as a full-time historical researcher, it was in the foreknowledge of those constraints which political sensitivity can impose on certain lines of investigation, however innocent they might appear to a visitor. I had, three years earlier, been present as an agent of the Northern Nigerian (Kaduna) Ministry of Education, and I now bore, of necessity, the imprimateur (in Hausa and English) of Kaduna to ask about matters that were, inescapably, often of a controversial nature. I was moreover a "European," thus by local definition the representative of some outer religious, economic, or political establishment. And none of the Border States had yet been host to a resident academic researcher.

My wife and I strove in several ways to dissociate ourselves in the public mind from the taint of government and in particular from its revenue-bearing activities

4. Smith, "Field Histories," p. 90.

of the past 60 years. We lived always in modest compounds, near the town center and well apart from the European (now senior service) headquarters or resthouse. My wife spent much of her time with families of my principal informants, cooking and chatting in Hausa with them. I acquired the Hausa title of sarkin zamanin da, or "man concerned with precolonial days" (as well as of sarkin aiki, "man in charge of work"—an address of sometimes wry distinction). And we both discouraged all mention of post-1900 events with a polite reminder of our unconcern. This measure was taken in full awareness that much of value would go unremarked, but in the hope that more would be gained via heightened confidence in our complete detachment from latter-day political affairs.

FIELD METHODOLOGY

A majority of the 14-month field experience was in the present-day capitals of Gombe, Katagum, and Hadejia, where I recorded narrative and descriptive data through interviews both with groups and with individuals.

Informants had been referred initially by the local emir or his counselors. I selected from these men and added others who on the basis of their knowledge, tested by sample questions, of particular subject areas appeared to have appropriate backgrounds and a sufficient concern with (or sense of) the past. Answers were checked whenever possible against those offered by comparably qualified men as well as against relevant statements in written sources. A group interview in an emirate capital engaged between five and seventeen persons for an average eight-hour day, and continued in every case during several months without interruption.[5] (In these periods I also met with rural-based elders when they attended the capital for some economic, political, and/or family purpose.) By talking with a carefully chosen group of informants over an extended span of time there developed a much wider ambience of mutual trust than would have occurred otherwise; of equal importance, we had the chance to explore given areas of concern at leisure and from a variety of perspectives. Because of my felt need to have all responses available soon after they had been rendered, I transcribed them in a private

5. The inclusive dates of these interviews appear, together with biographical data on the informants, on pp. 249–70.

shorthand and typed up the notes in English that same night, classifying them in the process.[6]

The narrative data came largely to consist of detailed chronicles of the reign of each nineteenth-century emir. Descriptive materials were assembled under nine general heads:

1. The formal structure and operation of state and local government, as well as informally active aspects that were significant to the conduct of this highly organized complex
2. The selection, ranking, and principal functions of successive emirs, central-administration officials, and the most prominent local chiefs, with near-complete lists of those men appointed to each office during the last century and particulars of their social and ethnic background, previous and/or subsequent political careers, and notable events associated with their terms of office
3. The royal courts—their membership, panoply, social and political practices, and relations to the emirates at large (so, too, each capital city—its residential patterns, municipal organization, and ethnic, social, and occupational divisions)
4. Taxation and tribute—their assessment, collection, and the uses to which the proceeds were put
5. Judicial organs; the execution of Islamic law; and the role, political and religious, of the Qadiriyya and Tijaniyya Muslim brotherhoods
6. Farming, craft, trade, and other non-officeholding occupations
7. The constitution and workings of markets and trade routes, articles and media of commercial exchange
8. The military in war and raiding—its recruitment, weapons, order in battle, and styles of combat
9. Relations with the sultan and the Sokoto court, Bornu, and contiguous emirates.

It was apparent early in my field-work experience how difficult is the assemblage, weighing, and interpretation of oral evidence for an area of such manifold cultural and physical dimensions, one that had a pronounced variety of ethnic character, religious and political allegiance, economic patterns, terrain, and even climatic influence.

6. A full set of my field notes, including the quantitative kind referred to below, is available on microfilm at the University of Ibadan library, where it was deposited in 1965. The notes are in typewritten form and arranged according to major categories of data.

I discovered, for example, that a significant share of descriptive recountings by local informants is on the order of "there were three (five, eight, twelve) markets in this emirate before the Europeans came"; or "most of the people in this land have been Muslims for many years"; and, less quantitatively, "he conquered the towns of X, Y, and Z on his next campaign"; "this man was powerful because of all the people under him"; or "that side of the river was nothing but empty bush in the old days." It was obvious that such declarations, however often they were made, could be "true" (or "false") in varying degrees, but even if "true" they lacked the qualities of definition, completeness, comparability, and perspective that alone might give a more adequate meaning to these kinds of data.

Similar defects were evident in the nature of much historical narrative. If a town is said to have rebelled against a particular emir, what can be known of its ethnic, religious, or economic attributes in that period, and how did these compare with the same categories of data for other towns in the area? What changes in settlement patterns or in administrative arrangements can be adduced to help explain why an emirate border zone is reported to have been politically quiescent during a certain reign but the scene of continuous tumult a generation later, while the opposite phenomena are described for an area adjacent to it? It soon appeared necessary to develop a means by which I could better assess the import as well as the accuracy of a large number of descriptive and narrative statements.

If one could fault the broad generalization of M. G. Smith (that a study of the system of officeholding provides "the fullest and most precise information regarding Zaria [Hausa-Fulani] government and history")[7] it would be, I considered, in the apparent equation of "history" with "government," the first thereby suffering at least a partial eclipse. There seemed to be much of precolonial history, even political history, which might lie obscured in the shadow cast by a highly concentrated focus on governmental structure and functions, however well conceived and employed. A proper study of Border State offices must yield a rich fund of insight, yet may preclude even more. The fullest and often the most precise information about these emirates' genesis and development would emerge, perhaps, from going beyond the nature of government alone into realms where the data were at once ubiquitous and capable of being exhaustively gathered, hence open to a much fuller comparative analysis.

I thus began to compile a register of every named settlement remembered for the closing years of the nineteenth century and to locate each of these on a map. Eventually some 2,500 towns, villages, hamlets, and wards were identified in this

7. Smith, "Field Histories," p. 90.

way. A variety of devices were utilized here, beginning with checklists drawn from tax and census returns, supplemented by several European travelers' maps and textual references of the 1800s, old administrative sketch maps, and other archival sources. About 80 per cent of place names given by the informants were mentioned spontaneously.

At the same time I began to record certain categories of data, or variables, for all settlements (constants) contained in the register. The variables chosen were of two kinds: (1) those which bore on aspects of emirate administration (that is, how political authority was allocated) and of ways that people were identified, by themselves and others; and (2) those bearing upon demographic, military, and commercial aspects of emirate life.

The variables for each settlement were

1. If a pre-nineteenth-century settlement, its *ethnic composition* by ca. 1850; if one of later origin, its ethnic character and from where the settlers migrated, who led them, and why they came; when expanded by the fusion of its founding ethnic group with one or more other ethnic groups after they arrived, like answers were sought

2. What *chief and/or central-government official* the settlement was directly under ca. 1900; for large estates, whether they had been transferred from one office to another before that date

3. For Gombe and Katagum emirates, the *proportions of Muslim to non-Muslim inhabitants* per settlement, or whether it was all Muslim or non-Muslim—again ca. 1900

4. *When the settlement was founded,* according to whether it existed before the jihad or was established in the reign of a particular emir or local chief

5. An estimate, by consensus (see below), of the *number of free adult (i.e., married) men* in each settlement ca. 1900–10, broken down where appropriate into discrete ethnic groups or subgroups; for Gombe and Katagum emirates, the estimated adult male slave population per settlement as well

6. Whether the settlement had a *market and/or Friday mosque,* and if so, in which emir's or local chief's time these were built

7. Whether the settlement had a *mud wall, a stockade, or no artificial enclosure.*

Each of these questions was asked of some 350 persons interviewed during visits to all urban and rural administrative centers of Gombe, Katagum, and (save where indicated above) Hadejia emirates, Each interview lasted two or three days (20–30 hours). Decisions regarding population estimates, date and source of settlement foundation, religion, markets, and Friday mosques were reached by (sometimes extended) discussion and a final consensus. Questions relating to fiefholders, ethnic character, and type or absence of an enclosure usually were answered at once, and by common assent. By meeting jointly whenever possible with all informants in a given district the number of elders knowledgeable of contiguous areas could be multiplied. And to raise the level of precision on several of these variables, where a town or village had separately named wards I treated these as different settlements—thus frequently avoiding over-large units of analysis. Locations were fixed by the use of contemporary maps and the agreement of local officials and merchants whose work brings them to all parts of their district.[8]

The age of most of these informants was in the range of 65–80. Several means are available to fix the approximate year of birth, for example, one's age when the sultan of Sokoto was killed at Bormi, eastern Gombe (1903), by an advancing British column or when a particular emir was enthroned. Age is, however, but one of several indexes which must be sought and weighed in assessing the accuracy of an answer; others may include a man's social and occupational background, his early residence, and present mental capacity. All save the last of these data were obtained at the outset of an interview.

THE VERIFICATION OF ORAL CENSUS DATA

Two fundamental criteria were followed in selecting these variables: how far they could be verified, and their potential utility in illuminating precolonial events.[9]

When seeking oral testimony of this kind, what checks are available to the

8. Maps published by the former Northern Nigerian (Kaduna) Government are often not of much utility, unless drawn from aerial photographs, and then for major towns and natural features alone. More useful are unpublished maps, surviving in local government offices and in archival reports, which tend to list far more place names, but even these frequently misplace settlement sites and should be used with due caution.

9. "In all approaches to methodology, two problems exist: *verification* and *validity*. Verification refers to the processes by which the accuracy, or *reliability*, of the recorded observation may be checked, and validity refers to the processes by which variables are allocated to the appropriate conceptual categories" (John N. Paden, "Social Science and Africa," in *The African Experience*, ed. John N. Paden and Edward W. Soja, 4 vols. [Evanston: Northwestern University Press, 1970], I, 613).

historian? Can he establish appropriate and adequate rules of evidence? How, in short, may the data be assessed?

The answer will of course differ with each variable chosen and has been considered here a function, *inter alia,* of how

(1) *controversial* (e.g., politically sensitive),
(2) *prestige-laden,*
(3) *near in time and space,*
(4) *memorable or personally significant,* and
(5) *clearly definable*

the content of each variable is to the generality of informants on each. The variables employed were a mixed but often associated group, with margins of error and measures of probability affected by one or more of these, and perhaps other, determinants.

The several techniques for securing and evaluating each set of data can be summarized as follows:

In the establishment of *ethnic character* I adopted local usage in distinguishing Fulani, Habe, and Barebari, and wherever possible these designations were broken down into their commonly assigned ethnic subcategories. A good majority of small and middle-sized settlements, and many larger ones, are said by their modern inhabitants (and by other informants) to have been mono-ethnic. When a settlement was not so mentioned, I recorded each ethnic group said to have included five or more free adult males.

Only if a settlement were abandoned earlier than, say, 1915, does it seem that nearness in time could play a significant part in distorting such data. As regards prestige, it can happen that someone has wrongly styled himself a Fulani or Arab or as being of another group of high rank when he is in fact of a lower-status origin. Yet unless all informants in a village area or larger administrative district, meeting jointly, wish to mislead on this point (and several checks are available), it is unlikely that falsification will occur on a settlement scale. Neither was there much reluctance apparent when declaring one's own actual ethnic identity (i.e., that of one's father), any more than one's major occupation or free/slave descent.

The question of who was the *fiefholder of a settlement* in the late nineteenth century is often more complex, at least on the surface. By asking what person or office the settlement was directly under (*karkashin sosai*) in that period, I developed a set of pyramid structures, each of varying breadth at the base and middle but ascending more or less evenly to its respective senior titled official.

Changes during the century (an uncommon event) were noted by reference to other data, and all answers for the penultimate and highest levels were checked with appropriate persons in each emirate capital. Those few discrepancies found could usually be traced to the frequent duplication of titles at different layers of authority in the hierarchical edifice.

None of the credibility factors had a significant impact here; political sensitivity, which might seem influential, to all appearances was not.

The *ratios per settlement of Muslim to non-Muslim free adult males* in the period ca. 1900 is the most difficult variable to assess the replies to, and I often doubted that such estimates were accurate enough to warrant their use. Although spot checks were also run for these responses, the limits of divergence where settlements were of mixed religious affiliation often exceeded 25 per cent.

Neither the "controversial" nor the "prestige" criteria are—against expectation—clear reasons for concern here: many settlements in Gombe and Katagum were said by their older residents to have lacked a Muslim presence by 1900, even when, as usually happens, they are accounted Islamized today. (So too a number of settlements are said now by their inhabitants to have been largely, or wholly, slave.) Rather, it seems that for settlements of a dual religious character ca. 1900, remoteness in time, lack of memorableness, and above all the problem of a uniformly accepted definition of Muslim and non-Muslim exert too strong an influence.

Times of settlement foundation were resolved, for those which fell in the nineteenth century, by reference to who led the first arrivals, whence they came, and why, and by placing together all those that fell prior to ca. 1800. It is an advantage here that informants habitually refer to the pre-jihad era as *zamanin Habe* ("time of the Habe") and to the period ca. 1800–1900 as *zamanin Fulani*. Again, nearness in time and memorability or lack of it appear the chief considerations in verifying responses.

The *estimated number of free adult males* at the turn of the century was asked on the assumption that figures would approximate to a usable degree the actual numbers for the period ca. 1900–10. Such figures are obviously not open to absolute verification (save through a perfectly executed genealogical charting of the settlement and a record of the birth date and/or time of death of each inhabitant in the past one hundred years). If fallible in practice, may the use of these estimates be justified? By taking sample checks on a settlement with different informants and by asking an informant the same question on widely separated occasions, I found that such estimates rarely deviated more than 25 per cent for the smaller, and 15–20 per cent for the larger, settlements; very often they were unchanged or within a margin of 10 per cent.[10]

It should be stressed that we are concerned here not with *absolute* population figures but with *approximate,* and then only as regards adult male totals per settlement. Such figures may also provide—by the single means now available—a rough guide to the *relative* size of each settlement ca. 1900. Those settlements reported to be of a roughly comparable magnitude can be lumped together and represented as belonging to a particular demographic quantum; that is, all those with estimates that fall within a certain range, e.g., 5–100 free adult males, would appear on the same point of a scale marked off by increments of 100 or, on a map, as circles of the same diameter. (The units of these increments are of course a matter of personal choice, one made here in light of visual considerations and the clear need to minimize chances of reading into the data more than is warranted by their quality.)

Of the five possible credibility factors, none but prestige and, perhaps, memorableness appear critical. The former can generally be coped with by spot checks, and the latter is undecisive if one allows for even a 20 per cent margin of error.[11] Neither does it seem that informants encounter much difficulty when referring to precolonial free as opposed to nonfree lineages. The British Northern Nigerian Slavery Proclamation of 1900 abolished the legal condition of slavery in the (then) protectorate; declared all persons born after April 1, 1901, to have the status of free men; and ordained that any slave who wished could be enfran-

10. Jan Vansina has remarked that while conducting a population census for the same general period in Central Africa, he concluded that such under- and over-estimates in a given area tend to cancel out (private conversation, Madison, Wisconsin, October, 1965).

11. Northern Nigeria was the scene of widespread famine in 1904–5 and 1914. The first of these famines, and perhaps the second as well, may be supposed to have altered the number of free adult males in each emirate, and their distribution, in such a way as to affect the estimates given in 1964–65 for the period ca. 1900. There might have been an appreciable decrease in gross population for the Border States, although archival sources do not suggest any significant rise in mortality or emigration. While the famine of 1904–5 is said in these reports to have caused a measure of demographic dispersion, this was not often, according to informants, of a permanent, large-scale, or long-distance character. Moreover, this question was asked always of the oldest informants, the majority of whom were at least 10–15 years of age in 1900. Finally, I took special care, whenever a settlement was said to have been founded or abandoned around the time Europeans first arrived, to establish whether famine was the causative agent.

chised. In practice few slaves claimed their freedom in the early 1900s. While their legal disabilities in Islamic law are no longer effective, lineages which had been classified as "slave" in the past are still often viewed by their co-resident "free" lineages as bearing the social status associated with the historical Muslim position on slavery.

I recorded *the presence or absence of a Friday mosque* at both local and central levels of each emirate, from laymen and clerics alike. The date (by reign) of construction is often linked with a special, well-remembered event, for example, the arrival of a particular divine or the advent of a new chief.

A possible element of prestige cannot be discounted here, although no evidence came to light that such a consideration ever led to the inaccurate ascription of a Friday mosque's precolonial presence or of its origin.

For *markets and their foundation times* I interviewed former long-distance and local traders at both emirate and district levels of administration. (It was impossible, despite some effort, to establish a usable measure of estimated end-of-century market volume.) I asked the same informants about major trade routes in this period, and these were given in terms of the usual overnight halting stations of caravans.

Remoteness in time should be considered here, at least for the date a market was founded and if, as may happen, no memory of its founder has been preserved. A more acute problem arises when a market was opened in the reign of an emir or local chief whose term of office overlapped the first several years of British rule.

Whether a settlement had a mud wall, stockade, or no artificial enclosure is a variable which in the Border States context finally was discarded. Mud walls and stockades often were allowed to decay soon after the introduction of a Pax Britannica, and many of these have now disappeared; others are said to have been reconstructed at different historical moments before then; and a number of settlements were moved to new sites nearby during the nineteenth century, either off a hill or to more fertile ground, with concomitant changes in the nature of their enclosure. Thus verification presented more problems than it seemed reasonable to pursue.

If we accept the five credibility factors proposed here, it still must be asked whether replies for each variable are in fact of a commensurate accuracy for the units of analysis (settlements) whatever their size and location. I have so concluded when there is no sufficient reason to suppose that (1) the level of area-by-area recall differs beyond certain allowable, and tested, limits, and (2) bias cannot be detected and allowed or compensated for by internal or external checks. It is unclear how any one category of data could prove *uniformly* accurate for all settlements, if by this we mean all things being fully accurate, not merely equal.

THE VALUE OF ORAL CENSUS DATA

The potential validity, or value, of settlement-by-settlement data of this kind in the consideration of narrative material can be illustrated with reference to the career of Mallam Jibril.

During the last 15 years of the nineteenth century, Gombe Emirate was increasingly engrossed by this militant religious-political figure. District notebooks, government reports, and local tradition loosely represent the measure of his inroads on Gombe as near-total, serious, or light. I catalogued each remembered settlement in the emirate according to whether he conquered it, failed in an attack on it, left it undisturbed, won it over through fear and propaganda, or forced its people to seek refuge elsewhere. Having at hand an ethnic, religious, administrative, and partial economic profile on which to impose this breakdown created a much fuller canvas, one to which the abundant narrative field notes could also be most profitably referred.

The value of these kinds of uniform data when researching the structure, content, and operation of societal institutions like those mentioned under the general heads of descriptive material above has been equally evident. A number of instances emerge in this work, but several of the more representative examples would be, how does one account for the widely acknowledged high rank of official X, who seems from the answers given here and elsewhere to have supervised only these few settlements? Why did a preponderance of late-nineteenth-century long-distance traders live in these wards of a capital, and what significance lies in the fact that all were from the same ethnic group? Or, can one explain why a largely Habe area appears to have gone unraided by the emirs even though it is said to have resisted Islamization?

The rewards of such a pointillist approach could be (and were) many-sided.[12]

12. I am aware of only one other published survey of this general kind attempted in Africa; see Michel Izard, *Traditions historiques des villages du Yatenga* (Paris: C.N.R.S.,

We might, for example, determine, with a measure of confidence unrivaled perhaps by other means, the following sorts of interrelationships:

1. Correspondences between estimated settlement size and ethnic character, period of immigration, and religious factors (Muslim to non-Muslim ratios, presence or absence of a Friday mosque and of an alkali, number of those who made the pilgrimage, and adherents of an Islamic brotherhood), with possible combinations of these variables

2. Demographic movements and their association with political events, administrative change, growth or decline of markets and trade routes

3. Allocation of fiefs in relation to ethnic groups and religious affiliation as well as their sites, amount, and individual size

4. The proportion of slaves to free adult males by particular emirate subarea, again with ethnic, religious, and other potential correlatives

5. Approximate size and other significant attributes of settlements conquered or raided by the emirs or their enemies—in effect, adducing a few of the more accessible geopolitical implications of certain military ventures

6. The relevance of physical geography and ecological factors to all of these variables.

The potential benefits of this method suggest that it might be extended with profit in scope and design. A few of the categories of data which could be essayed are types of dwelling (e.g., grass huts, mud compounds, and their several subdivisions); modes of dress; weapons; forms of transport; medicinals; water sources; artifacts; imports and exports; craft occupations; and cultivated crops. While there might in theory be no ceiling on the diversity of means or of matter that can engage the student of precolonial Africa, he will decide for particular methods and objects of inquiry of finite proportions when in the field. Whatever he chooses, the historian should be aware of the kinds of knowledge his informants dispose of and, at least as much, of his own limitations of training and temperament.

An obvious reward for northern Nigerian historiography would lie in the delineation of state (emirate) boundaries in the later nineteenth century. Robert

---

1965). Izard, with his wife Françoise and Yacouba Ouédraogo, has since 1964 conducted a historical survey of some 700 settlements in Yatenga, Upper Volta, including material on their constituent wards. Ethnic, social, religious, political, and administrative data on 113 of these settlements are recorded in the book cited, as well as traditions of the putative founder of each, how it was founded, and in whose reign (whether chiefly or royal).

Heussler has finely remarked of the written sources for this region and period how they

> are in general highly stylized and concerned almost entirely with religion, genealogy, constitutionalism, and fighting. They give us very little of the raw material on which systematic historical research depends—population figures, data on natural resources, agricultural productivity, crafts, communications, and basic political information such as the areas under the effective control of the various emirs. There is no accurate map of the Sokoto empire as a whole, much less a more detailed chart showing changes in emirate boundaries throughout the nineteenth century.[13]

I experimented with elaborations of the oral census procedure in several ways. Occupational estimates were taken for each precolonial capital (by ward) and the results plotted on scale maps drawn for the period ca. 1900 showing urban residential patterns. I also prepared scale maps of each metropolitan central market and palace at that time, with subsections, commercial and otherwise, included. All of these maps (see Appendixes IV–VI) were composed with the aid of divisional surveyors, guided by local elders.

So too, on a limited geographic front—some 250 settlements in Shira District, Katagum Emirate—I recorded estimated annual output for the decade 1900–10 of 53 cultivated crops, expressed in common standards of measurement convertible into modern units, and of 56 nonfarming occupations (religious, craft, hunting and fishing, commercial, etc.), either in like standards or by the number of practitioners. Shortage of time precluded a wider application of this trial, which offers, among other possibilities, the chance of calculating official annual proceeds from taxation of fiefs in that period. All high titleholders were enfeoffed, and some officials were in charge of collecting a fixed amount on certain farm or craft products.

It is essential for ease of interpretation to represent this kind of evidence graphically and in a manner that lends itself to uncovering meaningful associated features. The constants chosen here—individual towns, villages, hamlets, and wards—are shown on the end-pocket envelope maps with each drawn to a circle- or section-size graduated in radius or width according to its (estimated) end-of-

13. "Research on Pre-British Northern Nigeria: A Note on Limitations and Potentialities," *The South Atlantic Quarterly,* LXV (1966), 525.

century free adult male population. Other variables shown are ethnic character, fiefholder, markets and Friday mosques. These maps are designed to serve as a medium for the reader to see how the data arrange themselves areally and perhaps to allow him to draw a few of his own conclusions; they are not intended to replace or do the job of tabulated correlations. If all variables were represented on separate and translucent maps, gross correlations and cross-checks would emerge when they are superimposed one on another or viewed severally in sequence. Such maps could also be used together with others of geological and topographical features and soil formations, as these are available.[14]

THE VERIFICATION AND VALUE OF OTHER ORAL DATA

All five of the credibility factors mentioned above with reference to oral census data will have some bearing on how far we can verify narrative and descriptive statements about precolonial history. Of these five, only the first and second ("controversial," "prestige-laden") may have lessened in their effect with passage of time. Most if not all the oral data influenced by these factors have progressively shed their more prestigeful or contentious attributes, a process that might well recompense the reseacher for the longer span of years elapsed since 1900 as compared with fragmentary and unannotated archival reports. While this net gain applies with greater force to population estimates and fiefholding arrangements for the late nineteenth century, it is true as well of much narrative and perhaps even more of descriptive material. Exactitude in modern population counts has often been undermined by the wish of local chiefs to reduce the head tax levied by Native Authorities and by the countervailing wish of party leaders to secure a larger say at higher levels of decision-making. The trustworthiness of assertions about historical fiefs was early on affected by hopes of titled officials of receiving from their new sovereign increased sources of revenue after 1900. The same kind of advantages reside in the later collection of narrative/descriptive data concerning the precolonial Border States, wherever else political significance had been attached.

14. For a rare example of how revealing this technique can be, see J. Desmond Clark, *Atlas of African Prehistory* (Chicago: University of Chicago Press, 1967).

Conversely, a number of methodological problems encountered in the verification of oral census data are encountered here. Individual or collective bias may often be sensed and allowed or offset by the recourse of local and external (i.e., written) checks. We can usually fix an approximate date on occurrences from their coincidence with memorable precolonial events, like "before, during, or after the reign of X," or "around the time Y conquered Z town." Again, informants are chosen by virtue of their occupational background, social placement, youthful residence, etc., or those of their fathers. We should define our terms of discourse in a way mutually understood and acknowledged. And just as the field historian, when proposing a conclusion drawn from his comparison of oral census data, must refer to whatever defects may inhere in them, so he will, if alert, avoid mistaking the apparent accuracy of a given set of evidence for the true measure of their interdependence. Thus whether our focus is a non-Muslim group or a Habe chief a suggested correlation between ethnic character and acceptance of Islam is verifiable only if each variable in the compound falls within adequate margins of likelihood (as well as of relevance); the same criteria obtain in the case of narrative and descriptive statements.

The question of how we adjudge the value of oral testimony of a narrative or descriptive nature is perhaps more conventional. It has been posed, and variously answered, by social scientists as well as by historians of Africa. Problems which attend on the significance, congruousness, integrity, and power of illumination of certain areas of oral data are, I would propose, no different in kind than problems we confront with written documents, either "primary" or not. The final worth of a quantum of evidence is in both instances decided by those research goals we have set and by the quality of our other data. It is, in effect, a judgment at once referential and private we make in the evaluation of this material. Nor should the potential worth of any document, written or oral, be discounted: while narrative/descriptive responses cannot always be consonant with a given line of inquiry, those which fail an immediate purpose may, for example, have relevance to another line, open a fresh one, or reveal an unsuspected bias. In short, the burden of proof of validity is upon the observer; the demonstration, in his published work.

A final word on the position of oral documents in African, indeed in all modern, historiography. Manuscript and archival material, whether ascribed to a participant, unengaged witness, or nonobserver of the scene recorded, is inferior in several ways to the kind of testimony which living deponents can offer. Written documents inform (as well as misinform) but they do not usually define their terms or supply much background on the author's motivation for writing, his biographical nodes of reference, or his range of access to primary sources; we may even lack assurance that he did in fact provide the text at hand. While each of these normal concerns of the scholar might be answered from external (often oral) evidence, written documents share a further, still more awkward disadvantage: *they cannot explicate a given record and be cross-examined on it.* Most fieldworkers in Africa have been aware of this difference in the uses of written vs. oral data. Although a number of precolonial historians now make a virtue of hard necessity, few as yet have gone beyond an acknowledgment of the abundance of oral evidence into questions regarding its value, credibility, and nature.

Oral matter of the kind employed here does not qualify as demonstrably valid or accurate if by this we mean definitive. Rather, it is hoped that with more refined techniques such matter can help to establish historically useful truths along an expanding continuum of political, social, and economic affairs.[15] On grounds alone of my experience with field histories, it seems evident that most qualitative matter is enriched, made less improbable or incomplete, when laid against the more quantitative. I found in the course of assembling the latter a number of questions, unprovoked by traditional methods, were suggested by emergent correlations as well as by apparent (or actual) inconsistencies. What explained, for instance, the migration of so many Auyakawa from this area to that in the reign of Emir Haru? Or the founding of three markets within a ten-mile radius of Katagum during a single decade? There developed, that is, a constantly rewarding interplay between the pointillist and narrative/descriptive material, with each type illumined, and challenged or corroborated in particulars, by the other.

It has often been said that a multiplicity of methods should be exploited for precolonial African studies—a commonplace now, yet one not observed with strict fidelity by all African historians of the nineteenth century, partly owing to an overdependence on written sources (even when these are few and inadequate), partly because of a misvaluation of oral data. And where written documents from

15. "The probability in favour of a given hypothesis increases with the degree of convergence of data stemming from different sources or relating to different aspects of culture. . . . And in the last resort a probabilistic estimate will always guide the historian in his quest" (*The Historian in Tropical Africa,* ed. Jan Vansina, Raymond Mauny, and L. V. Thomas [London: Oxford University Press, 1964], pp. 71–72). Studying a time of such relative recency as the years 1800–1900 invites the creative use of local memory, either living or at the brief remove of one, two, or three generations.

this period are themselves rare, as in these emirates, a still higher degree of trial and error seems warranted.

The need is great, and the opportunity passing, for basic research that will be at once monographic and multidimensional, specific in content but imaginative in conception. No tool-kit which offers another way into the African past should willfully go untried.

CHAPTER 4

THE NIGERIAN SUDAN TO 1800

KANEM-BORNU

While the genesis and initial era of expansion of the Kanem-Bornu Empire (ca. A.D. 700–1350) fall outside our main concerns, there is evidence that even before the Maghumi (Saifawa) rulers of Kanem transferred west of Lake Chad in the fourteenth century they had counted among their vassal groups a (historically obscure) number of chiefdoms in the Nigerian savanna.[1] Yves Urvoy suggests that by 1300 Maghumi political dominion west of the lake was confined to a ribbon of settlements bordering the Yo (Wobe) River in the neighborhood of Geidam and that beyond this point lay a vaguely defined, always shifting zone of political influence.[2] By 1430 the Maghumi line and authority were stabilized enough in Bornu to make their presence felt in the emerging polities of Hausaland.[3] The "Kano Chronicle" states that Abdullahi Burja (ca. 1438–52) was the

1. "Diwan of the Sultans of Bornu," in *The Bornu Sahara and Sudan* by H. Richmond Palmer (London: John Murray, 1936), p. 91; and Heinrich Barth, *Travels and Discoveries in Northern and Central Africa,* 3 vols. (1857–59; London: Frank Cass, 1965), II, 583–84. Barth concludes that Dunama Dabalemi, the Maghumi king, ca. A.D. 1200, penetrated as far southwest of Kanem as the Benue River. The Bornu chronicler of a later reign implies that Dunama's power extended much farther, to the frontiers of Yorubaland, or some 500 miles southwest of Lake Chad (Ahmed ibn Fartua, "The Kanem Wars," in *Sudanese Memoirs,* trans. H. Richmond Palmer, 3 vols. [1928; London: Frank Cass, 1967], I, 16, and note by Palmer, 73).

2. *Histoire de l'Empire du Bornou* (Paris: Larose, 1949), p. 44.

3. Al-Makrizi, writing ca. 1400 but here probably dependent on earlier sources, asserts that an "Afunu" king is ruled by the mai of Kanem—*Afunu* being the Kanuri word for Hausa-speakers (quoted in Palmer, *Sudanese Memoirs,* II, 6). Barth interprets this "rule" as signifying "a certain degree of dependency on Kanem" (*Travels and Discoveries,* II, 586).

first Hausa king to pay tribute to Bornu and that "all the west" did so in his reign.[4]

A long period of civil war and local resistance, first in Kanem and later Bornu, finally ended ca. 1500 when Mai Ali (Ghaji) Dunamani centralized Maghumi state power. Ali imposed clear, effective lines of authority between each level of government, reduced the quasi-independent status of fiefholding titled officials, and built a new capital, Birni Gazargamu, on the Middle Yo.[5] But he preserved the formal territorial base of the highest imperial offices, which continued to constitute a grand council of twelve—in particular, those of the galadima, kaigama, yerima, and mestrema. The galadima of Bornu was in charge of Ghaladi, or all the vassal chiefdoms west of Birni Gazargamu, and the kaigama of all southern vassals west of the Shari.[6]

The early 1500s witnessed frequent, largely frustrated attempts to extend Bornu dominance as far west as the borders of Songhay, on the Niger Bend. A ruler of Kano who died ca. 1565 is recorded as having marched to Bornu where he occupied Birni N'guru—then, or later, headquarters of the galadima.[7] While nothing is yet known of the role of the Bolewa, Shira, Teshena, and Auyo kingdoms which lay between Hausaland and Bornu,[8] the last three date from these years their payment of tribute to Birni Gazargamu, via the galadima.

Far the best documented mai of Bornu is Idris Alooma (ca. 1580–1617). Idris revived the forward policy toward Kano, whose people, his imam contends, had been plundering west Bornu. He also campaigned vigorously among the N'gizim, an ethnic group which the imam divides in two sections: those on the west Bornu marches, called the Binawa, and those farther south, between Mugrum and Daura. The latter, the Southern N'gizim, are said to have defied Bornu authority by raiding "Fellata"—either Cattle Fulani who already had reached

4. "The Kano Chronicle," in Palmer, *Sudanese Memoirs,* III, 109. Abdullahi is credited with having "opened roads from Bornu to Gwanja [Gonja, northern Ghana]"; this is the earliest extant reference to long-distance trade between Hausaland and Bornu (*ibid.*).

5. Barth, *Travels and Discoveries,* II, 33–34; and Urvoy, *Histoire de l'Empire du Bornou,* p. 55.

6. *Ibid.,* pp. 38–40; Barth, *Travels and Discoveries,* II, 26–27, 591–92; and J. R. Patterson, "Assessment Report on Borsari District, Bornu Emirate, Bornu Province (1918–26)," NAK SNP 17/8 K.2041.

7. Palmer, *Sudanese Memoirs,* III, 112.

8. Ahmed ibn Fartua, *History of the First Twelve Years of the Reign of Mai Idris Alooma of Bornu (1571–1583),* trans. H. Richmond Palmer (1926; London: Frank Cass, 1970), pp. 30–31, 73–74.

the Gujba-Damaturu grassland or else Kanuri of the same area. Idris marched there in strength during several wet seasons, burned the Southern N'gizim compounds and crops, and compelled the submission of their Habe chiefs. The Binawa, or Western N'gizim, posed a more acute problem, as they not only were pillaging Muslim communities close to Birni Gazargamu but also had severed the main road southwest from the capital through Daniski to the Bolewa Kwararafa center of Kalam. Long-distance traders and other travelers bound for the "land of Fali" had to move by a circuitous northern route made hazardous by marauding Bedde and nomadic Tuareg bands. Aware of the punitive devastation wrought by Idris on their southern kinsmen, the Binawa surrendered and their paramount chief converted to Islam (although both ranks of N'gizim continued—and still are—non-Muslim).[9]

With a series of campaigns in the trans-Chadian Sudan, Idris completed the unification of the new Bornu Empire. He conquered or pacified Mandara and Marghiland, the Bulala of Kanem, the Budumma of Lake Chad, and the Tebu (Teda) of Bilma, as well as the Tuareg kingdom of Asben (Air). His most enduring contributions to Central Sudanic history, at once religious and technological, have been summarized elsewhere,[10] but several key features of Bornu government are apposite here, in particular the assignment of overall administration and defense of the border zones to four senior Bornu officials. We shall consider only the positions of the galadima and kaigama vis-à-vis the northwestern and southwestern marches of the empire after its political center of gravity was removed west of Lake Chad ca. 1385–1485. The office of Kaigaman Bornu was held from that period by the chief slave and military commander of the mai. His writ of authority came to reach as far as the southernmost frontiers of Bornu, which put him in close and profitable contact with much of present-day Bauchi, Gombe, and Adamawa emirates, and Biu Federation.[11] Almost the whole of this huge area was until the jihad composed of non-Muslim peoples and states

9. *Ibid.*, pp. 12–13, 19, 36–44, 69, 81–82; and Barth, *Travels and Discoveries,* II, 595–96. "The Land of Fali" is identified by Palmer as all the region of present-day Fika Emirate (southwest Bornu), southern Kano, and the Border States excluding Hadejia (see his note in ibn Fartua, *The First Twelve Years,* p. 74, as well as his *Gazetteer of Bornu Province* [London: Waterlow, 1929], p. 8, n. 1, and his Introduction to C. K. Meek, *A Sudanese Kingdom* [London: Kegan Paul, 1931], p. xix). According to Palmer, the Binawa were then living in a zone which extended from Teshena northeastward to the Lower Yo.

10. Ibn Fartua, *The First Twelve Years,* pp. 11–12, 20, 30–31, 33, 44.

11. J. R. Patterson, *Kanuri Songs* (Lagos: The Government Printer, 1926), pp. 14–16; and "Mai Daud," in Palmer, *Sudanese Memoirs,* II, 48.

that would have provided the kaigama with more than sufficient sources of wealth, from his share of tribute and from periodic invasions, to justify Barth's account of the office as one "possessing very great power."[12]

About 1625 Galadiman Bornu acquired his own town, Birni N'guru, close by the course of the Lower Yo and 100 miles west of Birni Gazargamu.[13] From there his successors developed into "almost independent vassals" of the mai, holding "immense power."[14] The galadima's realm comprehended all the northwest corner of the Bornu Empire, including the vassal kingdom of Damagaram (Zinder), Gumel, the Sosebaki states, Auyo, Shira, and Teshena, as well as chieftaincies of ethnic groupings like the Bedde and Western N'gizim. Still farther west he exercised on the mai's behalf a more titular hegemony over the emergent city-states of Hausaland.[15] Establishment of the galadima at N'guru seems to have been designed in part as a device for sustaining more easily in future the West-Central Sudanic exploits of Idris Alooma a generation earlier.

The two centuries (ca. 1617–1808) which followed the death of Idris were marked in the empire by a succession of ineffectual mais who seem to have been as devoted to the passive enjoyment of their imperial legacy as to its increase or even its preservation. By the mid-1700s Tuareg depredations had wasted much of the sahilian tracts of Bornu, and its vassal chiefs were enabled progressively to reclaim their independence.[16] Under Mai Ahmad (ca. 1793–1810),

12. *Travels and Discoveries,* II, 591.

13. G. J. Lethem, "Chronicle of the Galadimas of Bornu, Notes on," NAK SNP 10/5 2868 204p/1917; and "Special Report on Nguru District, Bornu Province," NAK SNP 10/7 3741 258p/1919. A town of that name located there may have existed before this date, since the defeat of Mai Ali by the first ruler of Kebbi ca. 1500 is reported to have occurred at "Onghoor" in northwest Bornu (Barth, *Travels and Discoveries,* II, 590), while the "Kano Chronicle" declares that Sarki Mohamma Kisoka (ca. 1509–65) briefly occupied "Birnin Nguru" (Palmer, *Sudanese Memoirs,* II, 113).

14. Barth, *Travels and Discoveries,* II, 555.

15. *Ibid.* p. 591; Barth says that he governed "the western countries" from N'guru to the Niger.

16. Urvoy, *Histoire de l'Empire du Bornou,* p. 86; and Louis Brenner, "The Shehus of Kukawa: A History of the Al-Kanemi Dynasty of Bornu" (Ph.D. diss., Columbia University, 1968), p. 22. Brenner concludes that while "at the turn of the [nineteenth] century Bornu was still considered the most powerful kingdom in central Africa . . . this power was more apparent than real" (p. 22). Mai Ali b. Hajj Dunama (ca. 1753–93) made several attempts to reassert Bornu's political dominance by launching punitive raids on the Bedde to the west and against Mandara on the southeast, in one of which his kaigama was defeated with great loss by an army said to have included "growing numbers of Fulbe (Fellata) . . . of the region of Dikwa and Mandara" (Palmer, *The Bornu Sahara,* p. 255). A dissenting view of Maghumi leadership in this period is

the land experienced an epidemic that killed vast numbers of people, and, soon after, a visitation more deadly in its political aspect—a rebellion of its Fulani subjects, inspired by the example of Shaikh Usuman dan Fodio and his lieutenants in Hausaland, but prepared for by several hundred years of waning influence abroad coupled with an advancing corrosion of royal authority at home.

THE HAUSA STATES AND THE ORIGINS OF THE SOKOTO JIHAD

By 1500 the main Hausa polities, notably Kano, Zaria, Katsina, and Gobir, "formerly independent small-scale chiefdoms," had, according to M. G. Smith, "become tributary city-states, Muslim in outlook and allegiance, units in the widespread system of Sudanic and Saharan trade, and committed to large-scale slave-raiding for tribute, commerce and local production by forced labour."[17] They were and remained until the jihad of 1804–10 in at least nominal subordination to the mai of Bornu, sending annual gifts through his galadima, though otherwise it would seem their own masters in both domestic and foreign affairs.[18]

The general chaos which prevailed on the Middle Niger after the conquest by Morocco in 1591 of the Songhay capital marked a watershed in northern Nigeria's encounter with Islam. In its wake there ensued a breakdown of long-established, orderly caravan traffic moving along the Western Saharan oases and transversely across the Western Sudan. Kano, Katsina, and Birni Gazargamu developed henceforth as new ports and transshipping stations for Sudanic and northern African goods, ushering in several centuries of rapid commercial growth at these major entrepôts. Equally significant in its effect on the Nigerian savanna, this shift led to a redefinition of those religious and cultural ties with North Africa which has endured since then: while Hausaland previously had been involved

---

given by Ronald Cohen. He suggests that later descriptions may in good measure "be a reinterpretation of Bornu history by the second [al-Kanemi] dynasty and their followers, who would naturally have played up the failures of the previous regime" when they took power (*The Kanuri of Bornu* [New York: Holt, Rinehart and Winston, 1967], p. 16).

17. "The Beginnings of Hausa Society, ca. 1000–1500," in *The Historian in Tropical Africa,* ed. Jan Vansina, Raymond Mauny, and L. V. Thomas (London: Oxford University Press, 1964), p. 342.

18. *Ibid.,* p. 348, n. 35.

with the broader Islamic world chiefly through a contagion of ideas, customs, and rituals filtered down West Sudanic routes of trade from the Maghrib, now commerce and its attendant carriers of Muslim tradition were to come south undeflected, the latter with a heavier orthodox coloration, from Cairo and Tripoli.[19] Arabic manuscripts of local origin bear witness, in their quality and number, to a high level of Islamic erudition in West Africa well before the modern era. Until the sixteenth century it seems that Muslim studies were confined largely to canon law and commentaries thereon. Later, a Muslim intelligentsia created a body of its own literature that included glosses on Islamic texts as well as chronicles of domestic royal or sacerdotal lineages. Thus, when from 1804 the Fulani warrior-scholars of northern Nigeria led, on the religious authority of Shaikh Usuman dan Fodio, a series of brilliantly executed campaigns against the Hausa kings and, less successfully, against Bornu, they were moving from positions of impressive doctrinal as well as military strength.[20] In six years all but two of the major Hausa dynasties had been dethroned and provincial emirs appointed by Usuman in their stead.

19. See John Hunwick, "The Influence of Arabic in West Africa," *Transactions of the Historical Society of Ghana,* VII (1964), 24–41; and Mervyn Hiskett, "Material Relating to the State of Learning among the Fulani before Their Jihad," *Bulletin of the School of Oriental and African Studies,* XIX (1957), 571–73. On the strength of a document regarding Timbuctu which he examined after his article appeared, John Hunwick suggests that in fact "contrary to what one might have expected, Egypt and Mecca and not the Maghrib were the centres of intellectual stimulation for Timbuctoo, the chief dispersion points of the Islamic sciences in West Africa." Hunwick observes that (a) Egypt in the fifteenth and early sixteenth centuries produced the finest scholarship of its time and genre, while Maghribi learning was then at a low ebb; and (b) pilgrims from the Western Sudan more often reached the Sahara via the Nigerian savanna than crossed it by a Mauritanian route. He further notes "the possibilities of an oriental (rather than Maghribi) influence in Hausa Islam through this pilgrimage traffic and the residence of the Timbuctoo *'ulamā* in Hausa towns on their return from the pilgrimage." If Hunwick's revisionist conclusion is accurate, we shall have to ascribe a far less significant role to Maghribi influence on the early development of Islam in the Nigerian Sudan (see "Further Light on Ahmad Bābā al-Tinbuktī," *Research Bulletin of the Centre of Arabic Documentation*, II [July, 1966], pp. 25–26).

20. As accepted exponents of Muslim canon law and guides to proper forms of Islamic ritual in communities often nominal in their understanding and usage of these, such clerics (*mallamai,* A. *'ulamā*) were popularly accorded the status thought due them and seem to have been ranked socially just below the local and other *sarakuna* by the mass of peasantry, craftsmen, and traders. Hence they formed a separate class in the social order, one potentially seditious in the view of many Habe chiefs—who themselves appear to have been rather slack in their observance of codified religious conduct.

SHAIKH USUMAN DAN FODIO

Shaikh Usuman was born during the middle years of the eighteenth century in the Hausa kingdom of Gobir. Descended from a long, distinguished line of Fulani divines of the Torodbe clan, he studied as a youth at Agades (Air) and then settled at Degel, 20 miles north of modern Sokoto. Between ca. 1774 and 1786 there gathered about him an ever-increasing band of student disciples, attracted by Usuman's knowledge and personality from various parts of the Western and Central Sudan. While at Degel he made regular circuits of the Gobir countryside, to proselytize and instruct the local Hausa, Fulani, and Tuareg. Around 1786–87 Usuman transferred his missionary work one hundred miles southward, to Zamfara, but five years later, his position at home secured by an understanding with Sarkin Gobir, he returned to Degel.[21]

The political influence of Gobir, already on the wane by this date, was further weakened in 1794–95 when the Gobirawa sustained a crushing defeat and their ruler was killed. The new sarki, Nafata, soon abrogated his father's agreement with Usuman—an event, it has been said, which "is usually taken in Sokoto as the first shot of the jihad." When the next king of Gobir, Yunfa (1803–8), attempted Usuman's assassination, he emigrated with his immediate following from Degel to another town some 25 miles northwest (February 21, 1804).[22] This act of the shaikh is often referred to in local tradition as corresponding in its religious import to the Prophet's own hijra (departure) from Mecca to Medina.[23]

In this period the Community of Believers who recognized Shaikh Usuman as their spiritual guide (H. *Sarkin Mussulmi*) was scattered widely, both in the environs of Gobir and elsewhere across the Nigerian Sudan. But when the wet-season crops had been harvested, those men around Usuman, and others, including a number of the Fulani resident in Bornu or on its western periphery, made preparations to carry out local jihads against the mai and the rulers of Habe polities of the western and southern hinterland of Bornu.[24]

21. Denis Murray Last, *The Sokoto Caliphate* (London: Longmans, Green, 1967), pp. 6–8.

22. *Ibid.*, pp. 8, 12–13.

23. Sidney J. Hogben and Anthony H. M. Kirk-Greene, *The Emirates of Northern Nigeria: A Preliminary Survey of Their Historical Traditions* (London: Oxford University Press, 1966), p. 380.

24. Last, *The Sokoto Caliphate*, pp. 16, 21–22, 29–30; and Roland A. Adeleye, *Power and Diplomacy in Northern Nigeria 1804–1906* (London: Longman Group, 1971), pp. 11–19.

THE FULANI OF NORTHEAST NIGERIA UNTIL THE JIHAD

All but one of the eight eastern emirates of the (former) Sokoto Caliphate have remained for some 150 years clearly defined Muslim areas, whose traditional rulers, now responsible to a new and secular higher authority, are each direct scions of the founding agnatic lineages.[25] In several instances these royal lines can be traced further back two or three generations from their dynastic progenitors. Evidence contained in oral tradition points to the likelihood that each governing kin group in the nineteenth century was descended from a clan (which itself may have been part of a larger social aggregate) of pastoral or semisedentary Fulani which had resided for many years in the northeast Nigerian grassland of the Lake Chad and the Gongola, Hadejia, Katagum, and Misau (Dingaya) river basins. While the original names of these Fulani descent groups and of their family subdivisions are no longer known, they can be separated out for convenience by observing the present-day local habit of referring to each in the context either of one of its earlier, remembered leaders or of the place where it camped in the wet seasons shortly before 1800.[26]

The pre-jihad chronicles of these several kin groups are now in great measure lost to memory, but a rough outline of major Fulani communities and their probable migration patterns in northeast Nigeria may be pieced out from the combined use of documentary sources and a rather more abundant supply of local traditions. The first apparent reference to a Fulani presence east of the region of Hausaland is found in a Bornu chronicle allusion to the arrival ca. 1250 of a pair of Islamic divines, "Fulani of Melle [Mali]," at the court of the ruler of Kanem (then reigning at Njimi, near Lake Chad).[27] One hundred and fifty

25. The exception, Marma Emirate, was conquered by and incorporated into Hadejia ca. 1854; see p. 142 below.

26. Derrick J. Stenning has noted of the pastoral Fulani clans of the "Great Forest" of western Bornu that until the colonial period their names were usually taken from those neighborhoods where they found themselves in the wet season, or else were nicknames (*Savannah Nomads: A Study of the Wodaabe Pastoral Fulani of Western Bornu Province, Northern Region, Nigeria* [London: Oxford University Press, 1959], p. 54). Another scholar, who conducted a similar study of pastoral Fulani in western Hausaland, writes that such clans tended strongly to adopt "the name of the village at or near which they had lived for at least a generation" (C. E. Hopen, *The Pastoral Fulbe Family in Gwandu* [London: Oxford University Press, 1958], p. 44).

27. Barth, *Travels and Discoveries*, II, 584–85; and ibn Fartua, *The First Twelve Years*, p. 79.

years later, the Arabic author al-Makrizi reported Fulani resident in the Kanem-Bornu area,[28] and it could have been this element which by 1573 was recorded by a native contemporary historian as living in northern Bornu.[29] Palmer suggests, perhaps on the evidence of these and similar Arabic writings, that a significant migration of Fulani pastoralists into Bornu should be dated from about the early 1400s; moving progressively eastward along the Sudanic-sahilian borderlands, after 1600 (he continues) they had passed south of the Yo (Wobe) River and soon formed numerous nomadic communities in western Bornu, especially around N'guru and in the Damaturu-Gujba-Daya complex, as well as farther south, in the Lower Gongola Valley.[30] Barth, who visited much of the Lake Chad Basin a century ago, cites the existence ca. 1550–1600 of two Fulani settlements in Baghirmi (southeast of the lake).[31] Baghirmi and the Mandara foothills due south of the lake are both given in Damaturu tradition as an alternative base of emigration by Fulani who reached there at some period in the 1700s.[32]

Such gradual, often piecemeal shifts of pastoral Fulani groups—what Stenning calls "migratory drift"—probably were similar in kind to the general course of removal and dispersion that seems to have characterized the progress of nomadic Fulani demographic patterns in much of the Western and Central Sudan before 1800.[33] Cattle-herding Fulani bands had spread eastward from the Senegambia region since the eleventh or twelfth centuries to find new grassland and water sources, to escape bovine epidemics, to evade the hostility and covetousness of

28. Palmer, *The Bornu Sahara*, p. 23. Palmer translated a *mahram*, or grant of privilege, conferred originally by Mai Ali (ca. 1472–1505) on a group of Fellata (Fulani) subject to Bornu (*ibid.*, pp. 36–37).

29. Ibn Fartua, *The First Twelve Years*, p. 79.

30. *The Bornu Sahara*, p. 258; and his note in ibn Fartua, *The First Twelve Years*, p. 79.

31. Barth, *Travels and Discoveries*, II, 549; III, 115.

32. G. J. Lethem, "Assessment Report on Allaguerno District, Bornu Emirate, Bornu Province," NAK SNP 10/7 3748 265p/1919.

33. Stenning describes three gradations of pastoral nomadic group movement: transhumance, migratory drift, and migration. Transhumance is characterized by a cyclical change of habitat to accommodate the annual dry-season lack of adequate herbage and water, the group concerned often or usually returning to the same wet-season camp each year. Migratory drift is a spatial extension of transhumance and occurs when the area encompassed by the regular transhumance cycle has been replaced by a new one. Migration is an abrupt, sometimes long-distance, shift of such nomadic routes and is occasioned less by ecological than by political or ideological stress. ("Transhumance, Migratory Drift, Migration: Patterns of Pastoral Fulani Nomadism," in *Cultures and Societies of Africa*, ed. Simon Ottenberg and Phoebe Ottenberg [New York: Random House, 1960], pp. 142–57).

more settled neighbors, or whenever the surrounding King's Peace was disrupted by foreign predators.[34] Those which entered the Nigerian savanna, beginning perhaps ca. 1300, appear to have maintained their custom of migratory drift through Hausaland and Bornu from the same divers causes that brought them east: the search for optimum ecological and community conditions for grazing and expansion of their herds. Until 1800 they seem to have remained aloof from direct engagement in the organized political societies of northern Nigeria; there are few recorded instances of Fulani participation in the prolonged contests for power and affluence among the Hausa or Kwararafa states before that date, or in Bornu earlier than ca. 1780.[35]

These immigrant Fulani predominantly had maintained a pastoral socioeconomic style of life and were for the most part un-Islamized. In contradistinction to individual Fulani who increasingly broke with this model by settling in Habe towns (the so-called *Fulanin Gida,* or Town Fulani), such groupings and their members are known to themselves as *Fulanin Bororo* or *Bororoje* (Cattle Fulani), or *Fulanin Daji/Jeji* (Bush Fulani), and to Kanuri as *Abore*. By means of a cautious extrapolation from an anthropological study of the Wodaabe Fulanin Bororo of western Bornu conducted by Stenning in the 1950s, which includes both a survey of their traditions of precolonial migration from Kano, Hadejia, and Katagum emirates and a critical summary of oral accounts of Wodaabe society before the jihad, we can infer something of the eighteenth-century human organization of other Cattle Fulani communities in northeast Nigeria.

The nuclear social and economic unit of this organization was the simple or compound patrilocal family.[36] Several such units, comprising an agnatic lineage group, might associate in carrying out the basic daily and seasonal round of their mobile activities. These joint occupations included those connected with the dry-season movement of herds to fresh pasturelands, e.g., building temporary camps while in passage; a common defense against cattle thieves; maintenance of sufficient livestock and working hands among the group's individual family units; supervision of marriage alliances for both sexes, especially at first marriage (the occasion for establishment of new families and herds within the group,

34. Stenning has summarized the most useful written sources for these geographical displacements and their principle causes (*Savannah Nomads,* pp. 21–22).

35. A major exception to this habit of political nonalignment was the involvement of local pastoral or semi-sedentary Fulani in sixteen-century conflicts over the royal succession in Kebbi (Barth, *Travels and Discoveries,* III, 115).

36. This and the next five paragraphs are drawn from Stenning, *Savannah Nomads,* pp. 4–6, 38, 41–42, 46–48, 53–55.

which, like all Cattle Fulani society, was endogamous); and regulation of inheritance of cattle on the death of a family head, inheritance being commonly patrilineal.

From among its family heads the lineage group chose a leader, or *ardo* (pl. *ardo'en;* in Hausaland, *ruga*), whose qualifications were based on a cluster of deciding factors. These included his age and genealogical placement vis-à-vis the former ardo, the number of his wives and children, the size of his family herds, and his degree of popularity with fellow household heads in the group. More often than not this meant that a new ardo was the son or brother of the man he succeeded. The ardo's functions were to represent his lineage group before similar groups; to secure the favor of local chiefs in communities where the group wished to pasture; to oversee arrangements for marriage and divorce within or outside the group; to insure that his people were effectively prepared to defend themselves from marauders; and to conduct meetings of family heads when the lineage group was ready to move camp, offering his advice and stating the consensus view on where they should go.

Because his position and authority were gained in large part by reason of his relative wealth in family members and cattle, the ardo's internal writ was vulnerable alike to radical change in his personal fortunes or in those of another herdowner, whose level of prosperity might come to exceed his own. Since no means existed for replacing an ardo, some of his followers might break away to form a new lineage group under a wealthier family head. When segmentation of the primary group occurred in this manner, the two resultant ensembles would still often spend the wet season together, but where they did not they soon drifted apart and no longer cooperated in areas of mutual concern.

Segmentation was but one of several ways by which the agnatic lineage group could be altered in size. Its membership was narrowed if, as frequently happened, a youth's father was unable to provide him with cattle on his first marriage, and he was forced to seek help from his mother's brother or his father's sister's husband, herding for the uncle and later, endowed with his gift of cattle, marrying into his lineage group. It could also be diminished when a family head's cattle were decimated by disease, and, unable to replenish the herd from his own group's resources, he and his family had to seek a patron within a more fortunate lineage group, thus transferring into it. Stenning concludes that, hence,

> the agnatic descent group was not a monolithic unit but was acutely sensitive to demographic and ecological fluctuations in the families of which it was composed. It functioned as a group by minimizing

> the effects upon its members of those fluctuations, by recruiting new members through birth, marriage, and incorporation, and by adjusting itself by periodic fragmentation to the conditions in which its subsistence was gained.[37]

Alternatively, the typical Fulanin Bororo wet-season camp was made up of a congeries of two or more lineage groups, that is, a clan. Here too the principle of association was agnatic descent, but of a more putative order, the several founders allegedly being of one father or grandfather. A second fictive device employed to form such a clan was that of asserting a different kind of ancestral connection by marriage, one that gave sanction as well to connubium of the living members of each lineage component. Among Wodaabe, as with Fulanin Bororo communities which founded the Border States, a clan often took its name from the place where it encamped in the wet season.

Each constituent group of the clan was led by its own ardo, and each was ranked in social importance according to how far back in generational depth it could derive its agnatic descent from one of the clan founders. Thus the senior lineage group (and the senior ardo) was the one generally accepted as having a direct line of descent from the earliest known or assumed male ancestor of the clan as a whole, while other groups (and their ardos) were classified by the genealogical position of their respective founders relative to that of the senior lineage group.

On the evidence provided by local descendants of the Cattle Fulani lineages and clans that established themselves after 1800 in year-round settlements under the central authority of Gombe, Katagum, and Hadejia, as well as from accounts by European observers of those that remained in southern Bornu and Adamawa, it would seem that most if not all of these groupings were, in the late eighteenth century, spending the wet season on pastureland that surrounded non-Fulani towns, either Habe or Barebari. Where, as in the Gongola-Benue region, the host population was both non-Muslim and outside the immediate reach of Bornu authority, the ardo of each unit (or the senior ardo) was not only accountable to the local chief (F. *ardido,* pl. *ardidai*) of the wet-season site for its good deportment but also for the rendering by its family heads of gifts to that chief, in the medium of cows or bovine products (milk, butter, possibly meat).[38] Where,

37. *Ibid.,* p. 53.

38. "Miscellaneous Notes on the People of Biu Division and Neighboring Country," NAK Biu District 134 L.1; "Notes on the Origins of Peoples of Bornu Province and Neighboring Country (1920–28)," NAK Biu District 135 L.2; E. J. Douglas, "Assess-

as farther north, officials of Bornu had more control over nomadic Fulani in the wet season, an agent of the mai, the *chima jeribe,* was in charge of collecting the Qur'anic tithe (*zaka*), usually called *jangali* in Nigeria when levied on pastoralists and paid in cattle, one chima being assigned to each group.[39] In either case the payment was emblematic of an ardo's subordinate political status, that is, was a form of tribute. In exchange, the Fulani were secured from molestation by thieves and slaveraiders and in their right of peaceful grazing. A like system obtained in Hausaland, where *jangali* was paid to local agents of central-government officials holding the pastureland as fiefs under the Hausa kings.

Well before the outbreak of a jihad in 1804 the Fulani communities of northern Nigeria had thrown up from their ranks a number of Muslim scholars, preachers, healers, and diviners.[40] These men, whose knowledge of Islamic canon law, tradition, and ritual vary today from the most superficial acquaintance to a deep and wide background in the religious sciences, can be grouped under the all-inclusive rubric of clerics, "holy men," or divines. At one extreme, they lack even the ability to read the Qur'an; at the other, they are theologians, masters of local branches of Muslim fraternities, and heads of scholastic institutions. A few have made the pilgrimage once or several times, thus gaining the honorific title of *alhaji.* Many have been trained in the making of talismans, astrology, the predictive reading of sand patterns, customary Islamic medicine, and other supernatural expedients.[41] Although a number are wealthy traders and farmers, most live on

ment Report on Shani District, Biu Division, Bornu Province," NAK SNP 17/2 1195 10160; and Informants IA: 2–4; IB: 1–4, 6, 11–14; IC: 2, 5, 12–14, 20, 23–25, 27–28, 30, 35, 38–40; ID: 1–5, 7–8, 11, 14, 17; IE: 8–12; IF: 1, 3, 6; IG: 2, 5, 7–8. A close observer of the Cattle Fulani in this region has written: "As regards the relationship of the Nomadic Fulani with the rulers, it would appear that the majority of, if not all, such tribes had, from long ago, representatives of their own in the towns of the ruling chiefs." These men (he continues), usually sons of ardos, had settled in non-Fulani towns as Muslim clerics. They provided the formal link between their still-nomadic clan groups and local authority (F. W. de St. Croix, *The Fulani of Northern Nigeria* (Lagos: Government Printer, 1945), pp. 7–8).

39. Informants as in n. 38 above; and M. G. Smith, "Pluralism in Precolonial African Societies," in *Pluralism in Africa,* ed. Leo Kuper and M. G. Smith (Berkeley: University of California Press, 1969), p. 109.

40. This paragraph and the next two are drawn from personal observation, supplemented by Stenning, *Savannah Nomads,* pp. 9–10. For the Western and Central Sudan as a whole, see J. Spencer Trimingham, *Islam in West Africa* (London: Oxford University Press, 1961), pp. 68–101.

41. Both Shaikh Usuman and Sultan Muhammad Bello condemned soothsaying, astrology, talismans, and several other modes of traditional Islamic "magic," on the grounds, *inter alia,* that no sanction is given them by orthodox Islamic sources and

donations of the Faithful, instruct young children, and/or receive a modicum of support from their immediate followers. Because of their specialized education, and particularly by virtue of an ascribed possession of holiness (A. *baraka;* H. *barka*), they are in constant demand to perform at weddings, funerals, and post-natal ceremonies, as well as to resolve disputes.

The more learned among them, the legists with a command of the *Sharī'a* and of standard commentaries on the law, the teachers of theology, and others having a sophisticated knowledge of Islamic doctrine (A. *'ilm*), are called in Hausa *mallamin ilimi,* an equivalent of the Arabic *'ulamā.* Those whose competence does not extend far beyond the recitation from memory of Qur'anic passages are known as *mallamin al-Kur'ani.* Today, any person with a claim to literacy in some language may be addressed as mallam, but in earlier times the title was reserved to men who could read the Qur'an but neither speak nor write Arabic. A senior grade of holy men, in Fulani the *gwonayi* (sing. *gwoni*), both read the Qur'an fluently and served as community reciters of it; a few had also acquired proficiency in spoken and written Arabic. At a still higher level was the *modibbo* (F.) or *shehu* (H.), well read in Qur'anic law and commentaries and an authority on proper Islamic practice. Together, such clerics formed a distinct social class in Fulani (as well as Kanuri and Hausa) society. They often traveled about the countryside or shuttled between the several centers of higher Muslim education, ministering to urban and rural Believers alike, teaching, propagating the Faith, doctoring, forecasting, officiating, and functioning as magistrates. Not all, or perhaps a majority, of these men were of Fulani extraction, but those who were played an especially central part in the local jihads of northeast Nigeria, not only in providing them a vital sanction and a divine rationale but also and often by serving as militant exponents of the new creed.[42]

---

that good Muslims should be undistracted in their practice of *'ibāda* (see Denis Murray Last, "A Note on Attitudes to the Supernatural in the Sokoto Jihad," *Journal of the Historical Society of Nigeria, IV* [December, 1967], 5–7).

42. The vexed question of how far the Sokoto jihad was in essence a Fulani thrust at political seats of power or a general movement toward social and/or religious reform has been considered, though not resolved, by several authors. See, e.g., Marilyn Robinson Waldman, "The Fulani *Jihād*: A Reassessment," *Journal of African History,* VI (1965), 333–55; and "A Note on the Ethnic Interpretation of the Fulani *Jihād,*" *Africa,* XXXVI (July, 1966), 286–91; Last, *The Sokoto Caliphate,* pp. 16–22; Adeleye, *Power and Diplomacy,* pp. 19–21; and H. A. S. Johnston, *The Fulani Empire of Sokoto* (London: Oxford University Press, 1967), pp. 95–102, 266. While a number of Hausa, Tuareg, and Habe did actively support the jihad in its earlier phase, it is evident that most of Shaikh Usuman's initial community, and almost all of its leadership beyond the immediate environs of Gobir, were composed of Fulani.

A CLASSIFICATION OF NORTHEAST NIGERIAN FULANI

Among the Fulani groups resident in Bornu and its western environs by 1800 we can identify nine more or less major categories. Some of these probably were already settled in towns, villages, or encampments of their own where they lived in the dry months as well as the wet and practiced a measure of small-scale agriculture during the rains, to move off with their cattle after the harvest for distances more limited than those covered by the still fully nomadic Fulani. Others seem to have gone even farther along the route of conversion to a sedentary mode of life and had been transformed as a whole into Town Fulani, often adopting at least a few of the economic and social customs of their long-settled Habe or Muslim neighbors. Yet a high proportion of the Fulani of northeast Nigeria appear to have continued as year-round pastoralists throughout the eighteenth century, and a number remain so today.[43]

The classification that follows would not of course preclude the manifest possibility of other Fulani communities in this period, nor are its component divisions always as clear-cut or self-contained as we might wish.[44] It is drawn from the current popular nomenclature as employed by informants when speaking of themselves or of their Fulani co-residents in a particular area.

1. The *Fulanin Bororo* were then pasturing in the open savanna parklands around N'guru, Marma, and Auyo.[45] From their ranks emerged the ruling families of Marma and Hadejia emirates. Descendants and early followers of those who founded Hadejia are commonly referred to as Fulanin Sambo, after the first emir of Hadejia, Sambo Digimsa dan Ardo Abdua; outside the emirate they and other Fulani of this region often are called simply Fulanin Hadejia.

2. The *Fulanin Mare* were so-called, it appears, from the place-name of one of their two known foci of wet- (and perhaps dry-) season habitation—the Mare or Dilara Plain on the southwest banks of Lake Chad. Their other known site was

43. Informants as in n. 38 above; and IIB: 3–5, 8; IIC: 7–10, 12–19; IID: 8; IIE: 1, 9–11, 13–14, 20; IIF: 1–4, 6, 8, 11–14; IIG: 6–7, 12–13; IIH, 2, 8–9; II I, 2–5, 10–16, 19–22, 24–28; IIJ: 1, 6, 8–9, 11–15; IIK: 1–2; IIIA: *passim.*

44. The Fulanin Gori, for example, who provided the nineteenth-century house of Galadiman Katagum (a high titled office) and who previously had lived in Beddeland, might be considered a separate category, although it appears they were relatively few in number. And the Fulanin Shira respectively of Katagum and Gombe might have been listed together.

45. See p. 133 below.

in the Damaturu-Gujba-Daya zone of southwest Bornu.[46] Ardos of this category provided the royal houses of Misau, Jema'are, and Adamawa emirates.

3. *Fulanin Kitaku* is an obscurely derived, omnibus term for the dozen or so lineage groups or clans then living in the extreme southwest of the Bornu Empire and in the Lower Gongola Basin.[47] They seem to have become semi-sedentary by the mid-1700s, and they produced in turn most of the governing elite of Gombe as well as the ruling dynasty of Muri Emirate.

4. The *Fulanin Shira* of the pre-jihad Habe kingdom of Shira subsequently incorporated into Katagum Emirate, and probably, together with the five groups below, had by the eighteenth century begun changing over to a more settled, agricultural economy.[48]

5. The *Fulanin Shira,* often called Fulanin Dukku, of the upper Gongola region made their camps in the environs of Kalam Town after an eighteenth-century migration there from west of Sokoto, via Shira Kingdom. Tributary to Kalam until the jihad, they had, despite their relatively large numbers and wealth in cattle, little direct share in the administration of Gombe Emirate.[49]

46. *Notes on the Tribes, Provinces, Emirates and States of the Northern Provinces of Nigeria, Compiled from Official Reports of O. Temple,* ed. C. L. Temple, 2d ed. (1922; London: Frank Cass, 1965), pp. 476–78; Hogben and Kirk-Greene, *Emirates of Northern Nigeria,* p. 472; Urvoy, *Histoire de l'Empire du Bornou,* p. 101, n. 5; and L. N. Reed, "Notes on Some Fulani Tribes and Customs," *Africa,* V (1932), pp. 426, 445.

47. Informants today are even more vague and uncertain about the origin or meaning of Kitaku than have been those interviewed by colonial district officers. Among the latter, Kitaku (or Kitiyen) were recorded as "serf-like" Fulani cattlemen herding for non-Muslim overlords in parts of southwest Bornu; as "Fulani slaves" who escaped from their Fulani masters, settled in Biu Emirate, and gradually acquired their own cattle; as immigrants from Malle (Mali)—the usual site of emigration quoted by Nigeria Fulani; and as partially settled, Islamized, and servile descendants of pure nomadic Fulani "pagans" (see W. O. P. Rosedale, "Assessment Report on Kanakuru District, Numan Division, Yola Province," NAK SNP 10/7 3752 275p/1919; J. H. Elder, in "Miscellaneous Notes on the People of Biu Division"; Douglas, "Shani District"; and E. A. Brackenbury, "Notes on the 'Bororo Fulbe' or Nomad 'Cattle Fulani'," Pt. II, *Journal of the African Society,* XXIII [July, 1924], 276–77). Brackenbury adds: "The word *Kitien* is said to have derived from the adjective *kitum,* which means 'ancient'; or from the word *Kitako,* meaning 'ancient custom' " (*ibid.*). De St. Croix defines "keteji" as "the almost humpless cattle of the Borgu [Bornu?] Fulani" (*Fulani of Northern Nigeria,* p. 71).

48. Informants IIC: 2, 10, 13, 18–19; IIF: 4; II I: 12–14, 16, 21, 24; IIJ: 1, 6, 8, 11–12.

49. Informants IF: 2–4, 6; P. Lonsdale, "Assessment Report on Gombe Town, Gombe Emirate, Central Province," NAK SNP 7/14 3607 7p/1913; and T. F. Carlyle, "History of Gombe Emirate, Central Province," NAK SNP 10/2 1179 445p/1914.

6. The *Fulanin Teshena* of the pre-jihad Habe kingdom of Teshena also became subjects of the emir of Katagum after ca. 1806.[50]

7. The *Fulanin Jafun,* usually called Jafunawa, were in the early 1700s migrants from the neighborhood of Jafun Town in eastern Kano. Their main concentration was at and around Hardawa Town (southeast Shira) and members of this group were under Katagum until 1913.[51]

8. The *Fulanin Sika* of what became central Katagum Emirate were a relatively small unit which had come under the Lerewa (Barebari) chiefdom of Guma'i before 1800.[52]

9. The *Fulanin Udubo* were resident near Udubo Town (east Katagum), another Lerewa center then paying tribute directly to Bornu.[53]

The Fulanin Bororo of the Auyo-Marma-N'guru zone, the Fulanin Mare, and the Fulanin Kitaku are known collectively as *Fulanin Bornu* in Hausa and *Fellata Bornu* in Kanuri and by themselves. The latter designation is far more often heard in the Border States, even today, and is used here.

BAREBARI OF THE BORDER STATES

The pre-jihad ethnic and political topography of those areas incorporated in the first half of the nineteenth century as Gombe, Katagum, and Hadejia emirates can be drawn as yet only in broad and irregular outline. Half a dozen major kingdoms and about an equal number of lesser Habe and Barebari chieftaincies or ethnic groupings are, however, at least partially discernable for the period ca. 1300–1800. These polities and peoples were (1) the Habe Kwararafa (Jukun and Bolewa) states of Kalam, Geri Kom, and Pindiga, with several Tera centers,

50. Informants IIB: 3, 5, 8.

51. Informants IIF: 11; IIH: 8–9; IIJ: 9, 13; H. Q. Glenny, "Historical Notes on the Jahun Fillane," in "History of Certain Emirates," 2 vols., NAK SNP 7/10 2761 1778/1909, II; H. C. Monro, "Assessment Report on Hardawa District, Katagum Division, Kano Province," NAK SNP 7/13 3521 5479/1912; and K. C. Vessey, "Re-assessment Report on Hardawa District, Misau Emirate, Bauchi Province," NAK SNP 17/3 4210 26847.

52. Informants IID: 8; IIE: 10; IIH: 2. They were so called because of their annual payment of tribute to Galadiman Bornu in the medium of the *sika, shika,* or *chika*—a local variety of woven grass mat.

53. Informants IIE: 1, 4, 9, 13–14, 20.

all in the Gongola Valley Basin;[54] (2) the Habe states of Auyo, Shira, and Teshena, between the Upper Gongola and the Sahil, together with Habe communities of Tangala-Waja, in southern Gombe division;[55] and (3) the Barebari known as Kwayamawa, Gizimawa (N'gizim), Kanuri, Lerewa, Mangawa, and Shuwa Arab, each found both concentrated and/or scattered in one or more of the Border States.

In Gombe ca. 1900–10 almost all Barebari peoples were of Kanuri stock, but they are said to have composed only one-fourteenth of the total free adult male population, and the great bulk of these appear to have reached there from Bornu during the previous half-century.[56] In Katagum at the same period, some two-thirds of the free Barebari adult males (one-fifth of all those in the emirate) were of Lerewa descent. Like the scattering of other Barebari in Katagum, they lived in settlements predominantly founded prior to 1800. In Hadejia, where the proportion of Barebari nuclear-family heads was about one-half of the whole, three-quarters were Mangawa and one-fifth Gizimawa. The Mangawa established themselves on Hadejia soil over a span of several hundred years, making a relatively large number of new settlements toward the end of the nineteenth century in northern Hadejia; there is written as well as oral testimony that Gizimawa had moved in strength into northeast Hadejia long before 1800.[57]

Barebari as a whole in all three emirates constituted some one-fifth of the entire free adult male population when Fulani governors were displaced by European. Only one of their ethnic subcategories, that of Kanuri, has been examined by linguists or anthropologists, and then in the Kanuri homeland of Bornu.[58] The Lerewa of Katagum would seem to be a nomadic offshoot or cousin to the Kanuri that moved west of the Lake Chad Basin and by 1800 had founded

54. For a short summary of the data on pre-jihad Kwararafa states, see pp. 81–86 below.

55. The evidence for Auyo, Shira, and Teshena is reviewed on pp. 103–7 below.

56. Percentages mentioned in this paragraph are shown and compared in tabular form in the end-pocket chart. Their computation is explained in Chapter 3, as are the sources of data on the foundation time of these settlements.

57. Recorded evidence of Gizimawa in this area by at least the fifteenth century is contained in the work of a contemporary (ca. 1600) Bornu historian, Ahmed ibn Fartua (*History of the First Twelve Years of the Reign of Mai Idris Alooma of Bornu [1571–1583]*, trans. H. Richmond Palmer [1926; London: Frank Cass, 1970], pp. 68–69).

58. See J. Lukas, *A Study of the Kanuri Language* (London: Oxford University Press, 1937); and Cohen, *The Kanuri of Bornu.*

several towns bordering the Misau River which figured prominently in the political growth of Katagum.[59]

For the Mangawa of Hadejia there are slightly more data at hand, useful even when inconsistent. Barth noted "the Manga nation seems to be the chief element of the Kanuri" and that as the Mangawa are not mentioned by name in the Bornu chronicles they probably are a late compound of several ethnic strains.[60] Fifteen years later Gustave Nachtigal found the Mangawa living within a district more than 200 kilometers broad in northern Bornu, and, although Kanuri-speakers, not—*pace* Barth—the largest segment of the Kanuri but rather "a separate strain," whose "appearance, customs, and culture are remarkably unified."[61] A careful observer of the early colonial period discovered three popular usages of the word "Manga" in Bornu: as it denotes those Kanuri-speakers who occupy a 400-mile-wide zone from north of Lake Chad southwest to Gumel; those whose ancestors before the jihad were in a servile relation with the rulers of Bornu; and those whose main economic activity has long been the mining of salt and potash north of the lake, together with their conveyance to and sale in markets throughout northeast Nigeria.[62] The first of these groups would include those Mangawa now settled in Hadejia Emirate, while a few trading members of the third group were resident in the precolonial market towns of each Border State.

59. J. M. Fremantle, "A History of the Region Comprising the Katagum Division of Kano Province," *Journal of the African Society,* X (1911), 302; and Temple, *Notes,* p. 258.

60. *Travels and Discoveries,* I, 556; II, 31; III, 35–36.

61. *Sahara und Sudan,* 3 vols. (Berlin: Paul Parey, 1879–89), II, 429–30.

62. G. J. Lethem, "Assessment Report on Machena District, Bornu Emirate, Bornu Province," NAK SNP 17/2 1962 12168.

PART II

CHAPTER 5

GOMBE: CA. 1800–41

KWARARAFA STATES OF THE GONGOLA BASIN

The Kwararafa peoples, whose polities and cultural influence extended for as long as 500 years from the Middle Benue Valley to as far north as Fika Emirate, have been of profound historical significance in the political and religious evolution of much of northern Nigeria. For at least a century they were the predominant military power in Hausaland, southern Bornu, and the lands between, while their spiritual authority survives today in several of the less Islamized ethnic communities of the Benue/Gongola region. Their importance in both these aspects often is obscured in published accounts of Nigerian history, for two reasons: 1) few chronicles or other documentation are available to students of the Kwararafa, and most which have been refer to the initial period of Kwararafa migrations into and over northeast Nigeria;[1] and 2) except for those Kwararafa who settled along the Benue valley—that branch denoted the Jukun—and those known as the Bolewa of Fika, no ethnographic studies are widely accessible.[2]

A second impediment to our knowledge of the Kwararafa place in northeast Nigerian history is that of deciding upon a consistent and "accurate" nomenclature. They are described in their ethnic totality as *Kwararafa* by Hausa- and Nupe-speakers, and as *Kwana* or *Gwana* by Kanuri. Moreover, the latter distinguish this

1. See, for example, "The Children of Taba'ul Awwal," and "Kings of the Land of Fika," trans. H. Richmond Palmer, in *Sudanese Memoirs* (1928; London: Frank Cass, 1967), II, 56–59, 70–73.

2. For the Benue and Fika branches of the Kwararafa, see C. K. Meek, *A Sudanese Kingdom* (London: Kegan Paul, 1931), *passim*, and *Tribal Studies in Northern Nigeria*, 2 vols. (London: Kegan Paul, 1931), II, 288–310.

collectivity from one of its ruling sacerdotal groups, which they term *Kona* or *Kwona,* but which are known as *Jukun* in Hausa.[3] They themselves appear to have no general designation for all of the people contained within this *omnium gatherum.* We have followed below the common Hausa forms, of Kwararafa and Jukun.

Sources for the pre-Fulani centuries of Kwararafa presence in the Gongola basin area are confined almost wholly to unpublished field notes prepared by two gifted colonial officials, T. F. Carlyle (1914) and R. C. Abraham (1926). Carlyle, then a district officer in Gombe and Tangale-Waja, assembled and synthesized oral traditions from Bolewa and Tera informants. Abraham, while serving the British government as an ethnographer, combined a wide number of such accounts with a command of Bolewa dialects to produce a much fuller, more credible profile of Bolewa political history.[4] Other background material may be found in several anthropological monographs by C. K. Meek, and in H. R. Palmer's explication of a few relevant Arabic manuscripts of Bornu and Hausa origin.[5] In view of the limited sources at hand, the brief outline given here is both macroscopic and highly provisional, relying as it does upon these four investigators.

Of the earliest-known inhabitants of the Gongola Basin area, only those now called Tangale, and who live on the southeast margin of Gombe Emirate, would seem to have survived ethnically intact. Other peoples that may once have resided in this area have either migrated elsewhere or lost their cultural identity by merging with immigrant Kwararafa of Tera and Bolewa stock.[6] Advanced parties of Kwararafa had begun, it appears, to reach the Kanem-Bornu longitudes from an eastward homeland about A.D. 1000. From Lake Chad, one Kwararafa branch moved farther west, eventually to found Daniski (Fika), Biri, and Ribadu towns

3. H. Richmond Palmer, Introduction to Meek, *A Sudanese Kingdom,* pp. xiv–xv, and *The Bornu Sahara and Sudan* (London: John Murray, 1936), pp. 27 n. 1, 248, and 255 n. 1. Palmer himself at times confused Bolewa with Jukun, and Jukun with Kwararafa (Introduction to Meek, *A Sudanese Kingdom,* p. xxxi; and *Sudanese Memoirs,* II, 59 n. 1).

4. T. F. Carlyle, "History of Gombe Emirate, Central Province," NAK SNP 10/2 1179 445p/1914; and R. C. Abraham, "Ethnological Notes on the Bolewa Group," NAK SNP 17/8 K.1119. L. L. Rickford provided a short summary of Abraham's historical sections, modified in places by reference to the subsequently published work of Meek and Palmer ("Notes on the Organization of the Bolewa Villages in Gombe Emirate, Bauchi Province," NAK SNP 17/8 K.2383).

5. See references contained in notes 1 and 2 above; and G. Merrick, "The Bolewa Tribe," *Journal of the African Society,* XVI (1905), 417–26. John Lavers of Abdullahi Bayero College, Ahmadu Bello University, has been the first professional historian to gather and analyze Bolewa (Fika) tradition.

6. Carlyle, "History of Gombe Emirate."

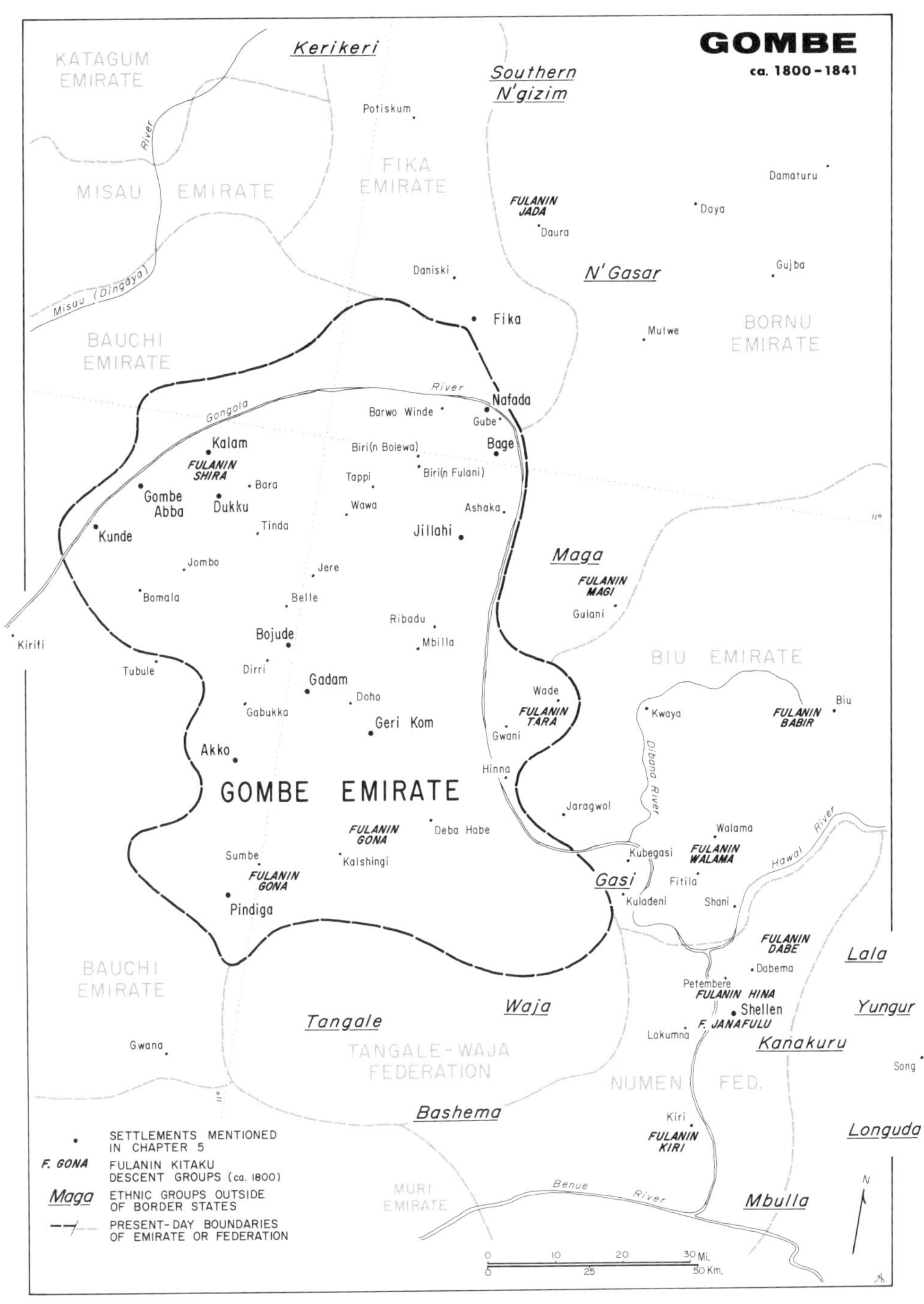
GOMBE
ca. 1800-1841
KATAGUM EMIRATE
Kerikeri
Southern N'gizim
Potiskum
MISAU EMIRATE
FIKA EMIRATE
River
Damaturu
FULANIN JADA
Daura
Daya
Misau (Dingaya)
Daniski
N'Gasar
Gujba
Fika
Mutwe
BORNU EMIRATE
BAUCHI EMIRATE
River
Nafada
Gongola
Barwo Winde
Gube
Kalam
Biri(n Bolewa)
Bage
FULANIN SHIRA
Biri(n Fulani)
Bara
Tappi
Gombe Abba
Dukku
Wawa
Ashaka
Tinda
Kunde
Jillahi
11°
Maga
Jombo
Jere
FULANIN MAGI
Bomala
Belle
Gulani
Ribadu
Kirifi
Bojude
Mbilla
BIU EMIRATE
Tubule
Dirri
Gadam
Wade
Doho
Biu
Gabukka
FULANIN TARA
Kwaya
FULANIN BABIR
Geri Kom
Gwani
Akko
Hinna
Dibana River
GOMBE EMIRATE
Jaragwol
FULANIN GONA
Deba Habe
Walama
Hawal River
Sumbe
Kalshingi
Kubegasi
FULANIN WALAMA
FULANIN GONA
Gasi
Fitila
Pindiga
Kuladeni
Shani
FULANIN DABE
BAUCHI EMIRATE
Lala
Dabema
Petembere
FULANIN HINA
Waja
Tangale
Shellen
Yungur
F. JANAFULU
Lakumna
Kanakuru
TANGALE-WAJA FEDERATION
Gwana
Song
NUMEN FED.
11°
Bashema
Kiri
FULANIN KIRI
Longuda
SETTLEMENTS MENTIONED IN CHAPTER 5
F. GONA
FULANIN KITAKU DESCENT GROUPS (ca. 1800)
Maga
ETHNIC GROUPS OUTSIDE OF BORDER STATES
PRESENT-DAY BOUNDARIES OF EMIRATE OR FEDERATION
MURI EMIRATE
Benue River
Mbulla
N
0 10 20 30 Mi.
0 25 50 Km.

on the Middle Gongola, as well as the old Jukun capital south of the Benue. A second branch, taking another westerly route, established in turn the kingdoms of Kalam (on the Upper Gongola) and Geri Kom (central Gombe), together with Tirwun and Kirifi towns still farther west, in present-day Bauchi Emirate.[7] Thus four centers of original Kwararafa settlement in the Gombe region are identifiable: Biri, Ribadu, Kalam, and Geri Kom.

By the mid-thirteenth century Bolewa and/or Jukun Kwararafa may already have been predominant in the Gongola-Benue riverain complex; a Katsina manuscript notes that Sarkin Katsina warred on the Kwararafa ca. 1250.[8] The "Kano Chronicle" provides at least eight references to the Kwararafa. The earliest records that Sarkin Kano Yaji (ca. 1349–85) ruled all the "pagan tribes" from Biri to Fanda and that only the Kwararafa near "the rock of Ata-gara" defied him successfully by taking refuge there.[9] (Palmer's inference that Ata-gara "almost certainly" was Kalam, though plausible, is unconfirmed by present evidence.)[10] A generation later Kwararafa are reported to have rendered Sarkin Kano tribute in slaves, and, shortly after, the legendary Queen Amina of Zaria is credited with having conquered "all the towns from Kwararafa to Nupe."[11] Kalam is first cited by name for Sarkin Kano Abdullahi's reign (ca. 1499–1509), and is mentioned again a century later; on both occasions the people of Kano are said to have raided there.[12]

Katsina, Kano, and Bornu chronicles agree that during the seventeeth century the Kwararafa became a formidable power in the Nigerian Sudan. They are said to have twice occupied Kano Town and attacked Katsina, but to have been defeated by Mai Ali of Bornu (ca. 1645–84) following a siege of Birni Gazargamu.[13] Their military ascendence appears to date from ca. 1600, when they "ate up the whole

7. Abraham, "Ethnological Notes"; Palmer, Introduction to Meek, *A Sudanese Kingdom,* pp. xxxi–xxxii, and *Sudanese Memoirs,* II, 59 n.

8. *Ibid.,* III, 79.

9. *Ibid.,* p. 106.

10. Palmer, Introduction to Meek, *A Sudanese Kingdom,* pp. xx, xxxii. Meek associates it with the site of Idah, on the Niger (*ibid.,* pp. 24–25).

11. Palmer, *Sudanese Memoirs,* II, 107, 109.

12. *Ibid.,* pp. 112, 117.

13. *Ibid.,* pp. 121–22, III, 83–84; Yves Urvoy, *Histoire de l'Empire du Bornou* (Paris: Larose, 1949), p. 84; and Heinrich Barth, *Travels and Discoveries in Northern and Central Africa,* 3 vols. (1857–59; London: Frank Cass, 1965), II, 598. An Arabic poem by the contemporary Katsina author Dan Marina tells how Mai Ali "drove back to their furthest borders the army of the Jukun" and "ransomed the whole Sudan from strife" (in Palmer, *Sudanese Memoirs,* III, 83–84).

country" and drove the inhabitants of Kano Town to seek refuge at Daura;[14] it probably was ended by, or soon after, the reversal in Bornu. For the next two hundred years they seem to have withdrawn from this wider political arena, being preoccupied with internal divisions and discouraged perhaps by a drying up of their slave markets to the south.[15]

However difficult it is to judge conclusively which of the Kwararafa states were engaged in these campaigns,[16] we do know something of events in the Gongola region during this era.[17] There is local evidence that the Bolewa kingdoms of Kalam and Geri Kom and the Jukun center of Pindiga on their southern boundaries were involved in a long competition to create or sustain an empire that would extend well beyond present-day Gombe Emirate. Kalam and Geri Kom had emerged first as rival states, dividing control of almost the entire Gombe area and large tracts of Bauchi, Tangale-Waja, and Biu (southwest Bornu). The Bolewa of Kalam early on founded Gadam, Bojude, Belle, and Jere, and conquered the independent Bolewa towns of Bomala, Bage, Bara, Jombo, and Barwo Winde, later subjecting as well the ancient Bolewa center of Ribadu. Geri Kom's dependencies came to include Gabukka, Doho, Tappi, Kirifi, and a number of other, now-deserted, Bolewa towns; Geri Kom also sent out colonists to Gadam, Bojude,

14. *Ibid.*, II, 116. Meek alludes to Zaria manuscripts which say that Sarkin Zaria was at one time tributary to the Kwararafa. There is oral evidence that the Kwararafa also attacked and drew tribute from the Habe states of Teshena and Misau, in present-day Katagum area. Palmer declares that the rulers of Bornu once paid tribute as well to the Kwararafa, but to the Benue Jukun branch (Introduction to Ahmed ibn Fartua, *History of the First Twelve Years of the Reign of Mai Idris Alooma of Bornu (1571–1583)*, trans. H. Richmond Palmer [1926; London: Frank Cass, 1970], p. 69).

15. Meek suggests the latter as a possible cause of their political retirement (*A Sudanese Kingdom*, pp. 28–29). He speculates, on the strength of a remark by Sultan Muhammad Bello to Clapperton, that a mainspring of the Kwararafa campaigns to Hausaland and Bornu was the desire to obtain slaves for purchase by coastal merchants and that with the beginnings of an international palm-oil trade from Gulf ports and a reduced commercial demand for Sudanic slaves, the Kwararafa political decline was intensified.

16. Palmer considers it probable that it was the Bolewa of Kalam who were involved in most if not all of the early Kwararafa campaigns to Hausaland, but that it was the Jukun of Pindiga who are the Kwararafa described in the "Kano Chronicle" as having occupied Kano in the late seventeenth century (Introduction to Meek, *A Sudanese Kingdom*, pp. xxxi–xxxii).

17. This paragraph and the next are based on Carlyle, "History of Gombe Emirate"; and Abraham, "Ethnological Notes."

and Dirri. For an undetermined span of time, perhaps as long as 300 years, the two Bolewa kingdoms fought a succession of border engagements with neither side gaining a permanent victory, although Kalam is said to have been the more successful in this protracted struggle.

Pindiga Town reputedly was founded by a prince of the main Jukun dynasty from the Benue area. His descendants began to carve out a new kingdom when Kalam and Geri Kom were already past their full strength, having all but exhausted themselves in fratricidal combat. The Pindiga Jukun apparently were much fewer in number than their Bolewa antagonists, and established only one other known settlement of enduring importance, Gwana (southeast Bauchi). However through skill at arms, and perhaps by virtue as well of their priestly authority, they were able to impose a mixed political-religious dominion over many Tera, Jera, Waja, Tangale, and Biu towns in the Lower Gongola Basin. They went on to sack Geri Kom, annexed all of its territory, and then enfeebled Kalam further by engrossing much of its domain. Pindiga tradition also refers to a successful expedition to Kano, when its king refused payment of tribute "to Kwararafa"; although said to have occurred in the reign of Muhammad Rimfa (ca. 1463–99), this could well be an allusion either to the conquest by Kwararafa of "all the [Kano] country" one hundred years later or to their occupation of Kano Town in the late 1600s.

THE FULANIN KITAKU OF SOUTHWEST BORNU

Because of their political and administrative significance as corporate members of precolonial state government in Gombe Emirate, we know far more of the social, economic, and religious activity of 11 Fulanin Kitaku descent groups in the several decades before they were led in a local jihad against the Kwararafa states of the Gongola region. All these groups appear to have adopted the semi-sedentary life-style of Cattle Fulani in transition from a purely nomadic to a largely agrarian way of subsistence. Many are said to have begun taking up elements of the non-Muslim (Habe) faiths and cultures of their more settled neighbors in the Lower Gongola Valley. But among their ardos a number would seem to have been lineage heads whose kin groups had developed a special regard for Islamic education, sending the most talented and ambitious sons, after a good Qur'anic training at home, to study either at Birni Gazargamu or some other scholastic center in Bornu.

These 11 Fulani Kitaku clans or clan-aggregates had roles of sharply varying importance in the jihad and subsequent evolution of emirate government in Gombe. They were and are called by the following names:

1. The *Fulanin Jada* were then living in Jada Ward of the N'gasar capital of Daura, one of the numerous hill towns in southwest Bornu and the most northern known site of Fulanin Kitaku settlement. Their leader by 1800, Bula, was titled *bauchi* rather than *ardo*—a further indication that his Fulani clansmen were already at some remove from exclusively pastoral concerns. Bula took a leading part in the Gombe jihad but later fell out with Buba Yero (the shaikh's flag-bearer) and died fighting the N'gasar. The Fulanin Jada who emigrated to Gombe Emirate in Buba Yero's reign were then put under several fiefholders, all unrelated to them.[18]

2. The *Fulanin Tara* were so called either because they were found ca. 1800 close to Tera settlements or because they had (according to other accounts) arrived there from Tarangara, near Marua on the Upper Benue. Having reached Teraland perhaps two generations before the jihad, they were by 1800 divided into three sections, each under a kinsman and known respectively by the names of their neighboring Tera hill towns of Hinna, Wade, and Gwani. The ardo of Wade branch when Buba Yero appeared there, Kaigama Buba Yele, was later appointed by him the first Madakin Gombe. His successor-descendants in that high office had their fiefdoms both in Teraland and wherever the Fulanin Tara migrated during the nineteenth century.[19]

3. The *Fulanin Jera* are said to have settled, or made wet-season encampments, around a number of Jera and Waja towns in the same period as the Fulanin Tara, their immediate neighbors to the north, reached the Gongola area. One branch (allegedly the largest) founded Kuladeni; another, Jaragwol; and a third, Kubegasi—all on high bluffs overlooking the river. Alkali Aliyu, a son of the ardo who built Kubegasi, became the first Sarkin Yakin Gombe. His successor-descendants in office had as fiefs all Jera, Waja, and Fulanin Jera settlements under Gombe.[20]

4. The *Fulanin Babir* were living in Biu Kingdom of southwestern Bornu before the jihad. Led by Ardo (later Bauchi) Gordi, many joined Buba Yero after a series of campaigns launched by Gordi in the Mubi and Marghi country east of

18. Informants IB: 1–2, 13–14, 32; IE: 12; IG: 5.

19. Informants IC: 12–14, 30–37; IE: 10–11; and Carlyle, "History of Gombe Emirate."

20. Informants IB: 3; IC: 38–40; IE: 8; and T. F. Carlyle, "Assessment Report on Waja Sub-District, Ako District, Gombe Emirate, Central Province," NAK SNP 10/1 661 715p/1913.

Biu. His fiefs included the new and principal Fulanin Babir town of Jillahi, and, briefly, western Biu.[21]

5. The *Fulanin Magi* resided among the Maga people of Gulani area, western Biu. Ardo (later Sarkin) Magi Buba Kari Banto led them across the Gongola with Buba Yero and served as the first Alkalin Gombe.[22]

6. The *Fulanin Walama*, from the Walama-Fitila zone of southwest Biu, were relatively few in number and, moving as a group, established only two settlements in Gombe Emirate. Their leader, Hamma Bano of Fitila, was given the (honorific) title of Ardo Walama when Buba Yero awarded him a flag.[23]

7. The *Fulanin Hina* of Shellen area (due south of Biu Town, on the left Gongola bank) were relatively few as well and also moved together, settling inside the new emirate capital of Gombe Abba. Like Ardo Walama, their chief, Mallam Mango, was not made a sarki or central-administration official but received the title of Ardo Hina or Ardo Maituta (*maituta,* flag-bearer). So too, he did not hold any fiefs apart from the ward occupied by his followers in Gombe Abba.[24]

8. The *Fulanin Dabe,* then living around Dabema, near Shellen, moved in the early years of the jihad into Gombe, where they founded several minor towns. Sarkin Dabe Idirisa and his successors had no other fiefs.[25]

9. The *Fulanin Janafulu* were composed of Buba Yero's immediate kin group and their following. Settled before the jihad in the environs of Shellen, they were closely enough related to the Fulanin Tara, Fulanin Jera, and Fulanin Kiri for Madaki Buba Yele, Sarkin Yaki Aliyu, and Hamma Ruwa (see below) to be spoken of generally as "brothers" of Buba Yero.[26]

21. Informants IB: 4, 6, 11, 19; IE: 13; and Hauptmann Kurt Strümpell, "Die Geschichte Adamauas nach mündlichen Überlieferungen," *Mitteilungen der geographischen Gesellschaft in Hamburg,* XXVI (1912), 57.

22. Informants IA: 2–5; IG: 4, 7; and P. Lonsdale, "Assessment Report on Gombe Town, Gombe Emirate, Central Province," NAK SNP 7/14 3607 7p/1913.

23. *Ibid.;* and Informants IA: 2–5; IE: 9; IG: 4, 7.

24. *Ibid.*

25. *Ibid.*

26. Informants IA: 2–5; IG: 4–7. According to C. E. Hopen, Fulfulde (the Fulani tongue) does not distinguish between kinsmen and clansmen; both are designated "children of the clan" (F. *bibbe lenyel*). If the specific kinship relation is known, however, "the appropriate referent is used rather than the more general term for clansman (*bandirao*)" (*The Pastoral Fulbe Family in Gwandu* [London: Oxford University Press, 1958], p. 79 n. 1). While the Fulanin Janafulu, Fulanin Kiri, Fulanin Tara, and Fulanin Jera are not remembered to have been at this period sections of a single

10. The *Fulanin Kiri* had taken their name from Kiri, a Kanakuru town which their hamlets adjoined. Their ardo, Hamma Ruwa, later broke with Buba Yero and was killed by him. His descendants then established Muri Emirate, south of Tangale-Waja.[27]

11. The *Fulanin Gona* were divided, one branch living near the Tera town of Kalshingi, the other at Sumbe, next to Pindiga. These branches shared appointments to the high office of Galadiman Gombe. The first galadima, Ahmadu Gona, and his successors made their first official home at Akko, 45 miles southeast of the capital. Their fiefs included those Tera communities not under Madakin Gombe, the part of Pindiga's realm that became subject to Gombe, and all Fulanin Gona settlements.[28]

---

clan, such a relationship is implied in the uniform assertion that all four men were "brothers" (*dengi*, relative, relatives). Such a reading would clarify an earlier assertion that Buba Yero "was of the Tara clan" (*Notes on the Tribes, Provinces, Emirates and States of the Northern Provinces of Nigeria, Compiled from Official Reports by O. Temple*, ed. Charles L. Temple [1922; London, Frank Cass, 1965], pp. 476–78).

27. See p. 100 below.

28. Informants ID: 1–4, 9, 11–12, 14, 18–19; P. Lonsdale, "Assessment Report on Ako District, Gombe Division, Bauchi Province," NAK SNP 7/13 3597 7252/1912; and Salihu Atiku Kumo, "A History of Akko District" (MS, copy in my possession, 1961).

The percentage figures derived for each of these 11 Fulanin Kitaku clans or descent groups, as expressed in terms of free adult males ca. 1900–10 per total Fulani and total emirate free adult male population in Gombe, are as follows:

Fulanin Kitaku	Per Cent of Total Fulani	Per Cent of Total Emirate
Fulanin Jera	8	5
Fulanin Jada	7.5	4.5
Fulanin Babir	6	3.5
Fulanin Tara	6	3.5
Fulanin Gona	6	3.5
Fulanin Magi	3	2
Fulanin Dabe	3	2
Fulanin Janafulu	2	1
Fulanin Walama	1	.5
Fulanin Hina	1	.5
Undifferentiated	2	1.5
	45.5	27.5

MODIBBO BUBA YERO (?–CA. 1841)

Buba Yero was born in the Shellen/Shani area at the confluence of the Gongola and Hawal rivers, ca. 1760–65.[29] His paternal grandfather, a native of Rai Buba (Cameroon), had migrated to Mayofaro (Adamawa), from where his son, Usuman Subande, transferred north across the Benue to Petembere, near Shellen. There, or at Lakumna nearby, Usuman married a daughter of Gongon, the Habe Kanakuru chief of Shellen, who later gave birth to Buba Yero.[30] Having learned as a child to read the Qur'an, Buba Yero left home to follow a more advanced Islamic curriculum at Birni Gazargamu. En route he was captured by non-Muslim N'gizim or Kerikeri close to the modern site of Potiskum, and enslaved for several years. Regaining his freedom, he arrived at the Bornu capital and studied for a while

29. Material on the family background, youth, and early career of Buba Yero is almost entirely oral, that is, unwritten or else recorded by colonial officials. The single major exception is an Arabic manuscript authored by the chief Muslim judge (*babban alkali*) of Potiskum (Fika), probably ca. 1925. This document, which chronicles the core events of Buba Yero's life, is denied in so many particulars by informants today that it must be used with caution (see Alkalin Potiskum Yakubu b. Halilu, "The History of Buba Yero of Gombe," trans. R. C. Abraham, in "History Notes on Gombe Division, Bauchi Province [1929–30]," NAK SNP 17/2 1979 12250). What follows is a critical distillation of this one document and of other oral sources (whether published, on file, or collected in the field). Only those names, events, and circumstances uniformly agreed upon by each reference are given here without qualifying addenda.

30. Yakubu b. Halilu, "History of Buba Yero"; "Notes for Revised Bauchi Provincial Gazetteer," NAK SNP 17/3 3456 21104; Informants IA: 1–6; IG: 4, 7; Lonsdale, "Assessment Report, Gombe Town"; Abraham, "Ethnological Notes"; C. O. Migeod, comp., *Gazetteer of Yola Province* (Lagos: The Government Printer, 1927), p. 12; J. G. Davies, *The Biu Book: A Collation and Reference Book on Biu Division* (Zaria: NORLA, 1954–56), p. 36; Rickford, "Organization of the Bolewa Villages"; Palmer, *The Bornu Sahara,* p. 258, and Introduction to Meek, *A Sudanese Kingdom,* p. xxvi; F. B. Gall, *Gazetteer of Bauchi Province* (London: Waterlow, 1920), p. 13; Carlyle, "History of Gombe Emirate"; Chiroman Gombe Babagoro dan Sarkin Gombe Abubakar, "A History of the Gombe Emirs" (MS, copy in my possession, 1960); Sidney J. Hogben and Anthony H. M. Kirk-Greene, *The Emirates of Northern Nigeria: A Preliminary Survey of Their Historical Traditions* (London: Oxford University Press, 1966), p. 465; and W. O. P. Rosedale, "Assessment Report on Kanakuru District, Numan Division, Yola Province," NAK SNP 10/7 3572 275p/1919. Buba Yero's place of birth is variously given as Petembere, between Shellen and Shani (Abraham; Informants; Migeod; Davies); Shani (Carlyle); Walama (Palmer); and Lakumna (Rosedale).

the religious sciences; alternatively, he was prevented from going there after his liberation.[31]

During this rather obscure young adulthood Buba Yero went for some years to further his education with Shaikh Usuman dan Fodio, then (ca. 1774–86), from a residence at Degel, preaching and gathering students in the rural hinterland of Gobir.[32] The length of his stay there is uncertain (estimates vary from seven to thirteen years), and it seems likely that he returned several times to Shellen while acquiring the Fulani religious title of *modibbo*. On completion of higher studies Buba resettled at Shellen, having been told by Shaikh Usuman to remain at peace with surrounding Habe communities of the Gongola Basin area. He disobeyed orders and attacked them on a wide front soon after.[33]

It is unclear what his grounds were for acting without proper authorization. The general account is that a quarrel between the Fulanin Janafulu and Fulanin Kiri (led respectively by Buba Yero and Hamma Ruwa) caused Gongon to intervene on the side of his grandson. Gongon was killed, and his Kanakuru followers then turned on both Fulani groups, driving them from Shellen and Kiri. The Fulani withdrew north, via Shani, to seek refuge or aid among the Fulanin Magi and Fulanin Walama of modern Gulani, and combined with them—and probably with

31. Informants IA: 1–6; IG: 4, 7; "Revised Bauchi Provincial Gazetteer"; Yakubu b. Halilu, "History of Buba Yero"; Babagoro, "A History"; Hogben and Kirk-Greene, *Emirates of Northern Nigeria*, p. 465; and Temple, *Notes*, p. 420.

32. Informants IA: 1–6; IG: 4, 7; Migeod, *Yola Province*, p. 13; Yakubu b. Halilu, "History of Buba Yero"; Abraham, "Ethnological Notes"; and Rickford, "Organization of the Bolewa Villages."

33. Informants IA: 1–6; IG: 4, 7; "Revised Bauchi Provincial Gazetteer"; Yakubu b. Halilu, "History of Buba Yero"; Abraham, "Ethnological Notes"; and Rickford, "Organization of the Bolewa Villages." Abdullahi dan Fodio recorded how Shaikh Usuman had permitted his community of followers to arm themselves in 1794–95 against the likelihood of molestation by Nafata, Sarkin Gobir, who on taking power that year, widely made public his unwillingness to compromise with Usuman ('Abdullah ibn Muhammad, *Tazyīn al-Waraqāt*, trans. Mervyn Hiskett [Ibadan: Ibadan University Press, 1963], p. 105). Roland Adeleye has remarked that in granting this measure of self-protection, Usuman shifted "the movement of [Islamic] reform from the plane of mere exhortation and protest to one of positive determination that the Muslim community and its ideals must survive, if need be by fighting for their survival." He concludes that "general acceptance [of the Shaikh's allowance by his people] was a revolution in the history of Islam in the Hausa states . . . [as] it marked the first definite departure of the course of Islamic revivalism in those lands from mere preaching to the fighting of *jihād*" (*Power and Diplomacy in Northern Nigeria 1804–1906* [London: Longman Group, 1971], p. 13).

the neighboring Fulanin Hina, Fulanin Dabe, and Fulanin Babir as well—under Buba Yero's overall command.[34]

A less immediate, more profound cause of Buba's premature conflict with Habe groups may be sought in events and political tendencies in southern Bornu which occurred, it would seem, not long before this emigration from the land of non-Muslim Kanakuru. Widespread traditions in Biu Emirate refer to the death at Fulani hands of its Babir king Garga Moda ca. 1760 and of his successor Garga Kopchi ca. 1793.[35] That Fulanin Kitaku elements might well have been an aggressive factor in this period is suggested by other traditions of Bauchi Gordi, the Fulanin Babir leader in the Gombe jihad. These relate that Gordi, born of an ardo and of a daughter of Sarkin Babir, was exiled as a youth because of intemperate behavior. With a few companions he traveled east, eventually defeating in battle a number of towns in the Marghi-Mubi region south of Lake Chad; he is said to have then joined Buba Yero. At a minimun, such oral documents indicate that Biu, adjoining Kanakuruland and for several hundred years the strongest known state in southwest Bornu, was, shortly before the Sokoto jihad, a potential site of Fulani-Habe conflict—a condition that may have spilled over its eastern frontier with the Marghi. So too, as regards Fulani then settled just south of Shellen, we can probably credit as symptomatic a Yola tradition that a short while before 1800 several ardos of the Wollabe'en clan around Song revolted from local Habe chiefs when the latter insisted upon their exercise of *jus primae noctis*.[36] This prerogative, reported elsewhere in northern Nigeria for non-Muslim chiefs vis-à-vis Cattle Fulani subjects, would likely have been a continuing source of ethnic grievance and friction.[37] Again, a Kanuri poem dating from the same period suggests that Fulani divines and their followers in Bornu (as in Gobir) were already an irritant on the establishment:

34. Informants IA: 1–6; IG: 4, 7; Rosedale, "Kanakuru District"; Davies, *Biu Book,* p. 36; and E. J. Douglas, "Assessment Report on Shani District, Biu Division, Bornu Province," NAK SNP 17/2 1195 10160.

35. Davies, *Biu Book,* p. 36; and H. Richmond Palmer, ed., *Gazetteer of Bornu Province* (London: Waterlow, 1929), p. 17.

36. Strümpell, "Die Geschichte Adamauas," p. 56. Strümpell, a German imperial resident in eastern Adamawa, compiled his article from oral data.

37. Anthony H. M. Kirk-Greene, *Adamawa Past and Present* (London: Oxford University Press, 1958), p. 128; and Migeod, *Yola Province,* p. 13. The Fulanin Shira of Gombe are said by informants to have left Kamenei from the same proximate cause in the mid-eighteenth century.

Verily a cloud has settled upon God's earth,
A cloud so dense that escape from it is impossible.
Everywhere between Kordofan and Gobir
And the cities of the Kindin [Tuareg]
Are settlements of the dogs of Fellata [Bi la'ila]
Serving God in all their dwelling places
(I swear by the life of the Prophet and his overflowing grace)
In reforming all districts and provinces
Ready for future bliss.
So in this year of AH 1214 [AD 1799] they are following
their beneficial theories,
As though it were a time to set the world to order by preaching.
Alas! that I know all about the tongue of the fox.[38]

Thus when Buba Yero assembled an army composed of several Fulanin Kitaku elements at Gulani and proceeded to war upon Habe communities his unauthorized action, though irregular, was not altogether unprecedented, nor, it could be said, premature. While the dating and exact sequence of Buba's early campaigns are at best difficult to arrange, by comparing a variety of citations from diverse parts of the Gongola-Hawal-Middle Benue region we can build an overall picture of his career at the turn of the century.

He appears first to have struck north and northeast from Gulani, raiding the few major towns which then lay between it and Damaturu, from the Gongola to the Marghi border.[39] Probably strengthened by spoil and new allies, the Fulanin Tara and Fulanin Jera, he next marched through Tera and Jeraland, Biu Emirate, and the settlements of his former Kanakuru hosts.[40] Continuing into Yungur, Longuda, Bashema, Lala, and Mbulla country, he now pushed as far south as the Benue,[41] where he was reached by a message from Shaikh Usuman recalling him

38. Palmer, *The Bornu Sahara,* p. 52.
39. Informants IA: 1–6; IF: 2–6; Carlyle, "History of Gombe"; and Lonsdale, "Gombe Town."
40. Informants IA: 1–6; T. F. Carlyle, comments in Rosedale, "Kanakuru District"; Rickford, "Organization of the Bolewa Villages"; and Abraham, "Ethnological Notes."
41. Informants IA: 1–6; F. A. Ruxton, "Notes on Fulani, Jukun, Wurobo and Ankwe Tribe Customs in Muri Province," NAK SNP 7/9 2679 6663/1908; Migeod, *Yola Province,* p. 12; J. M. Fremantle, ed., *Gazetteer of Muri Province* (London: Waterlow, 1920), pp. 22–23; Meek, *Tribal Studies,* II, 333; Davies, *Biu Book,* p. 37; Strümpell, "Die Geschichte Adamauas," p. 58; and Kirk-Greene, *Adamawa,* p. 131.

to Gulani. It is generally said in Gombe that Usuman, angered by his precipitous campaigns, denied Buba title to most of the territory east of the Gongola and honored Modibbo Adama by entrusting him instead with future rights of conquest in what later became Adamawa Emirate.[42] It is clear that Buba withdrew from operations east of the Hawal and, then or afterwards, abandoned any further claim on Biu and the Kanakuru. In so doing he established the future eastern boundary of his new state along the Gongola from Hinna to its junction with the Hawal.[43]

Moving his Fulani Kitaku forces to the right bank of the Gongola, Buba made Ribadu Town a main base of military action for about the next 16 years (ca. 1802–18).[44] Located on the southeastern frontier of Kalam State, Ribadu was already of mixed Bolewa and Fulanin Babir population,[45] thus affording Buba two evident strategic advantages. The Bolewa, who are said to have welcomed him and seem never to have been drawn effectively into the geopolitical orbit of Kalam or Geri Kom, might be expected to offer a compliant, if not actively supportive, wedge for whatever plans he then had to direct a jihad against the numerous Bolewa towns of the Upper Gongola Basin. And there was at hand in Ribadu a permanent Fulani presence which could prove useful if his initial thrusts toward the northwest should be turned back.

Soon after arriving at Ribadu, Buba received orders from Shaikh Usuman to begin a jihad.[46] The immediate object of his first authorized venture was Nafada Town, on the right bank of the Gongola Bend and, like Ribadu, of a mixed Bolewa-

42. *Ibid.;* and Informants IA: 1–6; IB: 1–4, 6, 11–14, 19, 32; ID: 1–4, 11–12, 14, 18–19; IE: 8–13; IG: 4–5, 7–8. According to oral tradition gathered at Yola ca. 1910, as Adama began his own local jihad in the middle Benue region he moved through Bata and Lala country, met Buba Yero at the Gongola, and with him then campaigned among the Yungur, Lala, Kibba, and Hona peoples (C. Vicars Boyle, "Historical Notes on the Yola Fulanis," *Journal of the African Society,* X [1910], 77).

43. Davies was told that Buba Yero had instructions from Shaikh Usuman to make the Gongola his southeastern frontier (*Biu Book,* p. 37). This account, from Biu informants, is disputed by those in Gombe, who say that Usuman specified the Dibana River (near Kwaya, west Biu) and that it remained the boundary with Biu until the mid-nineteenth century.

44. Informants IA: 1–6; IB: 9–10; IG: 5, 7; Carlyle, "History of Gombe"; "Revised Bauchi Provincial Gazetteer"; and Temple, *Notes,* p. 420.

45. Informants IA: 1–6; IB: 9–10; IG: 5, 7.

46. Yakubu b. Halilu, "History of Buba Yero," gives as the date of the (authorized) launching of the Gombe jihad, Thursday, the 8th of Rabi al-Awal, A.H. 1219 (June 17, 1804). This would have been several months before Shaikh Usuman began hostilities in the Gobir sector. Informants today state merely that it commenced a year or two after Buba Yero came to Ribadu.

Fulani ethnic character. A walled settlement founded in the eighteenth century by Fulanin Jada from Daura (Bornu), Nafada already contained a preponderance of Bolewa quarters, together with a few Kanuri, Fulanin Shira, and Fulanin Sika inhabitants.[47] Independent of Kalam and Pindiga alike, it was, by reason of its ethnic complexity and geographical position, vulnerable at once to internal divisions and to N'gasar, Kerikeri, and Bolewa (Fika) attack. Descendants of both the initial Fulani and Bolewa settlers maintain that a delegation of these two major residential groups asked Buba Yero to come there as sarki; he agreed, leaving most of his following at Ribadu, and remained about six years (ca. 1804–10) in Nafada.[48]

During the Nafada phase of the Gombe jihad Buba mounted a large expedition against the powerful neighboring Bolewa state of Daniski (later Fika Emirate); conquered the important northern Tera center of Bage, close to Nafada; raided Tangale-Waja to the south of Ribadu; and gave substantial aid to a successful campaign by the Fulanin Mare of the Damaturu-Gujba-Daya area to the northeast, which ended in their brief occupation of Birni Gazargamu and the flight of Mai Bornu.[49] The Daniski expedition (ca. 1805) followed upon a raid to Fika Town, whose chief, the son of Moi Daniski, and his heir-apparent, connived with the Fulani in their seizure of his father's capital. Just before and just after this major victory, Buba fought a number of engagements in the southwest corner of present-day Bornu Emirate: at Daura and Mutwe, in the Damaturu-Gujba-Daya complex, and with the Kerikeri and Southern N'gizim of modern Potiskum Division. The Tera of Bage were overcome with the help of a nearby Fulanin Jada settlement, but an attempt on Gube, the second Tera center in the vicinity of Nafada, failed. Of Tangale-Waja, it is remembered only that Buba carried the jihad there and captured large quantities of slaves in this period.

Whether Buba Yero personally was engaged in either the first or later Fulani occupations of Birni Gazargamu is discussed below. It appears likely, from the weight of independent corroborative evidence, that he and/or his eldest son, Suleimanu, were present on at least one of these occasions. We have the word of Sultan Muhammad Bello that shortly before the earliest Fulani conquest of the Bornu capital (ca. 1808), Buba led a sizable column comprised in part of Fulanin

47. Informants IB: 1–2, 30–33; and Saleh Jibril, "A History of Nafada District, Gombe Emirate" (MS, copy in my possession, 1961).

48. *Ibid.*; Informants IA: 1–6; IB: 1–2, 30–33; IG: 5, 7; Abraham, "Ethnological Notes"; and Yakubu b. Halilu, "History of Buba Yero."

49. This paragraph and the next are based upon *ibid.*; Informants IA: 1–6; IB: 1–2, 30–33; IG: 5–7; and Abraham, "Ethnological Notes."

Mare from Damaturu which (probably operating out of Nafada) "invaded Bornu and laid it waste."[50]

One important Bolewa town south of the Gongola had been reached by Islam prior to the jihad. A moi of Biri had, ca. 1700, married his daughter to Mai Bornu; their son, who succeeded his grandfather, built a Friday mosque there, and future mois of Biri were at least professing Muslims. Perhaps for this reason, or because, like Ribadu and Nafada, Biri had remained independent of Kalam and Pindiga and had a pre-existing Fulanin Kitaku (Jada) component, the reigning moi did not oppose Buba when he decided to shift his establishment there from Nafada.[51] A local king-list, written in 1912, indicates that Buba arrived at Biri ca. 1814, a date supported by other evidence.[52] He is said to have encamped for some two years close by, with the Fulanin Jada. Since there is no local memory today of Buba having conducted campaigns while at Biri, it may be that he now sought a brief pause to consolidate his gains before launching the next and climactic phase of the Gombe jihad.

From Biri, he marched west and took Wawa, a strongly fortified eastern gateway to Kalam State, together with several key satellite towns. After a year or two in the Wawa bush, he continued the westward advance and completed, without apparent difficulty, the subjugation of the rest of Moi Kalam's domain.[53]

By the eighteenth century Kalam had surrendered much of its political authority in the Upper Gongola Basin to the Pindiga Jukun.[54] A reduced but still formidable power, its cohesion as a Bolewa kingdom had been further weakened by the foundation in its geographical heartland of numerous Fulanin Shira towns and hamlets, beginning probably ca. 1750. This potentially subversive element in the body politic was concentrated in the plains below Kalam Hill, on top of which the Bolewa capital had been located.[55]

50. E. J. Arnett, *The Rise of the Sokoto Fulani, Being a Paraphrase and in Some Parts a Translation of the Infaku'l Maisuri of Sultan Mohammed Bello* (Kano: Emirate Printing Department, 1922), p. 101; and Informants IA: 1–6; IB: 1–4, 6, 11–14, 19, 32; ID: 1–4, 11, 14, 18; IE: 8–13; IG: 4–5, 7.

51. Informants IA: 1–6; IB: 24–25, 33–34; Abraham, "Ethnological Notes"; and T. F. Carlyle, "Assessment Report on Birri District, Gombe Division, Central Province," NAK SNP 7/13 3447 4196/1912.

52. *Ibid.*; and Informants IB: 24–25, 33–34.

53. Informants IA: 1–6; IB: 26–27; IG: 4–5, 7; Carlyle, "History of Gombe."

54. See p. 86 above.

55. Informants IA: 1–6; IF: 2–6. From this seemingly impregnable position, with a high surrounding wall and structures of earth and stone, Kalam had survived the earlier assaults of Kano and would have successfully discouraged whatever armed challenges were posed by Geri Kom or Pindiga.

Among the Fulanin Shira immigrants was an ardo whose son had married a daughter of Moi Kalam. Buba Yero is said to have come originally to Kalam Town area as a mallam, before the jihad and possibly on his way to or from Shaikh Usuman. He lodged with a brother of the ardo and on his return several decades later, as a flag-bearer in the Sokoto jihad, now stayed there again. Unable to reach Kalam by direct assault, Buba persuaded the moi to descend from his redoubt with the Bolewa army for negotiations below, and fell on them. The combined Fulani contingents killed, scattered, or enslaved the entire host.[56]

For about the next half-dozen years (ca. 1818–24) Buba Yero made Dukku Town, eight miles from Kalam, his military and political headquarters. Dukku had been the site of 11 Fulanin Shira hamlets, which he now brought together as one civic unit by having a wall built around them and appointing a single chief (F. *lamido*) above the several ardos (who became wardheads).[57] While at Dukku he exacted allegiance from all the Bolewa towns hitherto under Kalam and Pindiga for a radius of some 30 miles, including a few, e.g., Kirifi and Tubule, that subsequently were ceded to Bauchi Emirate.[58] Although most of the Fulanin Shira themselves are said to have followed him willingly in this period, a number, then as later, did not: the ardo of Tinda, for example, seized on the occasion of Buba's annual visit to Sultan Muhammad Bello to carry off the royal women and cattle, and dissident elements in Dukku itself were a recurrent source of tension and instability in the new state.[59]

Around 1824 Buba moved again, eight miles farther south, to begin the construction of Gombe Abba, which served as the emirate capital until 1913. The site chosen for it was both strategically suitable—close to the centers of Fulanin Shira and Bolewa population—and well situated to accommodate large numbers of Fulanin Kitaku, their families, and their servants and slaves.[60]

It was about 1824 that Buba Yero came into serious conflict with Yakubu, first emir of Bauchi, over the exact limits of their respective dominion along the Upper Gongola Valley. During the expansion of his new emirate eastward from the Jos Plateau foothills, Yakubu had joined with Buba in several campaigns on the western marches of the Kalam-Pindiga kingdoms. As related in Gombe, there was a general understanding among provincial leaders of the Sokoto jihad that whenever the capital of an ethnic community had been occupied by one of them, all its

56. *Ibid.*; Abraham, "Ethnological Notes"; and Carlyle, "History of Gombe."
57. Informants IA: 1–6; IF: 2–6; IG: 4–5, 7.
58. *Ibid.*; and Yakubu b. Halilu, "History of Buba Yero."
59. Informants IF: 2–6; and Abraham, "Ethnological Notes."
60. Informants IA: 1–6; IG: 1–8; and Carlyle, "Waja Sub-District."

satellite settlements were deemed part of the spoil. Many Jukun-ruled and Bolewa towns already by this date were subject to Bauchi, and Yakubu refused to let these go the way of Kalam (or, later, of Pindiga). Both sides appealed to Sultan Bello, who ordered Buba and Yakubu to leave their palaces on the same day and make the point where they met the common frontier. Yakubu left immediately on receiving the message, and was at the Gongola by the time the imperial edict arrived at Gombe Abba. Suleimanu dan Buba Yero was quickly dispatched with a strong column to intercept the Bauchi force, but in a pitched battle on the left river bank Yakubu routed him. Sokoto then sent representatives to demarcate the interemirate boundary, which left a number of Jukun and Bolewa towns on either side.[61]

EARLY EMIRATE GOVERNMENT IN GOMBE

When Buba Yero settled at Gombe Abba he was around 60 years of age and had been conducting an almost uninterrupted jihad for at least two decades. Thereafter he entrusted all operations against *dār al-ḥarb* to Suleimanu and to a younger son, Muhammadu Kwairanga.[62] Suleimanu especially had long experience of military life, having led portions of the Fulanin Kitaku in Bornu, Tangale-Waja, and on the Gongola. As Yeriman Gombe, he was now stationed at Wawa from where he conquered Gadam, Bojude, and other, less significant Bolewa towns of central Gombe; raided in the Waja Hills; and put down revolts by the Tera of Deba Habe and at Bojude. Muhammadu Kwairanga, residing at Akko, maintained constant pressure on Pindiga Town and took or retook a variety of Jukun, Bolewa, and Tera settlements to the south and southeast of Akko. The brothers often collaborated in this continuing effort to enlarge and consolidate *dār al-Islām* under Gombe; they were in turn greatly aided by a contemporaneous large-scale migration of Fulanin Kitaku into much of the grassland enclosed by the Gongola. Over time this phenomenon both hastened the conversion of Habe there to the faith

61. Informants IA: 1–6; IF: 3, 6; IG: 1–8; Yakubu b. Halilu, "History of Buba Yero"; S. M. Grier, section in "Assessment Report on Kirifi District, Central Province," by T. W. P. Dyer, NAK SNP 7/12 3269 5371/1911; and Carlyle, "History of Gombe." In this battle Suleimanu killed Sarkin Yakin Bauchi Mamman Kuso; it was fought at Buriburi, near the Upper Gongola, which then became an important landmark on the frontier.

62. Informants IA: 1–6; IG: 4–5, 7; and Carlyle, "History of Gombe."

of their new governors and made the latter, or at least their kinsmen, less casual in observance of Islam as they gradually were transformed into settled, Town Fulani. It also insured that wherever non-Muslim enclaves remained, these would be subject to close surveillance and control.[63]

Thus while Buba Yero encouraged Fulanin Kitaku movement into the emirate for security as well as religious purposes, he delegated to his nearest kin, Suleimanu and Muhammadu Kwairanga, over-all responsibility for the expansion and defense of its more outlying northern and southern zones. A third son, Mallam Buba, lived at Ribadu, on the eastern frontier; as a full-time scholar and teacher Buba did not engage in military affairs, but he could rely on the presence nearby of the large town of Mbilla, founded by a half-dozen or so Fulanin Kitaku groups when his father had been campaigning in the Gongola Bend.[64] The far Western sector of the nascent state, including the new capital as well as Dukku and Kunde (residence of the sarkin yaki), was readily defensible from these and numerous other Fulani settlements.

The earliest structure of emirate government, created simultaneously with Gombe Abba, reflected several ethnic and geographical imperatives. Ardos of the six largest Fulanin Kitaku ensembles were given direct authority over them. The sarkin yaki ruled the Fulanin Jera, the madaki the Fulanin Tara, the galadima the Fulanin Gona, Hamma Ruwa was head of the Fulanin Kiri, Bauchi Bula of the Fulanin Jada, and Bauchi Gordi of the Fulanin Babir. Similarly, those leaders of the four smaller clan groups were continued in charge: Sarkin Dabe (Fulanin Dabe), Sarkin Magi (Fulanin Magi), Ardo Walama (Fulanin Walama), and Ardo Maituta (Fulanin Hina). As their followers became less nomadic, the complexity and scope of administration increased for each of them: no longer first among equals, they acquired fiefs, titled subordinates, and, with the more affluent, ambitions that sometimes exceeded their means.[65]

All of these men had been lieutenants of Buba Yero in earlier phases of the jihad; two of them, Hamma Ruwa and Bauchi Bula, fell out with him after the move to Gombe Abba. Hamma Ruwa and the Fulanin Kiri had remained behind in the Middle Benue region when Buba was recalled north by Shaikh Usuman,

63. *Ibid.*; and Informants IA: 1–6; IIB: 26–27; IID: 1–4, 11–12, 14. Abraham mentions a fourth brother, Mohamman dan Buba Yero, who was stationed at Biri (northeast Gombe) and soon died in battle. He is remembered today only for the latter circumstance; his grave has been preserved in Biri Town.

64. Informants IA: 1–6; IB: 3–4, 6, 11–12, 19; IE: 8–11, 13; and Carlyle, "History of Gombe."

65. Informants IA–IG: *passim*.

and went on to conquer much of what later was incorporated as the emirate of Muri, founding a headquarters town of that name ca. 1817. As one of Buba's acknowledged "brothers," Hamma Ruwa had ambitions for his own son to succeed the modibbo. In the early 1830s both men were summoned by Buba to the capital, where they were executed on grounds of failing to render sufficient obedience. The Fulanin Kiri then secured from Sultan Bello permission to form a separate state, independent of Gombe authority.[66]

Bauchi Bula for his part had settled with a group of the Fulanin Jada near Gombe Abba at its foundation. A dispute with Buba Yero subsequently caused a number of them to cross permanently into Bauchi Emirate, while others returned with Bula to Daura (probably when it was taken, or retaken, by Suleimanu ca. 1830). The Fulanin Jada who remained on Gombe soil after Daura regained its autonomy a few years later were put under one or another of four separate fiefholders.[67]

In *Kitāb al-Farq,* an important expository work on the proper Islamic "foundations of government, and its ministers," Shaikh Usuman had enjoined his provincial subordinates to create only four state offices: that of the *wazīr* (*waziri*), or chief advisor to the crown; of the *qadi* (*alkali*), or judge; of the *walī al-shurta* (*walin shurat*), or chief of police; and of the collector of land tax or *kharāj* (*haraji*).[68] Following the general success of the jihad in west Hausaland, Usuman and Muhammad Bello appointed at Sokoto several additional titled officials, including a *muhtasib,* who served as "a kind of welfare officer and censor of morals"; a sarkin yaki, or commander of the army; a jailor; and a collector of cattle tax.[69]

Under pressure to accommodate his foremost ardos in the Gombe jihad, Buba

66. Informants IA: 1–6; IG: 4–5, 7; Temple, *Notes,* p. 499; Fremantle, *Muri Province,* p. 7; Gall, *Bauchi Province,* p. 13; Ruxton, "Notes on Fulani," and "Notes on the Tribes of the Muri Province," *Journal of the African Society,* VII (1908), 375; E. S. Lilley, "Assessment Report on Jalingo District, Muri Division, Muri Province," NAK SNP 7/14 3610 473p/1913; Kirk-Greene, *Adamawa,* pp. 153–54; and Hogben and Kirk-Greene, *Emirates of Northern Nigeria,* p. 447.

67. Informants IA: 1–6; IB: 1–2, 13, 32; IE: 12; IG: 4–5, 8; and G. J. Lethem, "Assessment Report on Allaguerno District, Bornu Emirate, Bornu Province," NAK SNP 10/7 3748 265p/1919.

68. Mervyn Hiskett, "*Kitāb al-Farq*: A Work on the Habe Kingdoms Attributed to 'Uthmān dan Fodio," *Bulletin of the School of Oriental and African Studies,* XXIII (1960), 570.

69. Denis Murray Last, *The Sokoto Caliphate* (London: Longmans, 1967), pp. 49–52. According to Last, Buba Yero was appointed sarkin yaki—amir al-jaish, or commander of the army—by Shaikh Usuman in his capacity as leader of the Gombe jihad, and he was the only one of several Sokoto lieutenants who retained that office until his death.

Yero soon departed from the shaikh's expressed wish and moved far beyond even existing practice at Sokoto. To have appointed but several of the Fulanin Kitaku to high administrative office would probably have encouraged more of the kind of dissension and eventual exodus from the emirate evidenced by the Fulanin Jada and Kiri. Hence, and with few exceptions, Buba allocated as fiefs most of the non-Muslim settlements (other than Bolewa) under his authority to the Fulanin Kitaku ardos who already had been made responsible for administering their own descent groups. This division of Habe fief areas was determined according to where each Fulani group had its main locus of residence before and/or after the creation of Gombe Abba. Thus all Jukun towns, and the Deba Habe segment of Teraland, were attached to the office of galadima; towns of the Gwani-, Hinna-, and Wade-associated Tera to that of the madaki; Jera, Gasi, and Waja towns to sarkin yaki; and, until their breakaway from the emirate ca. 1845, the Babir towns of west Biu to Bauchi Gordi; Kanakuru to Ardo Walama and Ardo Maituta; and Maga to Sarkin Magi.[70]

To his own lineage group and to less immediate relations, the Fulanin Janafulu, Buba reserved a majority of Bolewa towns. Wawa and its dependencies were placed under his waziri, while Nafada, Biri, and the Bolewa centers of the Kalam-Dukku region were given to Ajiyan Gombe. Both the first waziri and the first ajiya were considered "brothers" of the modibbo, as was the first Chiroman Gombe, who received the northern Tera communities of Bage, Gube, and Ashaka. The ajiya was also put in direct charge of Dukku and of the lamidos and ardos of all Fulanin Shira towns not the direct responsibility of Lamido Dukku. Non-Habe apart from those of the Fulanin Kitaku and Fulanin Shira, e.g., Kanuri, Fulanin Hadejia, and Shuwa Arab, were distributed as fiefs according to their location within a particular fief area, as were the scattered enclaves of Hausa settlers from Sokoto, Katsina, Bauchi, and Kano Emirates.[71]

All but two of these fiefholding titled officials lived in capital wards among their Fulani kinsmen, other followers, and slaves. Sarkin Yakin Gombe resided at Kunde, 10 miles away, and the galadima, at Akko. And all but the chiroma, waziri, and ajiya had been given standards by the modibbo in the early days of the jihad.[72] Such an award, similar in significance to that made by Shaikh Usuman to each of

70. Informants IA–IG: *passim*; and Carlyle, "History of Gombe." See map of Gombe Emirate ca. 1900 in end-pocket envelope for the allocation of fiefs to particular offices of central government by that date; the principle of ethnic distribution thus remained essentially unaltered during the nineteenth century.

71. *Ibid.*; and Informants IA–IG: *passim*.

72. Informants IA: 1–6; IG: 4–5, 7; and Lonsdale, "Gombe Town."

his prominent local deputies in northern Nigeria, would seem to have been at once a mark of formal recognition of their capacity and will to conduct a major phase of the Gombe jihad, and emblematic of their position as free, titled officials in emirate government. The flags were re-presented to successive occupants of each office at their investiture, a symbol of the (at least theoretically) permanent nature of the jihad.[73]

Several of the Fulanin Kitaku fiefholders were distinguished as well by their Islamic attainments. Hamma Ruwa, leader of the Fulanin Kiri, is said to have studied together with Buba Yero under Shaikh Usuman and was known also as a modibbo. Madaki Buba Yele was addressed as gwoni. Sarkin Magi Buba Kari Banto was appointed Alkalin Gombe. And the office of waziri was occupied by still another scholar. Of the four central-administration offices prescribed by the shaikh, only two, however, those of the *wazīr* and *qadi,* were in fact created in nineteenth-century Gombe. Collection of land tax was the responsibility of individual fiefholders, and three minor officials shared supervision of the metropolitan guard.[74]

73. Informants IA: 1–6; IG: 4–5, 7.
74. *Ibid.*

CHAPTER 6

KATAGUM: CA. 1805–46

THE HABE KINGDOMS OF SHIRA, TESHENA, AND AUYO

During that era (ca. A.D. 1000–1400) when the Kanem-based Maghumi clan had built an empire east and northeast of Bornu and the Hausa chiefdoms of northwest Nigeria were in process of growth toward more complex sociopolitical forms, three states emerged in the region of modern Katagum and Hadejia emirates. Sharing it seems a common origin and language, the capital town of each, Shira, Teshena, and Auyo, derived its name from an eponymous founder: Shiraka (Sheri, Shira), Teshe, and Auyo (Auwaya, Awuya). Uniformly said in local tradition to have been of royal Marghi descent, all three men are accounted to have arrived first at Shira Hill, where they defeated and eventually absorbed or dislodged a still more ancient colony of Habe settlers.[1] The sole Shira king-list known to have survived the jihad was discovered ca. 1883 to be defaced by rainwater, but it was reported a generation later to have placed the Marghian immigration 997 lunar years before Shira was taken by the Fulani, that is, ca. A.D. 940.[2] The Teshenawa

1. R. G. Ramage, "Historical Notes on Katagum Division, Bauchi Province (1929–33)," NAK SNP 17/1 1139 9715, and notes in P. G. Harris, "Anthropological Notes on the Teshena Tribe (1922–27)," NAK SNP 17/8 K.4195; F. W. H. Migeod, *Through Nigeria to Lake Chad* (London: Heath, Cranton, 1924) p. 260; *Notes on the Tribes, Provinces, Emirates and States of the Northern Provinces of Nigeria, Compiled from Official Reports by O. Temple,* ed. C. L. Temple, 2d ed. (1922; London: Frank Cass, 1965), pp. 32, 475; and J. M. Fremantle, "A History of the Region Comprising the Katagum Division of Kano Province," *Journal of the African Society,* X (April, 1911), 299–300.

2. *Ibid.*; and Ramage, "Historical Notes." The major spoken languages of Katagum now are Fula and Kanuri, but the Shirawa (Haben Shira) still prefer Hausa, which,

are quoted as remembering 70 rulers until the jihad;[3] and an Auyo traditional history, written or copied in the 1870s, put that town's date of foundation as A.D. 1211.[4]

Virtually nothing is recalled or on record of Teshena State but a vague reference to its occupation in the seventeenth century by Kwararafa.[5] It is apparent that by 1800 Teshena was far smaller in territorial extent than Shira and Auyo. Our present knowledge of Auyo is somewhat more detailed. There were visible fifty years ago remains of seven concentric Auyo town walls, the original, or outer, one being said to have been larger in circumference than the Kano wall. The locus of urban residence gradually contracted, owing perhaps to the encroachment of its surrounding marshland.[6] Auyo is mentioned twice in the "Kano Chronicle," once for the mid-seventeenth century, when Sarkin Kano marched there (probably on a slave-raid) and again for the reign of Sarkin Kano Babba Zaki (ca. 1768–76), when the Kanawa attacked Auyo Town but stopped short of destroying it because of the intercession of a high Kano official and two vassal chiefs.[7] The latter expedition is confirmed by a lineal descendant of the then king of Auyo, Abubakar, who claims that Babba Zaki was driven off and pursued across the Auyo frontier.[8]

The earliest recorded mention of Shira is also contained in the "Kano Chronicle": Abdullahi Burja (ca. 1438–52), reputedly the first Hausa sarki to pay tribute to Bornu, is said to have been the first ruler of Kano to marry a daughter of a Shira

---

according to Ramage and present-day local informants, had been the case well before 1900. The Shira tongue itself (Shirenci), now almost extinct, is said to have been used only by the rulers and their lineages of Shira Kingdom. This would suggest either a shorter dynastic line, or a very small group of immigrant leaders, or both. H. Richmond Palmer speculates that such immigrant Shirawa, together with their Teshena and Auyo counterparts (as well as the N'gizim and Bedde), arrived in the Border States region between the eleventh and thirteenth centuries A.D. from the southeast corner of Lake Chad, Marghiland, and Mandara (see comment by Palmer in Ramage, "Historical Notes").

3. Migeod, *Through Nigeria,* p. 263; and Fremantle, "History of the Region," X (1911), 302.

4. *Ibid.,* p. 300. Temple calculates the date as falling in the mid-fourteenth century (*Notes,* p. 32), while Migeod places it—on the authority of an Arabic king-list found at Auyo—in 1209 (*Through Nigeria,* pp. 264–65).

5. Ramage, notes in Harris, "Anthropological Notes."

6. Fremantle, "History of the Region," X (1911), 301.

7. H. Richmond Palmer, *Sudanese Memoirs,* 3 vols. (1928; London: Frank Cass, 1967), II, 121, 126.

8. Informant IIIG: 14.

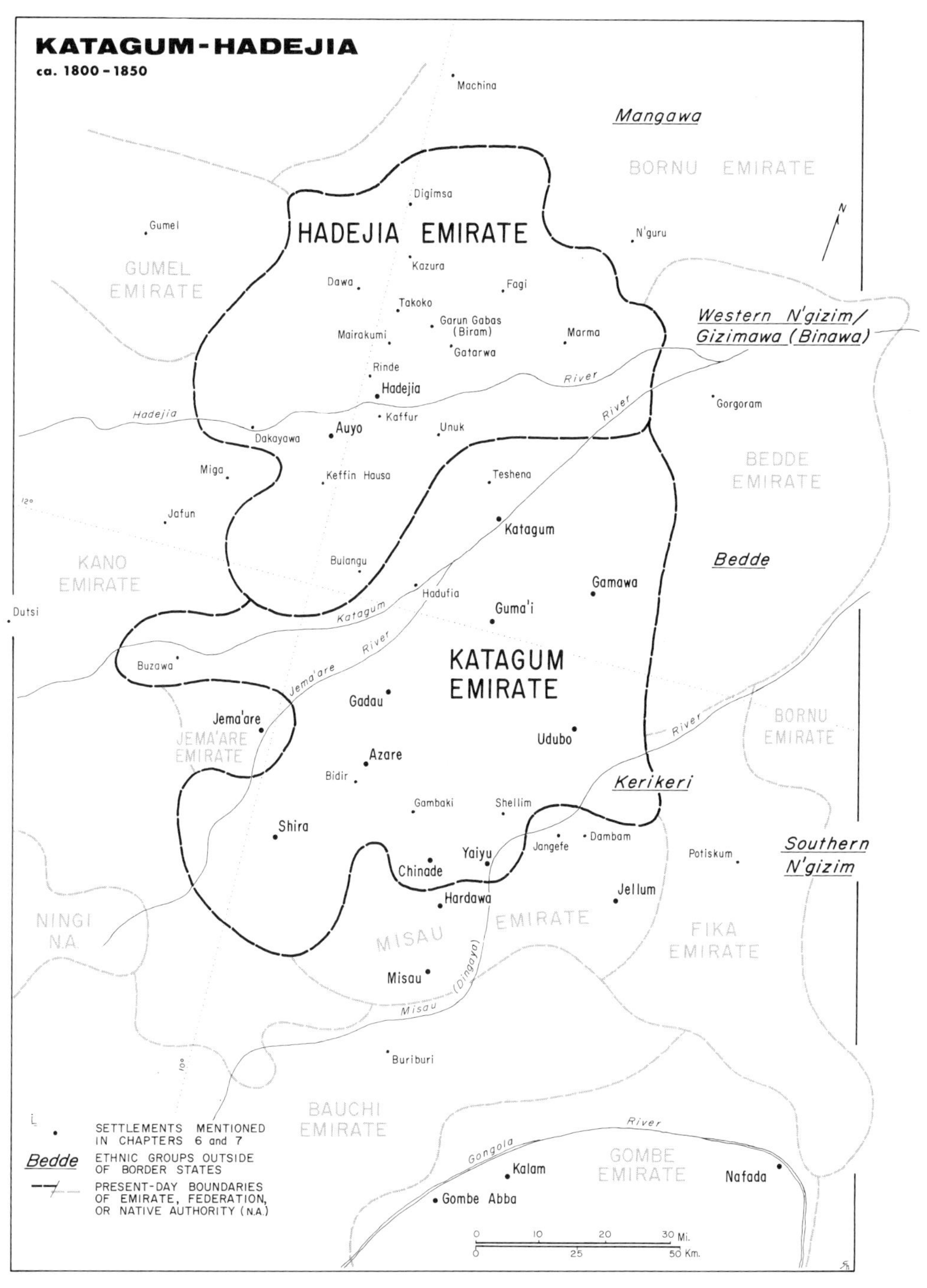
KATAGUM-HADEJIA
ca. 1800-1850
Machina
Mangawa
BORNU EMIRATE
Digimsa
HADEJIA EMIRATE
Gumel
GUMEL EMIRATE
N'guru
N
Kazura
Dawa
Fagi
Takoko
Garun Gabas (Biram)
Mairakumi
Gatarwa
Marma
Western N'gizim/ Gizimawa (Binawa)
Rinde
Hadejia
River
Hadejia
Kaffur
Auyo
Unuk
Dakayawa
Gorgoram
River
Miga
Keffin Hausa
Teshena
BEDDE EMIRATE
12°
Jafun
Katagum
KANO EMIRATE
Bulangu
Bedde
Gamawa
Hadufia
Dutsi
Katagum
Guma'i
River
Buzawa
KATAGUM EMIRATE
Jema'are
Gadau
Jema'are
JEMA'ARE EMIRATE
Udubo
River
BORNU EMIRATE
Azare
Bidir
Kerikeri
Gambaki
Shellim
Shira
Jangefe
Dambam
Potiskum
Southern N'gizim
Yaiyu
Chinade
Hardawa
Jellum
NINGI N.A.
MISAU
EMIRATE
FIKA EMIRATE
(Dingaya)
Misau
Misau
Buriburi
10°
BAUCHI EMIRATE
SETTLEMENTS MENTIONED IN CHAPTERS 6 and 7
Bedde
ETHNIC GROUPS OUTSIDE OF BORDER STATES
PRESENT-DAY BOUNDARIES OF EMIRATE, FEDERATION, OR NATIVE AUTHORITY (N.A.)
River
Gongola
GOMBE EMIRATE
Kalam
Nafada
Gombe Abba
0 10 20 30 Mi.
0 25 50 Km.

king,[9] an indication that Shira had already some wider geopolitical role—perhaps as a buffer against the emerging power of Bornu. Kano may have warred on Shira in the early 1500s,[10] and the Shirawa almost certainly would have been drawn into the several centuries of armed conflict between the Hausa kingdoms, Bornu, and the Kwararafa, lying as it did within a principal zone of east-west passage.[11] Although no reference to such a probability is found in either local tradition or chronicles, 'Abd al-Qadir b. al-Mustafa recorded an assault on Shira by Sarkin Gobir Barbari (ca. 1742–70) during his struggle with Kano and the capture of many Shira towns by Sarkin Gobir Yakubu (ca. 1795–1801).[12]

There is evidence that Fulani or Mandingo trader-missionaries traveled from Kano to Birni Gazargamu, and of Kanuri influence on Hausaland, beginning in the fifteenth century. A few Shirawa are said to have converted to Islam by 1500,[13] while another tradition holds that before the jihad Auyo Town had close to one thousand Qur'anic teachers.[14] It seems probable that rulers of Auyo, Shira, and Teshena were, like the Hausa kings, at least nominal Muslims by 1750. Auyo is alleged to have then included 18 town gates, a large market, and an Arab ward,[15] attributes which indicate elsewhere a lengthy involvement with long-distance trade and a much earlier date for the elite acceptance of Islam.

By the eighteenth century government in Shira appears to have encompassed to some degree an area of three to four thousand square miles, bounded on the north by Teshena and Auyo, on the east by divers Barebari chiefdoms and Kerikeriland, on the south by the states of the Gongola Kwararafa, and on the west by a line running close to Gaya and Dutsi in Kano Emirate.[16] A circumstance which might well have contributed appreciably to Shira's growth and relative independence of Bornu, Kano, and the Kwararafa was the presence of a belt of iron ore extending over 100 miles, from Buzawa on the west to eastward of Potiskum (Bornu frontier). Much of this belt lay in Shira kingdom; both local report and the number of slag heaps found there by Europeans when they arrived suggest that Shira (and

9. Palmer, *Sudanese Memoirs,* II, 110.

10. *Ibid.,* 113.

11. Ramage recorded a local tradition that Shira invaded the Kwararafa, its army reaching as far south as the Benue ("Historical Notes").

12. H. Richmond Palmer, "Western Sudan History," *Journal of the African Society,* XV (1915–16), 268–69.

13. Fremantle, "History of the Region," X (1911), 301; and Ramage, "Historical Notes."

14. Informants IIIG: 1–6, 8–9, 11, 14.

15. Fremantle, "History of the Region," X (1911), 302.

16. *Ibid.,* p. 301; and Ramage, "Historical Notes," and "Iron Currency," Jos Museum Files, June 6, 1928.

later Katagum) was a primary center for northeast Nigeria of iron-smelting and the manufacture of iron weapons, tools, and currency.[17]

Together with Auyo and Teshena, Shira was from at least the sixteenth century onward a vassal state of the mai of Bornu, paying him tribute through his galadima at N'guru.[18] Yet all three would likely have maintained a high measure of political autonomy, as did the Hausa provinces and those of the Sahil north of Auyo.

THE JIHAD IN BORNU

The Fulani jihad in Bornu was an outcome of several decades or more of ethnic conflict in northeast Nigeria, heightened by religious and social unrest of a kind which had surfaced in Hausaland in that same period. An undoubted expression of this may be found in the early, unauthorized effort of Buba Yero to carve out a Muslim Fulani state in the far southwest corner of Bornu as well as the Benue-Gongola Valley beyond. Its immediate cause, however, lay in the response of Cattle Fulani ardos of the N'guru-Marma-Auyo region to Shaikh Usuman's success in rallying support from nomadic Fulani and others of Kano, Katsina, and Daura (winter, 1804–5) and to Mai Bornu's dispatch through his galadima of offers to aid the embattled chiefs of these Habe kingdoms.[19]

17. Iron bars as a medium of exchange in the area probably were supplanted before the jihad by cotton strips and cowrie shells. The latter are said to have been introduced into Kano in the first third of the eighteenth century (Palmer, *Sudanese Memoirs,* II, 123) and to have reached Bornu between 1824 and 1851 (*Missions to the Niger,* ed. E. W. Bovill, Vol. II: *The Bornu Mission, 1822–25* [1826; Cambridge: At the University Press, 1966], 631; and Heinrich Barth, *Travels and Discoveries in Northern and Central Africa,* 3 vols. [1857–59; Frank Cass, 1965], II, 55). Clapperton wrote of his arrival at Katagum from Bornu, "Here we found, for the first time, kowrie shells in circulation as money; for hitherto native cloth, or some other commodity of standard price, had been the common medium of exchange" (Bovill, *The Bornu Mission,* p. 631).

18. Ramage, "Iron Currency," and "Historical Notes"; Fremantle, "History of the Region," X (1911), 301–3; Temple, *Notes,* p. 33; Migeod, *Through Nigeria,* p. 263; and Yves Urvoy, *Histoire de l'Empire du Bornou* (Paris: Larose, 1949), p. 62.

19. The fullest and most useful contemporary accounts now readily available of the Fulani jihad in Bornu are found in the "Infāq al-maisur fī ta'rīkh bilād al-Takrūr," written by Muhammad Bello dan Shaikh Usuman in 1812, and in the published, first-hand report of a young Bornuan eyewitness of several of its major events, 'Ali Eisami Gazirma (see E. J. Arnett, *The Rise of the Sokoto Fulani, Being a Paraphrase and in Some Parts a Translation of the Infaku'l Maisuri of Sultan Mohammed Bello* [Kano: Emirate Printing Department, 1922]; and S. W. Koelle, *African Native Literature*

In 1805 the galadima sent a column to relieve the by then hard-pressed sarki of Daura and was readying another to help defend Katsina and Kano.[20] A Fulani contingent led by Ardo Lernima of Marma—the galadima's agent for collection of cattle tithe in the N'guru-Marma savanna—intercepted his men and turned them back.[21] Strengthened by clan groups under Ardo Abdua and his sons Umaru and Sambo, Lernima then moved on N'guru. They defeated the galadima, who fled to Birni Gazargamu. There Mai Ahmad (ca. 1793–1810) hastily prepared to meet the new, western challenge to the empire by marshaling whatever military power continued at its disposal. Alarmed by the prospect of Ahmad fielding a superior force, the Fellata Bornu already committed to Usuman's cause now migrated, those Fulanin Mare of the Damaturu-Gujba-Daya area to join Buba Yero farther south and those Fulani in west Bornu to around Auyo and Marma, where Lernima and Abdua had maintained themselves in the face of raids from Bornu (and may again have driven the galadima out of N'guru).[22]

At this critical juncture, with the political situation fluid and the disaffection of his Fulani subjects still in some doubt, Mai Ahmad wrote one of their leaders, Alhaji Adamu, to seek an explanation of these events. He also requested Adamu

[London, 1854]). Two other important sources are B. G. Martin, "Unbelief in the Western Sudan: 'Uthmān dan Fodio's 'Ta'līm al-ikhwān,' " *Middle Eastern Studies,* IV (1968), 89–90; and Sarkin Misau Ahmadu dan Alhaji Tafida, "Tarihin Sarakunan Misau" [History of the Emirs of Misau] (Hausa MS, copy in my possession, dated 1926, of which an Arabic version, listed under Ahmad b. al-Hājj, "Tarīkh Missau" [History of Misau], is in the University of Ibadan Library [uncatalogued]). From the mid-nineteenth century there is material in Barth, *Travels and Discoveries,* and from the early twentieth in Captain Landeroin, "Du Tschad au Niger: notes historiques," in *Documents scientifiques de la mission Tilho 1905–9,* 3 vols. (Paris, 1911). However limited in their scope and often sparing in the details they provide, these authorities, when supplemented with oral traditions gathered over the past 50 years, enable us to follow in broad outline the course of Fulani attempts at forcing acknowledgment from the rulers of Bornu of Shaikh Usuman's position as Amir al-Muminin (Commander of the Faithful).

20. Arnett, *Rise of the Sokoto Fulani,* pp. 99–100.

21. *Ibid.,* p. 100; and Fremantle, "History of the Region," X (1911), 312. Lernima (or Lerlima) is usually said to have been given the title of Sarkin Fulani by Galadiman Bornu. Another source reports that he was also delegated responsibility for collection of tax or tribute in the Western N'gizim (Gizimawa/Binawa) towns, which lie between Marma and N'guru (G. C. Whitely, "Special Report on Bedde Emirate, Bornu Province," NAK SNP 10/8 4024 209p/1920). If true, this would suggest that some at least of the Cattle Fulani of the area no longer were living as pure nomads and may even have shifted their traditional position of using local pasturelands on the sufferance of their sedentary, non-Muslim neighbors.

22. Arnett, *Rise of the Sokoto Fulani,* p. 100.

to persuade Shaikh Usuman to prevent a continuance of Fulani migration from his domains, and to inform Usuman that he, Ahmad, was the sole and rightful Commander of the Faithful in Bornu. Muhammad Bello replied for his father and Adamu in a long message delineating the root causes of the jihad in Bornu. He did not refer to Ahmad himself as a practitioner of pagan customs, but he did accuse the Habe rulers of Hausaland of apostasy and sought Ahmad's support in combating them. At the same time he sent word enjoining the Fellata Bornu from a resumption of hostilities and instructed them to stay clear of the mai's territory. Bello's messenger was abused on his arrival at Birni Gazargamu, as Ahmad already was in motion westward to chastise the Fulani rebels of Marma and Auyo.[23]

From a base camp near N'guru, Ahmad ordered his galadima and kaigama to deal with Ardo Lernima. They did so with ease, but in a subsequent foray against Abdua's (reinforced) group the imperial army was routed, suffering severe losses; both commanders, with a number of other Bornu high officials, were killed. This victory, achieved on the western margin of the mai's empire ca. 1806–7, emboldened the Fulani of that region to offer a more direct challenge to Ahmad.[24]

23. *Ibid.*, pp. 100–101.

24. *Ibid.*, p. 101. In a work written December, 1813, to justify the Sokoto jihad within a traditional Islamic framework of values, Shaikh Usuman provided the following partial account of its initial phases in west Bornu and the mai's own explanation of what provoked the first outbreak of hostilities:

"We have not fully explained until now the cause of our conflict with them (people of Bornu). As for a detailed explanation of it, the Ghalādīma of Bornu equipped an army and sent it to Hadejīa. When it arrived there, one of our communities (*jamā'a*) there came out to defend themselves, and God helped them to victory. Then, after that, the Amīr of Bornū, Mai Ahmad, got busy and equipped a [second] army, and went himself with it until it reached W. t. kāl. Despatching his force against the community of [Ardo] Lerlima, he slaughtered men and women, young and old. While he was at that place, he sent an army against our community, the community of Ibn 'Abdur, which was a Q.d.r. They came out to defend themselves, and God gave them the victory. We had despatched Muhammad b. 'Alī to their king, to ask him the reason for their fighting against us, for the attack on our community, and the community of Ibn 'Abdur and the Muslim communities who were in their towns.

"Therefore, he wrote us this answer in a *wathīqa* (despatch) saying, 'As to the departure of the Amīr Ahmad on a raid to the westwards (al-Gharb), [it was carried out] in the spirit of chivalry (*hamīya*),' by which he meant the [perverse] spirit of the Age of Ignorance before Islam. And he declared, as to the cause of the fighting against the Muslim communities who were in their towns, 'its cause was that his Ghalādīma went to his Dayāma and told him falsely that the Amīr had ordered him to kill the Fallātīya (Fulani), so he had begun to slaughter them. That was why disorder had broken out in our towns—this was all that could be said to explain the origin of the disorder' (Martin, "Unbelief in the Western Sudan," pp. 89–90).

The leader of this second phase of the jihad in Bornu was Gwoni Mukhtar, an ardo of the Fulanin Mare clan(s) of the pastoral environs of Damaturu. According to a lineal descendant of Mukhtar, he was at least a third-generation modibbo and had as a youth inherited a Qur'anic school from his teacher and father-in-law at a Fulani settlement near Damaturu. There Mukhtar, with his own pupils and fellow ardos, was exposed to regular harassment by surrounding non-Muslim communities, and he obtained leave from Shaikh Usuman to begin a jihad in the area.[25] Other evidence would suggest that after the Fulanin Mare chiefs had gone south to find greater security with Buba Yero they returned on word of Mai Ahmad's reversal and, having chosen Mukhtar and a Mallam Buhari as joint commanders, soon made Daya their military headquarters.[26]

About this time the Cattle Fulani ardos of both the northern and southern wings wrote Shaikh Usuman to make plain why they held the injunction against further campaigns to be unjust. The Daya-based Fulanin Mare detailed a variety of alleged polytheistic customs in Bornu to demonstrate that its people were outside the pale of Islam. The Fulani under Lernima and Abdua reminded the shaikh that Mai Bornu was giving aid and comfort to Habe kings on their western flank. And both groups pleaded the right of self-defense against repeated attack by the mai and his "pagan" allies.[27] Meanwhile (and in partial substantiation of this argument) Ahmad had sent several columns to Daya, with sufficient success to induce them again to seek refuge southward. Rejoining Buba Yero they proceeded, under his leadership and alongside the Fulanin Kitaku, to ravage a number of towns in southwest Bornu.[28]

It was probably during the same year (ca. 1807) that Mallam Ibrahim Zaki assumed command of the northern half of the Bornu jihad. Seizing the initiative offered by their new mastery of the Auyo-N'guru-Marma region, Zaki and his

25. Ahmadu dan Alhaji Tafida, "Tarihin Sarakunan Misau"; and Ramage, "Historical Notes."

26. Arnett, *Rise of the Sokoto Fulani,* p. 101. 'Ali Eisami Gazirma relates how the chief of Daya—then a vassal of the mai—had ca. 1800 befriended the local Fulani divines and favored them over his own. When he refused several summonses from Birni Gazargamu, Mai Bornu attempted unsuccessfully to depose him by force. He was, however, removed by his younger brothers and five years later the Fulani, in response, "began a war . . . [and] gradually the Phula took the whole country of Daya" (Koelle, *African Native Literature,* pp. 212–18). 'Ali was then about 19.

27. Denis Murray Last and Muhammad A. al-Hajj, "Attempts at Defining a Muslim in 19th-century Hausaland and Bornu," paper delivered at the Annual Congress of the Historical Society of Nigeria, Lagos, December, 1964.

28. Arnett, *Rise of the Sokoto Fulani,* p. 101.

lieutenants now carried the war to the neighborhood of Birni Gazargamu and were almost able to occupy the capital.[29] To the south, Gwoni Mukhtar had in turn succeeded to full command of the Daya Fulani on Mallam Buhari's death; he led a combined force of Fulanin Mare and Fulanin Kitaku to Birni Gazargamu in 1808 and conquered it.[30] Mai Ahmad escaped with his courtiers and surviving soldiers, but, either then or a few months later, was obliged to relinquish authority to his son Dunama Lafiami.[31] Birni Gazargamu was pillaged by the Fulani; Mukhtar sent in the care of his son Muhammad Manga one hundred of each kind of spoil to Shaikh Usuman, and the future Wazirin Sokoto, Gidado, arrived soon after to collect the Bornu imperial treasure.[32]

29. *Ibid.*

30. *Ibid.* The date of this epochal event in Bornu history has been the subject of some dispute. Barth gives it as a Sunday in 1809 (*Travels and Discoveries,* II, 599). H. Richmond Palmer, citing copies of a letter from Al-Kanemi written soon after, makes it March 12, 1808 (13 Muharram 1223) (*The Bornu Sahara and Sudan* [London: John Murray, 1936], pp. 109–10, and *Gazetteer of Bornu Province* [Lagos: The Government Printer, 1929], p. 18). J. R. Patterson mentions March 31, 1808 (3 Safar 1223) ("Assessment Report on Geidam District, Bornu Emirate, Bornu Province," NAK SNP 10/6 3274 114p/1918); Urvoy, simply 1808 (*Histoire de l'Empire du Bornou,* p. 100); and 'Abd al-Qadir b. al-Mustafa, the fourth year of the Sokoto jihad, i.e., 1808–9 (Palmer, "Western Sudan History," p. 270). H. F. C. Smith, Denis Murray Last, and Gambo Gubio have more recently put "the most likely date" in March–April, 1808 (Muharram–Safar 1223) ("Ali Eisami Gazirmabe of Bornu," in *Africa Remembered, Narratives by West Africans from the Era of the Slave Trade,* ed. Philip D. Curtin [Madison: University of Wisconsin Press, 1968], p. 209 n. 23). Louis Brenner, also on the evidence of correspondence from al-Kanemi, believes that it must have been after May, in 1808 ("The Shehus of Kukawa: A History of the Al-Kanemi Dynasty of Bornu" [Ph.D. diss., Columbia University, 1968], p. 34 n. 4).

31. Koelle, *African Native Literature,* p. 222; Patterson, "Geidam District"; Landeroin, "Notes historiques," p. 358; and "The End of the Saifawa Dynasty" (Arabic MS, trans. Palmer in *Sudanese Memoirs,* II, 119). 'Ali Eisami, who witnessed the fall of Birni Gazargamu, recalled that following a four-hour battle on the west side of town the mai escaped through its eastern gate (Koelle, *African Native Literature,* pp. 221, 249). Ahmad died, of natural causes, shortly after.

32. Barth met an old man present at Birni Gazargamu then who recounted how the city had been "horribly sacked"; elsewhere Barth refers to its having been "given up to all the horrors accompanying the sacking of a town" (*Travels and Discoveries,* III, 26). But 'Ali Eisami notes that on the morning after Mukhtar's conquest, "a great preast of the Phula" told peasants living nearby: "Let everyone go and remain in his house, the war is over; let all the poor go, and each cultivate land!" (Koelle, *African Native Literature,* p. 250). The report of Muhammad Manga is from Ahmadu dan Alhaji Tafida, "Tarihin Sarakunan Misau"; and Ramage, "Historical Notes"; that of Gidado from Last and al-Hajj, "Attempts at Defining a Muslim."

Dispossessed of his capital and much of his wealth, Mai Dunama appealed for help to the one available source, al-Hajj Muhammad al-Amin ibn Muhammad al-Kanemi, generally known as Shaikh (Shehu) Laminu or al-Kanemi. A Muslim divine of Kanem, al-Kanemi had assembled a small band of fellow Kanembu and Shuwa Arabs on the western border of Lake Chad and was already engaged in hostilities with the Fulanin Mare of that district of Bornu. (He may also have been raided in this period by those of Gwoni Mukhtar.)[33] In May, 1808, al-Kanemi had written the Daya Fulani ardos to ask why they were acting aggressively and was unimpressed by their citation of Shaikh Usuman's apologia for the jihad.[34] Following the capture of Birni Gazargamu he wrote again, "beseeching them in the name of God and Islam to desist from their evil doing";[35] but they—presumably the Fulanin Mare under Mukhtar, although the more local branch could be meant here—did not desist. Given the circumstances, al-Kanemi responded quickly to Mai Dunama's plea.[36] At the same time he sent to a number of vassal chiefs of Bornu to join Dunama in the struggle to preserve the empire.[37]

While Dunama and al-Kanemi were making plans to liberate the capital, the Daya Fulani there had all but deserted Mukhtar and returned southward for the dry-season movement of cattle.[38] Left with a much-reduced force in the city, Mukhtar was unequal to its defense when a small detachment led by Dunama and a son of al-Kanemi arrived at the gates.[39] Probably in the winter of 1808–9 Birni Gazargamu was retaken, and Mukhtar slain.[40] Muhammad Manga, on the way

33. Barth relates that about this time al-Kanemi defeated the Fulani close to his new base at N'gurno, on Lake Chad (*Travels and Discoveries*, II, 600).

34. Last and al-Hajj, "Attempts at Defining a Muslim."

35. Arnett, *Rise of the Sokoto Fulani,* p. 101.

36. Brenner, working from sources gathered in Bornu, concludes that "vast portions of Bornu had now been overrun by the Fulbe and almost all the territory west and south of Birni Gazargamu had been laid waste" ("The Shehus of Kukawa," p. 35).

37. Landeroin, "Notes historiques," pp. 358, 429–30. Landeroin says that al-Kanemi wrote the chiefs of N'guru (?), Wacha, Miriya, and the Sosebaki states—all west of Birni Gazargamu; only the latter responded, coming in person with armed assistance.

38. Arnett, *Rise of the Sokoto Fulani,* p. 101.

39. According to Fremantle, Kanuri sources claim that Dunama had only 400 men against 8,000 Fulani warriors ("History of the Region," X [1911], 308). In view of the above, these figures may well be hyperbolic, and drawn from a statement by Denham that al-Kanemi had the former quantity at his command on his "first campaign" (Bovill, *The Bornu Mission,* III, 525).

40. The duration of the (first) Fulani conquest of Birni Gazargamu—and the related question of when it was reoccupied by Dunama—is, like the date of its capture, variously given in available sources. A period of 40 days is mentioned by the anonymous author of an Arabic manuscript, "The Peoples of Gujba" (trans. Palmer,

back from Shaikh Usuman to rejoin his father, met some of the Fulani remnants and took over Mukhtar's flag and position.[41]

A year or two later another successful attempt on the capital was mounted by Mallam Zaki and a section of the northern Fellata Bornu. Once again the mai fled east and sought refuge with al-Kanemi, who, with his following greatly enlarged, henceforth directed the Bornu resistance. They marched together to Birni Gazargamu, but Zaki had now abandoned the site.[42] His motives for having done so are variously suggested by documentary and oral evidence, but the general view is that he left on orders of Shaikh Usuman, who feared either a recurrence of Mukhtar's experience or that Zaki might establish himself in Bornu as a sovereign independent of Usuman's authority.[43] Al-Kanemi and Dunama passed well beyond the capital in pursuit of the northern Fellata Bornu and may have recovered some of the spoil at Teshena.[44]

Although Muhammad Manga twice raided as far as Birni Gazargamu in later

---

Sudanese Memoirs, II, 81); in Kanuri traditions collected at Bilma (north of Lake Chad) by M. Abadie (*La Colonie du Niger* [Paris, 1927], p. 387); by Landeroin ("Notes historiques," p. 430); by Fremantle ("History of the Region," X [1911], 308); and in oral accounts from Katagum and Gombe (field notes). Patterson ("Geidam District"); Palmer (*Sudanese Memoirs,* II, 119, and *The Bornu Sahara,* p. 259); and Derrick J. Stenning (*Savannah Nomads* [London: Oxford University Press, 1959], p. 32) all say about nine months. Last and al-Hajj propose seven months ("Attempts at Defining a Muslim").

41. Fremantle, "History of the Region," X (1911), 309; Ramage, "Historical Notes"; and W. F. Gowers, comp., *Gazetteer of Kano Province* (London: Waterlow, 1921), p. 33.

42. The date of the second Fulani occupation is even harder to establish from sources at hand than is that of the first. Mallam Zaki's arrival at Birni Gazargamu is put by Barth, Urvoy, and Stenning in the winter of 1811–12 (*Travels and Discoveries,* II, 600; *Histoire de l'Empire du Bornou,* p. 101; *Savannah Nomads,* p. 32); by Palmer in January, 1808 (*Gazetteer of Bornu Province,* p.12); by Patterson as "less than a year" after Mukhtar's death ("Geidam District"); by Landeroin ca. 1808–9 ("Notes historiques"); and by Ramage and Brenner early in 1810 ("Historical Notes"; "The Shehus of Kukawa," p. 39). So too the length of Mallam Zaki's residence there is disputed. The anonymous author of "The End of the Sefawa Dynasty" gives 40 days (Arabic MS, trans. Palmer, in *Sudanese Memoirs,* II, 119). A period of six months if offered by informants in Katagum (field notes), and by Landeroin ("Notes historiques," p. 359), and Yakubu b. Halilu ("Tarihin Mallam Zaki" [History of Mallam Zaki], [MS, copy in my possession, n.d.]). Palmer records 21 months (*Gazetteer of Bornu Province,* p. 13).

43. Informants IIA: 1–5; IIB: 1–9; Yakubu b. Halilu, "Tarihin Mallam Zaki"; and Fremantle, "History of the Region," X (1911), 313.

44. *Ibid.*; and Urvoy, *Histoire de l'Empire du Bornou,* p. 101.

years, this episode marked the end of Fulani exertions to include Bornu as a whole within the Sokoto Caliphate.[45] Thereafter the emirs of Gombe, Katagum, and Hadejia (as well as Jema'are and Misau) were content to forage for slaves, cattle, and horses and to stage reprisal attacks along the 200-mile, poorly delimited frontier with Bornu. The sultans of Sokoto more often than not maintained a largely effective understanding with their counterparts in Bornu that each empire would not go beyond such minor provocations. Dunama finally moved his court from Birni Gazargamu and founded a new capital, Birni Kafela, near al-Kanemi's own newly built headquarters-town of N'gurno, on the southwest bank of Lake Chad.

MALLAM ZAKI: THE FOUNDATION OF KATAGUM EMIRATE

The founder and first ruler of Katagum Emirate, Mallam Ibrahim Zaki,[46] was born at Yaiyu, a then-prominent town in the southeast corner of Shira Kingdom on the right bank of the Dingaya (Misau) River. His father, Muhammadu Lawan, is generally said to have been of mixed Fellata Bornu–Shuwa Arab ancestry.[47] Hence all descendants of Lawan describe themselves in ethnic terms as Arabs (*Larabawa,* s. *Balarabe*) rather than Fulani; in lineage terms they are known as *Lawanawa, Irin Lawan* (kin of Lawan), or *Fulanin Soro* (Fulani of the shade, i.e., those who are not expected to perform manual labor).

From his birthplace in Baghirmi, Lawan had traveled west as an itinerant student and Islamic preacher until he reached Nafada, on the Gongola Bend.[48] There he taught, proselytized, and married a daughter of the Bolewa chief after curing her of a tropical ulcer. Eventually he was forced to leave Nafada by his father-in-law, who had become apprehensive at his increasing popularity among the subject

45. *Ibid.*, n. 5; and Arnett, *Rise of the Sokoto Fulani,* p. 109.

46. He is almost always referred to in the literature and by informants today as Mallam Zaki, though considered to have been a modibbo. His full name was Ibrahim Zakiyu'l Kalbi. "Zaki," Hausa for "lion," seems to have been a childhood nickname; Shaikh Usuman is said to have lengthened it to Zakiyu'l, Arabic for "pure of heart" (Informants IIA–IIB: *passim*).

47. *Ibid.* Mallam Zaki's paternal grandmother is said to have been the daughter of a gwoni of Baghirmi (Yakubu b. Halilu, "Tarihin Mallam Zaki").

48. For the role of such men in Bornu Fulani society, see pp. 71–72 above.

Bolewa and Fulanin Jada there. With his young son, Muhammadu Bunni (an issue of the marriage), and several followers, Lawan then moved about 60 miles northwest to resume the career of a Muslim divine at Yaiyu. Here Lawan again used his medical knowledge to cure the local chief's daughter of an ulcer, and married her. Appointed to the office of imam of Yaiyu, he and Bunni proceeded to go about the countryside as missionary-doctors, serving the combined functions of Islamic teachers, healers, and soothsayers. Bunni concentrated at the Fulanin Jafun center of Hardawa, also marrying the chief's daughter after she had recovered from an illness of the same nature. Of Lawan's union at Yaiyu was born Mallam Zaki and of Bunni's at Hardawa, the third ruler of Katagum, Muhammadu Dan Kauwa.[49]

As at Nafada, Lawan at Yaiyu in time aroused the suspicion of his father-in-law and was constrained to found his own settlement nearby. From there Mallam Zaki traveled as a youth to study at Birni Gazargamu.[50] On his return home, he joined Dan Kauwa in taking up the missionary work of their fathers. Again the fear or jealousy evoked by this activity compelled a change of residence, and they moved some 15 miles northwest to Shellim, a major Lerewa town on the Shira-Udubo frontier. Here they gathered a considerable following, composed mainly of Lerewa but including Fellata Bornu and Fulanin Udubo. Evidently in this period Mallam Zaki paid regular visits to Shaikh Usuman dan Fodio (then in the Gobir hinterland), but it is uncertain whether he already had been given a standard and instructions to begin a local jihad when, from the base at Shellim, Zaki attacked Udubo unsuccessfully. In the wake of this initial reverse, he sought a new field of operations in the Auyo-Teshena region, some 60 miles farther northwest and by then a principal concern of Ardo Abdua, Umaru, and Sambo Digimsa of the Hadejia Cattle Fulani.[51]

Mallam Zaki and Dan Kauwa, now allied with the family of Abdua, may have taken part in its subjection of Auyo Town. They probably did receive armed assistance from Abdua's group when, about the same year (ca. 1805–6), they conquered the capital of Teshena.[52] Sarkin Teshena had earlier scorned Mallam

49. Informants IIA: 1–5; IIB: 1–9; IIF: 10–11; and Yakubu b. Halilu, "Tarihin Mallam Zaki."

50. According to Fremantle, his teacher was a Mallam Kiari, who also is said to have taught Modibbo Adama, founder of Adamawa Emirate, and Buba Yero ("History of the Region," X [1911], 309). Informants today in Katagum do not recall a Mallam Kiari, but point out that his name is a common one in Bornu, and means "old man" in Kanuri.

51. Informants IIA: 1–5; IIB: 1–9; IIF: 1–4, 10–11.

52. *Ibid.*; Informants IIIA: *passim*; and Ramage, "Historical Notes."

Zaki's request to marry his daughter, refusing, it has often been said, the offer of one thousand slaves. The sarki died in the struggle, and Zaki then married the girl, reportedly giving her that number of captives of Teshena royal blood to dispose of as she saw fit.[53]

With Teshena his military headquarters and strengthened by a fresh access of support from the Fulanin Teshena community and several Barebari chiefs in the neighboring area, Zaki next embarked on the conquest of Shira Town and its more important dependencies. Marching south, via Gadau and Azare, he arrived at Shira and encamped just beyond the outer fortifications.[54] At this point the local narrative accounts diverge into opposing versions of what ensued: while both sets agree that Zaki did not in fact subdue Shira by direct assault or a prolonged siege, one set claims that Sarkin Shira visited him in secret at his encampment and offered to pay the Muslim poll tax on conquered Habe (A. *jizya;* H. *jizi'a*) if the capital were spared—an offer he accepted;[55] the other set holds that Ibrahim Dabo (later emir of Kano), or, alternatively, a Mallam Zare (another, otherwise unidentified, flag-bearer in the jihad), was by then in possession of Shira Town and that Mallam Zaki persuaded him to relinquish it.[56] Whatever the actual circumstances, Shira became ca. 1807 a vassal town of Mallam Zaki and within several years was incorporated into the new emirate of Katagum.

Soon after the reduction of its capital, most settlements hitherto subject to Sarkin Shira—to the east and north, to the west and southwest as far as Kano Emirate, and southeastward to Misau—were subdued or surrendered peacefully. Zaki also acquired the Lerewa principalities which had paid annual tribute directly to the Galadiman Bornu, in particular Guma'i, Udubo, and Gamawa, along with their numerous satellite villages. It was during this period (ca. 1808–10) that he led the second Fulani expedition against Birni Gazargamu. On his return he moved to a newly built town, Katagum, eight miles east of Teshena, which was to remain for the next 100 years the emirate capital.[57]

53. Informants IIA: 1–5; IIB: 1–9; and Fremantle, "History of the Region," X (1911), 310.

54. Informants IIA: 1–5; IIB: 1–9; II I: 3, 25–28; H. F. Backwell, "Assessment Report on Galadiman Katagum District, Sub-District of Galadima, Katagum Emirate, Kano Province," NAK SNP 7/12 3260 5205/1911; and Yakubu b. Halilu, "Tarihin Mallam Zaki."

55. *Ibid.*; and Informants IIA: 1–5; IIB: 1–9; II I: 3, 25–28.

56. Gowers, *Gazetteer of Kano Province,* p. 31; Ramage, "Historical Notes"; Fremantle, "History of the Region," X (1911), 310; and H. F. Backwell, *The Occupation of Hausaland, 1900–1904* (1927; London: Frank Cass, 1969), p. 18.

57. Informants IIA: 1–5; IIB, 1–9; IIG: 6–8, 12–13; IIE: 1, 4, 9–10, 17, 20.

Before his death at Katagum ca. 1814 Mallam Zaki established 10 titled state offices. These formed the nucleus of central emirate government subsequently enlarged upon by Dan Kauwa. Three of the offices were among those enjoined on his provincial lieutenants by Shaikh Usuman: that of galadima, in Zaki's time the wazir of Katagum; of alkali; and of maidala, the chief of police. The remaining six offices were those of makama, in charge of all crown slaves; of ardo, responsible for supervising the collection of cattle tithe; of jarma, head of the royal bodyguard (whether at court or on campaign); of jekada, the chief messenger to Sifawa and Sokoto; of liman, that is, imam; of magatakarda, or chief scribe; and of chiroma, whose title appears to have been honorific.[58]

Zaki also appointed his nephew, Dan Kauwa, to the chieftaincy of Shira, putting him over all towns formerly under Shira except Chinade and Azare, which he gave as fiefs to his two eldest sons, Ismaila and Abdurrahman. (A third son, Wesu, received a less valuable appanage). Thus he initiated a policy which endured until 1905 of allocating fief areas to men of royal blood, a policy that appears in at least one respect to have been peculiar among the northeastern emirates to Katagum: the officials so appointed lived on their fiefs rather than in the state capital.[59]

SULEIMANU, OR LIMAN ADANDAYA (CA. 1814–16)

Mallam Zaki was succeeded by a younger brother, Suleimanu, commonly known as Liman Adandaya because of his learning and piety. As with Suleimanu's early career, the circumstances of his selection are obscure; it is said by all local informants that he was the only candidate whose name was submitted by the Katagum authorities for consideration by the sultan. Whether Dan Kauwa approved of their choice is unknown. As the senior surviving Lawanawa leader in the Katagum jihad he could well have felt unjustly passed over, but no evidence exists that he opposed the appointment once it had been made. Liman Adandaya's tenure in office was brief and marked by two serious revolts, both executed while he, Dan Kauwa, and the rest of his officials were visiting Sokoto.[60]

58. Informants IIA: 1–5; IIB: 1–9.

59. *Ibid.*; and Fremantle, "History of the Region," X (1911), 313, and *ibid.*, XI (1911), 193.

60. Informants IIA: 1–5; IIB: 1–9.

The first of these revolts was the doing of a wealthy Fulanin Teshena ardo settled in the capital. Possibly with the support of Sarkin Hadejia Sambo Digimsa, he moved into the palace and declared himself ruler of Katagum. On the urging of Liman Adandaya and his entourage, Sultan Muhammad Bello directed Sambo to have the ardo vacate the palace immediately. The order was carried out, several months after his entry.[61]

The revolt which soon followed was led by Tushim, who was a member of the Auyo royal lineage and thus in a position to rally support from dissident Habe chiefs of the Auyo-Teshena communities. He occupied the capital and proclaimed the end of Fulani hegemony in that area. Confronted by what must have appeared a far more subversive defiance of his authority, Bello sent the future Wazirin Sokoto Gidado with Liman Adandaya and Dan Kauwa (both still at Sokoto) to deal with Tushim and his allies. Sambo, Ardo Lernima of Marma, and the emir of Kano all offered their aid in the reconquest, and were promised a number of towns then under Katagum as recompense. The combined expedition overwhelmed Tushim's force, and he was killed outside the palace. With his death all effective Habe resistance collapsed, but Liman Adandaya was not allowed to continue in office; rather, Gidado announced at a public gathering in the capital the sultan's decision to replace him with Dan Kauwa, whom he thereupon invested as emir. The deposition seems to have been unopposed, although Liman Adandaya's immediate kin and personal following, which settled in a new extension of Katagum City that became known as the ward of Rakumanani (K. "say what you please"), remained a source of at least verbally expressed provocation to Dan Kauwa and his successors.[62]

AL-KANEMI AND THE BORDER STATES

Throughout the first decade of his long reign (ca. 1816–46) Dan Kauwa appears to have been too preoccupied with consolidating Fulani authority (in particular that of the Lawanawa) over the new state to hazard a resumption of

61. *Ibid.* The only other source to mention this event is Ramage, who says merely that the attempted takeover was "due to interference from Hadejia" ("Historical Notes").

62. *Ibid.*; Informants IIA: 1–5; IIB: 1–9; Backwell, "Galadiman Katagum District"; and Fremantle, "History of the Region," X (1911), 315.

the jihad in Bornu. The mais and Shaikh al-Kanemi were for their part diverted from any attempt at recovering the lost western provinces by a succession of critical challenges in the easternmost zone of the empire, where until 1824 Kanem and Baghirmi were engaged in almost continual rebellion. During these earliest years of Katagum's existence al-Kanemi's own efforts to establish effective control of the Bornu central government would have acted as another check to an imperial revanchist policy in that direction.[63]

Around 1820 al-Kanemi wrote Sultan Bello offering on the mai's behalf to settle their respective territorial claims on the other's domain:

> We profess the same religion, and it is not fitting that our subjects should make war on one another. Between our two realms lie the pagan Bedde people, on whom it is permissible to levy tribute; let us respect this limit. What lies to the east of their country shall be ours, and what lies to the west shall be yours. As for Muniyo, Damagaram, and Daura, they will continue to be vassals of the Sultan of Bornu, who in return will surrender to you all his pretensions to Gobir and Katsina.[64]

Bello accepted his terms, but neither side proved able, or perhaps willing, to abide very long by them.

Meanwhile, two leaders of the Fulani still in Bornu were striving to maintain a semblance of the jihad there. Muhammad Manga dan Gwoni Mukhtar had, after his raids to Birni Gazargamu (ca. 1809–11), been chased southward by al-Kanemi. Although defeated in battle around Damaturu, Manga successfully preserved it as a main base of operations against the Kerikeri and Southern N'gizim

63. Soon after returning from the pursuit of Mallam Zaki, Mai Dunama finally had abandoned Birni Gazargamu as being at once too far laid waste by the Fulani and too vulnerable to further assault. His brother, Muhammad Ngileruma, who replaced him a few months later as mai, transferred to a site conveniently near al-Kanemi's armed camp of N'gurno, and built a new imperial seat, Birni Kafela, close by the western banks of Lake Chad. In 1814 al-Kanemi moved with his family and courtiers from N'gurno to found his own new town, some 20 miles northwest; known as Kukawa, it served after 1820 as the effective capital of Bornu. At Birni Kafela, Ngileruma, Dunama (restored in 1813), and Mai Ibrahim—the last Maghumi sovereign (ca. 1818–46)—reigned without actual power, as al-Kanemi, taking to himself the title of Shaikh (Shehu), exercised full command of the empire until his death in 1837 (see Urvoy, *Histoire de l'Empire du Bornou,* pp. 103–7; and Brenner, "The Shehus of Kukawa," pp. 41, 62).

64. Landeroin, "Notes historiques," pp. 262–63 (my translation).

for about the next 15 years.[65] The second Fellata Bornu militant, Muhammad Wabi, was a son of Ardo Sale, head of the Fulanin Mare of the Dilara Plain near Lake Chad. Sale may have been host to al-Kanemi when the latter had first moved west of the lake, and according to several accounts they subsequently quarreled over Sale's refusal to let al-Kanemi build a permanent camp on his pasturing grounds. Despite his father's opposition, Wabi then visited Shaikh Usuman and received a flag. Now under Wabi's authority, the Dilara Fulani retired with their herds to the southwest, first joining Manga's Fulanin Mare around Damaturu and later forming their wet-season camps among the Kerikeri and Southern N'gizim of the Gijiri-Lafia Loi-Loi area. From here Wabi and his son, Sambolei, conducted their own, partially successful, jihad against the surrounding Habe communities, possibly aided at times by Dan Kauwa, Sambo Digimsa, and Ardo Lernima. Dan Kauwa is said to have warned Sultan Bello that the growing influence of Wabi and Sambolei in southwest Bornu might encroach upon towns claimed as tributary by Katagum. Whether to satisfy an already established emir, or because al-Kanemi had just disencumbered himself of Baghirmi and launched a new, aggressive policy toward the eastern emirates, Bello ordered Sambolei (on Wabi's death ca. 1824) to leave Bornu. Sambolei and his Fulanin Mare transferred to the western edge of Katagum, where they pastured on the left bank of the Jema'are River, founding a town and mini-state of that name some 10 years later.[66]

Manga remained until ca. 1826 at Damaturu. Constantly harried by local subordinates of al-Kanemi, and briefly deposed as a flag-bearer in the jihad by Wazirin Sokoto, he finally chose to lead his own Fulanin Mare out of Bornu. They wandered for about a year through Hadejia (Bulangu District) and Shira, where Manga's brother, Yerima Ahmadu, halted while he moved off with the main body to settle

65. Arnett, *Rise of the Sokoto Fulani,* p. 109; and Urvoy, *Histoire de l'Empire du Bornou,* p. 101 n. 5.

66. C. N. Monsell, "Assessment Report on Jema'are Emirate, Katagum Division, Kano Province," NAK SNP 10/1 582 631p/1913; John A. Burdon, *Historical Notes on Certain Emirates and Tribes* (*Nigeria, Northern Provinces*) (London: Waterlow, 1909), p. 70; Sidney J. Hogben and Anthony H. M. Kirk-Greene, *The Emirates of Northern Nigeria: A Preliminary Survey of Their Historical Traditions* (London: Oxford University Press, 1966), p. 493; Temple, *Notes,* p. 477; Gowers, *Gazetteer of Kano Province,* p. 35; Urvoy, *Histoire de l'Empire du Bornou,* p. 107; and Fremantle, "History of the Region," X (1911), 316.

Sambolei founded the emirate of Jema'are after he distinguished himself by killing Sarkin Maradi Rauda in battle while on campaign with an expedition from the Sokoto area against the kingdom of Gobir and the former Habe dynasty of Katsina (then established at Maradi). Sultan Muhammad Bello rewarded Sambolei with title to all the countryside within a half-day's march of his encampment at Gijip (close to the modern town of Jema'are).

a new town, Buriburi, under the nominal jurisdiction of Sarkin Bauchi Yakubu.[67]

When the Clapperton-Denham-Oudney expedition arrived at Kukawa from Tripoli in February, 1823, it found that al-Kanemi had been engaged for eight years in "a very desperate and bloody war with the sultan of Begharmi." Denham remained behind when his companions set out for Kano and Sokoto later that year and was an eyewitness to al-Kanemi's conclusive defeat of Baghirmi in March, 1824. Four months after this event, al-Kanemi assured Denham that "whatever I can do in the Soudan, remember I am ready. I have influence there certainly, which may increase, and probably shortly extend to Nyffe [Nupe]"—that is, to embrace all the Sokoto Caliphate. On his return to Kukawa, Clapperton reported the "sensation created throughout the neighborhood of Kano and Katsina, on his [al-Kanemi's] late defeat of the Begharmi force," and Denham observed, "I imagine he would find little difficulty in extending his empire in that direction." The expedition also provided a useful contemporary estimate of Bornu military strength, which comprised some 30,000 horsemen and 9,000 Kanembu foot-soldiers, equipped with spears, daggers, and shields. No muskets are mentioned, although another source refers to their use by al-Kanemi at this time.[68]

In the dry season of 1825–26 al-Kanemi took the field against Marma, territorially the smallest and most exposed of the eastern Fulani emirates. His action may well have been intended less as a regular campaign of liberation or conquest than as a preparatory, probing thrust. Sarkin Kano is said to have dispatched 5,000 cavalry and an equal number of infantry to assist Ardo Lernima, but a relieving force under Sambo Digimsa had already arrived in Marma, and al-Kanemi chose to retire without joining battle.[69]

Soon after, al-Kanemi set out again for the west. He bypassed Marma and marched directly on Hadejia, perhaps as a diversion for what seems to have been

67. Ahmadu dan Alhaji Tafida, "Tarihin Sarakunan Misau"; Ramage, "Historical Notes"; and Fremantle, "History of the Region," X (1911), 316.

68. Bovill, *The Bornu Mission,* pp. 475, 527, 529; and Landeroin, "Notes historiques," p. 363. In view of these eyewitness accounts, it is hard to accept Brenner's statement that al-Kanemi's whole intention was "to secure the western frontiers of Bornu and impose his own authority over those western provinces of the kingdom which had remained virtually a no-man's land since the first outbreak of Fulbe hostilities there twenty years before. . . . In fact, al-Kanemi had no intention of attacking Sokoto, or even Kano" ("The Shehus of Kukawa," pp. 77, 79). Another student of this campaign has concluded that al-Kanemi's "intention was to ally with Gobir and other enemies of Sokoto" and that it posed "the most serious threat of Bornu to the Caliphate throughout the nineteenth century" (Roland A. Adeleye, *Power and Diplomacy in Northern Nigeria 1804–1906* [London: Longman Group, 1971], p. 70).

69. Fremantle, "History of the Region," X (1911), 317.

his main object, the punishment of a rebellious ruler of Gumel, who was then raiding the western vassals of Bornu. After an initial reverse in Hadejia, al-Kanemi passed on and captured the Gumel chief. Meanwhile, the appearance of a large hostile army a few miles north of Katagum City brought its swift evacuation by Dan Kauwa, who fled south and combined with the Fulanin Mare under Sambolei. Arriving in Katagum from Gumel to find the capital deserted, al-Kanemi withdrew again to the east with large quantities of plunder, and Dan Kauwa returned.[70]

In the late autumn of 1826 al-Kanemi launched a third, more ambitious invasion of the caliphate. Before setting out from Kukawa he assured the emirs of Kano, Hadejia, Marma, and Katagum of his peaceful intentions toward them and Sultan Bello, stating that he was concerned only to chastise Manga and Sambolei, who, he alleged, were constantly raiding Bornu for slaves and cattle.[71] To lend his professions an added measure of credibility he went first to southwest Bornu, where the Habe communities (probably still a main source of tribute and spoil for the Fulanin Mare) were enlisted in his ranks.[72] He may then have proceeded in the same general direction toward Bauchi Emirate, in the guise of reaching Manga at Buriburi, though in fact with a view to outflanking Katagum and Kano. Richard Lander was told a few months later by Emir Yakubu of Bauchi of his defeat by al-Kanemi near the Bauchi capital—an event apparently confirmed by another nineteenth-century source but unmentioned elsewhere (the reference could also have been to Yakubu's initial setback in a fierce engagement that followed near Kano.)[73]

Entering Katagum Emirate at its southeast frontier with Misau, al-Kanemi made straight for Shira Town. Many of the Shira Habe, from Misau to Shira itself, rushed to his standard. Sarkin Shira Abdurrahman dan Dan Kauwa escaped to eastern Zaria, and al-Kanemi installed in his stead a son of the late Habe ruler of Shira Kingdom. Dan Kauwa again fled the capital, moving his troops back to Hadufia, a riverain town almost inaccessible to horses, even in the dry months.[74]

70. *Ibid.*, pp. 317–18.

71. Hugh Clapperton, *Journal of a Second Expedition into the Interior of Africa* (1829; London: Frank Cass, 1966), p. 242.

72. Fremantle, "History of the Region," X (1911), 318.

73. Richard Lander, *Records of Captain Clapperton's Last Expedition to Africa,* 2 vols. (London: John Murray, 1830), II, 90–91, 96; and Koelle, *African Native Literature,* pp. 238–40.

74. Informants IIA: 1–5; IIB: 1–9; IIF: 1–14; IIH: 2, 5–6; II I: 1–2, 7–8, 20, 23–28; IIJ: 1–12; Ramage, "Historical Notes"; Monsell, "Jema'are Emirate"; Gowers, *Gazetteer of Kano Province*, p. 31; and Fremantle, "History of the Region," X (1911), 318.

There is evidence that a substantial number of the conquered Habe of Kano Emirate also were prepared to join with Bornu. Sarkin Kano, then at Dutsi (on the Katagum-Kano border) to provide Dan Kauwa support, quickly returned to secure his own capital on hearing of al-Kanemi's approach via Shira.[75]

After routing the main Kano force, the survivors of which retired within Kano City, al-Kanemi was delayed by unknown causes a full month at Garko, 20 miles to the southeast. He never regained the initiative. In late January or early February of 1827, several hard, inconclusive engagements were fought near Garko between al-Kanemi's army and that of Yakubu. Both sides emerged with severe losses in men and matériel, but al-Kanemi, having lost the bulk of his cavalry, tents, and other essential equipment and being over 300 miles from Kukawa, was poorly situated for another such encounter, either against Yakubu or the nearby Fulani columns of Sarkins Kano, Katagum, Hadejia, and Jema'are. He turned back, making a successful withdrawal through southern Hadejia and northern Katagum.[76] Neither al-Kanemi nor his successors in Bornu were to attempt a second major expedition of conquest within the caliphate.[77]

DAN KAUWA (1827–CA. 1846)

With al-Kanemi's departure the combined strength of Bauchi and Katagum promptly restored Abdurrahman to Shira. The last Habe chief there was killed, and his brother, Abdulla Shiramami, escaped with his remaining followers to

75. *Ibid.*, p. 319. Wazirin Kano had already set out for or arrived at Kano, apparently to rally and coordinate Fulani resistance there (Clapperton, *Journal of a Second Expedition*, p. 242).

76. *Ibid.*, pp. 248–49, 252. Clapperton mentions several messages that arrived at Sokoto while he was there in mid-February, 1827, sent by the waziri. For a traditional account of the battle at Garko, as remembered in Bauchi, see Alhaji Mahmoud, chief imam of Bauchi, "A Light for Beginners and a Lamp for the Blind," trans. by Mallams Aliyu Lanle and Ibrahim Magaji, copy in my possession; written in the 1950s, it appears to be drawn from sections of an Arabic history of the early Bauchi emirs composed by a Mallam Mustapha, tutor to Sarkin Bauchi Yakubu's sons. A similar account, based on this apparent source as well, has been rendered into English in A. Schultze, *The Sultanate of Bornu*, trans. P. A. Benton (1913; London: Frank Cass, 1968), pp. 301–3.

77. To prevent further harassment by the Fellata Bornu, over the next decade al-Kanemi established a defensive barrier on his western border, supervised by slave officials (K. *kacellu*) (Brenner, "The Shehus of Kukawa," p. 82).

establish soon after a successor state at Dambam (in present-day Misau Emirate).[78] Dan Kauwa and Yakubu then moved farther east to punish Misau, whose Shirawa officials had not only aided al-Kanemi on his march toward Kano but had also expelled their Fulani subjects. Misau Town endured a three-year siege before it was finally starved into submission. The sole remaining independent Habe center in the Katagum-Hadejia area, it was leveled by the emirs, and the site was unoccupied for several years.[79]

Yakubu and Dan Kauwa both put forward a claim at Sokoto for the land which had been under Misau. Bello decided for neither party, but gave it instead to Muhammad Manga in recognition of his and Gwoni Mukhtar's long, distinguished services in the jihad as well as because the Fulanin Mare of Damaturu were as yet unable to found a state of their own. Manga transferred to Misau from Buriburi ca. 1832. Dignified with a new title, Sarkin Bornu ta Gabas (Emir of East Bornu), conferred by the sultan, Manga and those who followed him in office received as well certain collateral privileges of administration over all the Fulanin Mare who emigrated from the Damaturu area and had settled or pastured in other emirates.[80] Manga's successor, Ahmadu (ca. 1833–50), rebuilt Misau Town, and for some years continued the family tradition of raiding in western Bornu for slaves, cattle, and horses. Al-Kanemi returned at one point and burnt his capital in reprisal, but this and other punitive thrusts from Bornu left the more established northeastern emirates largely undisturbed.[81]

A far more serious threat to Fulani hegemony in the decade following the battle at Garko was offered by Abdulla Shiramami. After his flight in 1827 from Shira Town, Abdulla formed a royal Shirawa government-in-exile near Misau and began to raid as far south as Bauchi, Gombe, and Kano Emirates.[82] About 1830 he came at night to Azare, was admitted by its still predominantly Shirawa towns-

78. Informants IIA: 1–5; IIB: 1–9; II I: 1–2, 7–8, 20, 23–28; Ramage, "Historical Notes"; and Fremantle, "History of the Region," X (1911), 399. Monsell recorded that Sambolei of Jema'are killed the last Habe king of Shira ("Jema'are Emirate").

79. Ahmadu dan Alhaji Tafida, "Tarihin Sarakunan Misau"; Fremantle, "History of the Region," X (1911), 399; and Ramage, "Historical Notes."

80. As n. 79 above. For a discussion of this grant of privileges and its role vis-à-vis Katagum-Misau political conflict some 45 years later, see pp. 190–91 below.

The wording of Manga's (honorific) title—borne also by his successors at Misau—suggests that the Fulanin Mare of Damaturu had arrived there from the Dilara section of east Bornu or from the neighboring provinces of Baghirmi and/or Mandara. The emir of Katagum has traditionally been titled Sarkin Bornu as well, but without a more precise geographical referent.

81. Ahmadu dan Alhaji Tafida, "Tarahin Sarakunan Misau"; and Ramage, "Historical Notes."

82. "The History of Dambam," in Ramage, "Historical Notes."

men, and assassinated the sarki, Wesu dan Mallam Zaki. Abdurrahman was ordered from Shira by Dan Kauwa to prevent a second Habe revolt.[83] Overawed militarily, Abdulla took refuge with al-Kanemi, but within a few months had returned to the Misau area, having agreed to pay tribute to Sokoto. His quick shift in allegiance provoked an attack from Bornu, and he moved with the Shirawa court some 50 miles west of the Bornu frontier, outside al-Kanemi's immediate reach but well encircled by Fulani power. He then went to Sokoto for the annual gathering of all emirs and other prominent chiefs. Looking to insure the Border States permanently against future subversion by the Shirawa dynastic lineage, Bello announced his intention of settling Abdulla in one of them. Only Manga, however, who had just been awarded Misau and who may have seen a compliant, strong Habe leader as the best means of preserving it, was prepared to give him a place. Abdulla accepted, but used the gift of land as merely another base for renewed harassment of the neighboring emirates. Shortly after he moved once again, to Dambam, and revived his alliance with al-Kanemi.[84]

During the next several years Abdulla improved his economic posture by conquering a number of Kerikeri settlements in the region of Dambam. About 1835 Sultan Bello had the military of Kano, Hadejia, Katagum, Misau, and Jema'are organize for a joint assault on Abdulla. Supported by a column of Bornu troops (including, on one account, 60 musketeers) Abdulla successfully sustained a long siege at Jangefe, a local stronghold, and the Fulani had to abandon their effort. But Abdulla confined himself thereafter to expanding the boundaries of Dambam State in Kerikeriland.[85] The foremost nineteenth-century Kerikeri center, Jellum, had been occupied by Dan Kauwa on his triumphal progress eastward from Shira in 1827; it, and lesser Kerikeri towns, henceforth provided the Katagum officials their most lucrative ground of fresh slaves, either in payment of tribute or as spoil. Abdulla, though himself a Muslim and, after the battle of Jangefe, no longer prepared to strike at the Fulani directly, was, by virtue of his territorial demands on this vital reserve of new wealth for the northeastern emirates, a continuing source of vexation to them.[86]

83. *Ibid.*; Informants IIA: 1–5; IIB: 1–9; IIK: 1–5; and Fremantle, "History of the Region," 401.

84. *Ibid.*; and "History of Dambam," in Ramage, "Historical Notes."

85. *Ibid.*; and Fremantle, "History of the Region," X (1911), 401.

86. C. N. Monsell, "Reassessment Report on Dambam Emirate, Katagum Division, Kano Province," NAK SNP 10/1 689 743p/1913; Ramage, "Historical Notes"; and Informants IIA: 1–5; IIB: 1–9; IIE: 1–6, 9–14, 17–20; IIF: 1–14.

A British colonial officer remarked of the Jellum Kerikeri: "Their history until our arrival is a series of slave raids, sometimes bought off, sometimes successfully resisted, and sometimes succumbed to" (W. R. Crocker, "Pagan Administration in Misau Emirate, Bauchi Province [1934]," NAK SNP 17/4 39576/S.6).

CENTRAL GOVERNMENT IN KATAGUM UNDER DAN KAUWA

The only remembered appointment to office made by Liman Adandaya had been that of Mallam Zaki's youngest son as Yeriman Katagum, a position bearing no administrative functions and one that lay vacant some 50 years after he was given the fiefdom of Gamawa by Dan Kauwa.[87]

On Dan Kauwa's assumption of the crown ca. 1816 he transferred Abdurrahman dan Mallam Zaki from Azare to Shira and Abdurrahman's brother Wesu from a minor fief to that of Azare. When Abdulla of Dambam killed Wesu, the emir appointed Yusufa dan Mallam Zaki to succeed him, but eight years later he shifted Yusufa to Udubo and made his own son, Mamman Haji, Sarkin Azare. Shortly before, Dan Kauwa had put his eldest son at Shellim (where he died soon after), and the next senior, Kadr, at Gadau. Several of his younger sons were given less important fiefdoms, and one received the title of Chiroman Katagum, an office which seems to have carried no more privileges or responsibility than did that of Yerima.

Thus Dan Kauwa maintained and extended the general policy begun with Mallam Zaki of appointing Lawanawa *'yan sarki* to residential fiefholding positions located in strategic zones of the emirate. His initial appointments, at Shira and Azare, were made from outside his immediate house, either because none of his own sons were as yet of suitable age or, perhaps, owing to popular demand that two of Zaki's sons already in office be promoted. Even by 1830 he may not have been sufficiently secure from political exigencies to give Kadr, rather than Yusufa, the position at Azare; and when he later moved Yusufa to Udubo, it was on the avowed grounds that a strong Fulani captain was needed there to fend off extensive Kerikeri and Bedde raids in the east-central part of the emirate, while Yusufa agreed only on condition that not Kadr but rather Haji—a much younger son of Dan Kauwa—should succeed him at Azare.

87. The section that follows is based on materials provided by Informants IIA: 1–5 and IIB: 1–9, supplemented with two genealogical charts in Appendix 1 of Fremantle, "History of the Region," XI (1912), 193–94; and several others contained in "Pedigrees of the Principal Dynasties of Kano, Katsina, Katagum, Kazaure, Daura and Hadejia (1922–28)," NAK SNP 17/4 6117 38053; and "Genealogical Trees of the Ruling Families in the Northern Provinces—Katagum Emirate (1945)," NAK SNP 17/4 39576/S.6.

The policy of allocating resident chieftaincies to an increasing number of *'yan sarki* and their descendants was a feature of local government peculiar, among the eastern Fulani emirates, to Katagum in the nineteenth century. Several of the probable reasons for this unique arrangement are discussed below; a few of its more significant aspects will be outlined here.

There was peaceful though frequently warm competition between *'yan sarki* for these titles as the recipient, while answerable directly in matters of public concern to one of the higher officials at court, had by custom the privilege of retaining all revenue in taxes derived from his town and a sizable portion of that which accrued from all settlements under it. This prerogative was evinced on the first award of such an office, when the emir would send his appointee off with the admonition, "Go and earn your bread." As a young prince almost always was given a town of modest proportions at the beginning of his career, an appointment to such a town (and in time to every minor town) came to be known as a *jeka na yika* ("go and show what you can do"). Gifts of this kind obviously were made to provide junior *'yan sarki* with both a livelihood and an early opportunity of proving themselves.

From about age two until age seven, a prince was fed and otherwise cared for by his mother's best friend in the palace (her *babban abuya,* either a co-wife, co-concubine, or female retainer), who served thereafter as his *uwar daki.* She functioned as his patroness at court—an important advisor in his personal affairs, and one of his main avenues for attaining royal favor or moderating royal displeasure. As a youth he also acquired, from among the courtiers (*fadawa,* sing. *bafada*), an *uban daki* (pl. *iyayen dakuna*), or patron, who acted in a similar capacity. If the *dan sarki,* usually through the intercession of one or both of these guardians, secured (as often happened) a chieftaincy title that was administratively under his *uban daki,* the latter remained his male patron. But if the chiefdom was the responsibility of another official, that person became his new *uban daki* for as long as they both continued in office.

As the number of male Lawanawa increased over the later decades of the nineteenth century, two devices were employed to insure an adequate provision of income for them. *'Yan sarki* with titles to the larger fief areas like Shira, Azare, and Chinade more and more tended to appoint their sons to *jeka na yika*s attached to their own direct authority (sons of the reigning emir often were sent to Shira for this purpose). And a few of the princes living at the capital were given *jeka na yika*s nearby, without any change in their place of residence; the non-Lawanawa chiefs retained their positions, but the princes involved then became their new patrons.[88] Major *'yan sarki* fiefholders also took to sending their sons to live at the capital, in the hope they would benefit from this second device. In time it became increasingly difficult for a Lawanawa *dan sarki* whose father held no titled office, or a less important one, to obtain either kind of appointment.

Under Mallam Zaki and Liman Adandaya the administration of areas beyond the environs of Katagum City was left almost wholly to their several chiefs. Control from the center was limited to a loose and ill-defined supervision of military affairs and to the collection of cattle tithe and other taxes or tribute. Dan Kauwa expanded and rationalized this nascent system of royal government inherited from his uncles and introduced important new features.[89] He did so in large part by regularizing as a focal principle of centralized authority the concept of *"uban daki."* An *uban daki* ("father of the house" in its most literal sense, but more figuratively employed in another context to mean "master of the servant," as well as patron) had in the nineteenth-century Katagum state a connotation of "one's immediate superior." In one of its commoner local usages, the sarki of each provincial fief capital was, in matters of regional government, directly accountable to one or

88. Such a town was known as *kasar dan sarki* (land of the prince), as opposed to a *garin dan sarki* (town of the prince).

89. According to Informants IIA: 1–5, Mallam Zaki and Liman Adandaya were too concerned with religious affairs to attend vigorously to developing complex administrative arrangements, but Dan Kauwa, although learned, was—like Sultan Muhammad Bello—far more involved with affairs of state than were his predecessors in office. As with Gombe and Hadejia, the example of Katagum would support a recent contention that "administrative arrangements of the various emirates were worked out at the same time as the usually protracted wars of conquest and consolidation were going on. Indeed, most of the first emirs were noted and respected more for their role as learned and religious leaders (hence mallams) than as rulers" (Adeleye, *Power and Diplomacy,* p. 55).

Clapperton, who met Dan Kauwa at the capital early in 1824, described him as "a stout, tall fellow, blunt and good natured, and lavish in his promises." He wrote of the emirate that it could marshal some 4,000 cavalry and 20,000 foot-soldiers, wielding bows, swords, and spears (no mention of firearms). Its main products were cattle and grain, "which, with slaves brought from the adjoining territories of the Kafirs [non-Muslims], are the staple articles of trade." Katagum Town impressed Clapperton as "the strongest we had seen since we left Tripoli"; square in shape, with four gates and "defended by two parallel walls of red clay, and three dry ditches," it had a single mosque, "almost in ruins," but the palace, measuring 500 square yards, and the larger compounds, often two-storied, were made of brick, with flat roofs and windows. He estimated the urban population at seven to eight thousand, including foreign merchants (Bovill, *The Bornu Mission,* pp. 630–31). Dan Kauwa later extended the town walls, adding two more gates and several wards to accommodate new immigrant colonies (see map of Katagum City ca. 1900, Appendix V below).

another official at court, that is, his *uban daki.* The relation of an *uban daki* to a particular town provided him was expressed succinctly in terms of patronage or ownership: for example, *Waziri shi ne hanyar Shira* ("The waziri looks after, is the link with, Shira"); *Azare shi ne gidan waziri* ("Azare is the waziri's house").

Towns "belonging" in this fashion to an *uban daki* were his main source of income, principally in the medium of gifts rendered to secure his favor in present or future disputes among their inhabitants, in shares of taxes, fines, and indemnities levied, and in portions of the estates of deceased men of wealth. In turn the *uban daki* was responsible for the settlement of litigation between local chiefs or their townsmen when recourse to an alkali was deemed inappropriate; for the transmission of royal instructions to his provincial subordinates; and for keeping the emir advised of the politically more sensitive complaints or requests of the latter and their own people. In short, he served alike as an informal judge outside the established framework of Islamic jurisprudence and as an official conduit for the conveyance of information between his dependent chiefs and the throne. In both capacities, of course, the (unprescribed) opportunities for enhancing his affluence would have been rather considerable and were a function directly of the number and size of towns that were attached to his office, as well as of his own character.

Each *uban daki* of this kind had one or more agents (*jekadu,* sing. *jekada*), who lived at their master's residence in Katagum and represented him in dealings with the chief(s) he oversaw. When a chief had reason to consult his *uban daki* he sent a messenger to the capital to inform the appropriate *jekada,* who then usually spoke to his master. If the *uban daki* chose to settle the affair himself, he either told the chief's messenger (through the *jekada*) his decision, or sent the latter to investigate; but should it appear too serious a matter to be resolved in this manner, the *uban daki* referred it to the waziri or the emir directly, who often dispatched him, or another courtier, to the scene. In questions involving gross misbehavior and which a provincial alkali had not disposed of, if the official sent from the capital regarded the accused as culpable he was brought there, and the emir heard the case; if the royal judgment was unfavorable he was turned over to the maidala for imprisonment, fine, or execution.

According as the problem was accounted more or less severe by the several categories of officialdom, the process of referral may be represented as follows:

townhead—fiefholder—*jekada*—*uban daki*—(waziri)—emir
townhead—fiefholder—*jekada*—*uban daki*
townhead—fiefholder—*jekada*
townhead—fiefholder (often assisted by a local alkali)

The position of Sarkin Shira as compared with that of all other major fiefholders was unusual, and his special prerogatives in the nineteenth century help explain Barth's reference to Shira as "a considerable place, the capital of a province of the Fulfulde empire of Sokoto, and residence of a governor."[90] Among high provincial authorities (whether *'yan sarki* or not) he alone was empowered to appoint subordinate townheads without consulting his *uban daki* and/or the emir; and he could impose capital punishment, mutilation for crimes of theft, and, on certain occasions at Shira, wear a burnoose (*alkyabba*) over his head—privileges otherwise reserved for the emir. He could not, however, make war independently of the crown nor send the annual gifts directly to Sokoto; this and other contacts with the sultan were conducted in the accustomed way, through his father.

When Dan Kauwa moved from Shira to the palace the most influential state official was Galadiman Katagum Abunoboji, a Fulanin Gori leader from southwest Beddeland. Abunoboji had studied together with Mallam Zaki at Degel, but was not given a flag either by him or by Shaikh Usuman. Instead, he served as Zaki's chief advisor in public affairs, and received in fief a relatively large number of towns. His local standing was such that, *inter alia,* it is said that anyone condemned by the emir or chief alkali, even to death, could gain his freedom by touching the galadima's compound wall. Abunoboji died soon after Dan Kauwa's accession and the emir, while appointing a cousin of Abunoboji to succeed him, created the office of Wazirin Katagum, which came in time to exceed that of galadima in power and administrative authority—as reflected in the amount and affluence of those fiefholders beneath it. The first waziri, of but two in the nineteenth century, was Muhammadu Hamji, the son of a distinguished mallam of Katsina Habe descent. Hamji soon acquired most of the galadima's advisory and administrative role, becoming chief advisor to the crown as well as *uban daki* to all major *'yan sarki* officials. Dan Kauwa introduced a number of other titled offices of central government, the highest being those of madaki and sarkin yaki, both filled then and later by free nonroyals, The waziri, galadima, madaki, alkali, and liman constituted henceforth a throne consultative and electoral council. Ten of the new titles were given to military commanders, in particular that of sarkin yaki. The remaining were largely accorded palace functionaries, of whom the wombai (makama's chief deputy and the second-ranking slave official), sarkin dawaki (royal stablemaster), and majidadi (favorite messenger of the emir) were the most prominent.

Unlike nineteenth-century government in Zaria, there was no special nomen-

90. *Travels and Discoveries,* I, 625.

clature in use at Katagum (or at Gombe and Hadejia) to differentiate senior from junior officeholders.[91] Those who had one or several chiefs under their immediate authority were known as *hakimai* (sing. *hakimi*), and all others, together with untitled courtiers, were called *fadawa.* Sarkis and other titled officials everywhere in the emirate were collectively, as elsewhere in the Border States, referred to as *masu-sarauta* ("owners of titled office"). But if there was no sharply drawn verbal distinction between upper and lower officialdom, there did exist several clear means of visual demarcation to indicate relative placement or ranking within the central hierarchy. The most general of these was whether or not the appointee was turbanned at installation; nearly all but the most subordinate were. A second means turned on whether he saw the emir at regular intervals without first going through an intermediate (usually the waziri), that is, whether he was directly responsible to the crown. Of such men it was said, "he recognizes only the emir" (*ya san sarki kadai*), and with few exceptions this attribute was reserved for the highest officials. Another distinguishing mark was the number of drumbeats accorded the appointee at his installation ceremony; these ranged from twelve to eight. A fourth was the sequence in which officeholders greeted the emir each morning, and how they arranged themselves around the wall of his council chamber.

Several of the more ceremonial political innovations at Katagum before 1900 also appeared in Dan Kauwa's reign, including those attendant on the choice and investiture of high officials in central government. An aspirant for a vacant office at the capital would seek help from any courtier (slave or free), mallam, *dengin sarki,* or royal concubine, a device known as *kama kafa* (supplicating aid). One or more of these intermediaries who responded favorably then approached the emir in private, to offer cause for his giving their candidate preference; they might have recourse as well to Wazirin Katagum, who always advised him on such appointments.[92]

91. At Zaria, officials not of *dengin sarki* or of *mallamai* status who did not serve in the royal household or in chamber capacities were grouped into *rukuni* (senior) and *rawuna* (junior) rank-orders (i.e., the "public orders," composed of "the officials responsible for public order and administration") (M. G. Smith, *Government in Zazzau, 1800–1950* [London: Oxford University Press, 1960], pp. 39, 130).

92. On both occasions when a Wazirin Katagum was appointed, the emirs (Dan Kauwa and Haji) sought counsel on a broad front, including the sultan and his own advisors. The actual positions of Waziri Hamji and his successor, Sa'idu, were evident in their acknowledged power to veto a desired appointment by the emir by enlisting subordinate officials behind a different contender. It is said that had the emirs of Katagum deposed either Hamji or Sa'idu without clearly adequate reason, enough fiefholders and even townheads would likely have complained so vigorously to the sultan that he might have been persuaded to appoint a new emir. Informants IIA: 1–5; IIB: 1–9.

When the matter had been decided at throne level, all officeholders and the main provincial sarkis were summoned to hear the waziri announce it outside the palace at mid-morning. Later that day they were again assembled there, and Maidalan Katagum brought the man appointed forward to sit facing the waziri. Kilishin Katagum had been custodian of a fresh white gown, burnoose, and turban entrusted him by the emir, which he now gave the maidala, who removed the man's own turban. (Both gown and turban were of the same kind as those conferred on Sarkin Katagum at his installation, but the quality of burnoose varied with each office.) The ma'aji placed the new gown over the old, and Limanin Katagum wound the new turban around the appointee's head. The liman said a few cautionary words about serving the emir and people with rectitude, and Tambarin Katagum was then called in to beat his drum the appropriate number of times. After the waziri had sent word to the emir that everything was concluded, all those officially present moved into the palace, where the new officeholder paid homage before returning to his compound escorted by a tumultuous throng of royal slaves, musicians, and beggars.[93]

93. He also distributed kola nuts (*goron sarauta*) to all higher officials in the emirate, receiving back a slave, a horse, or cowries (and from lesser personages an article of dress, a cow, chickens, etc.). These gifts, referred to as *gudummuwar sarauta,* were made to provide him a degree of affluence commensurate with his new station.

CHAPTER 7

HADEJIA: CA. 1805–63

SAMBO DIGIMSA (CA. 1805–48): THE FOUNDATION OF HADEJIA EMIRATE

Due as much to the multiple causes of nomadic Fulani movements in the Nigerian Sudan before 1800 as to the slightness of oral data at hand for this region and period, we know little of when, how, and why the Cattle Fulani descent groups that included the family of Ardo Abdua first made their wet-season camps in the plentiful grazing land of the Auyo-Hadejia riverain savanna.[1] By the late eighteenth century they were pasturing near the Auyo capital and had entered upon an uneasy connection with Sarkin Auyo Jibrim, whose client chief of Hadejia Town recognized Abdua as head of the neighborhood Fulani. On the eve of the Sokoto jihad his eldest son, Umaru, settled at Rinde, an Auyakawa hamlet several miles from Hadejia, while a younger son, Sambo, was then at Digimsa, 30 miles north.[2]

Probably in 1805 Umaru sent Sambo to seek authority from Shaikh Usuman to conquer Auyo and its half-dozen or so minor Habe dependencies.[3] Sambo returned

1. Local informants today can offer no help on these matters. An earlier inquirer was told that what became known as the Fulanin Sambo (Digimsa) arrived from Machina in the mid- or late-1700s (H. M. Brice-Smith, "Assessment Report on Hadejia Town, Kano Province," NAK SNP 10/5 2847 181p/1917).

2. Informants IIIA: *passim*; IIIG: 1–6, 8–12; W. F. Gowers, comp., *Gazetteer of Kano Province* (London: Waterlow, 1921), p. 21; and J. M. Fremantle, "A History of the Region Comprising the Katagum Division of Kano Province," *Journal of the African Society,* X (1911), 312.

3. *Ibid.*; and Gowers, *Gazetteer of Kano Province,* p. 21. The kingdoms in question were Hadejia, Garun Gabas (the ancient Hausa city-state of Biram), Gatarwa, Kazura, Fagi, and Dawa. All six are said to have paid tribute directly to Bornu, although field notes indicate that Hadejia at least was a political client of Auyo.

with a flag, other insignia of office, and a commission designating Umaru the shaikh's lieutenant in a jihad against the local Habe.[4] Joined by their junior brother Yusufu and a few of the Rindawa, Umaru and Sambo first conquered a number of towns under Auyo and then defeated several of Sarki Jibrim's high officials.[5] After a short investment of Auyo itself they entered it with the aid of Jibrim's eldest son and then occupied Hadejia as well as three Habe chiefdoms nearby, Gatarwa, Garun Gabas (Biram), and Kazura.[6] At the death of Umaru ca. 1808 the process of founding an emirate whose borders were roughly coextensive with those of the former Auyo state had, it seems, been almost completed.

Unlike the Fulani commanders of local jihads in west Bornu, the Gongola-Benue region, and against the Shira-Teshena complex, neither Umaru nor Sambo (who succeeded him as leader of the jihad in Auyo area) was a mallam.[7] Sambo is even said to have lacked adequate knowledge of Arabic to read the Qur'an. Although he appointed an alkali and a liman at Hadejia Town when he made it his capital soon after, and built a Friday mosque there, a complementary contrast is found between Sambo's conception of proper Muslim state government and that of his contemporaries in office, Dan Kauwa and Buba Yero. Instead of the well-defined, hierarchal systems of central administration established at Katagum and Gombe Abba, he relied on a much less formally structured assignment of royal authority, surrounding himself with a relatively small entourage of court favorites, most of whom lacked either titles or fiefs. His two most significant appointments to office were those of his younger brother Yusufu as Sarkin Auyo and of his eldest son Garko as Chiroman Hadejia.[8]

4. Informants IIIA: *passim*; Fremantle, "History of the Region," X (1911), 310; and R. G. Ramage, "Historical Notes on Katagum Division, Bauchi Province (1929–33)," NAK SNP 17/1 1139/9715.

5. Informants IIIA: *passim*; and Barden Rinde Muhammadu, "Tarihin Fulanin Hadeja da Mulkinsu" [A history of the Hadejia Fulani and Their Government] (MS, copy in my possession [1953]).

6. *Ibid.*; Informants IIIA: *passim*; IIIG: 1–6, 8–12; Brice-Smith, "Hadejia Town"; and Barden Rinde Muhammadu, "Tarihin Fulanin Hadeja."

7. This paragraph and the next are drawn from *ibid.*; and Informants IIIA: *passim*.

8. Sambo's other appointments to central-government office were those of galadima (a Mangawa); madaki (Fulanin Sambo); ma'aji (Fulanin Damagaram); maidala (Auyakawa); sarkin yara (Fulanin Sambo); piriya (Auyakawa); and sarkin wanzamai (Auyakawa). All were of client status, and the distribution of ethnic designation would suggest that Sambo was at least partially concerned to balance the political weight of major ethnic groups in the nascent emirate. But he also put a number of *dengin sarki* and other followers over new Fulanin Hadejia settlements, as well as over existing Habe towns.

So too the physical aspects of Sambo's palace at Hadejia Town were on a far more modest scale that its counterparts at Katagum and Gombe Abba, and until the mid-century the capital as a whole appears to have been much less developed. In general style of life, Sambo continued until his death ca. 1848 to reflect the socioeconomic interests of a seminomadic Fulani ardo: he often left the court in the dry season to oversee the pasturing of his own cattleherds, while in the summer he preferred to remain on his farm at Mairakumi, 15 miles from the capital. Similarly, his Fulani subjects are said to have made few permanent settlements in this period and their ardos to have led them as before on dry-season journeys outside the emirate. When not looking after his farm and his cattle, Sambo engaged in the campaigns referred to above, paid the annual visit to Sokoto, or raided along the ill-defined Hadejia frontier with Bornu. He also conducted at least two expeditions into western Bornu: the one to Damaturu already mentioned, and another, even less fortunate in its results, to Geidam.[9]

When Sambo was in his seventies he abdicated (ca. 1845)[10] and, with Sultan Aliyu Babba's approval, turbanned Garko emir of Hadejia, appointing his second son, Abdulkadir, to follow Garko as chiroma and heir apparent. Garko died several years later, and Sambo, again with leave from Sokoto, conferred the emirship on Abdulkadir. But the latter died after a few months, and Sambo had to reassume office.[11] Half-blind and approaching his own end, Sambo had made Buhari, now the eldest surviving dan sarki, chiroma during Abdulkadir's brief reign, probably in deference to the precedents created with him and Garko. But he then decided to make a younger son, Ahmadu, his royal successor. It is widely reported that some days before his death Sambo prepared to insure this transition by telling Ahmadu to come alone to his room at Mairakumi to receive the blessing and

9. This enterprise, said to have been conducted jointly with Sarkin Jafun, resulted in the latter's death and their general defeat by al-Kanemi (H. Q. Glenny, "Historical Notes on the Jahun Fillane," in "History of Certain Emirates," NAK SNP 7/10 2761 1778/1909, Vol. II). Of the first nine years of Shehu Bornu Umar's rule (1837–46), Louis Brenner observes, "Several campaigns were launched on the western borders, but it was soon determined that Bornu and Sokoto had more to gain from friendly relations than mutual hostility and . . . [these years] saw a steady improvement of conditions on the border" ("The Shehus of Kukawa: A History of the Al-Kanemi Dynasty of Bornu," [Ph.D. diss., Columbia University, 1968], pp. 97–98).

10. According to Gowers, Sambo was 42 when he succeeded Umaru ca. 1808 (*Gazetteer of Kano Province,* p. 22). Clapperton, who met Sambo at Kano in February, 1824, thought him "about 50"; (*Missions to the Niger,* ed. E. W. Bovill, Vol. II: *The Bornu Mission, 1822–25* [1826; Cambridge: At the University Press, 1966], p. 662).

11. Informants IIIA: *passim*; Fremantle, "History of the Region," X (1911), 404; and Gowers, *Gazetteer of Kano Province*, p. 22.

chikara— a small bag of Fulani charms. (The combination of these gifts is considered to have signified among the Cattle Fulani a laying on of hands.) Buhari is said to have learned of the summons, gone to his father just ahead of the hour set for Ahmadu's visit, and by impersonating Ahmadu's voice secured for himself the dual manifestations of Sambo's political heir.[12] According to a contemporary chronicler and intimate of the Sokoto court, Buhari's claim to the throne was supported by Sultan Aliyu's waziri who, despite Sambo's implied wish, preferred Buhari in virtue of the latter's having sent him over the years a number of valuable presents.[13] In the event, Aliyu sanctioned the succession and Buhari was duly installed at Hadejia by the waziri.

BUHARI (CA. 1848–63)

Of all precolonial Hadejia emirs Buhari is far the best known to records and oral historians alike. The major events of his reign have been more fully remembered, in Hadejia and elsewhere, while a few of the most significant aspects of his career in successful rebellion from Sokoto were noted by two highly perceptive observers—Barth, and al-Hajj Sa'id, a mallam in close touch with the caliphal establishment.

Of Buhari's character and career until his accession we know little beyond an account of his learning to read the Qur'an as a child at Miga, a Kano provincial center 30 miles southwest of Hadejia Town.[14] Immediately on taking office he made, in league with Sarkin Misau, his baptismal raid against several towns on the Hadejia-Machina frontier.[15] Having plundered these, he turned southward

12. This (Jacob and Easau) account is widely given locally, with minor variations in the finer detail. A much longer version, beginning with the prophecy by Shaikh Usuman that if Sambo had a son the son would become an infidel and murderer, has been recorded as far south of Hadejia as Adamawa Emirate (see Rupert M. East, *Stories of Old Adamawa* [1935; Farnborough: Gregg Press, 1967], pp. 73–77).

13. Hajji Sa'id, *History of Sokoto,* trans. C. E. J. Whitting (Kano: Ife-Olu Printing Works, 1931), p. 28.

14. East, *Old Adamawa,* p. 74. Buhari is said to have remained until his death only a student of the Qur'an (*almajarin Alkur'ani*) (Informants IIIA: *passim*).

15. *Ibid.*; Sarkin Misau Ahmadu dan Alhaji Tafida, "Tarihin Sarakunan Misau" [History of the Emirs of Misau], trans. Abdulmumin Suleiman Jalingo (MS, copy in my possession, 1926); and G. J. Lethem, "Assessment Report on Machena District, Bornu Emirate, Bornu Province (1919)," NAK SNP 17/2 12168.

and, strengthened by armed support from Shehu Umar of Bornu, invaded the prosperous region of Miga, where he pillaged and burnt without regard for the sovereignty of Sarkin Kano Umaru or the Muslim faith of its inhabitants. After some delay, Umaru responded by marshaling a large counter-expedition (said at Miga to have included ten thousand horses) which Buhari put to flight.[16] Buhari then proceeded to devastate a wide portion of east Kano Emirate, marched to within 35 miles of the capital, and, according to Barth, arrived at one point outside the Kano Town walls.[17]

The swath of destruction and havoc wrought by this campaign is recounted vividly in Barth, who wrote of the "terror" and "state of misery" they had engendered. Barth noted how

> Predatory incursions are nothing new in these quarters, where several provinces and entirely distinct empires have a common frontier; but this, as the event proved, was rather a memorable campaign for the whole of this part of negroland, and was to become "the beginning of sorrows" for all the country around.[18]

From local sources there is additional evidence of this, for example, that a severe famine ensued ca. 1852 in the Miga-Jafun complex.[19] Only at Jafun Town does it appear that Buhari was checked from entering; at Miga, he broke through the battlements and killed the chief (making captive several years later his successor). But the eastern Kanawa rallied at Jafun under its sarki, who finally was able to help reduce the attacks from Hadejia to occasional forays, and who himself often took the offensive. By 1853 Buhari was too involved with military commitments on other fronts to stake all his ambition on a decisive encounter with Sarkin Jafun; rather, he stationed two high-ranking officers, the mabudi and jarma of Hadejia, at Keffin Hausa and Dakayawa respectively, from where they conducted regular patrols of the Miga-Jafun countryside and prevented both farming and grazing. The villagers are said to have been forced to abandon their homes *en masse,* causing still more widespread famine, which probably continued on a large scale

16. Informants IIIA: *passim*; and Glenny, "Jahun Fillane."
17. *Ibid.*; and Heinrich Barth, *Travels and Discoveries in Northern and Central Africa,* 3 vols. (1857–59; London: Frank Cass, 1965), I, 544.
18. *Ibid.*
19. Glenny, "Jahun Fillane." Barth alludes to a surprise attack from Hadejia on Zakara district, eastern Kano, in 1852, and to Buhari's capture of upwards of one thousand persons there (*Travels and Discoveries,* I, 533).

until about 1857, when Buhari and Sarkin Kano reached an agreement that ceded to Hadejia a number of towns on their common boundary.[20]

Soon after Buhari assumed office, Sultan Aliyu Babba had sent Magajin Rafin Sokoto to Hadejia to reconcile the emir with his brother Ahmadu who, supported by a strong local faction, had been pressing his claim to the throne. Buhari declined to meet the magaji at Dakayawa, the site from which nineteenth-century rulers of Hadejia conventionally escorted the sultan's representative into the capital. When the Sokoto party arrived alone at the palace, Buhari compounded his breach of protocol by having it taken directly, without a royal audience, to lodgings elsewhere in town. From there the magaji summoned Madakin Hadejia, who replied that he would come only with Buhari's permission—which had been refused, the emir insisting that the magaji return to the palace if he wished to see either of them. The magaji then asked the madaki to advise Buhari (referring to the emir by name instead of his title) to assemble all courtiers outside the palace to hear an important message from the sultan. Concluding that he was to be publicly rebuked and dismissed, Buhari ordered the magaji to leave Hadejia at once, on pain of execution.[21]

In view of Buhari's early acceptance of armed aid from the shehu of Bornu and his initial incursions into Muslim chiefdoms governed by a fellow emir, it is unclear why the sultan hesitated several years before deciding upon his deposition.[22] Meanwhile, Buhari had visited Sokoto in company with his first cousin, Sarkin Auyo Nalara (the son and successor to Yusufu dan Ardo Abdua). On the death of Sambo Digimsa, Nalara had presented himself at Sokoto as a suitable choice for the crown. As leader of Yusufu's lineage and sarki of Auyo Town, Nalara would have been a serious rival to both Ahmadu and Buhari. It appears that he and Buhari had fallen out openly at Hadejia and that Sultan Aliyu had mediated what was thought to be a permanent understanding between them. On their return from Sokoto the quarrel revived, and Buhari soon had Nalara killed on a charge of disloyalty.[23] It was this act of flagrant indifference to his own sovereign's explicit

20. Informants IIIA: *passim*; IIIC: 1, 5–7; and Glenny, "Jahun Fillane."

21. Informants IIIA: *passim.*

22. A major cause of the caliphal inaction has been offered lately by Roland Adeleye, who finds that rebellion dating from 1849 in Dendi, Zaberma, Arewa, and Kebbi, all on the western flank of the empire, combined with that of Buhari, "paralysed the Caliphate's control over those places" (*Power and Diplomacy in Northern Nigeria 1804–1906* [London: Longman Group, 1971], p. 69).

23. Informants IIIA: *passim*; and Fremantle, "History of the Region," X (1911), 404.

intention that seems to have persuaded the sultan to grasp the nettle by sending Wazirin Sokoto himself to deal with Buhari.

Al-Hajj Sa'id offers in explanation of the waziri's mission "the numerous complaints of their [Hadejia and Katagum's] people," and adds that the waziri usually came straight to Hadejia from Kano, but now traveled first to Katagum.[24] At Hadejia today the popular account is that while en route he picked up a force of Kano troops and then halted in southwest Hadejia, from where he sent a message to the capital asking Buhari to join him at Katagum Town for consultations.[25] Although Buhari was reluctant to leave the security of Hadejia, he finally arrived outside the gates of Katagum with a large column, which included all his court officials and many of the local chiefs. From their encampment, he sent word of his readiness to negotiate. The waziri replied with a letter from Sultan Aliyu announcing that his deputy had come with a message for all the people of Hadejia.[26]

Buhari was prepared to ride through one of the city gates when a praise-singer (*maroki*) of his, Dan Fatima, sang out: "Garba, when you enter, please greet Nalara and Sarkin Dutsi Bello for me."[27] The implied warning of imminent threat to his person is said to have dissuaded him from proceeding further; he wheeled about and, with most of the Hadejia army, began to march homeward. This refusal to confer with the sultan's highest court official inspired a section of the Katagum citizenry to follow the emir as he moved up the road toward his capital. They hurled "coward," "pagan," and other derisive epithets from behind, and killed a few of the rearguard. At Unuk, just inside the Hadejia frontier, Buhari's sarkin yaki retaliated in kind.[28] This episode is generally considered in both emirates to have been the immediate cause of the protracted Hadejia-Katagum hostilities which followed, ending only with Buhari's death some 12 years later.

Shortly after Buhari's return to Hadejia Town, the waziri advanced there with a mixed body of Katagum and Kano troops. The emir gathered his nearest followers and removed northward to Machina State, where he was provided a sanctuary. Ahmadu was installed in the capital as his successor by the waziri, who then rode

24. Hajji Sa'id, *History of Sokoto*, p. 27.

25. Informants IIIA: *passim*.

26. *Ibid.*; Hajji Sa'id, *History of Sokoto*, p. 27; and Fremantle, "History of the Region," X (1911), 404.

27. Informants IIIA: *passim*. Sarkin Dutsi Bello had been executed a short time before on orders of Sarkin Kano. Garba is a Hausa variant of Abubakar, one of Buhari's names.

28. *Ibid.*; Hajji Sa'id, *History of Sokoto*, p. 27; and Fremantle, "History of the Region," X (1911), 404–5.

to Kano, where he received a peace offering from Buhari in the form of horses and articles of dress.[29] The waziri's reply was brief and unequivocal: "You did not come to me as the Commander of the Faithful ordered. I will not accept anything from you." Al-Hajj Sa'id ascribes the waziri's rejection to his "love of wealth," claiming the Kano chiefs had bribed him to fight Buhari instead of accepting his overtures.[30] Sa'id's account, however plausible, would gain in credence if it were plain that Buhari was in fact seeking the pardon of Sokoto, or that the waziri had orders to conciliate him. There is no clear evidence for either surmise.

A year later (ca. 1852) Sultan Aliyu sent the waziri's brother, Dangaladiman Sokoto, to Hadejia, where he and Ahmadu were joined by contingents from Kano, Katagum, Misau, and Jema'are.[31] Buhari meanwhile had fallen out with his benefactor, Sarkin Machina, and, having seized a large quantity of spoil there, moved south again with a much-increased following. He encamped near Hadejia Town and sent word to Emir Sambolei of Jema'are, reminding him of the old friendship between him and Sambo Digimsa. Sambolei nonetheless took command of a joint attack on Buhari (the Battle of Takoko), in which the allied forces were driven beyond Hadejia and compelled to scatter. Ahmadu escaped to Kano Emirate but was overtaken and executed by Sarkin Arewan Hadejia Tatagana, Buhari's chief slave and military officer.[32]

Buhari now re-entered the palace. To secure his political position he again sought, and was given, armed support from Bornu.[33] The year after Takoko, ca. 1853, Sultan Aliyu organized a still larger combined expedition against him. Drawing upon the resources of almost every major caliphal state, Aliyu brought together under the waziri's command substantial levies from Sokoto itself, Zamfara, Zaria, Kano, and Bauchi, as well as from Gombe, Katagum, Misau, and Jema'are;[34] according to sources at Miga, the allies included some 20,000 horses

29. *Ibid.*; Informants IIIA: *passim*; and Barth, *Travels and Discoveries,* I, 544.

30. Hajji Sa'id, *History of Sokoto*, p. 28.

31. *Ibid.*; Wazirin Sokoto M. Junaidu, *Tarihin Fulani* [History of the Fulani] (Zaria: Gaskiya Corporation, 1957), p. 36; and Informants IIIA: *passim.*

32. *Ibid.*; Fremantle, "History of the Region," X (1911), 405; and Hajji Sa'id, *History of Sokoto,* p. 28.

33. Informants IIIA: *passim.* Sultan Aliyu then appointed Tukur, another junior brother of Buhari, emir of Hadejia. Having lived quietly from then onward in Kano and Katagum emirates, Tukur died in 1904; *ibid.*; Fremantle, "History of the Region," X (1911), 405–6; and Gowers, *Gazetteer of Kano Province*, p. 22.

34. Informants IIIA: *passim*; Hajji Sa'id, *History of Sokoto*, p. 28; "History of Certain Emirates"; Fremantle, "History of the Region," X (1911), 406; Ramage, "Historical Notes"; and Sarkin Misau Ahmadu, "Tarihin Sarakunan Misau."

alone. Galadiman Kano (later Emir) Abdullahi led the Kano party, and had Sarkin Miga serve as guide because of his knowledge of the approaches to Hadejia Town.[35] A near contemporary of these events (writing in the early 1950s) has confirmed their general outline as given in documents from Miga and provided a number of details.[36]

The loyalist units converged in southwest Hadejia and moved forward in a slow, confident procession toward the capital. Sarkin Miga was critical of his fellow chiefs' careless assurance that Buhari would prefer to stay within the town walls and cautioned Galadiman Kano to have all forces maintained on alert. But nothing was done to prevent a surprise assault, even when they had reached Kaffur, a village six miles from the city. The historian's account of what followed, though colored by passage of time, an obvious partiality, and at second hand, still is the best-preserved record of what may be considered the single most significant armed engagement in the northeastern emirates from Buba Yero's occupation of Kalam until 1900. He narrates that Buhari slipped his men quietly into position along a high ridge overlooking the broad plain that falls away south of the capital, and then had the praise-singer, Dan Fatima, drum a notice of their arrival to the unorganized mass of imperial soldiers which lay spread out at ease in the scrubland below.

> On hearing the drum-beat, Galadiman Kano's army began to flee. Instead of bridling their horses' fronts they bridled their tails. All was confusion as they attempted to save their lives. No one stood his ground. Some climbed into trees and were caught in them and killed or enslaved. Then a number of the horses and weapons were collected [by the Hadejawa]. On that day, even a woman received her own slave. The capture and enslavement of men continued for three days.

He concludes, "From this day onward Hadejia was renowned in war, and much feared," a judgment echoed by the local author of an Arabic history of Kano, who refers to the Battle of Kaffur as "the origin of Hadejia's greatness."[37] Al-Hajj Sa'id reports that in the general confusion and subsequent rout of the various columns,

35. Glenny, "Jahun Fillane."

36. Barden Rinde Muhammadu, "Tarihin Fulanin Hadeja." In 1964, Barden Rinde was considered by his family and neighbors to be at least 100 years old.

37. M. Ia'faru, "History of Kano," Arabic MS, trans. H. Richmond Palmer, The Palmer Papers, Jos Museum Library, No. 204, p. 17.

Buhari's men took one thousand horses and killed a son of Sarkin Zaria, three sons of Sarkin Kano, and seventeen sons of the Kano chiefs, as well as a grandson of Sultan Aliyu.[38] The waziri is said to have ridden at full rein as far south as Shira Town, a distance of over 70 miles.[39] For the decade or so that remained of his life, Buhari was free to conduct even major campaigns in the caliphate without armed interference by Sokoto, and with hardly more than token opposition from Hadejia's neighbors.

Probably in the dry season following Kaffur, Buhari seized on a minor dispute with the emir of Marma, a grandson of Ardo Lernima, to besiege him at his capital. He gained entry by the unorthodox means of tunneling beneath the town wall and carried out at dawn a general massacre of its Fulani inhabitants.[40] Those few that survived, both royals and commoners, were given a site by Sarkin Katagum Kadr on which to settle.[41] Thereafter Marma and its former subject settlements were constituent parts of Hadejia.

For about the next four or five years (ca. 1855–60) Buhari appears to have confined himself to raiding at will among the Bedde, Kerikeri, and Western N'gizim communities spread out along the northeastern border of the Sokoto empire.[42] There is some evidence that he concluded a treaty with the sultan in this period and, on the accession of Galadima Abdullahi as emir of Kano ca. 1855, with him as well.[43] But ca. 1860 Buhari led or dispatched another expedition to Miga, causing the sarki and his people again to evacuate that district. It remained largely deserted for perhaps three years, and this campaign would seem to have been one of a series of such exploits in eastern Kano during the early 1860s. There is recorded mention that by 1863 Jafun, Dutsi, Gaya, Kadimi, and Garko were the

38. Hajji Sa'id, *History of Sokoto*, p. 28.

39. Fremantle, "History of the Region," X (1911), 408.

40. *Ibid.*, p. 409; Informants IIIA: *passim*; IIF: 4–7; and "History of Certain Emirates." The greatly reduced political condition of Marma by the reign of Sultan Abubakar Atiku (1837–42) is clearly attested in a letter to him from Sarkin Marma Muhammadu Fema dan Ardo Lernima, in which he complains of his terrible hardship and want of assistance in dealing with his people's exigencies, and concludes by asking the sultan for the gift of a horse (Official Correspondence, Various Sultans of Sokoto, NAK Sokprof, File V, Box 25, No. 58).

41. Informants IIIA: *passim*; IIIF: 4–7; IIA: *passim*. The town, which still exists, was Mainarin Yamma. After the British occupation most of the exiles returned to Marma.

42. Informants IIIA: *passim*.

43. *Ibid.*; and Glenny, "Jahun Fillane."

sole provincial seats then still occupied between Kano Town and the west Hadejia frontier. A chronicler observes: "The whole country was a solitude, traveling was done only by night."[44]

Buhari's penultimate effort was also his most ambitious: the attempted subjection of Katagum Emirate. The usual account given locally is that he arrived at Teshena and asked the sarki's aid in a campaign against the Bedde capital of Gorgoram. When the Teshena cavalry had gone to join with his own, Buhari fell on the town just before dawn, killed its chief, and made it his war camp for six months while he laid siege to Katagum.[45] Faced by a shortage of food and other supplies he finally withdrew, again sending overtures of friendship to Sokoto. But he soon returned and marched through southern and central Katagum. On this campaign, widely recalled in both emirates, he unsuccessfully attacked Azare, conquered Bidir and the important long-distance trade center of Gambaki, and on his way back to Hadejia sacked Jema'are Town.[46]

The death of Buhari at Gorgoram ca. 1863 was a consequence, indirectly but in large measure, of his wish to offset the power conferred by him on the two leading slave officials and the position of his brother Serkio with the appointment of his eldest son, Umaru, to high office and Serkio's transfer to a post distant enough from the capital to reduce materially his chances for political maneuver.[47] At Buhari's succession to the throne Serkio, none of Buhari's sons as yet being of age to hold office, had inherited from him the title of Chiroman Hadejia. By 1863 Umaru was about 18 years old, and Buhari sought at once to help restore his own position of near-absolute power in state affairs and to place Umaru in strong contention to follow him as emir. Although he might have created for Umaru a new titled office, Buhari chose to appoint him to the traditionally pres-

44. *Ibid.*

45. Informants IIIA: *passim*; IIA: 1–5; IIB: 1–9; Fremantle, "History of the Region," X (1911), 408; and H. F. Backwell, "Assessment Report on Waziri District, Katagum Emirate, Kano Province," NAK SNP 7/13 3343 1433/1912.

46. Informants IIIA: *passim*; IIA: 1–5; IIB: 1–9; IIF: 1–4, 12; IIK: 1–5; Glenny, "History of Certain Emirates"; and H. F. Backwell, "Assessment Report on Azare District, Katagum Emirate, Kano Province," NAK SNP 7/13 3555 6249/1912. According to Sarkin Misau Ahmadu, Buhari advanced as far as Misau on this campaign, but was defeated with heavy loss by Yeriman Misau Sale (who shortly after became emir) ("Tarihin Sarakunan Misau").

47. Except where otherwise noted, this and the next three paragraphs are drawn from Informants IIIA: *passim*; and Barden Rinde Muhammadu, "Tarihin Fulanin Hadeja."

tigious one of Sarkin Auyo, which had lain vacant since Nalara's successor had fled the emirate in the mid-1850s, mindful of Nalara's fate.[48]

The slave officials in question, Sarkin Arewa Tatagana and Sarkin Yaki Jaji, were both appointees of Buhari. They had been his chief personal slaves in his youth, and Tatagana in particular was from an early period his favorite companion and counselor.[49] After the Battle of Kaffur, Buhari altered the loose and informal administrative arrangements of his father's time, distributing as fiefs among Tatagana, Jaji, the madaki, and the galadima his patrimony and the lands he acquired by cession or conquest. Tatagana held the largest number of towns and received from Buhari the greatest number of other gifts, in horses, cattle, and slaves of his own—to a point where it often was said by disgruntled royals and courtiers that Hadejia was in fact ruled by two emirs. Sarkin Yaki Jaji, whose office was under Tatagana's, shared with him the responsibility of field command in Buhari's absence, and hence a major part of the spoils of war. The free titled offices of madaki and galadima appear to have been of much less political or administrative consequence.[50]

When Buhari determined on the reduction of Gorgoram, he announced at Hadejia merely that a campaign would be undertaken against a few of the more vulnerable settlements in Beddeland. To his younger brother Haru he confided the real object of the expedition—the strongly defended Bedde capital—and said that if they were successful he would replace Sarkin Gorgoram dan Babuje with Serkio, give Auyo to Umaru, and reintegrate Hadejia into the caliphate. Having designs of his own on the emirship, Haru disclosed Buhari's intention to higher officials at court, and they, with Haru, decided to secure their political future by a timely act of desertion when the army arrived at Gorgoram.

As Buhari advanced at the head of one column through Gorgoram's western gate, his officials hung back. Supported by only a handful of the Hadejia troops, Buhari was struck down inside the wall. He was carried off by his personal guard and died on the road to the capital. Immediately they re-entered the palace Tatagana and Jaji proclaimed Umaru his successor. Because of the estrangement from Sokoto, Sultan Ahmadu Atiku was not officially notified of Buhari's death, nor

48. Glenny, "History of Certain Emirates."

49. For additional oral material on Tatagana, see M. Jirgi, *Sarkin Arewan Hadeja Tatagana* (Zaria: Gaskiya Corporation, 1954).

50. Buhari created six other central-government offices, all given to slaves. These were sarkin dawaki, jarma, shamaki, sarkin lifida, barde, and barua. In contrast, his successors together until 1902 established only five more (all but one—that of waziri—of slave status as well).

was he involved in the selection or turbanning of Umaru, but he sent a congratulatory message, and Hadejia returned to the caliphate.[51]

51. Roland Adeleye, viewing Buhari's career in the broader context of nineteenth-century caliphal development, concludes that it "is significant here not only because it failed but even more so because the isolation of Bukhari and the combination of other emirates against him demonstrated the cohesion of the Caliphate." He continues, "as long as the Caliph exercised his authority justly he was assured of the unanimous support of his emirs." In light of Buhari's consistent performance as a freebooter who posed a common threat to his fellow emirs and who often allied with Bornu (a major, enduring menace to their joint security), these judgments appear to draw upon somewhat narrow evidence (*Power and Diplomacy,* p. 95).

PART III

CHAPTER 8

GOMBE: CA. 1841–1900

GOMBE EMIRATE AT THE DEATH OF BUBA YERO

Shortly before he died at the new capital of Gombe Abba, Modibbo Buba Yero abdicated his official status of the sultan's chief deputy in the Gongola region in favor of his eldest son and designated successor, Yerima Suleimanu.[1] As the first ruler of Gombe to have the title of emir,[2] Suleimanu transferred his own establishment from Wawa to Gombe Abba. There he was turbanned and formally installed by the caliphal delegate to the emirate, Walin Sokoto.[3]

By this date (ca. 1841) the general contours of central and local government in Gombe State had been firmly etched out. Their shape can perhaps be most clearly discerned by considering two vital areas of administrative control: the systems of taxation and tribute and of selection or deposition of both Fulani and Habe officials of separate orders of political magnitude.

1. Informants IA: 1–6; IG: 4–7; Chiroman Gombe Babagoro dan Sarkin Gombe Abubakar, "A History of the Gombe Emirs," MS, copy in my possession, 1960; and T. F. Carlyle, "History of Gombe Emirate, Central Province," NAK SNP 10/2 1179 445p/1914. The usual date given for Buba Yero's relinquishment of official duties is 1841 (*ibid.*; R. C. Abraham, "Ethnological Notes on the Bolewa Group," NAK SNP 17/ K.1119; Sidney J. Hogben and Anthony H. M. Kirk-Greene, *The Emirates of Northern Nigeria: A Preliminary Survey of Their Historical Traditions* [London: Oxford University Press, 1966], p. 468; and H. D. Foulkes, notes in "Information Required for Compilation of Provincial Gazetteer, Bauchi Province," NAK SNP 17/2 10791, Vol. 1).
2. Buba Yero was and remains known only as Modibbo Gombe.
3. Informants IA: 1–6; IG: 4, 7.

Although Geri Kom and Pindiga had maintained their independence of Gombe, a majority of non-Muslim towns hitherto subject to them or to Kalam were now held in fief by one or another of the emirate's titled officials. Of such towns, by far the most numerous were Bolewa, and most of these had or soon acquired neighboring Fulani settlements.[4] Except at Biri and Ribadu, whose mois had given Buba essential aid in the earliest phase of the Gombe jihad, untitled Fulani headmen eventually assumed many of the Bolewa chiefs' political functions and prerogatives; but the latter were allowed to remain in office, and succession continued to be determined in the traditional manner, subject to approval by the particular fiefholder.[5] Leaders of the Tera and Jera communities (the next two largest Habe groups), being further removed on the whole from centers of Fulani colonization, appear to have preserved their customary chieftaincy institutions more fully intact.[6]

Western Tangale towns before the jihad seem to have been even less united by a single ethnic authority than were either Tera or Jera. They are said to have maintained in full their conventional apparatus of internal governance after 1800, though Galadiman Gombe, their Fulani overlord, dealt with them as a unit via the chief of Billiri. The eastern Tangale seem to have escaped the attentions of Gombe entirely.[7] Waja towns, divisible into those on the plain and those in the hills, stood in a more ambiguous relation with Gombe Abba: officially under the sarkin yaki, they still had enclaves of Fulanin Jera semipastoralists living much of the year in their midst, two of whose ardos acted as intermediaries between the Plain Waja and an agent of sarkin yaki. But ardos who lived among the Hill Waja remained throughout the nineteenth century in closer rapport with their non-Muslim hosts than with their Fulanin Jera kin groups at Kunde, and the Hill Waja themselves gave little if any tangible evidence of allegiance to Gombe.[8]

East of the Gongola, and apart from Bolewa, N'gasar, Tera, and Jera towns

4. See map of Gombe Emirate, ca. 1900, in end-pocket envelope.

5. Informants IA: 1–6; IB: 9–10, 13, 24–25, 33–34; IE: 1–2, 6–7; IF: 1, 3, 6; IG: 2, 4–5, 7–8; and Carlyle, "History of Gombe Emirate."

6. Informants IA: 1–6; IC: *passim*; IE: 5, 8, 10–11; IG: 2, 4–5, 7–8; and T. A. Izard, "Pagan Administration in Gombe Emirate, Bauchi Province (1933–34)," NAK SNP 17/3 3545 21103.

7. Informants IA: 1–6; ID:1–4, 7–9, 11–12, 14, 18–19; IG: 2, 4–5, 7–8; and A. B. Mathews, "Administration of Tangale-Waja, Bauchi Province (1933–36)," NAK SNP 17/3 3550 21108.

8. *Ibid.*; Informants IA: 1–6; IG: 2, 4–5, 7–8; and T. F. Carlyle, "Assessment Report on Waja Sub-District, Ako District, Gombe Emirate, Central Province," NAK SNP 10/1 661 715p/1913.

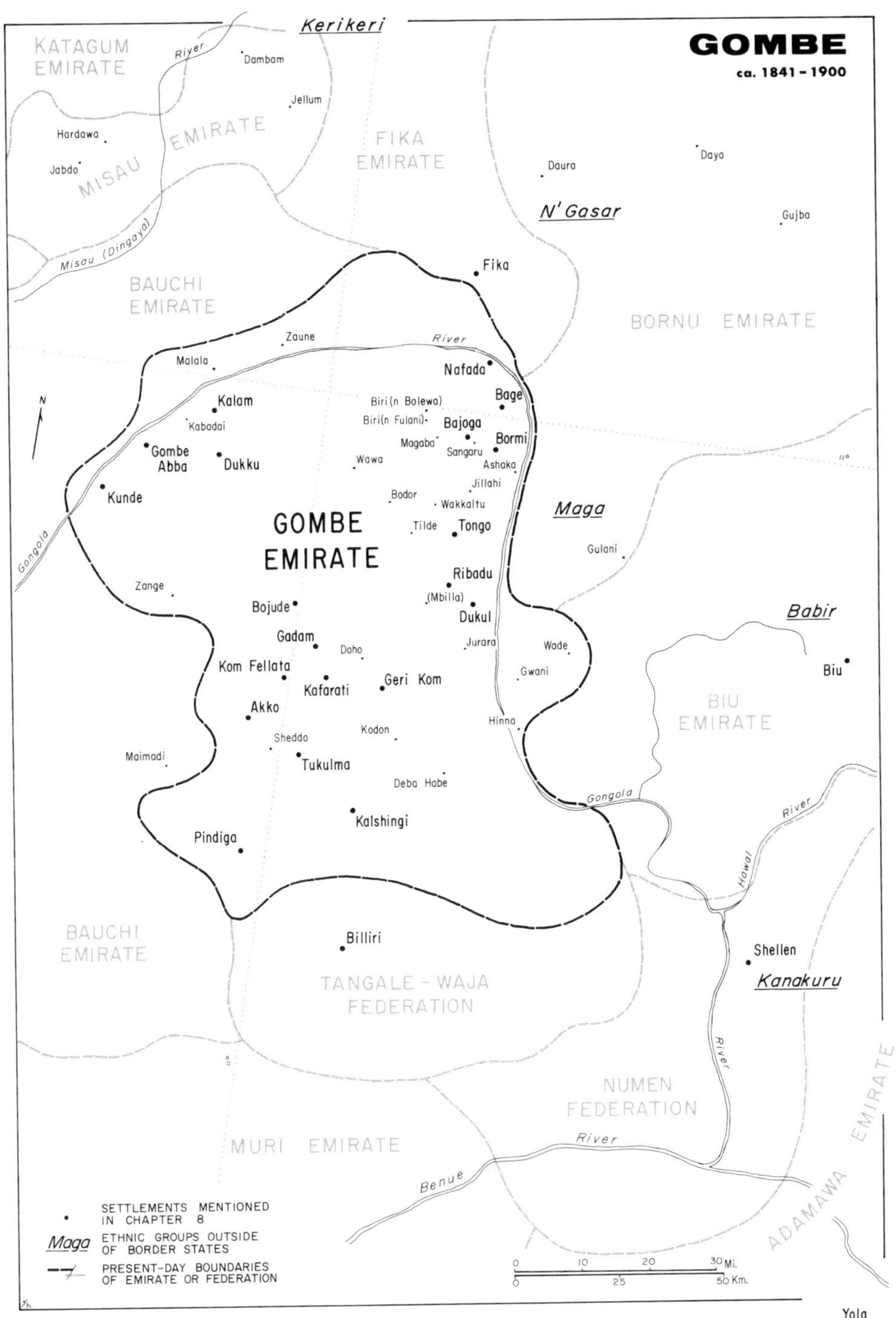

GOMBE
ca. 1841 - 1900
Kerikeri
KATAGUM EMIRATE
River
Dambam
Jellum
Hardawa
Jabdo
MISAU EMIRATE
FIKA EMIRATE
Daura
Daya
N' Gasar
Gujba
Misau (Dingaya)
Fika
BAUCHI EMIRATE
BORNU EMIRATE
Zaune
River
Malala
Nafada
Bage
Kalam
Biri(n Bolewa)
Biri(n Fulani)
Bajoga
Kabadai
Magaba
Sangaru
Bormi
Gombe Abba
Dukku
Wawa
Ashaka
Jillahi
Kunde
Bodor
Wakkaltu
Maga
GOMBE EMIRATE
Tilde
Tongo
Gongola
Gulani
Ribadu
Zange
(Mbilla)
Bojude
Dukul
Babir
Gadam
Jurara
Wade
Doho
Biu
Kom Fellata
Gwani
Kafarati
Geri Kom
Akko
BIU EMIRATE
Hinna
Kodon
Sheddo
Maimadi
Tukulma
Deba Habe
Gongola
River
Kalshingi
Hawal
Pindiga
BAUCHI EMIRATE
Billiri
Shellen
Kanakuru
TANGALE - WAJA FEDERATION
River
ADAMAWA EMIRATE
NUMEN FEDERATION
River
MURI EMIRATE
Benue
SETTLEMENTS MENTIONED IN CHAPTER 8
Maga ETHNIC GROUPS OUTSIDE OF BORDER STATES
PRESENT-DAY BOUNDARIES OF EMIRATE OR FEDERATION
0 10 20 30 Mi.
0 25 50 Km.
Yola

there, administrative control of the Maga, Babir, and Kanakuru probably was nominal even at the best of times. The ardido of Shellen was, by virtue of his blood connection with Buba Yero, supervised in some vague manner by one of the latter's own agents, while other Kanakuru settlements were loosely attached to either Ardo Walama or Ardo Maituta. The Maga of Gulani area were responsible in a like fashion to Sarkin Magi, and the western Babir to Bauchi Gordi.[9]

All of these Habe communities were considered to be in the political-administrative category of *kasar amana,* or "neutral land."[10] In exchange for immunity from attack by Fulani groups they rendered *jizya,* a form of tribute assessed annually on each town by its fiefholder and collected (on a per-settlement basis) through his agent there.[11] Payment was usually in the medium of cowries, cloth strips, or domestic animals (never, it is said, in slaves or a share of the food crop). In theory a local chief was allowed to keep one-tenth of the revenue thus produced, the fiefholder one-tenth of the balance, and whatever proceeds remained were divided by the emir among the mallams and poor of Gombe Abba, officials at Sokoto, and the royal treasury. In fact, much less a proportion of the whole is reported to have reached the capital each year.

The lamidos and ardos of Fulani towns were appointed by their respective fiefholders and could be deposed by them, although local opinion of wealthy households bulked large in both processes. Fiefholders of these and of non-Fulani Muslim towns had authority as well over assessment and collection of the several kinds of taxes imposed on adult male Believers.

SULEIMANU (CA. 1841–44)

Like his father, Suleimanu did not himself undertake any armed expeditions while reigning at Gombe Abba. He did, however, send Fulani columns under his younger brother Muhammadu Kwairanga (now the Yerima and still based at Akko) against the refractory Tera centers of Kalshingi, Deba Habe, and Kodon and against the Plain Waja.[12]

9. Informants IA: 1–6; IG: 2, 4–5, 7–8; and Carlyle, "History of Gombe."

10. This paragraph and the next are drawn from Informants IA: 1–6; IG: 2, 4–5, 7–8.

11. For the more usual meaning of *jizya* in Islamic law, see p. 28 above.

12. Informants IA: 1–6; IC: 1–5, 42–44; ID: 1, 3, 6–7, 9; and Carlyle, "History of Gombe" and "Waja Sub-District."

Having ruled about three years, Suleimanu was summoned by Sultan Aliyu Babba to Sokoto. According to present-day accounts in Gombe, he was to have been dismissed for withholding the annual gifts expected of each emir in the caliphate. On his refusal to attend the sultan, a letter of deposition, addressed to "the people of Gombe," was dispatched from Sokoto. Suleimanu was advised by his senior councilors that they and the rest of his people were afraid to continue the use of his name while offering prayers at the Friday mosque, as to do so would appear to commit them publicly to his evident rebellion from the head of the Community of Believers.[13] Unable to marshal adequate support from his own officials, the emir finally went to Sokoto, where he distinguished himself in a battle with Sarkin Gobir and was forgiven his dereliction by the sultan. He died at Kano ca. 1844, on the return journey to Gombe.[14]

MUHAMMADU KWAIRANGA (CA. 1844–82)

Muhammadu Kwairanga, who succeeded as emir on Suleimanu's death, was the third son of Buba Yero, born to a daughter of the Fulani conqueror of Daura Emirate while his father was campaigning in the Gulani area.[15] As Yerima under Suleimanu and with a notable record of military service in the Gombe jihad, Kwairanga's claims on the throne were far stronger than those of Mallam Buba, his surviving elder brother. (There were by this date no living sons of Suleimanu.) During his years of residence at Ribadu, Mallam Buba had remained aloof from the conduct of armed operations against Habe communities in the middle Gongola Basin and had been passed over when Buba Yero (in retiring) named a successor

13. Informants IA: 1–6; IC: 4–5, 7–8; and Babagoro, "History of the Gombe Emirs." For the common Islamic significance of this kind of omission, see p. 33 above.

14. Both present-day and earlier sources agree that Suleimanu reigned about three years. See Informants IA: 1–6; IG: 4–5, 7–8; Foulkes, "Information Required"; Abraham, "Ethnological Notes"; Carlyle, "History of Gombe"; and Alkalin Potiskum Yakubu b. Halilu, "The History of Buba Yero of Gombe" (Arabic MS, trans. R. C. Abraham, in "History Notes on Gombe Division, Bauchi Province [1929–30]," NAK SNP 17/2 1979 12250).

15. *Ibid.*; Informants IA: 1–6; IG: 4–5, 7–8. The maternal grandfather was Mallam Ishaku of Alkalawa, who had studied with Buba Yero at Degel and was given a flag by Shaikh Usuman (Hogben and Kirk-Greene, *Emirates of Northern Nigeria,* p. 151).

to Suleimanu as yerima. In the event, there is no evidence that Mallam Buba or any other *dengin sarki* actively opposed Kwairanga's appointment by Sokoto.[16]

The long reign of Kwairanga was marked less by his protraction of the effort to extend the geographic boundaries of effective emirate control and conversion to Islam than by his often successful measures to consolidate and enlarge the political authority of Buba Yero's immediate kin group, the Fulanin Janafulu, and to contain or diminish that of the other Fulani corporate units.

Maintenance of the local jihad was confined largely to the final reduction of Geri Kom and Pindiga towns; reassertion of an uncertain hegemony over parts of Tangale-Waja; and attempts to regain the submission of the moi of Fika, who, together with the chiefs of Daura, Gulani, Shellen, and a number of other Habe communities east of the Gongola, had refused payment of *jizya* soon after the death of Suleimanu. An accurate dating of these events is, on the evidence at hand, in good part conjectural, but their general outline can be defined with some precision.

The most important of Kwairanga's campaigns was launched at the Jukun stronghold of Pindiga, probably ca. 1870—the consummation of a task which had occupied him intermittently for upward of five decades, both in his career at Akko and as emir. With most of their subject population already absorbed into Gombe as "neutral land" (*kasar amana*), the Pindiga Jukun had endured, from a secure hilltop redoubt, repeated sieges and frontal assault by Fulani warriors.[17] The circumstances of Pindiga's conquest are obscure, though it seems that a general massacre followed. The few survivors then established a new settlement of the same name several miles below, and were put under Galadiman Gombe.[18]

With the political isolation of Pindiga in Buba Yero's time, the Bolewa of Geri

16. Informants IA: 1–6; IB: 9–10, 13; IG: 4–5, 7–8. Mallam Buba is said to have died several months after Kwairanga's installation. Two younger sons of the modibbo, Bappa Usuman and Bappa Isa, were still in their minority at this date.

17. Informants IA: 1–6; IF: 2, 4, 11–14, 17–19; IG: 4–5, 7–8; and Carlyle, "History of Gombe." The conflicting dates of Pindiga's overthrow given by Meek and Temple probably relate to earlier attempts to subject the fortress. Informants declare the Pindiga Jukun paid tribute intermittently to Gombe during the years preceding their conquest, and it may well have been that Kwairanga and his predecessors had tried, without much success, to enforce regular payment (see C. K. Meek, who puts the Fulani occupation of Pindiga ca. 1850; *A Sudanese Kingdom* [London: Kegan Paul, 1931], p. 32; and Carlyle, whose conjecture I follow here. A third reference, to 1841–44, seems even more doubtful than Meek's (see *Notes on the Tribes, Provinces, Emirates and States of the Northern Provinces of Nigeria, Compiled from Official Reports of O. Temple*, ed. C. L. Temple [1922; London: Frank Cass, 1965], p. 173).

18. Informants IA: 1–6; IF: 2, 4, 11–14, 17–19; IG: 8.

Kom had recovered their independence and were allowed to sustain it relatively undisturbed until Kwairanga learned of their plans to subvert the large, neighboring Bolewa town of Gadam. He burnt Geri Kom in reprisal, executed its moi, and forced those inhabitants not either killed or enslaved to found another town, Kafarati, nearby.[19] The moi of Fika revolted at what appears to have been rather early in Kwairanga's reign. For some 10 years thereafter Sarkin Nafada, the emir's chief resident official and military commander in the Gongola Bend, carried on an indecisive struggle with Fika. Ultimately, however, the mois were able to restore their exemption from regular payment of tribute.[20]

On the left Gongola bank, Kanakuru, Babir, and Maga communities held in fief by Ardo Walama, Ardo Maituta, Sarkin Magi, and Bauchi Gordi at Kwairanga's accession detached themselves in the 1840s from any meaningful measure of Gombe control. Except for the Hinna-Gwani-Wade enclave of Tera chiefdoms on that side of the river, the effective eastern boundary of the emirate lay henceforth at the water's edge.[21] Further south, Kwairanga led seven punitive expeditions to the Waja Plains, against as many towns there. Exacting submission from all but two of these, he recompelled them in token of this to send (through sarkin yaki's agent) a few gowns and horses each year to the capital. He also raided in person several western Tangale fief towns of the galadima which had been slow to produce their annual tribute of cocks and dwarf cattle via the chief of Billiri.[22]

DEMOGRAPHIC CHANGE IN KWAIRANGA'S REIGN

Despite these campaigns, the four decades or so which elapsed between the retirement of Buba Yero and the death of Kwairanga are remembered today as a period of relative peace in the emirate. They witnessed at least four significant

19. Informants IA: 1–6; IE: 1–4, 7; IG: 4–5, 7–8; and Abraham, "History Notes."
20. Informants IA: 1–6; IB: 1–2, 5, 9–10, 30–31; IG: 4–5, 7.
21. Informants IA: 1–6; IB: 4, 6, 11, 19; IC: 2–6, 11–14, 30–37; IE: 9–11, 13; IG: 4–5, 7; and Carlyle, "History of Gombe."
22. *Ibid.*; Informants IA: 1–6; IG: 4–5, 7; Carlyle, "Waja Sub-District"; Mathews, "Tangale-Waja"; Abraham, "History Notes"; P. Lonsdale, "Assessment Report on Ako District, Gombe Division, Bauchi Province," NAK SNP 7/13 3597 7252/1912; and Sarkin Misau Ahmadu dan Alhaji Tafida, "Tarihin Sarakunan Misau" [History of the Emirs of Misau] (MS, copy in my possession, 1926).

changes in the general pattern of Muslim habitation; three of these changes were characterized by the founding of new settlements on the part of Fulani already established in Gombe and one by a sizable immigration from southwest Bornu of Fulani and Kanuri settlers.

The first in time of these demographic movements occurred in the mid- or late-1840s, and was directly occasioned by a voluntary dispersion of Fulanin Kitaku descent groups from Mbilla, a large town, adjoining Ribadu, which had been founded a generation before at the high tide of the Gombe jihad. Their exodus appears to have been caused by a conjunction of internal political divisions among their several ardos and the removal of any exterior menace to the easternmost rim of the emirate, particularly from Biu. The Fulanin Kitaku now built half a dozen major towns, all within a 15-mile radius north and south of Ribadu. These new centers of Fulani power (and their clan-group constituents) were Jillahi and Jurara (Fulanin Babir); Bodor (Fulanin Jera); Tilde (Fulanin Tara and Magi); and Dukul and Tongo (Fulanin Tara, Magi, Dabe, and Walama). As had been the case for each metropolitan division of Mbilla, each town or ward thereof became a fief of its respective Fulanin Kitaku flag-bearer or his successor in the jihad.[23]

A second, perhaps equally significant shift of Fulani populations took place ca. 1850–55, when Alkalin Dukku led his family and their numerous followers 25 miles north of Dukku to establish three more centers of Fulanin Shira settlement on the Gongola: Malala, Zaune, and Kabadai, together with a number of ancillary towns or villages in the immediate neighborhood. At the alkali's behest all these were removed from the direct supervision of Lamido Dukku and put under Ajiyan Gombe. The area soon attracted still more Fulanin Shira, drawn by the alkali's reputation for learning and his great wealth.[24]

Another considerable transfer of people was involved in the founding of several major towns in the southwest corner of the emirate by Fulanin Gona and a second (undifferentiated) group of Fulanin Kitaku. Tukulma and Sheddo were settled around the mid-century by dissident Fulanin Gona elements from Akko, while Kom Fellata and two nearby satellites were built soon after Kwairanga persuaded a number of Fulanin Kitaku resident in that area before the jihad to return from their subsequent sites of colonization across the frontier with Bauchi. The Fulanin

23. Informants IA: 1–6; IB: 3–4, 6, 9–14, 19; IE: 8–9, 13; IG: 4–5, 7; Carlyle, "History of Gombe"; and Saleh Jibril, "A History of Nafada District, Gombe Emirate" (MS, copy in my possession, 1961).

24. Informants IA: 1–6; IF: 1–3, 6; Carlyle, "History of Gombe"; and A. H. Groom, "Assessment Report on Malala District, Gombe Division, Central Province," NAK SNP 7/13 3446 4195/1912.

Gona remained under the galadima, but Kom Fellata was given in fief to Yeriman Gombe.[25]

Probably as a by-product of the decade or so of hostilities between Fika and Nafada, the region enclosed by the right bank of the Gongola Bend saw in the middle years of the century the creation of about a dozen Kanuri and Fulanin Jada towns by emigrants from Bornu. Most of these were made fiefs of the local chiefs of Jillahi, Bage, and Birin Fulani.[26]

CENTRAL ADMINISTRATION UNDER KWAIRANGA

As with Mallam Zaki at Katagum and Sambo Digimsa at Hadejia, the structuring of central government in Gombe under Buba Yero was far less extensive and formalized than it became after the death of its founder.[27] Apart from his initial appointments of the Fulanin Kitaku flag-bearers to fiefholding titled offices; of three *dengin sarki* "brothers" as chiroma, waziri, and ajiya; of Suleimanu as yerima; and of several religious officials, Buba created only seven other state offices, all but one of them concerned with palace activities.

During the reign of Kwairanga some 25 additional central-government titled offices came into being. With one or two exceptions these were divided about equally among persons responsible for other palace functions; for military affairs; and for the general supervision of, and collection of taxes on, certain occupational pursuits. The most important politically of these new offices were those of magajin gari and ardo na'i. The first Ajiyan Gombe was married to Buba Yero's only daughter, and following the modibbo's death Suleimanu had given her in fief three towns near Wawa; she had received as well a pair of towns on the Middle Gongola from Mallam Buba and three more near Gombe Abba from Lamido Dukku. All these gifts are said to have been made in sympathy for her bereavement. When she died, they were inherited by a son born to her and the ajiya, who was then appointed the first Magajin Garin Gombe. The office of ardo na'i (initially en-

25. Informants ID: 1–4, 9, 11–12, 14, 18–19, 21–22; and Salihu Atiku Kumo, "A History of Akko District, Gombe Emirate" (MS, copy in my possession, 1961).

26. Informants IB: 1–2, 13, 18, 24–25, 32; and Carlyle, "History of Gombe."

27. This paragraph and the next five are drawn from Informants IA: 1–6; IG: 2, 4–5, 6–7.

trusted to a son of Kwairanga) was associated with assessment and collection of cattle tithe throughout the emirate and had attached as its fief towns Gadam, Bojude, Kafarati, Kom Fellata, and Doho.

Soon after Kwairanga was turbanned emir he instituted a local variation of the systems of *uban daki* already in being at Katagum and introduced later at Hadejia. As in Katagum this operated in two politically significant ways. At the level of central government it involved a strict separation of most fiefholders from the emir in the conduct of civic affairs by setting between the official and throne another official. Thus sarkin yaki, sarkin dabe, and ardo walama dealt with Kwairanga (and his successors) in matters of public concern through Ajiyan Gombe; the madaki, sarkin magi, and ardo maituta through the turaki; and the galadima through the yerima. Similarly, most non-Fulanin Kitaku flag-bearers—the lamidos of Nafada, Bage, and Dukku, for example—had to go through the ajiya or turaki when transacting such business at court. Any of these titled officials might be summoned to a royal audience on special occasions, but otherwise, and apart from the usual Friday visits of all those officials present in Gombe Abba, they lacked direct access to the emir.

By his interposition of trusted officials between himself and the major Fulanin Kitaku (as well as other) fiefholders, Kwairanga sought to help balance the rising administrative needs of Gombe State, the clan attachments of those Fulani who served the local jihad, and his own wish to concentrate power increasingly in royal hands. Although Buba Yero had ultimate authority as flag-bearer of Shaikh Usuman in most of the Gongola Basin area, he would have been more of a first among equals, an ardo writ large, than a secure, unchallengeable sovereign; Buba is widely said to have kept (as did Mallam Zaki) his traditional title, that of modibbo, and never acquired that of emir. While court, metropolitan, and provincial demands on Kwairanga multiplied, and with a growing band of princes to look after, he came naturally to delegate functions where they might offer the minimum risk of abuse. Hence when the first ajiya died early in Kwairanga's reign, he conferred the position on a favorite slave, who, with his lineal descendants, held it until the colonial period. The office of turaki had been from its origin occupied by a slave, and both it and that of ajiya developed in the second half of the century into far the most lucrative and influential of any filled by men of Habe extraction, rivaling if not surpassing in affluence and actual power those of the largest fiefholders and highest religious officials. Kwairanga also made the ajiya and turaki the patrons (*iyayen dakuna*) of his several sons, all but the two eldest of whom were sent to live in the compound of one or the other at about age seven to nine, where they remained until their first marriage. Afterward, and like nonroyal fiefholders at the capital, they communicated with or saw the emir only through an *uban daki,* and thus continued to their death (or appointment as Sarkin Gombe) in something of a client relation with the ajiya or turaki.

By the mid-century the ajiya and turaki were the senior Gombe slave officials in virtue of their positions as patrons to *'yan sarki* and client fiefholders alike. Within all four orders of central-government officials—royals (*dengin sarki*), clients (*barori*), slaves (*bayi*), and clerics (*mallamai*)—rank positions were manifest publicly in several ways. Again as at Katagum, most but not all titled appointees were turbanned during their installation, and a select few received as well a set number of beats of the ceremonial drum (*tambari*), ranging in Gombe from three to twelve both on that and certain other occasions. But the most precise gauge of relative standing among high officials within each rank-order was the sequence in which they entered the royal council chamber and saluted the emir on Friday morning, each order performing this act of political homage at successive intervals.

ABDULKADIR ZAILANI (CA.1882–88)

During the years between Muhammadu Kwairanga's death from illness ca. 1882 and the peaceful submission of Gombe to a small British expeditionary column in 1902, four of his sons followed him as emir: Abdulkadir Zailani (ca. 1882–88), Hassan (ca. 1888–95), Tukur (1895–98), and Umaru (1898–1905). The relatively short reign of each brother was scored by deep fissures in the body politic of Gombe State, which fed, and were in turn nourished by, a severe challenge to royal authority in the person of Mallam Jibril—a militant religious-political figure and sometime representative of Mahdist pretensions in the Gongola Basin area.

A conspicuous root of internal discord throughout most of the two decades may be found in those arrangements devised by Kwairanga to satisfy the ambitions of *'yan sarki* at Gombe Abba as they reached maturity and pressed him for titled roles in emirate government. When turbanned emir, Kwairanga had appointed Bello, his eldest son, as Yeriman Gombe, thus singling him out as heir-apparent. About the same time he established three new royal offices by making the next eldest prince, Abdulkadir Zailani, tafida; his third son, Hassan, santuraki; and the fourth, Mu'azu, ardo na'i. On Bello's death ca. 1850, Kwairanga promoted Zailani to yerima, Hassan to tafida, and made a still younger son, Tukur, the santuraki. Later he created yet another such office, that of dan buram, and conferred it on Tukur; it is probable that he did so because Tukur was by then his favorite among the senior *'yan sarki,* and as santuraki he would have appeared to hold lesser rank than Zailani or Hassan.[28]

When Kwairanga died at the capital, the highest government officials—the *manya-sarakuna*—gathered in the Friday mosque to recommend to Sokoto a successor. This group of electoral councilors was composed of the foremost clients in Gombe, that is, the Fulanin Kitaku fiefholders; titled *dengin sarki* (the chiroma, magajin gari, waziri, and ardo na'i); the leading mallams (the chief alkali and liman); and the head titled slaves (the ajiya and turaki). Thus each rank-order in Gombe state administration was represented by its senior members, with the exception of the *'yan sarki* officials. As the senior client fiefholder, sarkin yaki presided over the deliberations, which are said to have been long and inconclusive. Zailani, Hassan, and Tukur each had strong factional support, but Tukur, who was at Sokoto when his father died, returned with a letter from the sultan appointing him to the throne. Tukur arrived home to find that Zailani, already acting as emir, had moved into the palace and made Hassan his yerima and Umaru his tafida. He was persuaded to accept this *fait accompli* and informed the sultan that in view of Zailani's seniority in age and political rank he should be accorded first claim on the office. Wazirin Sokoto then sent a formal announcement to Gombe Abba of the sultan's choice of Zailani.[29]

During the initial months of his reign Zailani ordered the execution of several Gombe officials who had opposed his accession.[30] He subsequently deposed from their titles the sarkin yaki, galadima, madaki, and sarkin magi—all officeholders he inherited from Kwairanga. Since there was no precedent in the emirate for such royal behavior, these measures were even more disruptive of political harmony between the Fulanin Kitaku descent groups than would have been the case had a precedent existed. But whatever the local tradition, and despite his proclaimed motivations, Zailani had seriously alarmed thereby most ardos of his major Fulani

28. This paragraph and the next two are drawn from Informants IA: 1–6; IG: 1–8.

29. Zailani's acknowledgment of this letter has been preserved (Official Correspondence, Various Sultans of Sokoto, NAK Sokprof, File II, Box 25, No. 27).

30. None of those killed were among the higher officeholders, but the former Chiroman Gombe (deposed by Kwairanga), who returned from exile to Gombe Abba on Zailani's appointment, narrowly escaped with his life.

corporate followings, the Fulanin Jera, Gona, Tara, and Magi. None of their titled officials would be assured of remaining in office while he continued as emir. Zailani for his part may well have desired to associate new men with the administration of the largest fief areas, men of his own generation and making.

MALLAM JIBRIL

The political evolution of Gombe State in the last 15 years of the caliphate was to an overwhelming degree connected with the career of Mallam Jibril. Operating out of his newly built Mahdist fortress of Bormi, just south of the Gongola Bend and eight miles from the right bank of the river, Jibril conquered, won over, or caused the desertion of a high percentage of settlements under the Gombe sarkis. When a British-led force arrived at Bormi in 1902, Jibril was preparing a major campaign against Bauchi, one that might well have been designed as a prelude to armed expeditions much farther west in the caliphate.[31]

Mallam Jibril (also known as Jibrilla, Jibrillu, Mallam Zai, Mallam Gaini, and Modibbo Bormi) was of mixed Fulanin Shira/Jafun extraction. His father, a Muslim physician, had settled at the Hardawa village of Jabdo in southern Katagum, where ca. 1820 Jibril was born. Of his youth little has yet come to light, but it is generally agreed that when he reached adulthood Jibril was ordered by Sarkin Hardawa to abandon his farm and emigrate out of the area. With several companions and a few cattle he journeyed some 40 miles eastward, crossing into Kerikeriland and finally settling at Zai, a village then jointly governed by Fika Emirate and Katagum. In the mid-1880s Jibril was again asked to move his establishment; he soon returned, however, and, supported by the emirs of Katagum and Gombe, killed the chief of Zai and enslaved his Kerikeri subjects. He now proclaimed a jihad against other Kerikeri towns, received additional aid from Jema'are, Hadejia, and Misau, and, together with Haji of Katagum, occupied briefly the Kerikeri center of Jellum. A subsequent defeat of the Katagum forces by Kerikeri of Daya caused Haji to accuse Jibril of seeking to weaken him through a depletion

31. T. H. B. Forster, *Précis of Information Concerning Nigeria* (London: The War Office [1901?]), p. 118.

of his cavalry, and the mallam, with an enlarged band of followers, had to take refuge at Nafada.[32]

It has been suggested that Haji and Sarkin Misau were decided that Jibril had become too effective a rival in the rich slaving grounds of Kerikeriland as well as for the allegiance of non-Muslim towns in the region that paid them annual tribute.[33] If true, it is understandable that he then lived quietly for several years at Nafada, Tongo, Zange, and Bage, all towns of the Gongola Bend. During this period (ca. 1885–87) Haji sent an armed deputation to Gombe Abba with a message for the emir: "We have shot a guinea fowl, which has flown down here; give us our food and we shall return home."[34] Zailani refused, but Jibril and his people were harried by a few of the more powerful chiefs of the Gongola Bend, reportedly in fear that his continued presence among them would encourage others to join the growing band of religious enthusiasts already gathered around him.[35] Jibril is said to have then had about 100 followers and to have been recognized widely as a modibbo of charismatic endowments.[36] Then and later he often had recourse to a wide range of quasi-Islamic predictive, healing, or other traditional arts that mallams of northeast Nigeria still can deploy.[37] By 1887 he had persuaded Zailani to pro-

32. Informants IB: 5–9, 13–19, 22, 33–36; Abraham, "Ethnological Notes"; Alhaji Mahmoud, Imamin Bauchi, "A Light for Beginners and a Lamp for the Blind," trans. by Mallams Aliyu Lanle and Ibrahim Magaji, copy in my possession, 1960; Sarkin Misau Ahmadu dan Alhaji Tafida, "Tarihin Mallam Jibril" [History of Mallam Jibril] (MS, copy in my possession, 1926); J. M. Fremantle, "A History of the Region Comprising the Katagum Division of Kano Province," *Journal of the African Society*, X (1911), 417–18; R. S. Davies, "An Account of Mallam Zai," in his "Report on Gujba District, Bornu Emirate, Bornu Province," NAK SNP 10/7 3647 125p/1919; T. L. N. Morland, "Bornu Report B.M./8 of 1st May 1902," NAK SNP 15/1 18; and R. G. Ramage, "Historical Notes on Katagum Division, Bauchi Province (1929–33)," NAK SNP 17/1 1139 9715. For a much fuller account of Jibril's career until he moved into Gombe Emirate, one that differs in a few particulars with the short summary given here, see John E. Lavers, "Jibril Gaini, a Preliminary Account of the Career of a Mahdist Leader in North-Eastern Nigeria," *Research Bulletin of the Centre of Arabic Documentation* (University of Ibadan), III (January, 1967), 19–23.

33. Morland, "Bornu Report"; Ramage, "Historical Notes"; Davies, "Mallam Zai"; and Carlyle, "History of Gombe."

34. Sarkin Misau Ahmadu, "Tarihin Mallam Jibril."

35. Informants IB: 1–2, 5–9, 13–19, 22, 33–36; and Davies, "Mallam Zai."

36. *Ibid.*; Sarkin Misau Ahmadu, "Tarihin Mallam Jibril"; and Informants IH: *passim*.

37. See p. 71 above. Something of the aura and local ambiance which reportedly surrounded Jibril is conveyed in a passage, based on oral documents, from a British district officer:

"He [Jibril] discovered a pool of medicinal properties over which he claimed a

vide him with farmland at Bormi, a slave hamlet of Sarkin Magaba, and the emir sent 150 baskets of guinea corn as a token of his good will.[38] Jibril received as well permission to revive his attacks on Kerikeri towns north of the Gongola. He quickly raided across the river, accompanied by Dan Buramin Gombe Tukur, and returned a share of the booty with him to the capital. Several of the Kerikeri chiefs, aided by Moi Fika (and possibly with Jibril's encouragement), soon retaliated, laying waste a portion of Sarkin Bage's fief area.[39]

Jibril seized on this counterraid to induce all the neighboring settlements to join him at Bormi for their mutual security. Without asking leave of Sarkin Magaba, or his superior, Sarkin Bage, he erected a wall around Bormi and soon drove away the Magaba slave overseers. At the end of the second annual harvest he refused payment of tithe (*zaka*) to Sarkin Magaba, and Sarkin Bage appealed to Zailani for help in bringing Jibril to account. At the same time Jibril announced publicly his intention of freeing the poor and the oppressed from their bonds of excessive taxation by local chiefs and resident agents of the Gombe fiefholders. He pledged to everyone who chose to enlist in his cause an end to extortion, illegal judgments, and all other forms of alleged misrule.[40]

Zailani was then at Wawa on his annual tour of the emirate. He confidently brought together most high state officials and many provincial sarkis. Moving slowly at the head of a large army he passed via Ribadu and Bage to Sangaru, three miles from Bormi. On the day before the planned assault, Zailani confided to a brother of Ajiyan Gombe that when Bormi was taken he would appoint him

monopoly, selling curative potions to women who desired children, to men who were sterile, and even to those who suffered from more obvious ailments. To others who wished to read the future . . . he could draw upon astrology, having purchased from a trader from Darfur a dirty piece of yellow parchment which contained all the twelve equal parts of the Zodiac. . . . Now he was invoking unknown gods to whom he ascribed the most magical powers, now he was manufacturing numerous charms and amulets; Koranic suras [chapters] rubbed off slates and imbibed in water; pills and concoctions mixed from the dried bones of [*sic*] excreta of birds and animals; leather charms, containing complicated arabesques, drawn on paper and alleged to be antidotal to all manner of evils, for all of which the Mallam and his lieutenants never failed to find suitable purchasers, at considerable profit to themselves" (R. L. B. Maiden, *The Nasarawa Gate and Other Stories* [London: Brown Knight & Truscott, n.d.], pp. 66–67).

38. Informants IB: *passim*; Sarkin Misau Ahmadu, "Tarihin Mallam Jibril"; and C. L. Temple, "Report on Bauchi Province for April–June, 1902," NAK SNP 15/1 7.

39. Informants IB: 1–2, 5–9, 13–19, 22, 33–36; and Carlyle, "History of Gombe."

40. Informants IB: 1–2, 5–9, 13–18, 22, 33–36; and T. F. Carlyle, Appendix 1 to "Gombe Division Intelligence Report," in "Annual Report, Bauchi Province (1916)," NAK SNP 10/4 873 737p/1916.

ajiya there. Learning of this conversation, and unknown to the emir, the incumbent ajiya assembled all titled officeholders present that evening at Sangaru. Supported by the turaki, Sarkin Nafada, and Sarkin Bage—each of whom had good reason to fear deposition—the ajiya prevailed upon the rest to leave Zailani unattended on the battlefield the next day.[41] They rode out at dawn with the emir to Bormi, where the ajiya complained of an illness and halted well beyond the town wall. The other commanders followed his lead and refused the royal order to move forward. Angry, shamed, and almost alone, Zailani charged the main gate, where he was shot by a poisoned arrow. He died at Magaba a few hours later and was buried at Birin Bolewa. Yerima Hassan dan Kwairanga immediately sent for assistance to Sarkin Misau Muhammadu Manga II, and together they fought several hard, undecisive engagements in the environs of Bormi against those villagers newly allied with Jibril. Then, unable to conquer Bormi itself, Manga returned to Misau while Hassan, already turbanned in the field by Walin Sokoto, went back as emir to Gombe Abba.[42]

HASSAN (CA. 1888–95)

The personalities of Zailani and Hassan were in sharp contradistinction, yet each served in its way to facilitate the quick rise of Jibril's political fortunes. Zailani is described as "morose of nature,"[43] hardfisted, and ungracious in his dealings with people of all social strata; Hassan as too generous, unmindful of his own best interests, and the cause of much of Jibril's early success in the emirate. "In the time of Hassan the walls of Gombe Town and of the palace were left un-

41. *Ibid.*; Informants IA: 1–6; IB: 5–9, 13–19, 33, 33–36; IG: 1–8; Sarkin Misau Ahmadu, "Tarihin Mallam Jibril"; and Forster, *Précis of Information*, p. 118. According to present-day informants, Zailani had earlier seized a number of the turaki's horses and given them to the mabudi, an age mate and favorite of his whom he wished to appoint turaki. Sarkins Nafada and Bage are said to have been alarmed by the recent deposition of Sarkin Dukku. Several potential dissenters from the majority view were constrained to go along with it out of fear and because of their weakness relative to the power of the higher officials.

42. Informants IA: 1–6; IB: 5–9, 13–19, 22, 33–36; IG: 1–8; Sarkin Misau Ahmadu, "Tarihin Mallam Jibril"; Ramage, "Historical Notes"; and Carlyle, "History of Gombe."

43. *Ibid.*

repaired. The people became impoverished. He disliked fighting, and was prodigal of his wealth, scattering the riches inherited from Zailani.[44] Within a few months of Hassan's installation, Jibril had conquered Bajoga, Ashaka, and Magaba.[45] A correspondent from the capital, writing in the name of "the people of Gombe," informed Wazirin Sokoto of these portentious events, and of their "fear of [Jibril]." Enclosed in the message were letters from the Sarkins Nafada, Biri, and Bage, asking the waziri to consider what could be done to check his advance.[46] The sultan ordered all the eastern Fulani states to mount a concerted effort at crushing him. They responded readily, though (it appears) with an enthusiasm tempered by considerable unease. The emirs of Bauchi, Misau, and Gombe commanded in person their respective forces, but Haji of Katagum sent a column under Yeriman Chinade, Muhammadu of Hadejia sent one led by Sarkin Auyo, and the emir of Jema'are likewise sent a deputy. The sultan was represented by Magajin Wazirin Sokoto, while Sarkin Bauchi Umaru had over-all command of offensive operations.

In the winter of 1888–89, all of these allied detachments converged near Bajoga, where, joined by Hassan and his army, they encamped for a month or two. Only the troops of Hadejia ventured to stage a direct assault on Bormi Town; the rest were deployed around it in an attempt to starve out the inhabitants. The failure of so large a combined operation to conquer Bormi, and its dispersal after so brief a period, may be accounted for in several ways. An adequate provision of water, food, and animal rations to a mixed host of such magnitude would have been a task at least as formidable as that which confronted Jibril in supplying his followers. Again, rivalries already manifest among the half-dozen neighboring states represented at Bajoga were easily aggravated by their traditional fear and suspicion of one another. It was publicly known, for example, that after Sarkin Auyo's unsuccessful attack on Bormi he advised Hassan that as it was of moderate size the Gombe commanders should encounter no hardship in coping with Jibril themselves. Manga is said to have concluded that if the Misau party reduced Bormi, the major credit would go to Bauchi. And perhaps most divisive of all, it was

44. Informants IA: 1–6; IG: 1–8. The quotation is a composite of informant remarks. Characteristic of Hassan's liberality was a gift he is said to have made of one thousand guns and a large number of horses to his father-in-law, Sarkin Misau Sale (*ibid.*).

45. Informants IB: 1–2, 5–10, 13–18, 21–22, 28–29. Bajoga had been founded 10–15 years earlier, by a relative of Sarkin Bage (Informants IB: 17–18; Saleh Jibril, "History of Nafada"; and Carlyle, "History of Gombe").

46. Official Correspondence, Various Sultans of Sokoto, NAK Sokprof, File V, Box 25, No. 19.

commonly rumored that Sarkin Bauchi Umaru was treating in secret with Jibril, who is reported to have sent numerous presents and offered his daughter in marriage to him. Whatever the actual state of affairs may have been, the caliphal lieutenants finally accepted Jibril's assurance that he would leave Bormi if they withdrew. Each column retired homeward (laden, according to most accounts, with costly gifts), and Jibril at once launched a broad campaign against the most prominent Fulani towns in the Gongola Bend.[47]

In its political aspect, Hassan's reign at Gombe Abba was marked by almost unceasing adversity. By 1895 Jibril had mastered the entire eastern half of the emirate, save the Nafada fief area and some Tera settlements, and was poised to strike farther west, at Dukku and the capital. During the first six years or so following the aborted joint expedition to Bormi, he forcibly occupied or received the submission of (in sequential order) Jillahi, Wakkaltu, Tilde, Bodor, Wawa, Tongo, Dukul, and Jurara.[48] All of these towns except Wawa were considerable Fulanin Kitaku centers, and they became, along with Bormi, Bajoga, and Magaba, Jibril's future strongholds in Gombe.[49] When a town succumbed without resistance Jibril maintained its sarki and left there a Bormi agent; otherwise he executed the chief, replacing him with one of his own titled subordinates, generally a relative of Jibril or a high Bormi slave or client official.[50] This policy was efficient alike in persuading the sarkis of eastern Gombe to submit peacefully and as a device for compensating his more successful commanders with regular sources of income. Another spring of Jibril's military achievement lay in the tactics which he developed to prepare for and carry through a fresh campaign: agents were sent ahead to sow fear of his pitiless character and ferocity in arms, as well as awe at his religious-

47. *Ibid.*, File II, Box 8, Nos. 28, 32, 34, 35; Informants IA: 1–6; IB: 1–36; IIA: 1–5; IIB: 1, 5–6, 8; IIF: 1–8; IIIA: 7, 9, 14–15; IIIC: 1; Sarkin Misau Ahmadu, "Tarihin Mallam Jibril" and "Tarihin Sarakunan Misau"; Ramage, "Historical Notes"; Carlyle, "History of Gombe"; Alhaji Mahmoud, "A Light for Beginners"; Fremantle, "History of the Region," X (1911), 418; and Lavers, "Jibril Gaini," p. 25 n.

That Hassan may have been a reluctant party to this agreement is indicated by a letter he wrote Wazirin Sokoto: "We encamped round Mallam Jibril and invested Bajoga till it surrendered and asked for a truce with our leader, Sarkin Bauchi Umaru. He agreed, and we cannot oppose him as he is our leader. You should know that this conflagration will not stop until you try to extinguish it by every possible means; do not disregard it" (Official Correspondence, Various Sultans of Sokoto, NAK Sokprof, File II, Box 25, No. 16).

48. Informants IB: 1–36.

49. *Ibid.*; and Temple, "Report on Bauchi Province."

50. Informants IB: 1–36. Examples were the appointment of Sarkin Yakin Bormi as chief of Jurara; Galadiman Bormi to Birin Bolewa; and Jibril's nephew to Bajoga.

political mission, while his men advanced always by night, attacking at dawn to secure maximum surprise. And although equipped only with bows, spears, and swords, the Bormi troops are said to have been undeterred by the rifles and matchlocks of several hundred Gombe special forces.[51]

THE SUDANESE MAHDIYA AND THE SOKOTO CALIPHATE

Jibril's martial and diplomatic skills, when considered in tandem with Hassan's political ineptitude, make intelligible the sudden and general success of his takeover bid in the Gongola region. But another, perhaps even larger contribution was made by Jibril's claim to be—or at least to represent—the long-awaited Mahdi. Islamic history is replete with popular traditions associated with *al-Mahdi,* "the Rightly Guided One," whom Allah will send in the fullness of time "to fill the world with justice in lieu of injustice, which often meant the abolition of unauthorized practices and the enforcement of orthodox doctrines and conduct . . . [and] to achieve the conversion of the world to Islam."[52] His appearance would herald the coming of al-Dadjdjal ("an eschatological personage of the antichrist type")[53] and other harbingers, foretold in the Qur'an, of the final, Messianic era on earth; and it would be preceded by a period of universal tyranny and human suffering.[54]

51. *Ibid.*; and Informants IA: 1–6. For a more detailed account of Jibril's political and military organization, as well as the economic role of Bormi at this time in the Gongola Basin area, see Lavers, "Jibril Gaini," pp. 33–38. Lavers notes that "up until this time [ca. 1895] Jibril had confined his activities to the regions to the west of the River Gongola. This was probably due to two reasons: the country to the east of the river was heavily infested with tsetse fly and thus restricted the use of cavalry, and, secondly, the Bornu frontier system was still effective enough to prevent incursions into the western provinces. Rabih Zubayr's invasion of Bornu in 1893 completely changed the situation: the administration collapsed . . . and the whole frontier region fell into chaos and the situation was exacerbated by the rinderpest epidemic of 1887–1893. Jibril, always an opportunist, turned his attention east of the Gongola" (p. 27).

52. D. S. Margoliouth, "Mahdi," *Encyclopedia of Religion and Ethics* (New York: Charles Scribner Sons, 1926), III, 337.

53. Gustave E. von Grunebaum, *Medieval Islam* (Chicago: University of Chicago Press, 1961), p. 194, n. 50.

54. Traditions regarding al-Mahdi's personal attributes, the time and circumstances of his appearance, and those acts he will perform, have been varied and often inconsistent; a good short summary is provided by Margoliouth, "Mahdi," III, 336–40.

The years of Jibril's political ascendance in the Gongola region were nearly coincident with those of the reign at Omdurman of ʿAbdullah b. Muhammad (1885–98), heir to the east Sudanic Mahdiya proclaimed by Muhammad Ahmad in 1881. ʿAbdullah styled himself *Khalīfat al-Mahdī*, "the Successor of the Mahdi," and his relations with several West African personalities constitute an important (if as yet ill-documented) chapter in modern Nigerian history.[55] There is, however, sufficient evidence at hand to suggest the recent contention that major Western and Central Sudanic jihads of the nineteenth century "gave rise to the Sudanese Mahdia," and, what is of more significance here, that both Muhammad Ahmad and ʿAbdullah "sought support and expansion [outside the Sudan] mainly in the Niger-Chad region."[56]

As exerted by the leading spokesmen of the Sokoto jihad, this influence on the Mahdiya was largely intellectual in content, and its origins can be traced in a number of exegetical works by Shaikh Usuman, Abdullahi dan Fodio, and Muhammad Bello. Shaikh Usuman denied vigorously the assertion of some of his followers that he was "the expected Mahdi," reminding them, *inter alia,* of two classical preconditions for so exalted a rank: birth at Medina and lineal descent from the Prophet. But while Usuman would not acknowledge himself eligible for consideration, like most West African Muslims of his day he was confident of the imminence of the Mahdi's arrival, and he looked on the Fulani jihad as an essential adumbration of that arrival.[57] Toward the end of 1805 Bello was sent by Shaikh Usuman to bear his "good tidings about the approaching advent of the

---

Sunnite (orthodox) Muslim theology, which includes that of the Nigerian Sudan, looks to "a final restorer of the faith," but does not call him by the name of Mahdi, or any other name; rather, it was "in the hearts of the Muslim multitude that the faith in the Mahdi" was found. "In the midst of growing darkness and uncertainty—political, social, moral, theological—they clung to the idea of a future deliverer and restorer and of a short millenium before the end. . . . And as the need for a Mahdi has been felt, the Mahdis have always appeared" (D. B. MacDonald, "Mahdī," *Encyclopaedia of Islam* [London: Luzac & Co., 1936], III, 113, 115).

55. Saburi Biobaku and Muhammad al-Hajj, "The Sudanese Mahdiyya and the Niger-Chad Region," in *Islam in Tropical Africa*, ed. I. M. Lewis (London: Oxford University Press, 1966), pp. 425–41 *passim.*

56. *Ibid.,* pp. 426, 428–29.

57. Roland A. Adeleye, et al., "Sifofin Shehu: An Autobiography and Character Study of ʿUthman b. Fūdī in Verse," *Research Bulletin of the Centre of Arabic Documentation* (University of Ibadan), II (1966), 7–12, 28–31; and Muhammad A. al-Hajj, "The Thirteenth Century in Muslim Eschatology: Mahdist Expectations in the Sokoto Caliphate," *idem,* III (July, 1967), 109–11.

Mahdi" to all supporters of the jihad in Zamfara, Katsina, Kano, and Daura; to assure them of their special position as the shaikh's "vanguard"; and to offer his pledge that the Sokoto jihad would continue "until it gets to the Mahdi."[58]

Such authoritative pronouncements by the shaikh of an intimate casual tie between his movement of religious and political reformation with the Mahdi's appearance are said to have "inspired prophecies, written and oral, about the appointed day" that drew on more traditional Islamic sources to corroborate or embellish their chiliastic visions. A considerable Mahdist-oriented literature soon developed in the caliphate; it predicted the Mahdi would first reveal himself in the East, following "a period of drought, civil strife, and general turmoil in the Maghrib and the Niger-Chad region," and his coming would produce a massive departure of Muslims from these areas to the Nile Valley and to Arabia.[59]

In the reign of Sultan Abubakar Atiku (1837–42) there was a minor exodus of Nigerian Muslims to the Nile Basin in anticipation of the Mahdi's appearance, and the sultan had to announce that such actions were premature. During the next four decades or so Mahdist agitation continued in many parts of the caliphate, and a number of persons migrated eastward.[60] The best-known example of Mahdist activity in the northeastern emirates before Jibril's time occurred in the early 1880s, when Liman Yamusa, a modibbo of Dutsi Gadawur in eastern Kano, gathered around him a sizable group of Believers and proclaimed his intention of going to Mecca. Yamusa denounced the Hausa-Fulani sarkis as corrupters of the Faith and oppressors of the common people. His following increased as he moved toward the Kano frontiers with Jema'are, Hadejia, and Katagum, and the sultan quickly ordered those emirates on his route to intercept and apprehend him. Yamusa was seized at Gwadayi by Haru of Hadejia, Sale of Misau, and Abdulkadir of Shira; they confiscated his baggage and sent him under heavy guard to Sokoto, from where he was exiled to Bauchi.[61]

58. Muhammad Bello, quoted in Biobaku and al-Hajj, "The Sudanese Mahdiyya," p. 428.

59. *Ibid.*, p. 429. For a survey of Mahdist activity and influence in the Western and Central Sudan, see A. Le Grip, "Le Mahdism en Afrique Noir," *L'Afrique et l'Asie,* XVIII (1952), 7–10.

60. Biobaku and al-Hajj, "The Sudanese Mahdiyya," p. 429.

61. Informants IIA: *passim*; Sarkin Misau Ahmadu, "Tarihin Sarakunan Misau"; Ramage, "Historical Notes"; and Fremantle, "History of the Region," X (1911), 418. Lavers persuasively argues that Yamusa could not have begun the *hajj* "earlier than 1883," citing the present Emir of Misau's recorded statement that Hayatu bn. Sa'idu (see below) wrote Yamusa to leave Kano and join the Mahdi of the Nilotic Sudan ("Jibril Gaini," p. 20 n).

MALLAM HAYATU BN. SA'IDU

The Yamusa episode was linked closely with a far more significant outbreak of Mahdist unrest in the caliphate. Mallam Hayatu bn. Sa'idu, a grandson of Sultan Muhammad Bello, had to leave Sokoto after his father was denied the sultanate in 1877. Against the new sultan's wishes Hayatu set out for the east, avowedly on pilgrimage to Mecca. Turned back at Kano on orders from Sokoto, he then took a more southern route, crossed the Gongola at Ashaka, and reached Adamawa. The emir of Yola welcomed Hayatu as befitted a great-grandson of Shaikh Usuman, but after presenting him with a large personal equipage sent him on farther east, with a letter of introduction to the emir of Marua (Cameroon). Hayatu eventually founded his own town of Balda, south of Marua, and from there began to harass the Fulani rulers of Yola, Marua, and other local emirates.[62]

Meanwhile, the Mahdi Muhammad Ahmad had written to Sultan Umaru and Shehu Bukar of Bornu putting forward his claim on the loyalties of all Western and Central Sudanic Believers.[63] Counseled by their religious advisers (the legists in particular), they made no reply,[64] but Hayatu in 1883 answered a similar message without hesitation: "I and my father and all that belong to me swore allegiance to you before your manifestation was perceived. Shaykh 'Uthman dan Fodio recommended to us to emigrate to you, to assist you and help you when you were made manifest."[65] In the absence of any response to his call from either Bornu or the sultan, the Mahdi commissioned Hayatu to serve as his deputy and overlord "of all the

62. Denis Murray Last, *The Sokoto Caliphate* (London: Longmans Green, 1967), pp. 122–23; Hayatu bn. Sa'idu, "The Life History of M. Sa'idu bn. Hayatu" (MS, copy in my possession, n.d.); Hauptmann Kurt Strümpell, "Die Geschichte Adamauas nach mündlichen Überlieferungen," *Mitteilungen der geographischen Gesellschaft in Hamburg*, XXVI (1912), 74–75; G. J. F. Tomlinson and G. J. Lethem, *History of Islamic Political Propaganda in Nigeria* (London: Waterlow [1927]), pp. 7–8, 69; P. M. Holt, "The Sudanese Mahdia and the Outside World," *Bulletin of the School of Oriental and African Studies*, XXI, Pt. 2 (1958), 285–86; and Hogben and Kirk-Greene, *Emirates of Northern Nigeria*, p. 441. Strümpell, who cites oral tradition, says that Hayatu was not trusted at Yola, being "a man of penetrating judgment, great cunning and wonderful adaptability, but above all of insatiable ambitions." The most thorough account thus far published of Hayatu is by Martin Z. Njeuma, "Adamawa and Mahdism: The Career of Hayatu ibn Sa'id in Adamawa, 1878–1898," *Journal of African History*, XII (1971), 61–77.

63. Tomlinson and Lethem, *Islamic Propaganda*, p. 7.

64. Hayatu bn. Sa'idu, a grandson of Hayatu, claims that the sultan of Sokoto at first displayed interest in the Mahdi's correspondence, but was put off by Hayatu's subsequent involvement with the Mahdia ("Life History").

65. Quoted in Biobaku and al-Hajj, "The Sudanese Mahdiyya," p. 434.

people of Sokoto who were subjects of your great-grandfather, Usuman dan Fodio." Hayatu also received confirming letters of authorization for delivery to the leading sarkis and mallams in the caliphate.[66] (It was probably such a letter which inspired Liman Yamusa's attempt to emigrate from Kano). He now declared a jihad against all who refused to acknowledge the Mahdi, or his own position as his chief lieutenant west of Lake Chad.[67]

When the eastern emirs declined Hayatu's summons to join him, he wrote to Mallam Jibril, who may well have already identified himself with 'Abdullah's ambitions.[68] By 1890, Jibril, newly established as a political and religious force to be reckoned with in northeast Nigeria, was allied ideologically and perhaps acting in concert with Mallam Hayatu.

RABEH

From 1894 to 1900 the Chad Basin area was dominated politically by the militant figure of Rabeh, an early if uncertain partisan of the Mahdi and his

66. *Ibid.*; and Sarkin Misau Ahmadu, "Tarihin Sarakunan Misau." Muhammadu Manga II of Misau wrote Sultan Umaru of a message received from Hayatu summoning him to follow the Mahdi, and that on his refusal to comply Hayatu has written Jibril and others (Official Correspondence, Various Sultans of Sokoto, NAK Sokprof, File IV, Box 25, No. 24). Manga later reported another such letter, either from Hayatu or Jibril, which he referred to Sarkin Bauchi (*ibid.*, No. 26). The first-mentioned letter is quoted in part by Njeuma, who incorrectly refers to Manga as Emir of Gombe ("Adamawa and Mahdism," pp. 71–72).

67. Biobaku and al-Hajj, "The Sudanese Mahdiyya," p. 435.

68. See n. 66 above. The emirs' reluctance to ally with Muhammad Ahmad of the Nilotic Sudan or his Mahdist agents in the west seems due not only to their loyal heeding of Sokoto but also to the fact, well attested, that a number of commoners (as well as others) under caliphal authority had begun to emigrate eastward (Informants IA: 1–6; IIA: 1–5; IIB: 1–9; IIIA: *passim*). The episode of Liman Yamusa would likely have reminded the eastern emirs of how potent a summons to join Mahdist ranks farther east might be when issued by a charismatic religious figure in a time of social unrest or political unease. For the apparent influence of European encroachment in West and North Africa upon those in the caliphate made aware of it—and what this implied with reference to an appropriate Islamic response to occupation by a corps of Unbelievers—see Roland A. Adeleye, "The Dilemma of the Wazīr: The Place of the *Risālat al-Wazīr'ila Ahl al-'Ilm Wal-Tadabbur* in the History of the Conquest of the Sokoto Caliphate," *Journal of the Historical Society of Nigeria,* IV (June, 1968), 285–309, especially 287–92.

Khalifa.[69] Born at Khartoum in 1845, Rabeh had settled as a youth in the Bahr al-Ghazal, where he served an apprenticeship in slaveraiding with Zubeir Pasha, afterward (1870–73) the Egyptian governor of that province and of Darfur. When Zubeir Pasha's son rebelled against General Gordon (1878–79) and was killed, Rabeh led a small band of unappeased warriors farther west and several years later set up as an independent sultan at Dar Runga (between Wadai and Darfur).[70] In 1886, a year after the Mahdi's death, Khalifa 'Abdullah sent to Rabeh detailing the accomplishments and future prospects of the Mahdiya, but unwilling to hazard his freedom by entering on a connection with 'Abdullah that might render him the subordinate party, Rabeh did not reply.[71] Instead, he maintained a gradual westward movement, always in search of fresh slaving grounds beyond the reach of Egyptian or Sudanese administration, building as he went an increasingly formidable army out of his original following and their levies.[72] At the same time he utilized the Mahdist cause by representing himself as a confederate of the Khalifa, one who came wielding the *saif al-nasār,* or "sword of victory," said to have been given the Mahdi by Allah. His men wore the uniform and observed the prayer rituals (A. *ritāb*) of the eastern Sudanic Mahdists.[73]

In 1891 Rabeh invaded Wadai, but had to withdraw still farther west. With his occupation of Baghirmi in 1892 he was at last sufficiently strong and close to the West-Central Sudan to perceive a more lucrative field of spoliation. The next year he crossed over the Shari, defeated a strong column dispatched by Shehu Hashim, and (after a single reverse) leveled the nineteenth-century Bornu capital of Kukawa. Hashim's successor was executed, and although sporadic resistance

69. A comprehensive, authoritative work on the life of Rabeh has yet to be written —and may not be without a control of the Arabic, Kanuri, English, German, and French sources. Published accounts of his career are few and often marred by inaccuracy or bias, though collectively they provide a useful conspectus of major events and a number of suggestive details, in particular for the years in Bornu. See especially Max Freiherr von Oppenheim, *La vie du Sultan Rabeh* (Paris, 1902); A. D. Babikir, *L'empire de Rabeh* (Paris, 1950); and John E. Lavers, "Rabih ibn Fadlullah," in *Studies on the History of Islam in West Africa,* ed. John R. Willis (London: Frank Cass, 1972). Rabeh's Arabic name was Rabih ibn Fadl Allāh; he is frequently referred to in the literature and documents as Rabih Zubair.

70. Richard Hill, *A Biographical Dictionary of the Sudan,* 2d ed. (London: Frank Cass, 1967), p. 312.

71. Holt, "The Sudanese Mahdia," p. 285.

72. For a useful summary of his route in these formative years, see W. K. R. Hallam, "The Itinerary of Rabih Fadl Allah, 1879–1893," *Bulletin de l'I.F.A.N.,* XXX, Series B (1968), 165–80.

73. Tomlinson and Lethem, *Islamic Propaganda,* p. 69.

continued a short while, by 1894 Rabeh held effective control of most of the Bornu Empire. He as once set about preparing the conquest of the Fulani emirates on the eastern side of the caliphate.[74]

While still at Baghirmi, Rabeh had initiated a correspondence with Mallam Hayatu, seemingly designed to reconcile his claim to be the Mahdi's vicegerent in the West-Central Sudan with Hayatu's more palpable, authorized occupancy of that position.[75] The two men concluded an alliance of convenience, formally sealed by the marriage of Hayatu to a daughter of Rabeh. Within a few months Hayatu, operating from Balda, had mastered the Marua-Mandara region and was recognized by his new ally as the legitimate heir to the caliphate.[76]

Once firmly established in Bornu, however, Rabeh undertook on his own to open negotiations with Sultan Abdurrahman. From his fortress-capital of Dikwa (30 miles south of Lake Chad) Rabeh sent emissaries to Sokoto through Sarkin Katagum Abdulkadir.[77] He also forwarded several hundred musketeers to a number of the more powerful *sarakuna* on the west Bornu marches, including those in Beddeland and Gujba (the emir of Dambam had already submitted).[78] Receiving no favorable response from the paramount chief of the Bedde, he sent a force to Gorgoram, whose people fled, many of them to Hadejia. Muhammadu of Hadejia, in evident concern, then wrote the emir of Kano that Rabeh was reported marching on Kano City, via either Hadejia, Katagum, or Damagaram.[79]

These events, which occurred in 1896–97, followed on several years of relative calm in Bornu during which Rabeh had focused his energies on the adminis-

74. Boyd Alexander, *From the Niger to the Nile,* 2 vols. (London: Edward Arnold, 1907), II, 170–77; Hill, *Biographical Dictionary,* p. 312; and Yves Urvoy, *Histoire de l'Empire du Bornou* (Paris: Larose, 1949), pp. 126–27.

75. Hayatu bn. Sa'idu, "Life History."

76. *Ibid.*; Tomlinson and Lethem, *Islamic Propaganda,* p. 8; and Hogben and Kirk-Greene, p. 407.

77. Letters from the Emir of Hadejia Muhammadu to the Emir of Kano Aliyu, G. O. K. 1/2/126, 127, tr. in S. S. Waniko and M. S. D. Ilyasu, *A Descriptive Catalogue of Early Lugard-Sultan of Sokoto Correspondence, Including a Description of 131 Arabic Letters Found in Sokoto in 1903* (Kaduna, 1961).

78. *Ibid.,* 1/2/121, 122, 123, 124, 125; H. F. Backwell, *The Occupation of Hausaland, 1900–1904* (1927; London: Frank Cass, 1969), pp. 59–62; and Fremantle, "History of the Region," XI (1912), 192.

79. Waniko and Ilyasu, *Descriptive Catalogue,* 1/2/123, 125. Roland Adeleye, citing this and similar correspondence to Sokoto from the eastern emirs, notes their "panic and confusion," a "wave of fear" that deepened still further when Rabeh's men were said to be aiming at Kano via them (*Power and Diplomacy in Northern Nigeria 1804–1906* [London: Longman Group, 1971], pp. 177–78).

trative organization of his capacious trans-Chadian empire.[80] That Rabeh neglected to pursue his apparent intention of invading the eastern Fulani emirates can be largely accounted for by the appearance of another, more serious challenge—a European armed presence in the Central Sudan.

In 1897 a French military mission, commanded by Lieutenant Gentil, sailed down the Shari and arrived on the southern banks of Lake Chad. Gentil had made treaties with a number of local rulers on his way there from the Congo, including the sultan of Baghirmi.[81] Rabeh, who reached Kusseri (at the Shari-Logone confluence) a day after the French steamer passed by on its return voyage southward to Fort Archambault, had to be content with destroying the capital of Baghirmi a few months later, as an example to other chiefs within his empire who might be tempted to traffic with Europeans.[82]

Le Comité de l'Afrique Française then conceived an elaborate strategy designed to eliminate Rabeh from the Chadian scene. It organized three separate expeditions, intended to converge on Bornu from Algeria, Niamey, and Fort Archambault. Before they could join up, however, Rabeh wiped out a mixed French-Baghirmi column just north of the fort (July, 1899), and three months later fought a heavy but inconclusive engagement with Gentil nearby.[83] Rabeh then retired to Dikwa, having learned of the approach on Kusseri, from west and north, of the two other French columns.[84]

Meanwhile, Hayatu had been persuaded by Rabeh to transfer to Dikwa for the common defense of their *dār al-Islām* (1897). Once there he quickly discerned that his position no longer was that of an ally of Rabeh, each having equal status in the Mahdist jihad, but rather one of dependency.[85] He therefore accepted an invitation from Mallam Jibril to remove to Bormi, where a number of his followers had already been provided a new base of operations.[86] Hayatu is also reported to have now proclaimed himself Mahdi,[87] and to have urged Sarkin Bauchi to invade Bornu.[88] Choosing a moment when Rabeh was in the field against Gentil and Baghirmi (winter, 1897–98), he set out from Dikwa, escorted by a few associates

80. Urvoy, *Histoire de l'Empire du Bornou,* p. 127.
81. E. Gentil, *La chute de l'empire de Rabah* (Paris, 1902), pp. 139–40.
82. Alexander, *Niger to the Nile,* II, 171–72.
83. Gentil, *La chute,* pp. 126–30, 139–40, 149–65.
84. Alexander, *Niger to the Nile,* II, 175.
85. Hayatu bn. Sa'idu, "Life History"; Strümpell, "Die Geschichte Adamauas," p. 76; and Tomlinson and Lethem, *Islamic Propaganda.*
86. *Ibid.,* p. 69; Hayatu bn. Sa'idu, "Life History"; and Informants IB: 15–18, 21–22.
87. Tomlinson and Lethem, *Islamic Propaganda,* pp. 69–70.
88. Strümpell, "Die Geschichte Adamauas," p. 76.

and a light guard of Bormi cavalry furnished by Jibril.[89] His party was intercepted by Fadlallah, Rabeh's eldest son, when several miles from the city; Hayatu was killed in the skirmish that followed, and Fadlallah wounded.[90]

TUKUR (1895–98)

The selection of Hassan as emir ca. 1888 had been decided and approved at a time when the higher state officials were united in opposing what they viewed as an immoderate exercise of the royal prerogative to dismiss them from office. As yerima under Zailani, and the late emir's oldest surviving brother, Hassan must have appeared to both the officials and the sultan the most congruous choice to succeed him. His personal character, at once generous and yielding, would—if only by contrast with that of Zailani—have rendered Hassan still more acceptable as a successor. And the fact that none of Zailani's sons yet held sufficiently high office to be considered instead, while none of Hassan's were old enough at his accession to replace him as yerima, probably worked as additional arguments in his favor.[91]

When Zailani had appointed Hassan to follow him as yerima, he had filled the vacancy thus created by giving the post of tafida to still another (but previously untitled) son of Kwairanga, Umaru. Tukur, who remained dan buram rather than advancing along the *'yan sarki* ladder, acquired thereby a second major public grievance against Zailani. When Hassan was turbanned emir he promoted Tukur over the head of Tafida Umaru by appointing him yerima; it is unclear whether he did so out of a sense of redressing an inequity or because he wished to conform to the apparent desire of their father, but an important side effect was the embitterment of Umaru and a subsequent defection by several of the highest emirate officials.

On Hassan's death in the palace ca. 1895, Tukur was immediately chosen emir

89. *Ibid.*; Hayatu bn. Sa'idu, "Life History"; Tomlinson and Lethem, *Islamic Propaganda,* p. 70; and Informants IB: 15–18, 21–22.

90. *Ibid.*; Strümpell, "Die Geschichte Adamauas," p. 76; Hayatu bn. Sa'idu, "Life History"; and extract from a letter written by W. P. Hewby, dated August 10, 1898, in "Bornu Provincial History," NAK SNP 15/14. Hewby reported that "it seems a prevalent idea that [Hayatu's death] had been arranged by Rabeh himself before leaving for Logone."

91. This paragraph and the next are drawn from Informants IA: 1–6; IG: 4, 7.

by the electors and installed by Walin Sokoto. With the crown's effective authority now confined to little more than half of Gombe state, Jibril was preparing to strike at those towns in the Gongola region that remained outside his orbit of influence or control. Hence Tukur, in an effort to rally maximum support from all his officials (and perhaps by prearrangement), appointed Umaru to succeed him as yerima. But several months later, for unexplained reasons, he deposed Umaru on charges of disobedience, and put a younger brother, Jalo, in that position. Exiled to Bauchi, Umaru sought to organize a revolt against Tukur, and finally moved back across the border to Kom Fellata, a large fief town of the yerima which had remained loyal to him. When Tukur marched there in force, Galadima Bubawa (living at Akko nearby) denied that Umaru was in the neighborhood. The emir, informed otherwise by his agents, remained away from the capital about a year, partly to hold Umaru and his faction in check and partly to besiege Kafarati, a town three miles east of Kom Fellata and then occupied by followers of Jibril. Tukur returned home only on hearing that a column of Jibril's men had burned the central market at Gombe Abba. Within three months Tukur was dead, of uncertain causes.[92]

UMARU (1898–1922)

The death of Tukur gave rise to a severe constitutional crisis in Gombe which continued, together with ever more serious inroads from Bormi on its integrity as an emirate, until the arrival some three years later of a British armed presence in northeast Nigeria.[93] Umaru was favored to succeed as emir by a preponderance of the electors, but there was vigorous advocacy for Jalo as well, led by the ajiya (his *uban daki*) and supported by most of the lower officials at court. The arguments for Umaru were framed in terms of his seniority in age and in tenure as yerima and of his being a more learned and militant figure than Jalo. Umaru's cause was championed by the turaki (his *uban daki*), and also by Galadima Bubawa, Alkalin Gombe, the waziri, and Sarkin Magi—all of whom were, like

92. Informants IA: 1–6; ID: 1–4, 9, 11, 13–14, 18–22; IG: 4, 7; Chiroman Gombe Babagoro, "History of the Gombe Emirs"; and Salihu Atiku Kumo, "History of Akko District."

93. This paragraph and the next two are drawn from references given in n. 92 above, together with Carlyle, "History of Gombe."

Umaru, recent adherents of the Tijaniyya brotherhood. Sarkin Yakin Gombe, dissatisfied with both candidacies, remained at Kunde while the rest of the council deliberated. When the majority view finally prevailed, Galadima Bubawa returned to Akko and had Umaru (still at Kom Fellata) brought to him there. Bubawa gave the emir-designate a horse and equipage, swore his allegiance, and sent him with a heavy escort to the capital. Umaru first resided a few months in the ajiya's compound, to demonstrate publicly his authority over the chief slave-official, and then moved into the palace.

Six months after Umaru's installation Galadima Bubawa came to Gombe Abba to make the annual dry-season homage prefatory to joining the emir on his visit to Sokoto. He was accompanied by a large mounted entourage that included Ardo Bayo, leader of the rival house of Fulanin Gona, that of Kalshingi Town. A few years before, Bayo and a group of Akko dissidents had founded the sizable market town of Tukulma, where he acquired a strong economic position, based on local salt deposits, which enabled him to undermine Bubawa's authority among the Fulanin Gona. While at the capital, Bubawa asked Umaru to punish Bayo for having broken away from Akko, but the emir, already afraid of appearing subservient to his benefactor, denied the request. The galadima then invited Sarkin Misau Muhammadu Manga II to assist him in reducing Tukulma, under the pretext of their jointly raiding a number of Tangale settlements. Manga accepted, and Bubawa left Gombe Abba, openly declaring himself in a state of rebellion. At Maimadi (Bauchi Emirate) Manga conferred on Bubawa the new title of Sarkin Kudun Misau ("chief of the south of Misau"), and they marched together on Tukulma—which Bubawa had promised to hand over to Manga. But the town successfully resisted their combined siege, and Manga soon went back to Misau, leaving behind some 200 cavalry to help Bubawa maintain his defiance of Umaru.

The emir now deposed Bubawa and made Bayo his galadima. He also transferred with most of the high officeholders to Tukulma, which served for nearly two years as his military command post (1899–1901). During this period Manga died, but his successor at Misau, Ahmadu, continued to exert steady pressure on Umaru by leading several raids on towns in the Akko area opposed to Bubawa and by supplying the latter with additional armed support. Probably at the instigation of the sultan, Sarkin Bauchi attempted to mediate what bade fair to expand from a well-sustained act of rebellion against an emir into a full-scale war involving two of the caliphate's member-states.[94] Each element in the dispute was, however,

94. See letters from Sarkin Bauchi Umaru to Sarkin Gombe Umaru, in "The Arabic Official Correspondence between the Emir of Gombe, Umaru, son of Kwairanga, and the Sultan of Sokoto and other Various Emirs in the Fulani Empire," NAK Bauprof,

already aware of the British advance into northern Nigeria, and of German and French activities around Chad. Hence when Bayo died in 1901 the way to reconciliation was open; Bubawa again acknowledged Umaru as his emir, and he was in turn reappointed galadima.[95]

Box 4, Nos. 154–56, 160. For additional detail on the involvement of neighboring emirates, drawn from this and similar correspondence, see Adeleye, *Power and Diplomacy,* pp. 92–93. Adeleye finds the origins of Galadiman Akko's revolt "still shrouded in mystery," and "no evidence to substantiate the claim that 'Umar had been unjust to the Galadima." The uses of oral history, especially when juxtaposed against written documents, are again suggested here.

95. For a well-documented, finely organized, and thoughtful account of European encroachment on the eastern emirates from 1894–1899, see *ibid.*, pp. 165–209.

CHAPTER 9

KATAGUM: CA. 1846–1900

ABDURRAHMAN (CA. 1846–51)

By the middle 1840s, or when Emir Dan Kauwa died in his palace, Katagum State was a recognizably unified political and administrative member of the Sokoto Caliphate. Its frontiers, particularly toward the east, may have been rather ill-defined, but its relations with neighboring emirates as well as with Bornu were on the whole peaceful, and its military position could fairly be said to have been well secured. Domestically, the Lawanawa governing elite and their immediate followers appear to have achieved a like measure of peaceful accommodation with non-Muslim chiefs who rendered them tribute (*gaisuwa*), and thus to have ensured the new state against a revival of those revolutionary conditions that had almost engulfed it some 20 and 30 years earlier.

On Dan Kauwa's death (ca. 1846) a royal electoral council is said to have referred only one name to Sokoto for consideration as his successor: Abdurrahman dan Mallam Zaki, first cousin of Dan Kauwa and sarki of Shira fief since the late emir's promotion from there to the throne of Katagum.[1] The council's decision, and the subsequent appointment of Abdurrahman by Sultan Aliyu Babba, had several notable political features. First, supreme authority in the emirate formally reverted to Mallam Zaki's immediate lineage; second, the position of a Sarkin Shira as heir apparent to Sarkin Katagum was thereby enhanced; and third, a precedent which endured for some 60 years was established in the manner of selecting a new emir.

1. The precolonial Katagum royal electoral council apparently first convened on this occasion. Then and thereafter it was called together at the death of an emir by Galadiman Katagum, who summoned, through the maidala and makama respectively,

According to present-day informants, Dan Kauwa and Wazirin Katagum Hamji were agreed that Abdurrahman—who was already well advanced in years—should, in view of his age, relative affluence, and filial tie with Mallam Zaki, have precedence over Dan Kauwa's two most qualified sons, Sarkin Gadau Kadr and Sarkin Azare Haji. If true, their understanding was undoubtedly founded on certain political realities. Excluded for three decades from the highest state office, Mallam Zaki's titled sons were unlikely to bear without open dissent or rebellion a further denial to one of them of the now-vacant throne. In a complementary sense Dan Kauwa's own titled sons could well have considered the selection of someone the age of Abdurrahman as no more than a short-term deferral of their chances to inherit the crown; they appear to have acceded gracefully to his appointment by Sokoto, perhaps on the understanding that the crown would be returned (as it was) to Dan Kauwa's line after the new emir died.

Assuming that Waziri Hamji did favor Abdurrahman, a majority of the council might have been counted upon to support his nomination. The council is said to have been guided at this time by the waziri, galadima, madaki, alkali, and liman (all of whom were Fulani but non-Lawanawa appointees of Dan Kauwa); the last two officials were, according to oral as well as Islamic tradition, eminent scholars, and Abdurrahman's reputation for learning and wisdom would likely have predisposed them to follow the waziri's lead. Of all the major central-administration officials, only Dan Kauwa's chief slave, Makaman Katagum, is reported to have actively opposed the council decision, and he fled the emirate on its approval by the sultan.

Abdurrahman's relatively short reign of six years saw few administrative changes in the emirate. He created no important titled offices, and made only three appointments to central-government positions.[2] He did, however, attempt to provide his elder brother, Ismaila dan Mallam Zaki, with a critical advantage when the next royal succession was determined by transferring him from the chieftaincy (yerima) of Chinade to that of Shira, and he replaced Ismaila at Chinade with one of his own sons.

During his first years as emir, Abdurrahman was able to pursue without distraction an active policy of raids, either slaving, punitive, or religious, along the Kata-

all other free and slave officials in the capital. Only the highest of these, however, took an active role in discussions and participated in voting, e.g., the galadima, makama, madaki, waziri, alkali, liman, and wombai. This paragraph and the next three are drawn entirely from Informants IIA: 1–5; and IIB: 1–9.

2. These were the key positions of makama, alkali, and liman. The latter two offices were filled on the deaths of their incumbents.

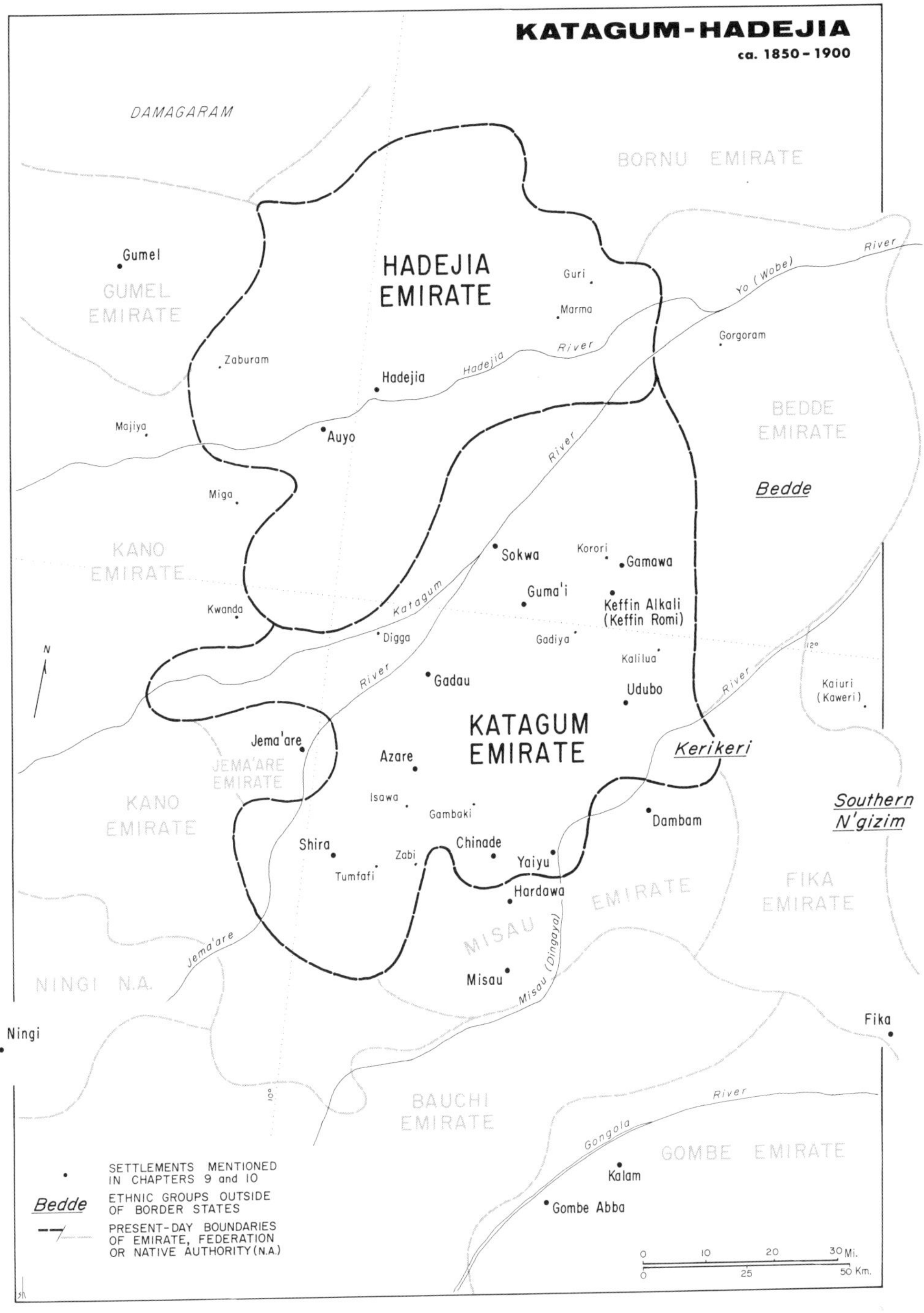
KATAGUM-HADEJIA
ca. 1850-1900
DAMAGARAM
BORNU EMIRATE
HADEJIA EMIRATE
Gumel
GUMEL EMIRATE
Guri
Marma
Yo (Wobe) River
Gorgoram
Hadejia River
Zaburam
Hadejia
Majiya
Auyo
BEDDE EMIRATE
Bedde
Miga
KANO EMIRATE
Sokwa
Korori
Gamawa
Guma'i
Keffin Alkali
(Keffin Romi)
Kwanda
Katagum River
Digga
Gadiya
Kalilua
Gadau
Udubo
Kaiuri
(Kaweri)
KATAGUM EMIRATE
Jema'are
Azare
JEMA'ARE EMIRATE
Kerikeri
KANO EMIRATE
Isawa
Gambaki
Southern N'gizim
Dambam
Shira
Zabi
Chinade
Yaiyu
Tumfafi
Hardawa
MISAU EMIRATE
FIKA EMIRATE
Jema'are
Misau (Dingaya)
NINGI N.A.
Misau
Ningi
Fika
BAUCHI EMIRATE
Gongola River
GOMBE EMIRATE
Kalam
Gombe Abba
SETTLEMENTS MENTIONED IN CHAPTERS 9 and 10
Bedde ETHNIC GROUPS OUTSIDE OF BORDER STATES
PRESENT-DAY BOUNDARIES OF EMIRATE, FEDERATION OR NATIVE AUTHORITY (N.A.)
0 10 20 30 Mi.
0 25 50 Km.

gum-Bornu frontier. The most significant politically of these expeditions was against the Southern N'gizim center of Kaiuri (Kaweri), a town which had twice broken away from Katagum, once after the death of Mallam Zaki and again on the turbanning of Abdurrahman. Kaiuri and its satellite settlements were recompelled to pay tribute to Katagum, but when Sultan Aliyu Babba was informed of this he ordered the emir to relinquish his rights there to Shehu Umar of Bornu, as a gesture of amity from the Sokoto Caliphate.[3] His other initial campaigns were to Kerikeri towns, which remained collectively the most lucrative source of fresh slaves to the northeastern Fulani states.[4] In the final three years of his reign, Abdurrahman was preoccupied with events across the northern Katagum borderlands that followed on Buhari's appointment as Emir of Hadejia. He died at the capital soon after helping Wazirin Sokoto install Ahmadu dan Sambo Digimsa in Hadejia Town.[5]

KADR (CA. 1851–68)

With the death of Abdurrahman the house of Dan Kauwa regained the crown, which has continued in its possession to the present day. Settlement of the royal succession of ca. 1851 was marked as well at the procedural level by two innovations that were to endure until 1905.[6] Members of the electoral council nominated for the sultan's consideration more than one candidate by referring to Sokoto the names of four titled *'yan sarki*: Sarkin Shira Ismaila dan Mallam Zaki; Sarkin Udubo Yusufa dan Mallam Zaki; Sarkin Yaiyu Ahmadu Jatau dan Abdurrahman (dan Mallam Zaki); and Sarkin Gadau Kadr dan Dan Kauwa. In

3. Informants IIA: 1–5; IIB: 1–9; R. G. Ramage, "Historical Notes on Katagum Division, Bauchi Province (1929–33)," NAK SNP 17/1 1139 9715; and J. M. Fremantle, "A History of the Region Comprising the Katagum Division of Kano Province," *Journal of the African Society,* XI (1911), 70. The assertion of D. J. Stenning that "by 1846 Sokoto and Bornu had reached accord over the jurisdiction of the western [Bornu] marches" and that "henceforth these territories were no longer the subject of dispute between the Fulani Empire and Bornu" might be qualified in light of events which followed there during several subsequent decades (*Savannah Nomads: A Study of the Wodaabe Pastoral Fulani of Western Bornu Province, Northern Region, Nigeria* [London: Oxford University Press, 1959], p. 68).

4. Fremantle, "History of the Region," XI (1911), 70; and Informants IIA: 1–5; IIB: 1–9.

5. See p. 139 above.

6. This paragraph and the next two are drawn from Informants IIA: 1–5; IIB: 1–9.

an apparent effort to avoid a potential imbalance of power (or at worst a civil war) between the two royal houses of Lawanawa, Waziri Hamji is said to have written Sarkin Gadau Kadr's name above the others in the council letter addressed to the sultan, and, in his own private message to Wazirin Sokoto, to have stated explicitly his preference for Kadr. Both of these practices were followed by the Waziri of Katagum during the remainder of the century.

Although Ahmadu Jatau was the eldest son of the late emir, and both Yusufu and Ismaila outranked Kadr in age, position, and administrative experience, the ensuing appointment of Kadr by Sokoto failed to produce any overt opposition from Mallam Zaki's lineal descendants. Several political circumstances may be adduced to explain their passivity. Survival of the emirate itself was in the early 1850s—as for most of the following decade—gravely threatened by the depredations of Buhari. Murray Last has pointed out that Buhari's career, "although effective in itself, shows the over-all strength of the Sokoto hegemony . . . [since] despite favorable circumstances, it spread no further."[7] It is probable that his revolt and subsequent invasions of Katagum soil would have tended far more to unite than to divide the titled *dengin sarki,* in a common defense of Lawanawa rule as much as of the principle of Sokoto's political and religious legitimacy.

With the approval of the sultan, and possibly with prior agreement of Yusufa and his supporters, Kadr at once deposed Ismaila from the chieftaincy of Shira and conferred it on Yusufa.[8] Ahmadu Jatau was transferred from Yaiyu to Gadau, a posting much nearer the capital. Thus of Kadr's three major rivals in the emirate—all of whom belonged to Mallam Zaki's house—one (exiled to Kano) was removed from the scene, another was put in line to succeed him, and the third was brought under close observation. But within a year Kadr was sufficiently secure in office to dismiss Yusufa as well from Shira and send him to live in Bauchi. He then gave Shira fief to his own younger brother, Sarkin Azare Haji dan Dan Kauwa, and appointed (at Haji's request) a junior son of Mallam Zaki to Azare. None of Kadr's sons was as yet old enough to hold more than a small town (*jeka na yika*).[9]

7. *The Sokoto Caliphate* (London: Longmans Green, 1967), p. 160.

8. The deposition of Ismaila was publicly justified on the grounds that he had been seizing young girls in Shira to serve him as concubines (rather than buying them as slaves). The decision was made officially at a meeting in Kano over which Sarkin Kano presided, when Kadr and Ismaila were on their way home from Sokoto. The sultan is said to have already been consulted by Kadr, and given his approval.

9. See above, p. 127. Kadr's appointment three years later (ca. 1855) of Berinde dan Dan Kauwa to the chieftaincy of Udubo—which then ranked second only to Shira among *'yan sarki* fiefs—would not have placed him in serious contention to suc-

The first 12 years of Kadr's reign (ca. 1851–63) are commonly described in the emirate as a time of widespread physical privation and frequent (although usually impermanent) demographic displacement. A large number of settlements were exposed to slave and cattle raids by lieutenants of Buhari, while many were sacked or burnt. Inhabitants of *jeka na yikas* often abandoned their compounds to seek refuge within the nearest walled town, and farming and animal husbandry were suspended for months at a time.[10] While *'yan sarki* and other officials appear to have remained loyal, the Jafunawa (Fulani) center of Hardawa revolted. Kadr is said to have gone there in force, and to have negotiated a peaceful accord with its part-Lawanawa chief.[11] The Lerewa of eastern Katagum solicited help from Bornu against Hadejia, and on one occasion Kadr was defeated near the Bornu frontier by two generals of the Shehu. (After Buhari's death he went there again to reassert the royal authority, but met with mixed success.)[12]

Almost the sole military successes remembered for Kadr were achieved by Adamu dan Ladan Ibiranjo, whom Abdurrahman had appointed Alkalin Katagum and whose father, a Kanuri immigrant, had been the muezzin (H. *ladan*) to Mallam Zaki. Around 1850 Adamu established Keffin Alkali (later merged with the larger town of Keffin Romi), in central Katagum, which soon came under attack by Hadejia, Bornu, and Gorgoram. Relieved temporarily of his legal duties, Adamu quickly assumed the role of Kadr's most effective military commander. He ravaged a number of towns in southeast Hadejia, western Bornu, and Beddeland, and wounded in battle Chiroman Hadejia Serkio dan Sambo Digimsa.[13]

Kadr's death at the capital ca. 1868 brought forward again four major contenders for the crown.[14] These included his three eldest surviving brothers (and sons of

---

ceed Kadr: as Sarkin Diga, Berinde had recently gone to Hadejia with most of his townsmen and sold them as slaves to Buhari. Although he went unpunished on his return, Berinde did not receive consideration from the electoral council when it met after Kadr's death.

10. Informants IIA: 1–5; IIB: 1–9; II I: 1, 25–28.

11. Informants IIA: 1–5; IIB: 1–9; and Fremantle, "History of the Region," XI (1912), 70.

12. *Ibid.*, and X (1911), 408; H. F. Backwell, "Assessment Report on Galadiman Katagum District, Sub-District of Galadima, Katagum Emirate, Kano Province," NAK SNP 7/12 3260 5205/1911; and Informants IIA: 1–5; IIB: 1–9; IIF: 2–5, 9–14, 18–20; IIG: 6–8, 11–13.

13. H. F. Backwell, "Assessment Report on Waziri District, Katagum Emirate, Kano Province," NAK SNP 7/13 3343 1433/1912; Ramage, "Historical Notes"; and Informants IIA: 1–5; IIB: 1–9; IIG: 1–3; IIIA: 1–20.

14. This paragraph and the next are drawn from Informants IIA: 1–5; IIB: 1–9.

Dan Kauwa)—Sarkin Shira Haji, Sarkin Guma'i Alhassan, and Sarkin Sokwa Abubakar—as well as Sarkin Gadau Ahmadu Jatau dan Abdurrahman dan Mallam Zaki. The electoral council was sharply divided among their respective candidacies, but Waziri Hamji placed Haji's name at the top of the list submitted to Sokoto and informed Wazirin Sokoto that Haji was his own choice.

Wazirin Sokoto Abdu Dan Nana had married a sister of Sarkin Guma'i Alhassan, and, although Haji was senior to Alhassan in both age and administrative rank, Dan Nana advised the sultan to appoint Alhassan emir. While the sultan was in process of deciding for Haji, Dan Nana replied himself to the council in a message that appointed Alhassan and bore the official seal of the Sokoto chancery. When Magajin Wazirin Sokoto reached Kano en route for Katagum, Sarkin Kano Abdullahi read the waziri's letter, detained the magaji's party, and wrote the sultan that Haji would be a far better alternative. The sultan responded that he favored Haji and sent his own representative to Katagum with a message designating him Kadr's successor. Sarkin Kano's action is said to have been motivated in turn by the fact of his daughter's marriage to Haji, although he offered in explanation of his preference the argument that Haji was a man of superior talents and breeding while Alhassan did not behave as a true *dan sarki*, often consorting with commoners and hence an unsuitable choice.

HAJI (CA. 1868–96)

With the unexpected removal of Sarkin Hadejia Buhari ca. 1863, Katagum had been relieved of a grave 10-year challenge to its constitutional integrity. When Haji assumed the crown some five years later the emirate was again at peace with Hadejia, and he was free to recommence the local jihad in those Habe communities across the northeast and eastern state boundaries which had for long successfully opposed the separate and combined assaults of Katagum, Hadejia, and Misau, as well as of Bornu. His baptismal raid, however, was directed instead against several of the more important Lerewa towns east of the capital and of Gamawa which had been constrained in the period of Buhari's ascendance to seek protection from Bornu, and had since paid tribute to the Shehus at Kukawa (although one of them, Kalilua, had allied itself with Dan Babuje of Gorgoram). After calling three times on the Lerewa chiefs to renew their allegiance to Katagum, Haji chastised them in a joint expedition with Sarkin Hadejia Haru.[15] Most of the Lerewa there chose to emigrate into Bornu, and for the next 60 years large tracts of land in the northeastern corner of the emirate remained without regular habitation.[16]

Haji also moved at once to secure his southeastern flank against increasingly troublesome Kerikeri inroads on the large fief area of Udubo and at the same time to provide his second and favorite son, Abdulkadir, with high office.[17] He did this by shifting Berinde dan Dan Kauwa from the chieftaincy of Udubo to that of Shira; transfering Ahmadu Jatau dan Abdurrahman (dan Mallam Zaki) from Gadau to Udubo; and appointing Abdulkadir first to Gadau and then (several years later) to Azare.[18] These redeployments, which did violence to no traditional pattern of royal behavior in Katagum, answered two obvious political needs of the emir. Ahmadu Jatau, a well-tested and locally renowned warrior-prince, could be entrusted with the precarious military affairs of Udubo region. (It is said that Haji was concerned as well to spare any of his sons prolonged exposure to physical danger.) Second, as none of Haji's sons yet held an important administrative post, and as he knew that Berinde would not be an attractive candidate to succeed him—either to the council or the sultan[19]—Haji put Abdulkadir in a titled position that ranked lower than Berinde's but from which he might, in view of the latter's unpopularity, be elevated directly to the throne or else follow Berinde at an earlier date in the chieftaincy of Shira. To have appointed his chosen successor as emir to the state's highest fiefholding office without first providing him a lesser one would have been considered an excessively provocative change in the accustomed procedure for selection of a new Sarkin Shira. In the event, on the death of Berinde ca. 1874, Abdulkadir was promoted to that position.

For most of his reign Haji also continued the tradition of attending, after the harvest was in and with his main officeholders, a meeting near Sokoto of all the sultan's chief lieutenants in the Fulani emirates. These visits were usually the occasion for a resumption of the Sokoto jihad against neighboring states still beyond the sultan's authority, in particular Gobir, Maradi, and Argungu. Four such campaigns are especially remembered in Katagum. One, in the time of Sultan Abubakar

15. Letter from Haji to Wazirin Sokoto Ibrahim Khalilu, NAK G.O.K. (Series), Kadcap, Box 30, No. 63; Fremantle, "History of the Region," XI (1912), 71; and Informants IIA: 1–5; IIB: 1–9; IIG: 6–8, 11–13.

16. *Ibid.*; and Backwell, "Waziri District."

17. This paragraph and the next are drawn from Informants IIA: 1–5; IIB: 1–9.

18. The chieftaincy of Azare fell vacant ca. 1870 on the death of Moman dan Mallam Zaki.

19. See p. 183, n. 9 above.

Atiku na Rabah (1873–77), was commanded by Haji and resulted in the destruction of several important towns in Gobir and the turning back of a joint Maradi-Gobir invasion. Haji again distinguished himself during an expedition against Maradi in Sultan Mu'azu's reign (1887–91).[20] But on two other campaigns, one with Sultan Ahmadu Rafa'i (1867–73) and a second ca. 1892 at Argungu, the Katagum forces sustained heavy losses at the hands of Sokoto's adversaries; the Fulani reverse at Argungu has been accounted "a disaster."[21]

An equally serious external threat emerged in the northeast quadrant of the caliphate around 1880, from the largely Habe zone between Zaria, Kano, and Bauchi emirates. Some 40 years earlier a group of mallams living in eastern Kano had refused on Qur'anic grounds to pay what they alleged was an excessive assessment of *zaka* by the emir. Emigrating across the southeast frontier of the emirate, they were soon forced to take refuge in the Ningi Highlands, 60 miles north of Bauchi City. Within several years one of the mallams, Hamza, united most of the Ningi settlements and those of other neighboring non-Muslim clans, but he was killed and his following scattered by Sarkin Bauchi ca. 1844. The surviving mallams rallied in time, and by 1880 they and their successors in Ningiland had plundered, burnt, or enforced payment of tribute—often in secret—from numerous towns in Zaria, Bauchi, and Kano.[22]

The most successful of the Ningi sarkis was Haruna, a great-grandson of one of Hamza's original band from Kano. After a series of highly profitable raids as far west as the walls of Zaria Town and well into Kano Emirate, Haruna turned ca. 1882 toward the northeast, and invaded Shira district with a large force at the end of the wet season. Haji was then on his annual tour of the emirate (preparatory to his departure for Sokoto), and learned of Haruna's arrival near Tumfafi. Although

20. This paragraph is drawn from Informants IIA: 1–5; IIB: 1–9; and Fremantle, "History of the Region," XI (1912), 71.

21. Last, *The Sokoto Caliphate*, p. 129.

22. The material in this paragraph and that which follows on the origins and nineteenth-century development of Ningi State is drawn from J. F. J. Fitzpatrick, "Assessment Report on Ningi District, Bauchi Division, Central Province," NAK SNP 10/2 1169 431p/1914; G. H. Payton, "Reorganization of Ningi District," NAK C.M.B. Prof 1, Box 34, 805 815, Vol. II; and Abdulkadir Akabi, "Notes on the History of Ningi Chiefdom" (Hausa MS, trans. Ibrahim Musa Ningi, copy in my possession, 1960). See too H. A. S. Johnston, *The Fulani Empire of Sokoto* (London: Oxford University Press, 1967), pp. 198–99. Johnston remarks: "The Ningi raids were fleeting, it is true, and inflicted no permanent damage. Nevertheless, they distracted the attention of the Fulani from the more serious dangers in the north and provided further evidence of the decline of their fighting power" (p. 199).

urged by his advisers to summon contingents from Shira, Azare, Hardawa, and Chinade, Haji decided to do battle with the relatively few men in his entourage. At the Battle of Tumfafi the Katagum party was overwhelmed by Haruna. Among those killed were Haji's sarkin yaki, galadima, madaki, and dandelma, while the wounded included Waziri Hamji; the emir himself narrowly escaped capture, but the standard given him by the sultan became a prize of war.[23]

On Haji's return to the capital he was excused by the sultan from proceeding to Sokoto, and all the surrounding emirates, as well as Bornu, dispatched gifts of fresh horses, armor, and gowns to compensate him and the Katagum officials.[24] A year or two later he enlisted the emirs of Hadejia and Jema'are in a major attempt at retaliation, but Haruna defeated their armies a few miles south of Shira. As the disorganized allies were fleeing the field, Haji with a few of his retainers fell into an ambush, and their lives were saved only by the swift intervention of Yeriman Chinade.[25] Haruna died ca. 1886; subsequent chiefs of Ningi appear to have raided in Shira district for slaves and other spoil with hardly more than token opposition.

To the east, against Beddeland and Bornu, Haji fared little better in his determination to carry forward the local jihad. Around 1869 he sent a column to support Emir Haru of Hadejia, who was marching on Gorgoram to avenge Buhari. Although a section of the Katagum force managed to scale the Bedde capital walls —a tactic for which the emirate had long been celebrated—the Fulani assault was hurled back. During the later years of Haji's long reign, and perhaps even earlier (by Kadr's time), the Bedde chiefs had occupied an ambiguous position vis-à-vis the rulers of Katagum, Hadejia, and Bornu.[26] Most of the Bedde clan groups had been welded together by one of their leaders, Babuje (d. ca. 1842), into what an

23. Informants IIA: 1–5; IIB: 1–9; II I: 1–8, 23–28; Fremantle, "History of the Region," X (1911), 416; W. F. Gowers, comp., *Gazetteer of Kano Province* (London: Waterlow, 1921), p. 31; and Ramage, "Historical Notes."

24. *Ibid.*; and Informants IIA: 1–5; IIB: 1–9.

25. *Ibid.*, and IIF: 4–6; and Fremantle, "History of the Region," X (1911), 414.

26. The data which follow on Bedde history in the nineteenth century are drawn from W. P. Hewby, "Bornu Province Monthly Reports, 1903, April–May," NAK SNP 15/1 48A; J. R. Patterson, "Assessment Report on Borsari District, Bornu Emirate, Bornu Province (1918–26)," NAK SNP 17/8 K.2041; G. C. Whiteley, "Special Report on Bedde Emirate, Bornu Province," NAK SNP 10/8 4024 209p/1920; and R. C. Campbell-Irons, "Assessment Report on Bedde District, Bornu Province," NAK SNP 10/2 1006 242p/1914. Clapperton passed through Beddeland in 1823. He observed later that its people, "although speaking the language of Bornou, and acknowledging

observer has called a "Pan-Bedde confederation," probably in response to several decades of regular demands for tribute from Bornu and the Fulani emirates alike. About 1825 Babuje had founded a new town and the first Bedde capital, Gorgoram, which, like most other Bedde settlements, was rendered nearly impregnable by its massive fortifications and, even more, its encircling swamps. Owing to a dense pattern of sizable streams that help feed the Katagum River, and which overflow on a broad front in the wet months of June through October, much of the land in present-day Bedde Emirate is inundated for at least half the year.[27] From their waterlogged redoubt the Bedde chiefs, notably the founder of Gorgoram and his son, Dan Babuje (ca. 1842–93), repelled assaults by the Hadejia emirs, al-Kanemi, Shehu Umar, and Haji; often went over to the offensive; and (as at Kalilua) were able to persuade a few of the border towns under Katagum to shift their allegiance. But whenever the Fulani raided the drier, extreme southwestern Bedde settlements, Dan Babuje sent gifts to Hadejia or Katagum.

Like his father, Dan Babuje accounted himself a good Muslim, yet when he sought permission to marry a daughter of Haji, it was denied on the grounds that no Fulani emir would countenance the joining of his line with that of a demonstrated pagan. Dan Babuje replied by launching the only remembered nineteenth-century Bedde attack on Katagum City area. He chose a moment when Haji was at Sokoto and, finding the capital gates shut, enslaved a number of persons just across the Katagum River from the capital.[28]

Immediately to the south of Beddeland, the Southern N'gizim had remained since the conquest of Shira Kingdom by Mallam Zaki in an at least nominal tribute-paying relation with Katagum, although (like the Bedde) they were often exposed to raids or exactions by slave-generals of Shehu Bornu. Soon after the failed expedition of Sarkin Hadejia Haruna to Gorgoram, Bukar Kura, a son of Shehu Umar and his principal fiefholder in the west Bornu marches, forcibly occupied

---

a kind of nominal sovereignty of the Bornuese sultan, . . . are every where regarded as a race of outlaws, whom it is incumbent on every good Mussulman, Bornuese, or Felatah, to enslave or murder" (E. W. Bovill, ed., *Missions to the Niger,* Vol. II: *The Bornu Mission, 1822–25* [1826; Cambridge: At the University Press, 1966], p. 621).

27. Of Gorgoram itself a former resident noted, "March is about the earliest one can enter dry-shod" (Whiteley, "Special Report"). And Clapperton remarked of Beddeland as a whole: "Their country is of small extent, defended by impenetrable morasses and forests, by which alone they preserve a precarious and dangerous independence" (Bovill, *The Bornu Mission,* p. 621).

28. Informants IIA: 1–5; IIB: 1–9.

the Southern N'gizim towns. Haji was again at Sokoto on the annual visit, and his resident agent there hastily agreed to have the Bornu-Katagum boundary moved farther west, to a ridge overlooking the Misau (Dingaya) River, where it remained.[29]

KATAGUM-MISAU HOSTILITIES

Political relations between the rulers of Katagum and Misau had long been hostile when, ca. 1878, Haji complained to the sultan that Sarkin Misau Sale was raiding Muslim rather than "pagan" towns in Dambam.[30] The chief source of the emirates' reciprocal enmity lay in the grant in perpetuity of extra-territorial privileges made 45 years earlier by Sultan Muhammad Bello to the house of Gwoni Mukhtar.[31] According to the terms of this apparently unique concession, the emirs of Misau were to hold certain fiscal and administrative rights in all settlements founded anywhere in the caliphate by those immigrants from the east who belonged to, or identified with, the Fellata Bornu clan groups (and their clients) which had supported the local jihad of Mukhtar and of his successor, Muhammad Manga.

A large preponderence of these new towns were established inside the frontiers of Katagum (most others being in Kano and Bauchi);[32] and while the chiefs of Katagum were invested by Sokoto with ultimate rights over allocation of farm and grazing lands within each town's precincts, adjudication of all disputes arising from this, and collection of taxes on the use of such lands (together with *zaka* and craft taxes), Misau retained full authority over the appointment and deposition

29. *Ibid.*; Fremantle, "History of the Region," X (1911), 415; and Gowers, *Gazetteer of Kano Province,* p. 31. A letter from Shehu Umar of Bornu to Sultan Mu'azu (1877–81) preserved in the Sokoto archives may well refer to this campaign and its boundary settlement; see A. D. H. Bivar, "Arabic Documents of Northern Nigeria," *Bulletin of the School of Oriental and African Studies,* XXII (1959), 333.

30. Sarkin Misau Ahmadu dan Alhaji Tafida, "Tarihin Sarakunan Misau" [History of the Emirs of Misau] (Hausa MS, copy in my possession, 1926); and Ramage, "Historical Notes." Fremantle suggests that a primary cause of this enmity was the fact that the emirs of Misau and Katagum were both referred to in the caliphate as Sarkin Bornu ("History of the Region," X [1911], 400); this inference is denied in Katagum today.

31. See p. 124 above.

32. For the location and relative size of these settlements ca. 1900, see map of Katagum Emirate ca. 1900 in end-pocket envelope.

of local chiefs, provision of public works and military defense, and other forms of taxation, including *kudin jini* (fines derived from the settlements of disputes which involved physical injury), *kudin gado* (or *rabon gado,* death duties), and—what had become far the most profitable of all sources of revenue among the Fellata Bornu—*jangali,* or cattle tithe.[33]

Acting on Haji's complaint, the sultan asked Sarkin Kano to investigate whether towns recently attacked by Sale were, in fact, Muslim.[34] They were found to contain no mosques of any kind, but Haji was unsatisfied, and when Sarkin Shira Abdulkadir proposed shortly after to marry a daughter of Sale, he was denied permission by Haji. A few months before Sale's death ca. 1886, Haji wrote Wazirin Sokoto suggesting his deposition, on the grounds that he was unable adequately either to govern the people of Misau or to obey the sultan's regulations.[35] The waziri's response is unknown, but when Sale was killed in Tangale-Waja and succeeded as emir of Misau by Muhammadu Manga II, Haji proved more successful in his lobbying to have revoked what he must have considered an undue encroachment on the Katagum royal treasury. Manga had quickly shown signs of becoming another Buhari: he quarreled with the sultan's representative after his installation over what presents should be given Sokoto, expropriated without proper warrant the estates of many of his subjects, and appeared in general to be moving toward open rebellion.[36]

Fearing that he might be deposed at the annual meeting of all emirs, Manga sent his junior brother to speak for him there. Sultan Umaru, probably in response to Manga's failure to explain in person his questionable conduct, advised the emirs of Bauchi, Katagum, Hadejia, and Kano that until he sought pardon of Sokoto they were free to collect *jangali* and to exercise full supervisory functions in Fellata Bornu towns within their domains.[37] On his way homeward Sarkin Bauchi arranged to see Manga in Shira District, where he reported the sultan's annoyance and order, and urged him to apologize at once; he assured Manga, however, that, as

33. Informants IIA: 1–5; IIB: 1–9; III: 1–8, 23–28.

34. Sarkin Misau Ahmadu, "Tarihin Sarakunan Misau"; and Ramage, "Historical Notes."

35. *Ibid.*; and Informants IIA: 1–5.

36. Official Correspondence, Various Sultans of Sokoto, NAK Sokprof, File IV, Box 25, No. 6. This letter also refers to reports that Shehu Bornu Hashim was preparing to march westward, and had sent agents ahead to facilitate his advance (Hashim took office in 1885).

37. Ramage, "Historical Notes"; Fremantle, "History of the Region," X (1911), 418–19; and Sarkin Misau Ahmadu, "Tarihin Sarakunan Misau."

a friend, he would not himself deprive Misau of any part of its regular income.[38] Soon after, Manga wrote Sarkin Bauchi to ask his intervention with the emirs of Kano, Hadejia, and Katagum, who (he alleged) were seizing his main source of revenue.[39]

It was almost certainly about this time that Sarkin Shira Abdulkadir expelled all the Misau agents (*jekadu*) in his district and enslaved the Fellata Bornu of Jalori Town.[40] These actions provided Manga a pretext for marching on Zabi, Tumfafi, and Isawa, each within 15 miles of Shira Town, Isawa being perhaps the wealthiest of all those Katagum settlements partially under Misau. Haji in turn dispatched Sarkin Azare to Isawa, Sarkin Sokwa to Zabi, and Sarkin Udubo Ahmadu Jatau to Gambaki. As the senior official now in the field, Ahmadu Jatau was charged with a joint defense of southern Katagum, but he displayed an uncharacteristic want of enthusiasm for an immediate confrontation.[41] It has been claimed that his reluctance was influenced by propaganda from Misau alleging that Haji anticipated his defeat—and possibly death—in battle, and his replacement at Udubo with a son of the emir;[42] at all events, Jatau informed Manga that he would return home if the Misau army withdrew as well. The offer was accepted, and, although minor engagements occurred for several years thereafter between Manga's lieutenants and the Katagum *'yan sarki,* more serious combat appears to have been successfully averted.[43]

Sarkin Jema'are, a relative by marriage to both Haji and Manga, at last persuaded the latter to meet Wazirin Sokoto at Kano.[44] It would seem that a message from Sarkin Kano to the waziri, reporting how the Misau *jekadu* had continued their annual collection of *jangali* in Kano Emirate, dates from this period, since it refers as well to an enclosed message from Manga that conveyed "his final decision."[45] A peaceful accord was negotiated, and the waziri announced that all extra-territorial rights awarded Misau had been restored.[46]

38. *Ibid.*
39. Official Correspondence, No. 37.
40. Sarkin Misau Ahmadu, "Tarihin Sarakunan Misau"; Informants IIA: 1–5; II I: 1–8, 23–28; and Fremantle, "History of the Region," X (1911), 419.
41. *Ibid.*; and Informants IIA: 1–5; IIB: 1–9.
42. Ramage, "Historical Notes."
43. Informants IIA: 1–5; IIB: 1–9; and Fremantle, "History of the Region," X (1911), 419.
44. *Ibid.*
45. Official Correspondence, File VII, Box 24, No. 107.
46. Fremantle, "History of the Region," X (1911), 419; and Sarkin Misau Ahmadu, "Tarihin Sarakunan Misau."

About 1895, or shortly after the Kano Civil War, Manga's leading Fellata Bornu official in Katagum Emirate, Sarkin Isawa, revolted from his authority with the open connivance of Shira and Azare. Manga was now able to secure the personal aid of Sarkin Kano Aliyu against Haji, and together they went to Isawa, razed the town, and beheaded a son of Sarkin Azare. Manga is said to have promised Aliyu a major part of any spoil they might take in the area, but following the capture of a few minor settlements Aliyu chose to reconcile Manga with Haji. Owing perhaps to the local prestige Aliyu had gained from his victory in the Kano Civil War, Haji agreed to cease interference with Misau affairs in the emirate.[47]

ABDULKADIR (1896–1905)

Haji's appointment of Abdulkadir to the chieftaincy of Shira had been designed, *inter alia,* to procure for him a commanding position when the royal succession was next determined. His subsequent appointment of Wazirin Shira Sa'idu to follow Hamji as Wazirin Katagum may have been made for that purpose as well. Endowed with an unbending and often erratic personality, Abdulkadir had marked himself out in the popular mind as unfit to assume the crown,[48] but he could be assured of Sa'idu's loyal support at the capital. His main rivals for the emirship were Haji's younger brother, Sarkin Sokwa Abubakar dan Dan Kauwa, and a descendant of Mallam Zaki, Sarkin Udubo Ahmadu Jatau dan Abdurrahman. In the years leading up to Haji's death in 1896, all three contenders acquired strong factional support from among the Katagum *sarakuna,* at both the central and local administrative levels.[49]

Ahmadu Jatau had twice been included on the slate of nominees referred to Sokoto; he now stood well above either Abdulkadir or Abubakar in length of tenure in high office, and he was far the most senior titled member of Mallam Zaki's lineage. But during the interregnum Jatau went blind, and thus became

47. *Ibid.*; H. F. Backwell, "Assessment Report on Azare District, Katagum Emirate, Kano Province," NAK SNP 7/13 3555 6249/1912; and Ramage, "Historical Notes."

48. Abdulkadir was and is referred to generally by the nickname of Gagara Dafuwa, Hausa for "impossible to cook," i.e., indigestible. He was often called to the capital by Haji and cautioned against repeating an arbitrary or Islamically illegal act performed at Shira (Informants IIA: 1–5; IIB: 1–9; II I: 1–8, 23–28).

49. This paragraph and the next are drawn (unless otherwise noted) from Informants IIA: 1–5; IIB: 1–9.

ineligible to succeed him. The electoral council therefore divided in sentiment between the partisans of Abdulkadir and those of Abubakar. Among the highest officials Abdulkadir was favored by the waziri, alkali, makama, and madaki, and Abubakar by the galadima, liman, wombai, and maidala. Hence the list submitted to the sultan contained the names of both men, together with those of two potential compromise candidates, Yeriman Chinade Muhammadu Baffa (a grandson of Dan Kauwa) and Sarkin Azare Usuman dan Abdurrahman. Although Waziri Sa'idu wrote Abdulkadir's name ahead of the rest, Sultan Abdurrahman preferred Abubakar and sent Magajin Wazirin Sokoto to Katagum with a letter appointing him.[50] On the magaji's arrival disorders broke out in the capital, and he informed Wazirin Sokoto that it would be unwise to proceed with Abubakar's installation. Probably mindful of events which had followed on similar circumstances at Kano three years before,[51] the sultan dispatched his waziri in person, with orders to have Abdulkadir turbanned instead and to have Sarkin Azare Usuman dan Abdurrahman promoted to Shira and Abubakar to Azare.[52] Thus (at the sultan's command) the eldest surviving titled offspring of Mallam Zaki's lineage was put in direct line to succeed Abdulkadir, while Abubakar, although denied the crown and a position as heir-apparent, was given what had by then become the second most important *'yan sarki* fief.[53] Abdulkadir's eldest son, Muhammadu, whom he had intended to make Sarkin Shira, received the much less important district of Sokwa—to which his father soon added a number of towns hitherto under Shira. Of the major

50. When Abdurrahman was a young man with no title, he and Emir Haji had competed for the hand of the same daughter of Sultan Umaru. The girl was married to Haji, who later divorced her, and after Abdurrahman became sultan (1891–1902) she married him. This is alleged by informants to have been the principal ground of Abdurrahman's enduring ill will toward Haji's son. Sidney J. Hogben and Anthony H. M. Kirk-Greene have observed that Abdurrahman "is widely known as Mai Kano or Danyen Kasko. The latter epithet in Hausa refers to the fact that in the same way as an unbaked pot will not hold water, so can the person thus nicknamed neither keep a confidence, nor finish properly what he undertakes. . . . Of all the Sultans, his reign was the least popular, and his incompetence brought Sokoto into disrepute and ridicule" (*The Emirates of Northern Nigeria: A Preliminary Survey of Their Historical Traditions* [London: Oxford University Press, 1966], p. 407).

51. See p. 208–9 below on the origins of the Kano Civil War.

52. Letter from Wazirin Sokoto Buhari to Sultan Abdurrahman, NAK G.O.K. (Series), Kadcap, Box 47, No. 6. For an English translation, see H. F. Backwell, *The Occupation of Hausaland, 1900–1904* (1927; London: Frank Cass, 1969), pp. 18–19.

53. In the second half of the century Azare came to surpass Udubo in rank as a major fief area.

central-administration officials who had opposed the new emir's appointment, he deposed the galadima and the liman, several fled the emirate to escape other punitive measures,[54] and the remainder were reconciled with him.

THE KATAGUM CIVIL WAR

The nine-year reign of Abdulkadir (1896–1905) was described soon after his death as "a time of good harvest and of plenty, except for the Yakin Gamawa. Even in the famine of 1903 there was enough in the markets for buyers from the south."[55] The Yakin Gamawa, or Katagum Civil War, had its genesis late in Haji's reign, when Rabeh had just conquered Bornu and was concerned to equip his new followers by reopening the major long-distance trade routes between the Chad area and Hausaland.[56] Katagum Emirate fast became a vital entrepôt for the transshipment of goods to and from Dikwa. A sizable commerce developed in the export by Kano merchants of grain, kola nuts, gowns and turbans, perfume, and especially gunpowder; in return, Rabeh's agents provided slaves, cattle, horses, salt, natron, and other traditional imports from Bornu to the caliphate. The sultan, alarmed by accounts of Rabeh outfitting an army for use against the eastern emirs with uniforms, powder, and foodstuffs obtained from their own economies, directed them to deny admission to all Bornu traders. Sarkin Kano Aliyu readily complied, but Haji equivocated, shifting the main Katagum city market 20 miles southeast of the capital, to Gamawa Town, a major stop on the Bornu-Kano high road; he also refused Aliyu's demand that any Kano merchants found using the Gamawa

54. Traditionally these included public humiliation, imprisonment, or *waso*—plundering of the official's compound.

55. Fremantle, "History of the Region," XI (1912), 71.

56. The remainder of this paragraph, and the next three paragraphs, are drawn from Informants IIA: 1–5; IIB: 1–9; IID: 1–2; IIF: 1–14; IIG: 1–14; IIK: 1–5; Ramage, "Historical Notes"; Backwell, "Sub-District of Galadima"; and Fremantle, "History of the Region," XI (1912), 63–64. British and French archival sources report that (1) trade between North Africa and Bornu was halted in the wake of Rabeh's occupation; and (2) Rabeh sought a base of commercial activity at Misau and that same year (1895) had designs on the Gombe-Adamawa region (cited in Roland A. Adeleye, *Power and Diplomacy in Northern Nigeria, 1804–1906* [London: Longman Group, 1971], p. 176).

market be stripped of their goods and the wealthier returned under guard to Kano. Two reasons have been assigned to explain Haji's failure to observe these injunctions: his growing vulnerability to punitive measures from Dikwa and the large access of revenue based on a steep rise in the amount of caravan and market tolls collected by Haji's agents along the Katagum frontiers with Bornu and Kano, and in Gamawa itself.

Aliyu renewed his demand when Abdulkadir assumed office. Apparently because he could afford less than his father to risk offending both the sultan and Sarkin Kano, Abdulkadir told Sarkin Gamawa Magaji dan Alkali Adamu to confiscate the goods of all Kano traders within his fief area. Magaji's only response was to detain the royal Katagum messenger, and when the emir wrote Sokoto that Magaji had become arrogant in his new affluence, the sultan's brother was sent to investigate. He was met at Gamawa by vehement complaints from Magaji and representatives of the four senior *'yan sarki* provincial chiefs (Sarkins Shira, Udubo, Chinade, and Azare) that Abdulkadir and Sarkin Sokwa Muhammadu were acting oppressively.[57] The sultan then summoned Abdulkadir for what he termed consultations, but, fearing dismissal if he went to Sokoto, the emir had Waziri Sa'idu go in his stead, to plead his case and laden with costly gifts. Sa'idu returned with another letter of summons and a warning from Wazirin Sokoto that Abdulkadir probably would be deposed on arrival. Yet Sa'idu, the galadima, madaki, alkali, and liman all urged him to obey, on the chance that he might thereby dissuade the sultan from such a course; they argued that for him to refuse again would leave Sokoto no alternative. The makama, wombai, and other high slave officials, together with his palace retainers (both slave and free), advised him not to proceed, but to remain at the capital and, if need be, ally himself with Rabeh; he followed their counsel, once more sending a surrogate who bore fresh gifts and a letter of apology for the sultan. The decision had already been taken, however; the provincial sarkis were instructed by Sokoto—even while the emir's deputy was enroute there—to ignore Abdulkadir and until further notice to regard Yeriman Chinade Muhammadu Baffa as the sultan's wakili (representative) in Katagum. With few exceptions, most notably at Sokwa and Hardawa, the resident fiefholders agreed.

During the late 1890s Magaji of Gamawa had acquired the strongest political

57. Muhammadu in particular appears to have been a profound source of anxiety in fief areas outside his own. Among his exploits was the looting of Zubuki (Gadau), whose chief he released only on representations to the emir from Sarkins Shira and Azare (*ibid.*, p. 65; and Ramage, "Historical Notes").

power base of any provincial lord in the emirate. His position, founded initially on the transfer by Haji of the capital's central market, had been greatly enhanced after 1894 by a large-scale migration and resettlement at Gamawa of displaced Kanuri from the Chad area and by his procurement in bulk of weapons and horses from Bornu.[58] Early in 1900 Magaji's arsenal was further augmented when several hundred armed followers of Rabeh escaped to Gamawa following Rabeh's death at Kusseri. Hence when the sultan a few months later divested Abdulkadir of authority over all the Katagum fiefholders, delegating it for the interregnum to Yeriman Chinade, Magaji, although of nonroyal and Kanuri descent, appears to have resolved on a forcible takeover of the emirship. He rode to Gadiya (12 miles southwest of Gamawa) at the head of a force that reportedly numbered some 1,000 cavalry, 1,000 archers, and 500 musketeers and was joined there by lesser columns from Shira, Azare, Udubo, and Jema'are Emirate. Before the allies could unite in turn with the yerima, they were scattered by a much smaller army under Makaman Katagum and Sarkin Sokwa Muhammadu. The yerima reached Gadiya the next day, to discover that Magaji had put up in Sarkin Gadiya's compound and arranged separate lodgings for him. Custom required that whenever two officials stayed over in the same town, the one of higher social rank lived with its chief while the other received quarters elsewhere. The yerima therefore concluded that Magaji, although a client and thus unacceptable as Abdulkadir's successor, had designs on the throne. He went back to Chinade and took no part in the subsequent struggle.

With his army disabled, Magaji now retired behind the walls of Gamawa and solicited fresh recruits and matériel from Beddeland and the Kanuri towns in Bornu. The chiefs loyal to Abdulkadir took up positions at Korori, several miles west of the town. But as each camp maneuvered for tactical advantage, news arrived that Sarkin Hadejia Muhammadu was marching on the capital, and Sarkin Sokwa, together with Abdulkadir's court officials, quickly rode back to defend it. Galadiman Hadejia had meanwhile persuaded his emir to send messages instead to Abdulkadir and Magaji offering to conciliate their dispute. Still confident of victory, Magaji declined his good offices, although he did accept reinforcements. The Katagum army then returned to Korori, and by a well-calculated strategem of plundering the countryside was able to provoke Magaji to open combat. In the

58. Gamawa Town is said to have doubled its population, and the wall to have been extended to include the new market. Fremantle adds that Magaji courted Rabeh's good will by sending him and his western lieutenants numerous gifts (Fremantle, "History of the Region," XI [1912], 64; and Informants IIG: 1–14).

second battle of Gamawa (fought a month after the engagement near Gadiya) Magaji's host was again defeated, and he himself was among the several hundred slain on both sides. Abdulkadir's lieutenants collected enormous spoil from the Bornu traders concentrated at Gamawa, but the townsmen were spared further punishment.[59] Notwithstanding, Magaji's son led most of them into Hadejia, and Emir Muhammadu wrote Abdulkadir that he would avenge Magaji by ravaging the capital.[60] Before he could act, however, the sultan (influenced perhaps by his receipt of a considerable share of the booty seized at Gamawa) announced that Abdulkadir had been pardoned and should be reacknowledged emir by all the dissident Katagum officials. Abdulkadir's political primacy in the emirate was confirmed shortly after when his main rival, Abubakar, died and he could transfer Muhammadu from the fiefdom of Sokwa to that of Azare.

59. Muhammadu sent Magaji's head to Abdulkadir in proof of his death. It was placed on a pole and centrally displayed in the capital for several months, as a deterrent to other potentially rebellious *sarakuna*.

60. The son was later stripped of his properties at Hadejia and returned to Katagum, where Abdulkadir gave him a minor chieftaincy. Sarkin Korori, a member of the traditional ruling house of Gamawa, succeeded Magaji there. Informants IIG: 1–14; and Backwell, "Waziri District."

CHAPTER 10

HADEJIA: CA. 1863–1900

HADEJIA AT THE DEATH OF BUHARI (CA. 1863)

To a far greater extent than either Gombe or Katagum emirates, Hadejia in the first half of the nineteenth century may be said to have been more an Islamic realm in the making than a unified commonwealth bound to the rest of the Sokoto Caliphate by well-tempered links of ethnic, civil, and religious identity. The Fulani sarkis of Gombe under Buba Yero, and those of Katagum under his contemporary, Dan Kauwa, had by 1845 centralized political authority in their own hands, laid the foundations of stable government, and established those institutional media essential to a general observance of Muslim doctrine and law. The case of Hadejia Emirate in this period was clearly otherwise, and the contrasts in pace of administrative growth as compared with Gombe and Katagum were just as clearly associated with differences in the relative size and the style of life of Hadejia's Fulani component.

By the late 1800s Fulani appear to have constituted about three-fifths of the adult male population in Gombe and some two-fifths of that in Katagum, while in Hadejia they are said to have formed only 15 per cent of the total.[1] There is evidence of a substantially smaller proportion of settled Fulani men in Hadejia at the close of Buhari's reign and most of these, having made the transition from the status of pastoral nomads to a more sedentary culture, still moved with their cattle outside the emirate during the long dry season of October through May.[2] The one town which had any sizable Fulani settlement in Sambo's reign (d. ca. 1848) was the capital; and even this seat of royal authority is described as having

1. See table "Ethnic Percentages," in end-pocket.
2. See p. 135 above.

then been little more than a collection of rude mud-walled compounds uniformly roofed with grass or thatch, the "palace" itself being physically indistinguishable from most other dwellings.[3] The structure of central government at Hadejia over these four decades would seem to have been equally rude in design, at least by comparison with coeval structures developed at Katagum and Gombe Abba. In outline if not in its principal functions Sambo's court might be likened to the wet-season encampment of a wealthy cattle Fulani ardo, enlarged by an accretion of free and slave retainers and different in kind only in that it included a handful of other titled officials. So too Hadejia informants can, in contrast with those of Katagum and Gombe, recall few examples of Islamic divines who lived at the capital before the late nineteenth century.

The years of Buhari's ascendance (ca. 1848–63) were, as regards the pattern of central government, a transitional period during which the number of administrative offices was doubled, estates were allocated in a well-defined manner to most of these offices, and their incumbents were enriched not only by the award of such fiefdoms but also through shares of the plentiful booty (especially in slaves) procured on Buhari's campaigns.[4] A sharp increase of affluence at Hadejia City in the 1850s was reflected in the construction of numerous slave quarters as well as of mud-roofed homes for leading officials and merchants. The royal compound grew radically in size and opulence; all of the large, rectangular flat-topped buildings of the precolonial palace area date from Buhari's time, as do most features of royal household management found at Hadejia by 1900. Yet in 1863 the emirate as a whole was even less a recognizably unified, Islamic state than it had been some 15 years earlier.

UMARU II (CA. 1863–65)

The death of Buhari and the immediate enthronement of his eldest but youthful son, Umaru, by the two highest slave officials at court had enabled Hadejia

3. Informants IIIA: *passim.*

4. This paragraph is drawn from Informants IIIA: *passim,* especially 1, 3–4, 6–7, 9–10, and 18–20 (the latter three being palace women). Heinrich Barth found in the 1850s that "tens of thousands of unfortunate people, pagans as well as Mohammadens, unprotected in their well-being by their lazy and effeminate rulers, have from the hands of Bokhari [Buhari] passed into those of the slave-dealers" (*Travels and Discoveries in Northern and Central Africa,* 3 vols. [1857–59; London: Frank Cass, 1965], I, 544–45).

to resume its position as a loyal dependency of Sokoto.[5] The Sultan's confirmation in office of Umaru soon after provided in turn the legally essential ground for an act which had disregarded most of the usual criteria in the Border States of eligibility to inherit a crown: physical maturity, an extensive entourage, a record of administrative achievement, and well-demonstrated martial prowess. Some or all of these qualifications were already possessed by two of the late emir's brothers, Chiroman Hadejia Serkio and Haru,[6] both of who at once set about to deprive Umaru of his strongest political champions—the head slaves, Sarkin Arewa Tatagana and Sarkin Yaki Jaji. Their effort was aided by the latter's intensified rivalry when Buhari died, and by a widespread public fear that in the absence of a sovereign long-experienced in the skills of war and diplomacy, Hadejia would fall victim to the aggressive attentions of Sarkin Damagaram (Zinder) or the Shehu of Bornu.[7]

On his return from a successful baptismal raid in Beddeland (ca. 1864), Umaru confronted the gravest military challenge of the entire nineteenth century to Hadejia's survival as an emirate. Tenemu of Damagaram (a sahilian province of the Bornu Empire due north of Kano) had for several decades—and often in contravention of the shehu's desire—been engaged in a largely victorious effort at annexing the kingdoms of his Fulani and Tuareg neighbors. To this end he assembled at Zinder an armory which appears to have been unique in the precolonial Central Sudan. Muskets, flints, sulphur, lead, and firing caps were imported across the Sahara from Tripoli, while at Zinder itself Tenemu introduced the manufacture of cannon, gun carriages, powder, and iron balls. When, following the death of Buhari and a disastrous campaign into Kano, Tenemu decided on the subjection of Hadejia City, he is reported to have commanded at least 6,000 musketeers and 40 cannon.[8]

Word of Tenemu's approach caused a general panic in the emirate capital. Umaru was urged by the chiefs and fiefholders to lead them in a common defense at the Hadejia-Gumel frontier, but he chose to remain in the palace with most of his retinue and high officials. Tatagana and Jaji were dispatched at the head of several thousand cavalry to Zaburam, an important border town, where they were able to delay the enemy progress long enough for Umaru to strengthen his metro-

5. See pp. 144–45 above.

6. In British records and publications Haru is more often called Haruna, but he is always referred to locally by the short form.

7. Informants IIIA: *passim.*

8. Captain Landeroin, "Du Tschad au Niger: notes historiques," in *Documents scientifiques de la mission Tilho 1905–9,* 3 vols. (Paris, 1911), II, 444–46; and M. Abadie, *La Colonie du Niger* (Paris: 1927), pp. 125–26.

politan bulwarks and lay in additional stores. Tenemu invested the city for about a month, without making either a frontal assault or an offer to negotiate its surrender. He then retired to Zinder, either in obedience to the shehu's order or because Umaru had persuaded him through gifts and his apparent readiness to endure a protracted siege. Although Tenemu returned the next year and razed the northeastern Hadejia Gizimawa center of Guri, there were no further major hostilities during the nineteenth century between Damagaram and the emirate.[9]

On a charge of intriguing to usurp the office of emir, Umaru now stripped Chiroma Serkio of his title and wealth, exiled him to Kano, and gave both to Haru.[10] Advised by the new chiroma that Sarkin Arewa Tatagana was an equal threat to his security and had been in correspondence with the shehu of Bornu, Umaru then had Sarkin Yaki Jaji murder Tatagana and appointed Jaji Sarkin Arewa. Haru soon convinced Umaru that Jaji himself was too powerful a subordinate; he therefore had him killed by another slave official, who in turn became sarkin arewa. Two more slave officeholders are said to have been marked for assassination in the same way, but Umaru at this juncture displayed strong evidence of mental derangement, and Haru was able to convince most of the court that in view of his odd behavior—no less than for their own safety—he should be deposed.[11]

Riding back from the royal farm one evening Umaru found the city gates closed

9. Informants IIIA: *passim*; Barden Rinde Muhammadu, "Tarihin Fulanin Hadeja da Mulkinsu" [A history of the Hadejia Fulani and Their Government] (Hausa MS, copy in my possession, 1953); W. F. Gowers, comp., *Gazetteer of Kano Province* (London: Waterlow, 1921), p. 23; J. M. Fremantle, "A History of the Region Comprising the Katagum Division of Kano Province," *Journal of the African Society*, X (1911), 411; and H. Richmond Palmer, in The Palmer Papers, Jos Museum Library, No. 191.

10. Informants IIIA: 1–20; Barden Rinde Muhammadu, "Tarihin Fulanin Hadeja"; and Fremantle, "History of the Region," X (1911), 410. At Kano, ex-Chiroma Serkio was soon joined by most of his clients and slaves, who managed to bring him the greater part of his cattle and other movable property. Umaru followed them to Kano, where he offered to let Serkio resettle as a private citizen at Hadejia. Serkio agreed, but when he arrived at the Hadejia River (then in flood) with his people and goods, they were ferried across, and he was denied passage. Serkio went alone to Katagum, and died there some years later (*ibid.*; and Informants IIIA: *passim*).

11. Several months after Jaji was killed Umaru fired a gun from the palace roof, a custom, dating from Sambo's time, which signaled the summoning of all warriors in town for an expedition or to defend the capital. When the army had assembled, Umaru ordered it to march toward a field near Hadejia Town where his cattle were pastured and to assault them and the herders, offering to let any soldier keep whatever spoil he might capture (*ibid.*).

on him. With Galadiman Hadejia and the new sarkin arewa he went first to the town where his maternal kin were established, and a few weeks later, joined by numerous partisans, to Zinder. Meanwhile, Haru was installed in the palace by the officials who remained at the capital. He secured the assistance of Sarkin Jema'are and together they scattered the loyalist forces of Umaru, whose restoration Tenemu had now agreed to support. Although Umaru and Tenemu entered western Hadejia several months later in strength, few towns rallied to their cause. Acknowledging the obstacles to a further advance, they marched south into Kano Emirate and plundered Miga. Umaru then asked asylum of Sarkin Kano, who gave him a place where he lived at peace with his successors at Hadejia until his death some 50 years afterward.[12]

HARU (CA. 1865–85)

Although recognized as emir by the remaining officials on Umaru's exclusion from the capital, Haru declined to assume the prerogatives and regalia of office until his position was clarified at Sokoto. He wrote Sultan Ahmadu Atiku and the waziri, who sent the latter's representative, Sarkin Rafi, to Hadejia with a letter authorizing him to enter the royal chambers but not to sit on the throne. Haru was also instructed to bring all the Hadejia officeholders to a pending annual conference of the emirs. Having supported Buhari during his long rebellion and deposed Umaru without leave from the Sultan, the officials were apprehensive of being detained or imprisoned on their arrival. They agreed to obey only after a messenger returned from Sokoto with a Qur'an upon which the Sultan had taken an oath that no harm would befall them.[13]

Tukur dan Sambo Digimsa, Buhari's younger and Haru's older brother whom the sultan had appointed Emir of Hadejia some 12 years before, now left Katagum and appeared uninvited at Sokoto with most of his followers.[14] He appealed for renewed recognition of his royal title, but Sultan Ahmadu accused him of cowardice

12. *Ibid.*; Barden Rinde Muhammadu, "Tarihin Fulanin Hadeja"; Fremantle, "His tory of the Region," X (1911), 410; Gowers, *Gazetteer of Kano Province*, p. 23; and H. Q. Glenny, "History of Certain Emirates," NAK SNP 7/10 2761 1778/1909, Vol. II.
13. Informants IIIA: *passim*.
14. Tukur had been appointed ca. 1853 on the death of his and Buhari's brother Ahmadu but had since been living at Yayari, in Katagum, which Emir Kadr gave him as a place of exile; see p. 140, n. 33, above.

in the struggle with Buhari and awarded all of his slaves, horses, and weapons to Haru on condition they be used in the service of the jihad.[15] He then turbanned Haru and appointed the new emir's eldest son, Muhammadu, Sarkin Marma, presenting him with all the symbolic ensigns of royalty but a sword, and announced that he could—like his father—don the special, hooded burnoose on each festival day. The sultan also excused Haru, who was then about 60, from attendance at future meetings in Sokoto and asked that Muhammadu come in his place.[16]

Sultan Ahmadu's uncommon grant to Muhammadu, like his ratification of the popular choice of Haru as emir, was probably influenced by several considerations of state. Hadejia Emirate had for 16 years (or since the passing of Sambo Digimsa) been the scene of sharp, often sanguinary conflict, between its *'yan sarki*; during most of this period the effective sovereign was in open, successful rebellion from Sokoto, while his successor, although loyal, had demonstrated no talent for government. After Umaru's expulsion Haru had given clear proof of fidelity to the sultan —even if his behavior toward Umaru, his immediate overlord, had been equivocal. And in favoring Muhammadu with tokens of especial regard, the sultan helped to ensure that on Haru's death (which might occur soon) there would follow a short, politically undisturbed interregnum and the accession of another obedient and experienced ruler.[17]

His age notwithstanding, Haru was to hold office about 20 years. Only the first half of his reign was occupied by an active pursuit of the jihad, and for the decade or so from ca. 1875 until his death in the palace no engagements of consequence have been recalled.

Shortly after his joint expedition with Emir Haji of Katagum against the Lerewa center of Kalilua (ca. 1868),[18] Haru mounted a far more ambitious campaign to Gorgoram, the precolonial Bedde capital. He vowed to punish the killers of Buhari and to subdue, finally, the strong coalition of non-Muslim Bedde towns on Hadejia's eastern flank with Bornu. The second of these goals, although fully consonant with Islamic teaching, had another and perhaps a still stronger motiva-

15. Informants IIIA: *passim*. Several members of this group assert that Haru and Tukur were each asked separately by Wazirin Sokoto if he would accept the sultan's appointment of his rival; Tukur did not reply, but Haru said that Islam required the acceptance of any choice, even a woman, made by the amir al-muminin.

16. *Ibid.*

17. It may be that his entitlement of Muhammadu as Sarkin Marma also avoided an awkward constitutional problem; in so doing, he tacitly recognized Buhari's unauthorized incorporation of Marma Emirate within Hadejia.

18. See pp. 185–86 above.

tion. Hadejia City was throughout the late decades of the nineteenth century the principal entrepôt for commodities shipped between Kano and Bornu.[19] Bedde chiefs who rose to power in the marshlands which separated Bornu and the caliphate had since the 1830s extracted heavy tolls from caravans moving across their frontiers with Hadejia. Long-distance traders in Hadejia appealed to Haru for relief, while the emir himself was unable to levy as high a duty on certain imports as he might have wished lest their passage be diverted to Zinder or Gumel.[20] Thus a clear economic as well as religious and political need existed to chastise or conquer the "Pan-Bedde Confederation." Haru summoned all his major fiefholders, but the Hadejia army was crushed near Gorgoram by Sarkin Bedde Dan Babuje and a number of its leaders slain. For the remainder of the nineteenth century an unofficial concord prevailed between Hadejia and Gorgoram, with only Bornu hazarding a major effort to reduce the Bedde.[21]

Haru's defeat and the loss of several of his key officials soon contributed to a fresh confrontation with a far-western vassal of Bornu. The Muslim kings of Gumel, a state founded in the mid-1700s between Damagaram and Hadejia by Habe immigrants from Kano, had since 1804 maintained a precarious independence of Fulani rule by accepting the patronage of Bornu.[22] Around 1871–72 Sarkin Gumel Abdullahi was emboldened to challenge Haru, allegedly by a promise of the shehu that if successful he would be allowed to incorporate Hadejia as part of his realm.[23] Abdullahi may also have anticipated that following hard on the Bedde victory, a second Hadejia reversal might encourage more long-distance traders to concentrate at Gumel. He is said to have sent Haru a message which noted that Tenemu had encamped 40 days with impunity outside his capital, and warned Haru that Gumel's power exceeded that of Damagaram; either Hadejia must

19. Informants IIIA: 1–17; and H. M. Brice-Smith, "Assessment Report on Hadejia Town, Kano Province," NAK SNP 10/5 2847 181p/1917.

20. Informants IIIA: 1–17.

21. *Ibid.*; Gowers, *Gazetteer of Kano Province,* p. 23; and Fremantle, "History of the Region," X (1911), 414. Among the *sarakuna* who fell in this battle were Sarkin Auyo and Shamakin Hadejia. About 1882 Shehu Bukar ravaged a number of Bedde settlements (*ibid.,* p. 415).

22. *Notes on the Tribes, Provinces, Emirates and States of the Northern Provinces of Nigeria, Compiled from Official Reports of O. Temple,* ed. C. L. Temple, 2d ed. (1922; London: Frank Cass, 1965), p. 482; Gowers, *Gazetteer of Kano Province,* p. 25; J. A. Burdon, *Historical Notes on Certain Emirates and Tribes (Nigeria, Northern Provinces)* (London: Waterlow, 1909), p. 46; and Sidney J. Hogben and Anthony H. M. Kirk-Greene, *The Emirates of Northern Nigeria: A Preliminary Survey of Their Historical Traditions* (London: Oxford University Press, 1966), pp. 355, 357.

23. Glenny, "History of Certain Emirates."

submit, or the Gumel horses would urinate on its palace grounds. Haru replied that both he and Abdullahi were given their kingdoms by Allah, Who enjoined acts of war between good Muslims.[24] In the event, Abdullahi's invasion proved abortive and a disaster: he died fighting at Zaburam (the border town where Umaru's vanguard had bought precious time against Tenemu's advance), and Haru's prestige in northeast Nigeria was restored.[25]

For the next several years Haru conducted a series of highly profitable raids in Kerikeriland. About 1875 he withdrew on grounds of ill health from personal leadership of the local jihad, entrusting this burden to Muhammadu, to whose title of Sarkin Marma he now added that of Wazirin Hadejia. The office of chiroma had been promised by Haru to still another of Sambo's sons, Maina Adamu, in exchange for his active support when Umaru was exiled. Haru failed to honor this pledge, Adamu exiled himself to Katagum, and the position—traditionally conferred on the royal heir-apparent—remained vacant throughout Haru's reign; it was not awarded Muhammadu partly in order to placate the faction that Adamu left behind in the capital and partly because Muhammadu already held a title having an equal if not superior historical importance.[26]

Although Sultan Ahmadu Atiku had publicly signified his wish that Muhammadu follow Haru as emir, the latter's next eldest son, Abubakar, soon established a rival claim on the succession.[27] With Haru's physical decline Abubakar drew strong backing from those officeholders who, for one reason or another, disapproved of the choice of Muhammadu. The contest was sharpened by a fundamental cleavage of interests between sarkin arewa, Muhammadu's *uban daki* (patron), and Galadiman Hadejia, Abubakar's *uban daki*—respectively the foremost slave and free court officials. Lacking a title and junior in age, Abubakar through Galadiman Hadejia seized upon an event at Sokoto in a vain effort to replace Muhammadu in their father's esteem. During the mid-1870s Muhammadu won a critical victory for Sultan Abubakar Atiku in a campaign against Maradi and was dignified with the honorific title of Sarkin Yakin Sarkin Mussulmi ("Leader in War of the Comman-

24. Informants IIIA: 1–17; and Barden Rinde Muhammadu, "Tarihin Fulanin Hadeja."

25. *Ibid.*; Informants IIIA: 1–17; Fremantle, "History of the Region," X (1911), 413; Glenny, "History of Certain Emirates"; and Gowers, *Gazetteer of Kano Province,* p. 23.

26. Informants IIIA: 1–17; and Barden Rinde Muhammadu, "Tarihin Fulanin Hadeja."

27. This paragraph and the next two are drawn from *ibid.*; and from Informants IIIA: *passim.*

der of the Believers"). Writing from Sokoto, Galadiman Hadejia misinformed Haru that Muhammadu had been designated emir in his stead and that he was resolved to send Haru into exile. There is evidence that the emirs of Kano and Katagum, alarmed by Haru's progressive enfeeblement and the prospect of Bornu or Damagaram profiting by another succession crisis at Hadejia, each wrote from Sokoto as well that Muhammadu was appointed emir.

The sultan is reported to have told Sarkin Kano Abdullahi to give Muhammadu one million cowries when they reached Kano, in further appreciation of his services against Maradi. Abdullahi doubled this figure on their arrival, and Muhammadu outfitted his entourage with fresh horses, clothing, and weaponry from Kano market. Unaware that Haru was all but convinced of an act of betrayal, Muhammadu sent him word of his impending return and of the purchases made. Haru posted all the warriors left at Hadejia at the palace gate, rode alone to the eastern city wall, and remained there while Muhammadu's party reentered the city from the southwest. Muhammadu was informed at once of these dispositions and concluded (correctly) that his father was prepared to flee on hearing the sounds of a struggle in front of the palace. He therefore rode himself unescorted through town, dismounted at Haru's feet, and did homage.

Haru lived on as emir another 10 years or so, and died ca. 1885 in his palace. No less prolonged was the competition of the two eldest *'yan sarki* and their factions to secure popular favor by dispensing gifts. Abubakar's adherents were roughly identifiable with those officials who lived on the eastern side of town, and Muhammadu's with those on the west. The first of these groups was not informed of Haru's death until the second had placed Muhammadu on the throne and proclaimed him emir to the public.

MUHAMMADU (CA. 1885–1906)

A new civil war at Hadejia was narrowly avoided by Muhammadu's possession of three powerful though symbolic assets: the palace, seniority in age and experience, and preferment by several successive sultans of Sokoto. Residence in the royal chambers conferred the shadow if not the substance of royal authority; convention afforded him, as the oldest and only titled *dan sarki,* a claim on the crown superior to that of his brother; and—what may have been the most efficacious advantage of all—Sultan Umaru was unlikely to condone the reversal of a *fait accompli* which had enthroned at Hadejia a favorite of the Sokoto court.

Muhammadu was, furthermore, already past 60, and Abubakar's following could hope for a second, higher chance of success in the near future.

But, as his father had done, Muhammadu ruled some 20 years. During the first two he established effective command of the local jihad by raiding extensively in Kerikeriland as far south as the borders of Fika. Then, having promoted the image of a vigorous longevity, he appointed his eldest son, Sambo, to the long-vacant office of Chiroman Hadejia and stripped Abubakar of all his wealth. With a single horse and servant, Abubakar went immediately to Katagum, where his full-sister was married to Emir Haji, but left voluntarily after Muhammadu threatened an attack if he was not expelled.[28]

HADEJIA AND THE KANO CIVIL WAR

The selection as sultan in 1801 of Abdurrahman ("Danyen Kasko"—"unbaked pot") and the death of Sarkin Kano Muhammad Bello in 1893 led directly to severe political disorders in Kano Emirate which involved Hadejia as well as Sokoto. Usually referred to as the Yakin Yusubenchi, the Kano Civil War of 1893–95 strained the constitutional fabric of the caliphate and divided loyalties over much of northeast Nigeria.[29]

Bello's favorite son, Galadiman Kano Tukur, had secured the good will of Sultan Abdurrahman by his role in a battle with Argungu, and his position as heir-apparent was strengthened when Bello sent Abdurrahman special gifts.[30] In the late summer of 1893 Wazirin Sokoto Bukhari arrived at Kano, probably en route

28. *Ibid.;* Barden Rinde Muhammadu, "Tarihin Fulanin Hadeja"; Gowers, *Gazetteer of Kano Province,* p. 23; and Fremantle, "History of the Region," XI (1912), 74. Abubakar died in Kano City in the 1920s.

29. The roots of this conflict have been traced in recent scholarship to the length of Sarkin Kano Abdullahi's reign (1855–83), which enabled several of his titled sons to acquire large followings and considerable wealth by the time of his death. The sons accepted the appointment by Sokoto of Abdullahi's brother Muhammad Bello (1883–93) as his successor but looked forward to a restoration in power of their father's line after Bello died. See Denis Murray Last, *The Sokoto Caliphate* (London: Longmans Green, 1967), pp. 134–35; and Roland A. Adeleye, *Power and Diplomacy in Northern Nigeria 1804–1906* (London: Longman Group, 1971), pp. 97–103.

30. Last, *The Sokoto Caliphate,* p. 135; and Hogben and Kirk-Greene, *Emirates of Northern Nigeria,* p. 203.

to mediate the Katagum-Misau dispute.[31] Finding the emir on his deathbed, he remained there until Bello died. At Abdurrahman's direction but against his own better judgment, the waziri then turbanned Tukur. Yusufu, Tukur's cousin and chief rival for the crown, at once left the capital with his own brothers and many of the titled officeholders.[32] Yusufu pitched a war camp a few miles east of Kano, and is reported to have asked armed assistance from the sarkis of Damagaram, Gumel, and Ningi—all states hostile to the caliphate.[33]

According to a later Wazirin Sokoto, he also contacted Muhammadu and, after Waziri Bukhari declined an offer of aid by Hadejia, went there in hopes of enlisting Muhammadu in his cause. The waziri followed, and Muhammadu urged him either to replace Tukur with Yusufu or expect a sanguinary contest for the Kano succession. Bukhari pleaded that he was no more than a servant of the sultan, and to accede would put him in a state of rebellion.[34] Muhammadu's posture at this stage appears to have been equally ambivalent: although he sided with Yusufu he would not risk an act of defiance of Sokoto by giving Yusufu armed support. Murray Last has observed that since Abdurrahman's appointment of Tukur "was of doubtful justice as well as being unrealistic, he found little sympathy among the Emirs by whom alone his decision could have been enforced."[35]

Waziri Bukhari's own account of his conference with Muhammadu varies in only one major detail, its location, which he places at Gunduawa, a town close to Yusufu's war camp. Bukhari adds, however, that Muhammadu agreed to have one

31. See p. 192 above. "When I entered Kano city I sent my messenger to Sarkin Bornu [i.e., the emir of Misau or of Katagum] to let him know of my arrival in Kano, and to say that I would come up to him when I left Kano" (Wazirin Sokoto Muhammadu Bukhari, "The Tukur Revolt," Arabic MS, trans. Roland Adeleye, NAK Kadcap, Box 2, No. 30).

32. *Ibid.*; and Last, *The Sokoto Caliphate,* p. 135.

33. *Ibid.*

34. Wazirin Sokoto M. Junaidu, *Tarihin Fulani* [History of the Fulani] (Zaria: Gaskiya Corporation, 1957), pp. 62–66.

35. *The Sokoto Caliphate,* p. 134. Letters from Waziri Bukhari to Muhammadu of Hadejia, asking him to dissuade or prevent Yusufu from his acts of "oppression" and "injustice," have survived (Official Correspondence, Various Sultans of Sokoto, NAK Sokprof, File II, Box 25, No. 13; and G.O.K. [Series], Kadcap, Box 30). Muhammadu's position of studied ambivalence was shared by other concerned emirs, who followed a policy that has been called one of "practical neutrality," offering at most a "placid compliance" with Sokoto and "pious wishes for a change of heart" in Yusufu's camp. The lesson drawn by Adeleye from this war is "the powerlessness of the Caliph to enforce a whim considered unpopular and unjust by the emirates. . . . The Yusuf revolt succeeded because the Caliph's cause won no deep sympathies or support . . . and the emirates tacitly supported Yusuf" (*Power and Diplomacy,* pp. 100, 102).

of his messengers go with the waziri's to the sultan and to return home with the Hadejia forces, leaving Yusufu behind; he also describes how after the conference Muhammadu sought to prevent an assault on Kano City by Yusufu, and, when some of the Hadejia troops were killed by Yusufu in the process, Muhammadu accused him of "treacherous and hypocritical" behavior. From other evidence it seems clear that Muhammadu chose at this point to adopt a position of careful neutrality in the Yakin Yusubenchi, and he remained at Hadejia until it was ended about a year later.

In the summer of 1894 Yusufu died, and a brother, Aliyu, took over command of his faction. Within several months Aliyu had driven Tukur from the capital, and in March, 1895, Tukur was killed in battle. Aliyu then sent to Sokoto asking forgiveness; at Kano, Bukhari installed him as emir and wrote all the eastern emirates of his pardon by the sultan.

Prior to his conference with Bukhari, Muhammadu is widely reported to have met with Yusufu and been offered the fertile eastern Kano provinces of Miga, Kwanda, and Majiya in exchange for his active support against Tukur. Muhammadu accepted, and despite his subsequent withdrawal from the struggle he claimed possession of these lands after Aliyu took office on the ground that he had provided Yusufu's party significant diplomatic service by interceding with Bukhari and the sultan. Aliyu refused to acknowledge this claim as valid, and for the next seven years (1895–1901) there were frequent skirmishes and punitive raids along the Hadejia-Kano marches, which sometimes engaged both Muhammadu and Aliyu in person. But as each emir was determined to prevent a more serious collision, the conflict never enlarged into full-scale war.[36]

Meanwhile, caravan trade across Hadejia Emirate was severely affected; Muhammadu could ill afford to meddle with Kano merchants using the markets under his control (and is said to have threatened to execute whoever did molest them), but long-distance traders from Hadejia were made unwelcome in Kano, and those who traveled there anyway had to go via Shira or Gumel.[37] Since Hadejia's affluence depended in good part on its geographic placement vis-à-vis Kano and Bornu, it is doubtful that Muhammadu gained much by his exertions to keep the disputed provinces. And it seems likely that a central cause of the prosperity of

36. Fremantle, "History of the Region," XI (1912), 62–63; Glenny, "History of Certain Emirates"; Gowers, *Gazetteer of Kano Province*, p. 23; and Informants IIIA: 1–17.

37. *Ibid.*; and Fremantle, "History of the Region," XI (1912), 63.

Gamawa Town in the late 1890s would have been the preference of Rabeh's agents for trading in Katagum rather than Hadejia Emirate.[38]

Reference has been made to Muhammadu's well-founded anxiety in 1897–98 that Rabeh was poised to strike westward from Dikwa and invade Kano through Hadejia, Katagum, or Damagaram, and to the desertion earlier of Gorgoram by Mai Duna, the paramount Bedde chief, at the approach of an advance Bornu column.[39] Rabeh's lieutenant had then appointed a brother of Duna to rule at Gorgoram, while Muhammadu gave Duna refuge and, jointly with Emir Haji of Katagum, tried unavailingly to restore him by force of arms.[40] When a year later Duna died, the fear of a massive attack on the Border States region had just receded. Muhammadu could now resume his forays into eastern Kano and himself threaten Haji's successor with an attack on the Katagum capital (1900).[41]

CENTRAL GOVERNMENT IN LATE-NINETEENTH-CENTURY HADEJIA

We have seen that a formal system of delegating certain royal prerogatives in Hadejia was inaugurated by Sambo Digimsa (ca. 1808–48), but that it acquired the most typical feature of central government in the Border States—administration via a titled cadre of fiefholders—only during the time of Buhari.[42] The reasons for this relatively slow growth of a more complex and rational mode of emirate-wide organization have been outlined; the shape it assumed after 1860 was prefigured in those changes introduced by Buhari in the course of the previous decade.

There is evidence from several different sources that a number of the Hadejia officeholders enjoyed between 1850 and 1863 an unprecedented access of wealth, especially in the form of enslaved prisoners taken on Buhari's campaigns to Muslim and Habe communities alike.[43] At the same time these campaigns, and the militant response they often provoked, would have generated a greater diffusion of political

38. See p. 195 above.
39. See p. 173 above.
40. Informants IIIA: 1–17; and Fremantle, "History of the Region," XI (1912), 74.
41. See p. 198 above.
42. See p. 200 above.
43. Informants IIIA: 1–17; and see p. 200 above.

authority as the aggressive and defensive concerns of Hadejia Emirate were increased. The fact that all major state offices created in this period had a primarily martial character is (in light of other data) of less enduring significance than Buhari's appointment of slave captains and his attachment of fiefdoms to each of them. For while the grants of such high offices may well have been prompted in part by a wish to award his most reliable and effective warriors the honor of prestigeful titles, the attendant grant of estates enabled him—and subsequent precolonial emirs—to govern their overwhelmingly non-Fulani provinces through a corps of officials all but one of whom were titled slaves. Perhaps the most notable dividend which this arrangement conferred on Haru and Muhammadu was the relative absence of competitive domestic loci of power in Hadejia. Late-nineteenth-century emirs of Gombe often were threatened with subversion of their authority by prominent fiefholders either of royal descent (and thus eligible to replace them) or who represented large nonroyal Fulani clan groups that might, if provoked, break away from the crown and be recognized at Sokoto as forming autonomous polities of the caliphate.[44] In Katagum, the distribution of important fiefdoms among *'yan sarki* had led even earlier to the establishment of regionally based centers of rival political influence and by 1900 had given rise to more than one civil crisis. Haru and Muhammadu both experienced internal dissent or opposition while they held the emirship, but that none of their high officials or co-descendants from Sambo appears to have rebelled is firm evidence of how effective the principle of devolving authority upon titled slaves proved to be.

After Buhari the manifest role of *'yan sarki* in public life was confined to the exercise of a single office, that of Chiroman Hadejia.[45] But since (as the example of Abubakar demonstrates) nonpossession of a title did not bar a *dan sarki* from legitimate pursuit of the crown, Haru adopted another aspect of the *uban daki* systems already found at Katagum and Gombe Abba. He sent each of his sons at about age seven to live with one or another of the leading fiefholders in the capital. As at Gombe Abba, the *uban daki* performed as a guardian of the young prince in his care: he fed and clothed him, arranged his first marriage, and then gave him a compound. Thereafter he served the *dan sarki* as a chief confidant, adviser, and channel to the royal presence. He also made him the major link (*babban jekada*) between the staff of deputies to his wealthier towns and himself.

44. Recollections of how the Fulani Kiri founded Muri Emirate after seceding from Buba Yero's authority are still green among older informants in Gombe; see p. 100 above.

45. This paragraph and the next three are drawn from Informants IIIA: 1–17.

About one-fifth of all remembered Hadejia settlements at the end of the nineteenth century were assigned in this way to *'yan sarki* by their patrons, and these provided the adult princes with their main source of income. The chain of command leading upwards from such towns can be summarily represented as follows: town head—*jekada—dan sarki—uban daki—emir.*

As in Gombe and Katagum, the level of administrative authority at which a given issue would be resolved was, broadly speaking, determined by the seriousness or scope of its political resonance. But where in those emirates a wide range of public disputes and questions of appropriate social conduct was often adjudicated in provincial courts or, less formally, by local mallams, even during Muhammadu's reign there was only one Muslim judge, the Alkalin Hadejia, and a handful of other men trained in Islamic precepts before whom a legal action might be brought under canon law (the *Sharī'a*).[46] Two important correlates of this relative weakness of an institutionalized Islam were a disproportionate amount of oppression (*zalunci*)—seizure of property (*wasau*), unjust fines, and similar corrupt behavior—on the part of Hadejia officials and the absence of clerical influence on the choice of a new emir.

Although Haru appointed Muhammadu Wazirin Hadejia, this title, second only to the sovereign's at Katagum and Sokoto, went unemployed again after Haru died. Yet while he and Muhammadu continued Buhari's practice of relying predominantly on titled slaves to oversee the operations of state government,[47] the

46. Haru was both a *mallamin al-Kur'ani* and a *mallamin ilimi,* having studied at Misau after Buhari took power. He is said to have been the first emir of Hadejia to send his children to Islamic schools and to give active encouragement to the founding of mosques and training of teachers in the emirate. Until his reign the capital Friday mosque was a large hut built of grass mats lashed together with rope and supported by wooden pillars; he erected one made entirely of mud-brick. The only other Friday mosque of this construction in Hadejia was at Auyo. Both Katagum and Gombe emirates had at least a half-dozen each by the mid-nineteenth century.

47. A common explanation today of why Hadejia was peculiar among the Border States in the great power held there by slave officials is of interest as another variant on the kind of "mythical charters" found operative in a number of non-Western societies. It is said by informants that when Sambo Digimsa was preparing to leave Hadejia to secure a standard from Sheikh Usuman, all his brothers declined to join him on the ground that they already had enough wealth. He arrived at Usuman's compound with only his slaves and reported his brothers' excuse. The Shaikh then asked that everyone pray for the slaves of Hadejia, prophesying that henceforth they would be masters of free men. In fact, it seems that none of Sambo's appointments to high central office were made from a slave lineage; those titled officials remembered today (nine altogether) were of *dengin sarki* or client status. See above, p. 134, n. 8.

highest subordinate emirate office came to be that of Galadiman Hadejia, filled in their time by leaders of a free Auyakawa lineage. The galadima served both emirs as a *vizier* in the classical sense recommended by Shaikh Usuman dan Fodio;[48] he was Haru's chief councilor at court, and his precedence of rank was clearly manifest in the ceremonial codes of the palace. Under Muhammadu the galadima was in fact a less significant personage than several other titleholders, but the office itself retained an at least formal pre-eminence.

That none of the high officials of nonroyal descent was a Fulani would seem to confirm the impression conveyed by informants that until the late nineteenth century few year-round Fulani settlements were founded in the emirate and that most of these were hamlets composed of one or two simple or compound families who socioeconomic interests continued to center on the care and increase of their cattle. Emirs before Muhammadu are said frequently to have expropriated at will the livestock and other possessions of nomadic Fulani bands which made wet-season camps in Hadejia. Instead, Muhammadu encouraged Fulani residence on a much wider, more permanent scale by refraining from such acts of oppression, and a number of Fulani towns were established in his reign, particularly south and west of the capital. It is likely that even without the imposition of foreign rule in 1903, the ethnic character of central government at Hadejia by 1960 would have been far closer to that of Katagum and Gombe.

48. See p. 100 above.

APPENDIXES

APPENDIX I

GOMBE EMIRATE

MAJOR 'YAN SARKI APPOINTMENTS

	EMIR	YERIMA	TAFIDA	DAM BURAM	SANTURAKI
ca. 1841	(Suleimanu/BY) (BY)	Kwairanga/BY (BY)			
1842					
1843	[Kwairanga/BY]	[Bello/MK (MK)]			
1844			Zailani/MK (MK)		Hassan/MK (MK)
1845					
1846					
1847					
1848					
1849					
1850		Zailani/MK (MK)	Hassan/MK (MK)	Tukur/MK (MK)	Tukur/MK (MK)
1882	[Zailani/MK]	Hassan/MK (Zailani)	Umaru/MK (Zailani)		Vacant
1883					
1884					
1885					
1886					
1887					
1888	[Hassan/MK]	Tukur/MK (Hassan)		[Tukur/Hassan (Hassan)]	
1889					
1890					
1891					
1892					
1893					
1894					
1895	[Tukur/MK]	(Umaru/MK (Tukur)) Jalo/MK (Tukur)	Vacant		
1896					
1897					
1898	[Umaru/MK]		Gabdo/MK (Umaru)	Sarki/Umaru (Umaru)	Kwairanga/Umaru (Umaru)

( ) Deposed
[ ] Died in office

/ Followed by father's name

BY = Buba Yero
MK = Muhammadu Kwairanga

Name in parentheses below that of dan sarki: Emir who appointed him to that office

APPENDIX II

KATAGUM EMIRATE

MAJOR 'YAN SARKI APPOINTMENTS

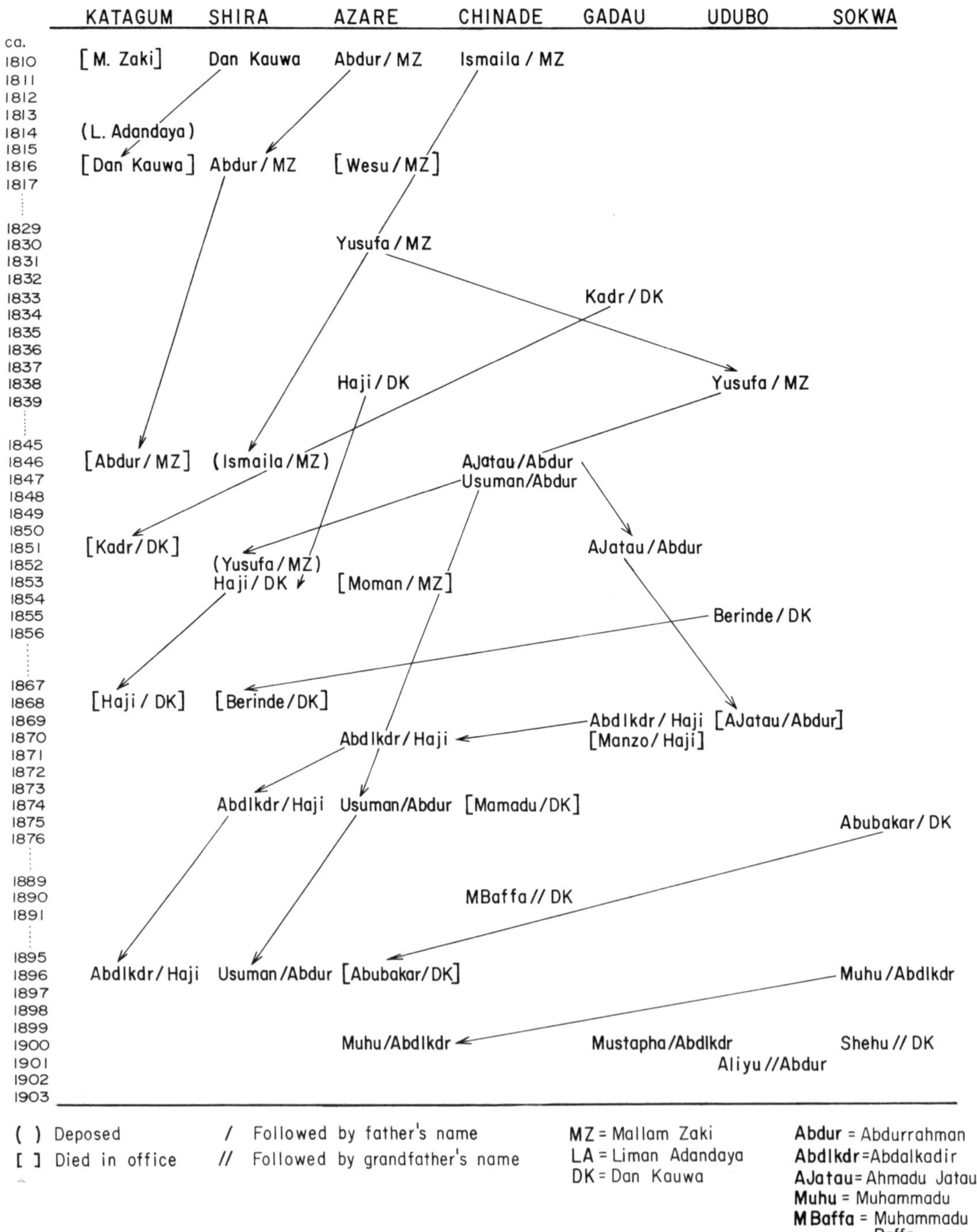

APPENDIX III

DESCENDANTS OF ARDO ABDUA

MENTIONED IN THE TEXT

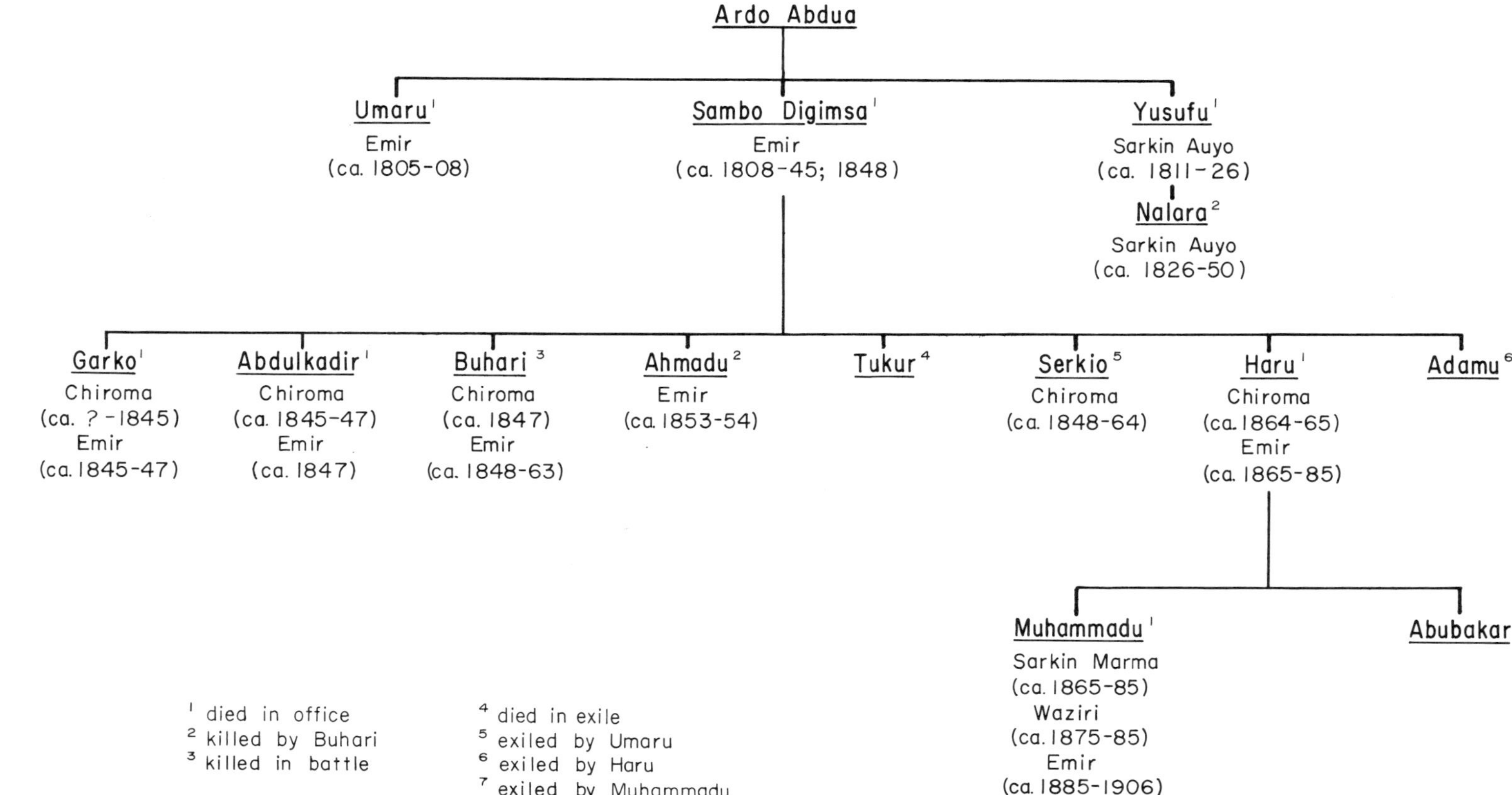

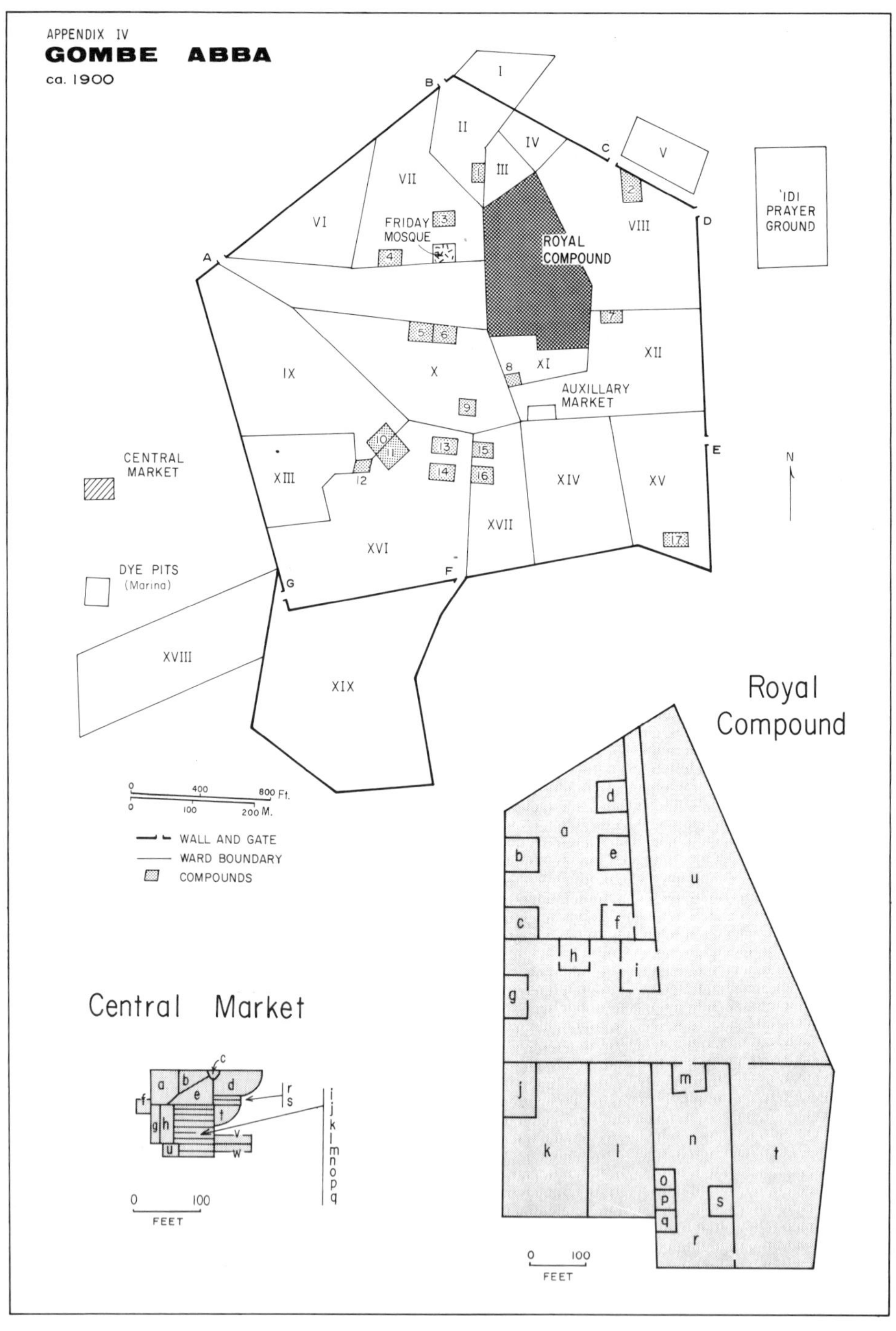

APPENDIX IV
GOMBE ABBA
ca. 1900
I
II
III
IV
V
VI
VII
VIII
IX
X
XI
XII
XIII
XIV
XV
XVI
XVII
XVIII
XIX
A
B
C
D
E
F
G
FRIDAY MOSQUE
ROYAL COMPOUND
'IDI PRAYER GROUND
AUXILLARY MARKET
CENTRAL MARKET
DYE PITS (Marina)
N
0 400 800 Ft.
0 100 200 M.
WALL AND GATE
WARD BOUNDARY
COMPOUNDS
Royal Compound
Central Market
0 100
FEET

APPENDIX IV
KEY: GOMBE ABBA (CA. 1900)

Wards (unguwoyi;
sing. *unguwa)*

I. Ung. Magi (1)
II. Ung. Magi (2)
III. Ung. Sengo
IV. Ung. Wulgu
V. Ung. Toloyel
VI. Ung. Shagale
VII. Ung. Tara
VIII. Ung. Hina
IX. Ung. Walama
X. Ung. Janafulu
XI. Ung. Puya (Palace)
XII. Ung. Malle
XIII. Ung. Dabe
XIV. Ung. Gona
XV. Ung. Siratiwo
XVI. Ung. Kanoma
XVII. Ung. Bardo Fittinder
XVIII. Ung. Daulewo (Dauleri)
XIX. Ung. Bardo Fittiyasi

Gates (kofofi; sing. kofa)

A. K. Madi
B. K. Tara
C. K. Wulgu
D. K. Hina
E. K. Siratiwo
F. K. Bardo Fitti
G. K. Kanoma

Compounds (gidaje; sing. gida) of high officials

1. G. Sarkin Magi
2. G. Santuraki
3. G. Madaki
4. G. Magajin Gari
5. G. Waziri
6. G. Turaki
7. G. Ardo Maituta (Hina)
8. G. Chiroma
9. G. Dam Buram
11. G. Ardo Walama
12. G. Ajiya
13. G. Sarkin Dabe
14. G. Tafida
15. G. Yerima
16. G. Alkali
17. G. Ardo Na'i
18. G. Liman

Miscellaneous

10. Auxiliary market

Royal-Compound (fada) Divisions

a. Open space *(fili)*
b,d,e,f. Rooms of Kwairanga's four wives; later emirs lodged their wives with one or another of their concubines
c. *Soron yini;* round mud-walled and roofed room with cupola top, to provide a shaded quarter in the hot season
g. *Soron Ajiya*; waiting room of Ajiyan Gombe
h. Quarters of Salaman Sarki and Sintali; also waiting room of Turaki and the *yam bindiga* (musketeers)

i. *Soron Fulanin Mata*; quarters for wives of deceased emirs
j. Quarters of Sarkin Gida
k. Quarters of Kachellan Tumbe, Barde, Sarkin Zegge, Baraya, Dan Rimi, Garkuwa, Korofi, Mabudi, Shamaki, and Sarkin Rafi
l. Quarters of Sarkin Dawaki, and royal stable
m. Entrance hut (*soro*; pl. *soraye*) to o,p, and q; also quarters of Jekadiya
n. Open space
o,p,q. *Turakar sarki*; royal bedrooms
r. Grave of Modibbo Bubba Yero
s. Entrance hut to o,p, and q
t. Quarters (huts) of royal concubines (*kawarakwarai*); the southern half was given to the *'yan turaka,* or younger, more favored women; Kwairanga is said to have had about 100 concubines; Zailani, 65; Hassan, 60, and Tukur 45; each emir had four wives
u. Open space; also quarters of Buma, the concubine in charge of all others belonging to Emirs Zailani, Hassan, Tukur, and Umaru

Central-Market Divisions

a. Sweets (*alewa*) and honey (*zuma*)
b. Wrestlers (*'yan kokawa*) and dancers
c. Potash (*kanwa*) and Bornu salt (*mangul*)
d. Pots (*tukwane*); soup ingredients (*kayan miya*); clay water-carriers (*butar kasa*); petty-goods vendors (*kashe-kashe*); sour milk (*nono*); ghee (*man shanu*); small fried cakes made from rice, bulrush millet, or guinea-corn flour (*masa, waina*); bean-flour cakes (*kosai*); small cakes made from peanuts, Bambara nuts, or bean flour (*abakuru*); and peanut oil (*man gyada*)
e. Mortars (*turame*) and pestles (*tabare*) for corn; mats (*tabarmi*) and beds (*gadaje*); double-matting headgear (*kabidai*) and plaited grass bags (*ash-asha*); mats from Lere Town, in Bauchi (*tabarmin Lere*); corn stalks (*karare*) and ropes (*igiyoyi*); and straw Fulani hats (*malafu*)
f. Thin strips of meat, sun-dried and roasted (*kilishi*)
g. Bits of meat spitted on stick and roasted (*tsire*) and innards (*hanji*)
h. Raw-meat sellers (*mahauta*)
i. Paper (*takardu*); needles (*allurai*); kola nuts (*goro*); mirrors (*madubai*); antimony cases (*kiratandu*); petty-goods vendors (*'yan koli*); bitter lemons (*lemon tsami*); and garlic (*tafarnuwa*)
j. Soap (*sabulu*); galena (*tozali*); silver (*azurfa*); gum (*karo*); and copper (*tagulla*)
k. Barbers (*wanzamai*) and tobacco (*taba*)
l. Leather-workers (*dukawa*); saddles (*sirada*); smithing tools (*kayan kira*); hoes with hafts (*faretani* and *kotochi*); and writing slates (*alluna*)
m. Red saddles (*jar fata*); bit straps (*kilasamadu*); large needles (*babban allura*); tanned skins (*fata*); and silken decorations for horses (*alharinin dawaki*)
n. Indian hemp (*rama*; *Hibiscus cannabinus*)

o. Plaited halter ropes (*tukakken igiyan*)
p. Grass mats (*zanaki*) and forked sticks (*gwafanni*)
q. Ladders (*tsanunuka*) and firewood (*itachen wuta*)
r. Onions (*albasoshi*) and bitter tomatoes (*yalo*)
s. Guinea corn (*dadawa*); salt from Bauchi (*gishirin Wase*); fish (*kifi*); and salt from Gombe (*gishirin Tukulma*)
t. Roasted peanuts (*soyeyen gyada*); Bambara nuts (*guzaye*); fruit of the tigernut (*aya; Cyperus esculentus*); type of sweets (*dakuwa*) made from tigernuts or peanuts; sweet potatoes (*dankali*); cassava (*rogo*); white-flowered benniseed (*ridi*; *Sesamum indicum*); pumpkins (*kabeyi*); okra (*kubewa*); red sorrel (*yakuwa*); bitter tomatoes (*gauta; Solanum sp.*); peppers (*barkono*); seeds (*kalwa*) of the locust-bean tree (*dorawa; Parkia filicoidea*); circular mats for covering vessels (*fayafayai*); circular gourds (*kore*); calabash ladles (*ludayi*); long gourds (*zunguru*) worn by women on arms to guard newly hennaed hands; gourds used as ink pots (*kurtun tawada*); long gourd-trumpets used by women and Fulani (*shantuna*); and gourd-bottles (*butochi*)
u. She-goats (*awaki*); sheep (*tumaki*); donkeys (*jakuna*); and cattle (*shanu*)
v. Strips of white cotton cloth (*fari*); circular mats used for covering vessels (*fayafayai*); baskets (*kindai*); cotton thread (*zare*); cotton (*auduga*); black leather-dye (*kufi*); henna (*lalle*); baskets made of young dum-palm or its fronds; and red dye (*jaje*)
w. Calabashes (*kore*); guinea corn (*dawa; Sorghum vulgare*); bulrush millet (*gero*; *Pennisetum typhoideum*); millet (*maiwa*; *Pennisetum spicatum*); maize (*masara*); rice (*shinkafa*); peanuts (*gyada*); fruit of the tree *Cordia abyssinica* (*alilliba*); desert-date tree (*aduwa*; *Balanites aegyptiaca*); fruit of the shea tree (*kadanya*); fruit of the tree *Detarium senegalense* (*taura*); black, plum-like fruit of the tree *Vitex cienkowskii* (*dinya*); small, yellow plum-like fruit of the tree *Ximenia americana* (*tsada*); fruit of the jujube tree (*magarya*; *Zizyphus jujuba*); fruit of the tree *Zizyphus spina-christi* (*kurna*); tamarind fruit (*tsamiya*); pods and leaves of the baobab tree (*kuka*; *Adansonia digitata*); seeds of the locust-bean tree (*kalwa*); and gum (*karo*).

APPENDIX V

KATAGUM CITY

ca. 1900

To IDI PRAYER GROUND
To DYE PITS (Marina)
FRIDAY MOSQUE
ROYAL COMPOUND
CENTRAL MARKET
A B C D E F G
I II III IV V VI VII VIII IX X XI XII XIII XIV XV XVI XVII XVIII
1 2 3 4 5 6 7 8 9 10 11 12 13 14 15
N
0 400 800 Ft.
0 100 200 M.
WALL AND GATE
WARD BOUNDARY
COMPOUNDS

Royal Compound

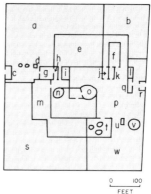

a b c d e f g h i j k l m n o p q r s t u v w
0 100
FEET

Central Market

a b c d e f g h i j k l m n o p q r s t u v w x y z a' b' c' d' e' f' g' h' i' j' k' l'
0 100
FEET

APPENDIX V
KEY: KATAGUM CITY (CA. 1900)

Wards (*unguwoyi*; sing. *unguwa*)

I. Ung. Kamfuri
II. Ung. Rimindi
III. Ung. Sarkin Marma
IV. Ung. Kukadi (1)
V. Ung. Magagaya
VI. Ung. Sittikiram
VII. Ung. Rakumanani
VIII. Ung. Waziri
IX. Ung. Barwadi
X. Ung. Kofar Bayi
XI. Ung. Katagum Gana
XII. Ung. Yarcham
XIII. Ung. Majema
XIV. Ung. Kofar Fada
XV. Ung. Kukadi (2)
XVI. Ung. Pawari
XVII. Ung. Sarkin Yaki
XVIII. Ung. Hadejawa

Gates (*kofofi*; sing. *kofa*)

A. K. Yamma
B. K. Babi
C. K. Sambo
D. K. Gabas
E. K. Yarcham
F. K. Maitandu

Compounds (*gidaje*, sing. *gida*) *of high officials*

1. G. Alkali
2. G. Hardo
3. G. Waziri
4. G. Sarkin Yaki
5. G. Wombai
6. G. Liman
8. G. Lifidi
11. G. Makama
12. G. Galadima
13. G. Madaki
14. G. Barua
15. G. Shamaki
16. G. Maidala

Miscellaneous

7. Friday mosque
9. *Shiranyi* (F.); room where all the *fadawa* waited for the emir to leave the palace interior; also used by persons (except royal wives and concubines) to rest and chat in, and by the emir to turban new officials—now called *zauren fadawa* (H. a thatched round entrance-porch to the palace, used by courtiers); called *dabi* in Sokoto
10. Auxiliary mosque

Royal-Compound (*fada*) *Divisions*

a. *Kewaye*; contained the huts of junior palace slaves and servants (about 35 in Abdulkadir's reign), with their families; also had an enclosure where *dengin sarki*, and relatives of those living in the *Kewaye*, were buried
b. *Gada*; contained some 20 outdoor corn bins (*rumbu*; pl. *rumbuna*) for storing millet; husking and winnowing were performed here

c. *Soron Kofa* (H.)—also called *jodunga mere* (F.); used by *fadawa* and other palace personnel when the *shiranyi* was full. Also, where straw (*tattaka*) was stored for dry-season use by the royal horses; *hakimai* and *sarakuna* left their entourages before entering the palace interior; the *tambari* drum was beaten 7 times on the two 'Idi festival days and other important occasions (e.g., when the emir returned from Sokoto or a victorious campaign); the emir made public announcements here and received the ceremonial charges of mounted officials on the 'Idi festivals
d. *Adadan huta*; resting place of the emir, *'yan sarki,* and *fadawa* in the hot season
e. Open field (*fili*)
f. *Gidan Mai Hatsi*; quarters of the senior female palace slave (Mai Hatsi) and of some 10 concubines supervised by her; also the center for distribution of millet throughout the palace
g. *Soron Juma'a*; room where the emir rested after Friday prayers and was greeted by junior officials
h. *Soron Kanawa*; a corridor; also where the emir saw anyone he wished to confer with in private
i. *Zauren Beddawa*; quarters of several old women (*kwaramai*; sing. *kwarama*) who served as messengers inside and from the palace
j. *Gidan yamba*; quarters of the senior slave girl (*makulliya*) and a few of her juniors (*makulla*)
k. *Turaka*; royal bedroom and storeroom
l. *Soron jekadu*; quarters of the (male) palace messengers
m. *Muri*; the royal stable, with hut for storing equipages (*kayan dawaki*)
n. Hut where Emir Abdulkadir slept in the daytime, and where he might receive any important visitor
o. *Kudandan Haji*; quarters of the Babban Jekadiya; also where other *kayan dawaki* and royal properties were stored
p. Open field
q. *Soron fadanchi*; where the emir conferred with his *hakimai* and tried cases brought before him
r. *Soron kofa*; a small entrance hut
s. *Kewaye*; see "a" above
t. *Gidan matan aure*; quarters of the royal wives (3 in 1900) and their servants and slaves, together with some of the royal concubines (58 altogether when Abdulkadir died)
u. *Makawanchin sarakuna*; burial place of emirs Dan Kauwa, Kadr, and Haji
v. *Zauren Makama*; where the slave officials had their mid-morning meal

Central-Market Divisions

a. Seeds of the baobab tree (*gwargwami*)
b. Flour (*buri*)
c. Sasswood (*gwaska*)

d. Mats (*tabarmi*)
e. Potash (*kanwa*)
f. Firewood (*itachen wuta*) and carpenters (*masassaki*)
g. Bornu salt (*mangul*)
h. Circular gourds (*kore*)
i. Balls of cooked flour (*fura*) for mixing in milk
j. Honey (*zuma*)
k. Kola nuts (*goro*)
l. Tobacco (*taba*) and tobacco blossoms (*furanni*)
m. Slaves (*bayi*)
n. Indigo (*shuni*)
o.–p. Petty-goods vendors (*'yan koli*)
q. Fish (*kifi*)
r. Peppers (*barkono*) and seeds (*kalwa*) of the locust-bean tree
s. Cotton (*auduga*)
t. Wrestlers (*'yan kokawa*)
u. Cassava (*doya*)
v. Barbers (*wanzamai*)
w. Spitted-meat (*mazarai*)
x. Strips of white cotton cloth (*fari*)
y. Notions (*kashe-kashe*)
z. Fruit of the tigernut (*aya*) and dates (*dabino*)

a′. Onions (*albasoshi*)
b′. Sellers by measure (*arkomai*)
c′. Sugar cane (*takanda*)
d′. Raw-meat sellers (*mahauta*)
e′. Leather-workers (*dukawa*)
f′. Horses (*dawaki*)
g′. Open space
h′. Donkeys (*jakuna*)
i′. Cattle (*shanu*)
j′. She-goats (*awaki*)
k′. Sweets (*alewa*)
l′. Pots (*tukwane*)

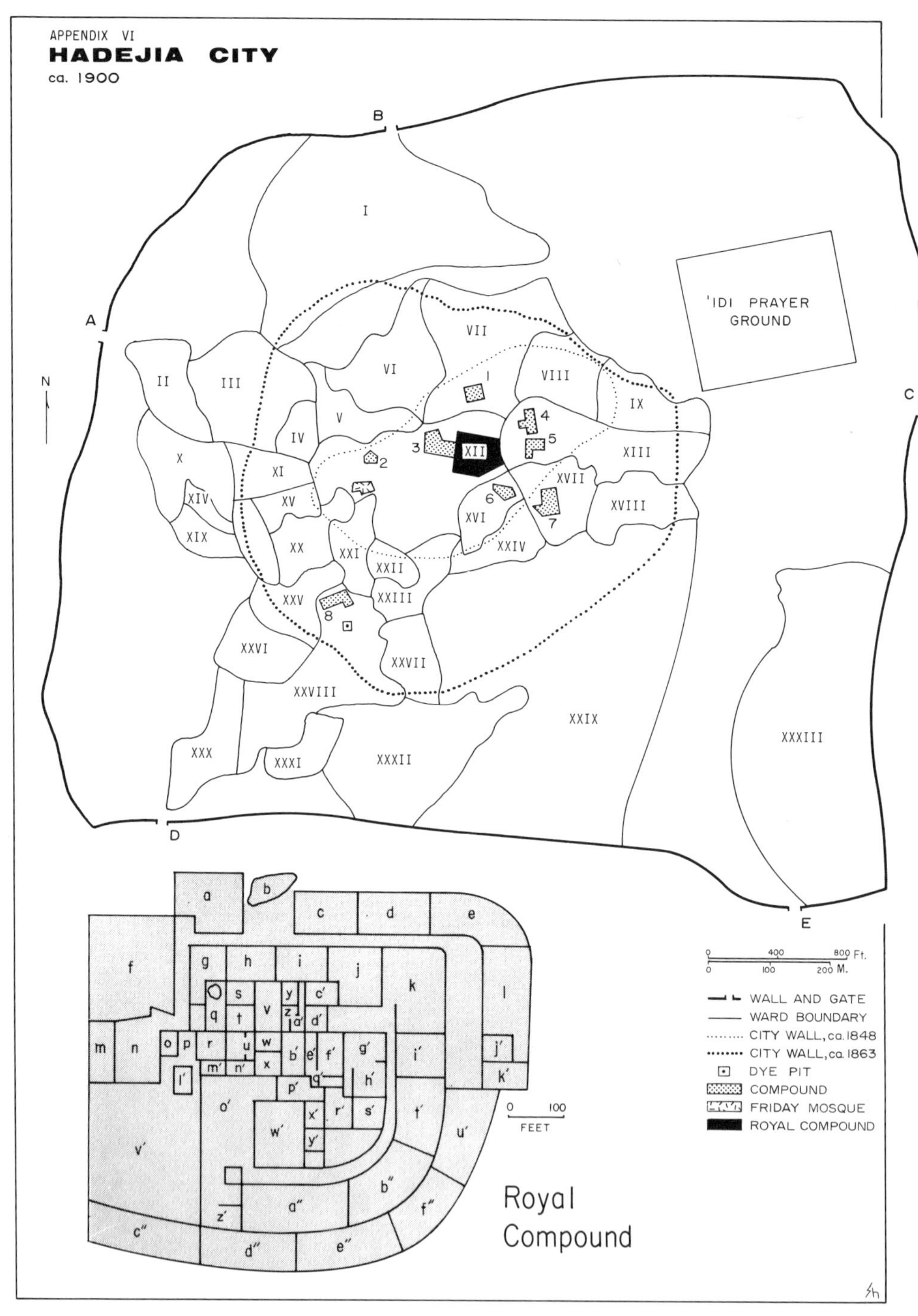

APPENDIX VI
HADEJIA CITY
ca. 1900
'IDI PRAYER GROUND
WALL AND GATE
WARD BOUNDARY
CITY WALL, ca. 1848
CITY WALL, ca. 1863
DYE PIT
COMPOUND
FRIDAY MOSQUE
ROYAL COMPOUND
Royal Compound
FEET

Appendix VI
Key: Hadejia City (ca. 1900)

Wards (*unguwoyi*; sing. *unguwa*)

I. Ung. Gagurmari
II. Ung. Rinde
III. Ung. Tagurza
IV. Ung. Makwalar Jarma
V. Ung. Kwarin na Ganda
VI. Ung. Kilabakori
VII. Ung. Durumin Gamma
VIII. Ung. Ma'aji
IX. Ung. Ilallah
X. Ung. Dubantu
XI. Ung. Badderi
XII. Ung. Fada
XIII. Ung. Bayi
XIV. Ung. Sarkin Ruwa
XV. Ung. Makama Kigo
XVI. Ung. Makwalar Aishe
XVII. Ung. Kwarin Madaki
XVIII. Ung. Piriya
XIX. Ung. Sarkin Makera
XX. Ung. Kasuwar Kofa
XXI. Ung. Tudun Barde
XXII. Ung. Kwarin Manu
XXIII. Ung. Kasuwar Kuda
XXIV. Ung. Atafi
XXV. Ung. Fandum
XXVI. Ung. Kuburu
XXVII. Ung. Wunti
XXVIII. Ung. Angku
XXIX. Ung. Jigawar Tsaba
XXX. Ung. Yayari
XXXI. Ung. Makafi
XXXII. Ung. Garko
XXXIII. Ung. Fantai

Gates (H. *kofofi*; sing. *kofa*)

A. K. Rinde
B. K. Gagurmari
C. K. Gabas
D. K. Talata
E. K. Kogi

Compounds (*gidaje*; sing. *gida*) *of high officials*

1. G. Alkali
2. G. Liman
3. G. Tafida
4. G. Sarkin Arewa
5. G. Galadima
6. G. Sarkin Dawaki
7. G. Sarkin Auyo
8. G. Sarkin Pawa

The wall of ca. 1900 was completed in Haru's reign, ca. 1882, in response to a threatened invasion by Shehu Bukr of Bornu.

Royal-Compound (fada) Divisions

a. *Gidan Kabo*; quarters of Mallam Kabo, a *chukurami* (K. special palace messenger)
b. A pond
c. *Gidan Abdulkarimu*; quarters of Mallam Abdulkarimu, a *chukurami*
d. *Gidan Idiyo*; quarters of Idiyo, a *chukurami*
e. *Gidan Mabudi*; quarters of Muhammadu dan Majeri, a *chukurami*
f. *Gidan Shamaki*; quarters of Shamakin Hadejia
g. *Murin arewa*; northern royal stables
h. *Gidan manya*; large room unused in Muhammadu's reign
i. *Matan sarki*; large room unused in Muhammadu's reign; built by Haru for one of his wives, a daughter of Sultan of Sokoto Umaru
j. *Matan Sarki*; large room unused in Muhammadu's reign
k. *Gidan lemo*; a lemon grove; fowl were also kept here
l. *Mayankar shanu*; royal cows were slaughtered here
m. *Zauren kofar maitsatsewa*; main entrance and entrance room to the palace
n. *Mabugan tambura*; where the *tambari* drum was beaten on Sallah days, and for one to two weeks thereafter; also whenever the emir rode out to his farm, or to war, to announce this publicly (*tambura* = *tambari*)
o. *Soron Tambari*; quarters of Tambarin Hadejia, and where he kept his five or six *tambari* drums
p. *Filin Shamaki*; where Shamakin Hadejia usually sat
q. *Machiyar tuwo*; where palace slaves and servants ate
r. *Soron babban gwani*; where the emir and other high officials were turbanned
s. *Soron mallamai*; where mallams, local or visiting, might confer
t. *'Yan jira*; a waiting room
u. *Soron chiyawa*; storeroom for grass used as fodder
v. *Mai yashi*; a well
w. *Soron baka*; storeroom for bows and arrows
x. *Sararin baina*; a field near the stairway to the second story of the palace
y. *Baina*; a second story, used by the emir for resting on hot nights, viewing the new moon, or sighting the approach to Hadejia City of friends or hostile forces
z. *Banten baina*; ornamental edge of upper story

a′ *Filin koromai*; open space with small stream
b′ *Baina*; see "y" above
c′ *Soron koromai*; room enclosing small stream
d′ *Soron koromai*; see "c′" above
e′ *Banten baina*; see "z" above
f′ *Babban soro*; where the emir relaxed with his women and children
g′ Open space (*fili*), with latrine
h′ Open space

i′ *Zauren arewa*; quarters of three concubines (two of them in charge of the third, Sarkin Arewa's daughter)
j′ *Gidan Mallam Likari*; quarters of Mallam Likari, a *chukurami*
k′ *Kofar rahogo*; entrance and entrance room from rear of the palace
l′ *Soron muri*; enclosed portion of the royal stables
m′–n′ *Soron chiyawa*; see "u" above
o′ Open space
p′ Open space
q′ *Soron Mai Dinga*; room where the *'yar sarki* waited before greeting their father
r′ *Soron maikyaure*; general store room
s′ Open space
t′ *Zauren 'yan turaka*; concubine quarters (Muhammadu is said to have had some 30 concubines, and two wives, ca. 1900)
u′ *Rahogo*; storeroom for corn (*hatsi*)
v′ *Muri*; royal stables
w′ *Unguwar Maisoro*; quarters of the Maisoro, or chief concubine, and eight other concubines
x′ *Filin 'yan turaka*; open space where concubines took the air by day
y′ *Soron 'yan turaka*; room where concubines met to relax and work together
z′ Open field, where deer were kept

a″ *Zauren tsaka*; quarters of four concubines, including the mother of Chiromans Hadejia Sambo and Usuman
b″ *Zauren gabas*; quarters of Muhammadu's head wife (*uwargida*) and three concubines
c″ *Shamaki Asan*; quarters of Shamakin Sarkin Marma in Haru's reign; after (Sarkin Marma) Muhammadu became emir, it housed the royal flag-bearer on campaigns
d″ *Gidan Kalumbu*; quarters for Kalumbu, a slave of the Chiroma
e″ *Gidan Mamman Sale*; quarters of Mamman Sale, a slave of the Shamaki
f″ *Gidan Malumbi*; quarters of Malumbi, a slave of the Shamaki

REFERENCES

BIBLIOGRAPHY

UNPUBLISHED

Official

Abraham, R. C. "Ethnological Notes on the Bolewa Group." NAK [Nigerian Archives, Kaduna] SNP 17/8 K.1119.

———. "History Notes on Gombe Division, Bauchi Province (1929–30)." NAK SNP 17/2 1979 12250.

"The Arabic Official Correspondence between the Emir of Gombe, Umaru, son of Kwairanga, and the Sultan of Sokoto and other Various Emirs in the Fulani Empire." NAK Bauprof Box 4.

Backwell, H. F. "Assessment Report on Galadiman Katagum District, Sub-District of Galadima, Katagum Emirate, Kano Province." NAK SNP 7/12 3260 5205/1911.

———. "Assessment Report on Azare District, Katagum Emirate, Kano Province." NAK SNP 7/13 3555 6249/1912.

———. "Assessment Report on Waziri District, Katagum Emirate, Kano Province." NAK SNP 7/13 3343 1433/1912.

"Bornu Provincial History." NAK SNP 15/14.

Brice-Smith, H. M. "Assessment Report on Hadejia Town, Kano Province." NAK SNP 10/5 2847 181p/1917.

Campbell-Irons, R. C. "Assessment Report on Bedde District, Bornu Province." NAK SNP 10/2 1006 242p/1914.

Carlyle, T. F. "Assessment Report on Birri District, Gombe Division, Central Province." NAK SNP 7/13 3447 4196/1912.

———. "Assessment Report on Waja Sub-District, Ako District, Gombe Emirate, Central Province." NAK SNP 10/1 661 715p/1913.

———. "History of Gombe Emirate, Central Province." NAK SNP 10/2 1179 445p/1914.

———. Appendix 1 to "Gombe Division Intelligence Report." In "Annual Report, Bauchi Province (1916)." NAK SNP 10/4 873 737p/1916.

Crocker, W. R. "Pagan Administration in Misau Emirate, Bauchi Province (1934)." NAK SNP 17/4 39576/S.6.

Davies, R. S. "An Account of Mallam Zai." In "Report on Gujba District, Bornu Emirate, Bornu Province." NAK SNP 10/7 3647 125p/1919.

Douglas, E. J. "Assessment Report on Shani District, Biu Division, Bornu Province." NAK SNP 17/2 1195 10160.

Fitzpatrick, J. F. J. "Assessment Report on Ningi District, Bauchi Division, Central Province." NAK SNP 10/2 1169 431p/1914.

Foulkes, H. D. Notes in "Information Required for Compilation of Provincial Gazetteer, Bauchi Province." NAK SNP 17/2 10791, Vol. I.

"Genealogical Trees of the Ruling Families in the Northern Provinces—Katagum Emirate (1945)." NAK SNP 17/4 39576/S.6.

Glenny, H. Q. "History of Certain Emirates." NAK SNP 7/10 2761 1778/1909.

———. "Historical Notes on the Jahun Fillane." In "History of Certain Emirates." 2 vols. NAK SNP 7/10 2761 1778/1909.

Grier, S. M. Section in "Assessment Report on Kirifi District, Central Province," by T. W. P. Dyer. NAK SNP 7/12 3269 5371/1911.

Groom, A. H. "Assessment Report on Malala District, Gombe Division, Central Province." NAK SNP 7/13 3446 4195/1912.

Harris, P. G. "Anthropological Notes on the Teshena Tribe (1922–27)." NAK SNP 17/8 K.4195.

Hewby, W. P. "Bornu Province Monthly Reports, 1903, April–May." NAK SNP 15/1 48A.

Izard, T. A. "Pagan Administration in Gombe Emirate, Bauchi Province (1933–34)." NAK SNP 17/3 3545 21103.

Lethem, G. J. "Chronicle of the Galadimas of Bornu, Notes on." NAK SNP 10/5 2868 204p/1917.

———. "Assessment Report on Allaguerno District, Bornu Emirate, Bornu Province." NAK SNP 10/7 3748 265p/1919.

———. "Special Report on Nguru District, Bornu Province." NAK SNP 10/7 3741 258p/1919.

———. "Assessment Report on Machena District, Bornu Emirate, Bornu Province." NAK SNP 17/2 1962 12168.

Lilley, E. S. "Assessment Report on Jalingo District, Muri Division, Muri Province." NAK SNP 7/14 3610 473p/1913.

Lonsdale, P. "Assessment Report on Ako District, Gombe Division, Bauchi Province." NAK SNP 7/13 3597 7252/1912.

———. "Assessment Report on Gombe Town, Gombe Emirate, Central Province." NAK SNP 7/14 3607 7p/1913.

Mathews, A. B. "Administration of Tangale-Waja, Bauchi Province (1933–36)." NAK SNP 17/3 3550 21108.

"Miscellaneous Notes on the People of Biu Division and Neighboring Country." NAK Biu District 134 L.1.

Monro, H. C. "Assessment Report on Hardawa District, Katagum Division, Kano Province." NAK SNP 7/13 3521 5479/1912.

Monsell, C. N. "Reassessment Report on Dambam Emirate, Katagum Division, Kano Province." NAK SNP 10/1 689 743p/1913.

———. "Assessment Report on Jema'are Emirate, Katagum Division, Kano Province." NAK SNP 10/1 582 631p/1913.

Morland, T. L. N. "Bornu Report B. M./8 of 1st May.1902." NAK SNP 15/1 18.

Muhammadu Bukhari, Wazirin Sokoto. "The Tukur Revolt." Translated by Roland A. Adeleye. NAK Kadcap, Box 2.

"Notes for Revised Bauchi Provincial Gazetteer." NAK SNP 17/3 3456 21104.

"Notes on the Origins of Peoples of Bornu Province and Neighboring Country (1920–28)." NAK Biu District 135 L.2.

Official Correspondence. NAK GOK (Series), Kadcap.

"Official Correspondence, Various Sultans of Sokoto." NAK Sokprof.

Patterson, J. R. "Assessment Report on Geidam District, Bornu Emirate, Bornu Province." NAK SNP 10/6 3274 114p/1918.

———. "Assessment Report on Borsari District, Bornu Emirate, Bornu Province (1918–26)." NAK SNP 17/8 K.2041.

Payton, G. H. "Reorganization of Ningi District." NAK C.M.B. Prof 1, Vol. II.

"Pedigrees of the Principal Dynasties of Kano, Katsina, Katagum, Kazaure, Daura and Hadejia (1922–28)." NAK SNP 17/4 6117 38053.

Ramage, R. G. "Iron Currency." Jos Museum Files. June 6, 1928.

———. "Historical Notes on Katagum Division, Bauchi Province (1929–33)." NAK SNP 17/1 1139 9715.

Rickford, L. L. "Notes on the Organization of the Bolewa Villages in Gombe Emirate, Bauchi Province." NAK SNP 17/8 K.2383.

Rosedale, W. O. P. "Assessment Report on Kanakuru District, Numan Division, Yola Province." NAK SNP 10/7 3752 275p/1919.

Ruxton, F. H. "Notes on Fulani, Jukun, Wurobo and Ankwe Tribe Customs in Muri Province." NAK SNP 7/9 2679 6663/1906.

Temple, C. L. "Report on Bauchi Province for April–June, 1902." NAK SNP 15/1 7.

Vessey, K. C. "Reassessment Report on Hardawa District, Misau Emirate, Bauchi Province." NAK SNP 17/3 4210 26847.

Whiteley, G. C. "Special Report on Bedde Emirate, Bornu Province." NAK SNP 10/8 4024 209p/1920.

Yakubu b. Halilu, Alkalin Potiskum. "The History of Buba Yero of Gombe." Translated by R. C. Abraham. In "History Notes on Gombe Division, Bauchi Province (1929–30)." NAK SNP 17/2 1979 12250.

Unofficial

Abdulkadir Akabi. "Notes on the History of Ningi Chiefdom." Translated by Ibrahim Musa Ningi. 1960. MS, copy in my possession.

Ahmadu dan Alhaji Tafida, Sarkin Misau. "Tarihin Mallam Jibril" [A history of Mallam Jibril]. 1926. MS, copy in my possession.

———. "Tarihin Sarakunan Misau" [History of the Emirs of Misau]. Translated by Abdulmumin Suleiman Jalingo. 1926. MS, copy in my possession.

Alhaji Mahmoud, Imamin Bauchi. "A Light for Beginners and a Lamp for the Blind." Translated by Aliyu Lanle and Ibrahim Magaji. 1960. MS, copy in my possession.

Babagoro dan Sarkin Gombe Abubakar, Chiroman Gombe. "A History of the Gombe Emirs." 1960. MS, copy in my possession.

Hayatu bn. Sa'idu. "The Life History of M. Sa'idu bn. Hayatu." MS, copy in my possession.

Muhammadu, Barden Rinde. "Tarihin Fulanin Hadeja da Mulkinsu" [A history of the Hadejia Fulani and their government]. 1953. MS, copy in my possession.

Palmer, H. Richmond. The Palmer Papers. Jos Museum Library.

Saleh Jibril (Salihu Bajoga). "A History of Nafada District, Gombe Emirate." 1961. MS, copy in my possession.

Salihu Atiku Kumo. "A History of Akko District, Gombe Emirate." 1961. MS, copy in my possession.

Yakubu dan Halilu, Alkalin Potiskum. "Tarihin Mallam Zaki" [A history of Mallam Zaki]. MS, copy in my possession.

PUBLISHED

PRIMARY

Official

'Abdullah ibn Muhammad. *Tazyīn al-Waraqāt.* Translated by Mervyn Hiskett. Ibadan: Ibadan University Press, 1963.

Adeleye, Roland A., et al. "Sifofin Shehu: An Autobiography and Character Study of 'Uthman b. Fūdī in Verse." *Research Bulletin of the Centre of Arabic Documentation* (University of Ibadan), II (1966), 1–35.

———. "The Dilemma of the Wazīr: The Place of the *Risālat al-Wazīr'ila Ahl al-'Ilm Wal-Tadabbur* in the History of the Conquest of the Sokoto Caliphate." *Journal of the Historical Society of Nigeria,* IV (June, 1968), 285–309.

Arnett, Edward J. *The Rise of the Sokoto Fulani, Being a Paraphrase and in Some Parts a Translation of the Infaku'l Maisuri of Sultan Mohammed Bello.* Kano: Emirate Printing Department, 1922.

Backwell, H. F. *The Occupation of Hausaland, 1900–1904.* 1927. Reprint. London: Frank Cass & Co., 1969.

Bivar, A. D. H. "Arabic Documents of Northern Nigeria." *Bulletin of the School of Oriental and African Studies,* XXII (1959), 324–49.

———. "The *Wathiqāt ahl al-Sudān*: A Manifesto of the Fulani Jihad." *Journal of African History,* II (1961), 235–43.

Hajji Sa'id. *History of Sokoto.* Translated by C. E. J. Whitting. Kano: Ife-Olu Printing Works, 1931.

Hiskett, Mervyn. "*Kitāb al-Farq*: A Work on the Habe Kingdoms Attributed to 'Uthmān dan Fodio." *Bulletin of the School of Oriental and African Studies,* XXIII (1960), 558–79.

Ibn Fartua, Ahmed. *History of the First Twelve Years of the Reign of Mai Idris Alooma of Bornu (1571–1583)*. Translated by H. Richmond Palmer. 1926. Reprint. London: Frank Cass & Co., 1970.

Junaidu, Wazirin Sokoto M. *Tarihin Fulani* [History of the Fulani]. Zaria: Gaskiya Corporation, 1957.

Martin, B. G. "Unbelief in the Western Sudan: 'Uthmān dan Fodio's 'Ta'līm al-ikhwān.' " *Middle Eastern Studies*, IV (1968), 50–97.

Palmer, H. Richmond. "Western Sudan History, The Raudthat ul Afkâri." *Journal of the African Society*, XV (1915–16), 261–73.

Unofficial

Alexander, Boyd. *From the Niger to the Nile*. 2 vols. London: Edward Arnold, 1907.

Barth, Heinrich. *Travels and Discoveries in Northern and Central Africa*. 3 vols. 1857–59. Reprint. London: Frank Cass & Co., 1965.

Bovill, E. W., ed. *Missions to the Niger*. 4 vols. Vols. II–IV: *The Bornu Mission, 1822–25*. 1826. Reprint. Cambridge: At the University Press, 1966.

Clapperton, Hugh. *Journal of a Second Expedition into the Interior of Africa from the Bight of Benin to Soccatoo*. 1829. Reprint. London: Frank Cass & Co., 1966.

East, Rupert M. *Stories of Old Adamawa*. 1935. Reprint. Farnborough: Gregg Press, 1967.

Gentil, E. *La Chute de l'Empire de Rabeh*. Paris, 1902.

Hiskett, Mervyn. "Material Relating to the State of Learning among the Fulani before Their Jihad." *Bulletin of the School of Oriental and African Studies*, XIX (1957), 550–78.

———. "An Islamic Tradition of Reform in the Western Sudan from the 16th to the 18th Century." *Bulletin of the School of Oriental and African Studies*, XXV (1962), 577–96.

Hunwick, John E. "Further Light on Ahmad Baba al-Tinbuktī." *Research Bulletin of the Centre of Arabic Documentation* (University of Ibadan), II (July, 1966), 19–26.

Ibn Khaldun. *The Muqaddimah*. Translated by Franz Rosenthal. 2d ed. 3 vols. Princeton: Princeton University Press, 1967.

Koelle, Sigismund W. *African Native Literature*. London, 1854.

Lander, Richard. *Records of Captain Clapperton's Last Expedition to Africa*. 2 vols. London: John Murray, 1830.

Landeroin, Captain. "Du Tschad au Niger: notes historiques." In *Documents scientifiques de la mission Tilho 1905–9.* 3 vols. Paris, 1911.

Nachtigal, Gustave. *Sahara und Sudan.* 3 vols. Berlin: Paul Parey, 1879–89.

Palmer, H. Richmond. *Sudanese Memoirs.* 1928. Reprint (3 vols. in 1). London: Frank Cass & Co., 1967.

———. *The Bornu Sahara and Sudan.* London: John Murray, 1936.

Patterson, J. R. *Kanuri Songs.* Lagos: The Government Printer, 1926.

Smith, H. F. C., Last, Denis Murray, and Gubio, Gambo. "Ali Eisami Gazirmabe of Bornu." In *Africa Remembered, Narratives by West Africans from the Era of the Slave Trade,* edited by Philip D. Curtin, pp. 199–216. Madison: The University of Wisconsin Press, 1968.

Smith, Mary. *Baba of Karo: A Woman of the Muslim Hausa.* London: Faber & Faber, 1954.

Strümpell, Kurt Hauptmann. "Die Geschichte Adamauas nach mündlichen Überlieferungen." *Mitteilungen der geographischen Gesellschaft in Hamburg,* XXVI (1912), 46–107.

SECONDARY

Official

Burdon, John A. *Historical Notes on Certain Emirates and Tribes (Nigeria, Northern Provinces).* London: Waterlow, 1909.

Davies, J. G. *The Biu Book: A Collation and Reference Book on Biu Division.* Zaria: NORLA, 1954–56.

Forster, T. H. B. *Précis of Information Concerning Nigeria.* London: The War Office [1901?].

Fremantle, J. M., ed. *Gazetteer of Muri Province.* London: Waterlow, 1920.

Gall, F. B., ed. *Gazetteer of Bauchi Province.* London: Waterlow, 1920.

Gowers, W. F., ed. *Gazetteer of Kano Province.* London: Waterlow, 1921.

Izard, Michel. *Traditions historiques des villages du Yatenga.* Paris: C.N.R.S., 1965.

Keay, R. W. J. *An Outline of Nigerian Vegetation.* Lagos: The Government Printer, 1959.

Krzywon, Anthony M. "Agricultural Notebook for Gombe Emirate." Mimeographed. Gombe, 1959.

Lely, H. V. *The Useful Trees of Northern Nigeria.* London: Crown Agents for the Colonies, 1925.

Meek, Charles Kingsley. *Tribal Studies in Northern Nigeria.* 2 vols. London: Kegan Paul, 1931.

———. *Land Law and Custom in the Colonies.* London: Oxford University Press, 1949.

———. *Land Tenure and Land Administration in Nigeria and the Cameroons.* London: H.M.S.O., 1957.

Migeod, C. O., comp. *Gazetteer of Yola Province.* Lagos: The Government Printer, 1927.

Palmer, H. Richmond, comp. *Gazetteer of Bornu Province.* London: Waterlow, 1929.

St. Croix, F. W. de. *The Fulani of Northern Nigeria.* Lagos: The Government Printer, 1945.

Smith, J. M. "Agricultural Notebook for Southern Katagum Division." Mimeographed. Azare, 1960.

Smith, M. G. *The Economy of Hausa Communities of Zaria.* London: H.M.S.O., 1955.

Temple, Charles L., ed. *Notes on the Tribes, Provinces, Emirates and States of the Northern Provinces of Nigeria, Compiled from Official Reports of O. Temple.* 2d ed. 1922. Reprint. London: Frank Cass & Co., 1965.

Tomlinson, G. J. F., and Lethem, G. J. *History of Islamic Political Propaganda in Nigeria.* Report and Appendices. London: Waterlow [1927?].

Waniko, S. S., and Ilyasu, M. S. D. *A Descriptive Catalogue of Early Lugard-Sultan of Sokoto Correspondence, Including a Description of 131 Arabic Letters Found in Sokoto in 1903.* Kaduna, 1961.

Unofficial

Abadie, M. *La Colonie du Niger.* Paris, 1927.

Adeleye, Roland A. *Power and Diplomacy in Northern Nigeria 1804–1906: The Sokoto Caliphate and its Enemies.* London: Longman Group, 1971.

al-Hajj, Muhammad A. "The Thirteenth Century in Muslim Eschatology: Mahdist Expectations in the Sokoto Caliphate." *Research Bulletin of the Centre of Arabic Documentation* (University of Ibadan), III (1967), 100–13.

Aluko, S. A. "How Many Nigerians? An Analysis of Nigeria's Census Problems, 1901–63." *The Journal of Modern African Studies,* III (1965), 371–92.

Anderson, J. N. D. *Islamic Law in Africa.* 1954. Reprint. London: Frank Cass & Co., 1970.

Arnold, T. W. *The Caliphate.* 1924. Reprint. New York: Barnes & Noble, 1966.

Babikir, Arbab. *L'empire de Rabeh.* Paris, 1950.

Biobaku, Saburi, and al-Hajj, Muhammad. "The Sudanese Mahdiyya and the Niger-Chad Region." In *Islam in Tropical Africa,* edited by I. M. Lewis, pp. 425–41. London: Oxford University Press, 1966.

Boyle, C. Vicars. "Historical Notes on the Yola Fulanis." *Journal of the African Society,* X (1910), 73–92.

Brackenbury, E. A. "Notes on the 'Bororo Fulbe' or Nomad 'Cattle Fulani'." *Journal of the African Society,* XXIII (1924), 208–17; 271–77.

Clark, J. Desmond. *Atlas of African Prehistory.* Chicago: University of Chicago Press, 1967.

Cohen, Ronald. "From Empire to Colony: Bornu in the Nineteenth and Twentieth Centuries." In *Profiles of Change: African Society and Colonial Rule,* edited by Victor Turner, pp. 74–126. *Colonialism in Africa, 1870–1960,* vol. 3. Cambridge: At the University Press, 1971.

———. *The Kanuri of Bornu.* New York: Holt, Rinehart and Winston, 1967.

———. "Power, Authority and Personal Success in Islam and Bornu." In *Political Anthropology,* edited by Marc Schwartz, Arthur Tuden, and Victor Turner, pp. 129–39. Chicago: Aldine Publishing Company, 1966.

———. "Slavery among the Kanuri." *Trans-action,* IV (January–February, 1967).

———. "Social Stratification in Bornu." In *Social Stratification in Africa,* edited by Arthur Tuden and Leonard Plotnicov, pp. 225–67. New York: The Free Press, 1970.

Encyclopaedia of Islam. Leiden: E. J. Brill, 1927, 1936.

Falconer, J. D. *The Geology and Geography of Northern Nigeria.* London: Macmillan, 1911.

Fremantle, J. M. "A History of the Region Comprising the Katagum Division of Kano Province." *Journal of the African Society,* X–XI (1911–12).

Gaudefroy-Demombynes, Maurice. *Muslim Institutions.* London: George Allen & Unwin, 1961.

Greenberg, Joseph H. *The Languages of Africa.* 2d ed. Bloomington: Indiana University Press, 1966.

Hallam, W. K. R. "The Itinerary of Rabih Fadl Allah, 1879–1893." *Bulletin de l'I.F.A.N.,* XXX, Series B (1968), 165–80.

Heussler, Robert. "Research on Pre-British Northern Nigeria: A Note on Limitations and Potentialities." *The South Atlantic Quarterly,* LXV (1966), 523–31.

Hill, Richard. *A Biographical Dictionary of the Sudan.* 2d ed. London: Frank Cass, 1967.

Hogben, Sidney J., and Kirk-Greene, Anthony H. M. *The Emirates of Northern Nigeria: A Preliminary Survey of Their Historical Traditions.* London: Oxford University Press, 1966.

Holt, P. M. "The Sudanese Mahdia and the Outside World: 1881–89." *Bulletin of the School of Oriental and African Studies,* XXI, Pt. 2 (1958), 275–90.

Hopen, C. E. *The Pastoral Fulbe Family in Gwandu.* London: Oxford University Press, 1958.

Hunwick, John. "The Influence of Arabic in West Africa." *Transactions of the Historical Society of Ghana,* VII (1964), 24–41.

Johnston, H. A. S. *The Fulani Empire of Sokoto.* London: Oxford University Press, 1967.

Jirgi, M. *Sarkin Arewan Hadeja Tatagana.* Zaria: Gaskiya Corporation, 1954.

Kirk-Greene, Anthony H. M. *Adamawa Past and Present.* London: Oxford University Press, 1958.

Khadduri, Majid. *War and Peace in the Law of Islam.* Baltimore: Johns Hopkins Press, 1955.

Last, Denis Murray. *The Sokoto Caliphate.* London: Longmans, Green and Co., 1967.

———. "A Note on Attitudes to the Supernatural in the Sokoto Jihad." *Journal of the Historical Society of Nigeria,* IV (1967), 4–13.

Last, Denis Murray, and al-Hajj, Muhammad A. "Attempts at Defining a Muslim in 19th-century Hausaland and Bornu." Paper delivered at the Annual Congress of the Historical Society of Nigeria, Lagos, December, 1964. Revised article published in *Journal of the Historical Society of Nigeria,* III (1965).

Lavers, John E. "Jibril Gaini, A Preliminary Account of the Career of a Mahdist Leader in North-Eastern Nigeria." *Research Bulletin of the Centre of Arabic Documentation* (University of Ibadan), III (1967), 16–39.

———. "Rabih ibn Fadlullah." In *Studies on the History of Islam in West Africa,* edited by John Ralph Willis, Jr. London: Frank Cass & Co., 1972.

Le Grip, A. "Le Mahdism en Afrique Noir." *L'Afrique et l'Asie*, XVIII (1952), 3–16.

Levy, Reuben. *The Social Structure of Islam*. Cambridge: At the University Press, 1957.

Lukas, Johannes. *A Study of the Kanuri Language*. London: Oxford University Press, 1937.

Maiden, R. L. B. *The Nasarawa Gate and Other Stories*. London: Brown Knight & Truscott, n.d.

Meek, Charles Kingsley. *A Sudanese Kingdom*. London: Kegan Paul, 1931.

Merrick, G. "The Bolewa Tribe." *Journal of the African Society*, XVI (1905), 417–26.

Migeod, F. W. H. *Through Nigeria to Lake Chad*. London: Heath, Cranton, 1924.

Newman, Paul. "Linguistic Relationship, Language Shifting, and Historical Inference." *Afrika und Übersee*, LIII (1967), 217–23.

———. *A Grammar of Tera*. Berkeley: University of California Press, 1970.

Njeuma, Martin Z. "Adamawa and Mahdism: The Career of Hayatu ibn Sa'id in Adamawa, 1878–1898." *Journal of African History*, XII (1971), 61–77.

Paden, John. "Social Science and Africa." In *The African Experience*, edited by John Paden and Edward Soja. Vol. I. Evanston, Ill.: Northwestern University Press, 1970.

Palmer, H. Richmond. "Notes on the Kororofawa and Jukun." *Journal of the African Society*, XI (1912), 401–15.

———. Introduction to *A Sudanese Kingdom*. By Charles Kingsley Meek. London: Kegan Paul, 1931.

Prothero, R. Mansell. "African Ethnographic Maps, with a New Example from Northern Nigeria." *Africa*, XXXII, no. 1 (1961), 61–66.

Reed, L. N. "Notes on Some Fulani Tribes and Customs." *Africa*, V (1932), 422–53.

Rosenthal, Erwin I. J. *Political Thought in Medieval Islam*. Cambridge: At the University Press, 1962.

Ruxton, F. H. "Notes on the Tribes of the Muri Province." *Journal of the African Society*, VII (1908), 374–86.

Schacht, Joseph. "Islam in Northern Nigeria." *Studia Islamica*, VII (1957), 123–46.

Schultze, A. *The Sultanate of Bornu.* Translated by P. A. Benton. 1913. Reprint. London: Frank Cass & Co., 1968.

Smith, M. G. Introduction to *Baba of Karo: A Woman of the Muslim Hausa.* By Mary Smith. London: Faber & Faber, 1954.

———. "The Beginnings of Hausa Society, A.D. 1000–1500." In *The Historian in Tropical Africa,* edited by Jan Vansina, Raymond Mauny, and L. V. Thomas, pp. 339–57. London: Oxford University Press, 1964.

———. "Exchange and Marketing among the Hausa." In *Markets in Africa,* edited by Paul Bohannan and George Dalton, pp. 299–334. Evanston: Northwestern University Press, 1962.

———. "Field Histories among the Hausa." *Journal of African History,* II (1961), 87–101.

———. *Government in Zazzau, 1800–1950.* London: Oxford University Press, 1960.

———. "Hausa Inheritance and Succession." In *Studies in the Laws of Succession in Nigeria,* edited by J. D. M. Derrett, pp. 230–81. London: Oxford University Press, 1965.

———. "The Hausa of Northern Nigeria." In *Peoples of Africa,* edited by James L. Gibbs, pp. 119–55. New York: Holt, Rinehart and Winston, 1965.

———. "The Hausa System of Social Status." *Africa,* XXIX (1959), 239–51.

———. "Pluralism in Precolonial African Societies." In *Pluralism in Africa,* edited by Leo Kuper and M. G. Smith, pp. 91–151. Berkeley: University of California Press, 1969.

———. "Slavery and Emancipation in Two Societies." *Social and Economic Studies,* III (1954), 239–90.

Stenning, Derrick J. *Savannah Nomads: A Study of the Wodaabe Pastoral Fulani of Western Bornu Province, Northern Region, Nigeria.* London: Oxford University Press, 1959.

———. "Transhumance, Migratory Drift, Migration: Patterns of Pastoral Fulani Nomadism." In *Cultures and Societies of Africa,* edited by Simon Ottenberg and Phoebe Ottenberg, pp. 139–59. New York: Random House, 1960.

Trimingham, J. Spencer. *Islam in West Africa.* London: Oxford University Press, 1961.

Tumin, Melvin M. "Ethnic Group." In *A Dictionary of the Social Sciences,* edited by J. Gould and W. L. Kolb. Glencoe, Ill.: Free Press, 1964.

Urvoy, Yves. *Histoire de l'Empire du Bornou.* Paris: Larose, 1949.

Vansina, Jan. *Oral Tradition: A Study in Historical Methodology.* 1961. Translated by H. M. Wright. Chicago: Aldine, 1965.

———. "Once Upon a Time: Oral Traditions as History in Africa." *Daedalus,* (Spring, 1971), 442–67.

Vansina, Jan, Mauny, Raymond, and Thomas, L. V., eds. *The Historian in Tropical Africa.* London: Oxford University Press, 1964.

von Grunebaum, Gustave E. *Medieval Islam: A Study in Cultural Orientation.* Chicago: University of Chicago Press, 1961.

———. *Islam: Essays in the Nature and Growth of a Cultural Tradition.* New York: Barnes & Noble, 1961.

von Oppenheim, Max Freiherr. *La Vie du Sultan Rabeh.* Paris, 1902.

Waldman, Marilyn Robinson. "The Fulani *Jihād*: A Reassessment." *Journal of African History,* VI (1965), 333–55.

———. "A Note on the Ethnic Interpretation of the Fulani *Jihād.*" *Africa,* XXXVI (1966), 286–91.

Woodhouse, C. A. "Some Account of the Inhabitants of the Waja District of Bauchi Province, Nigeria." *Journal of the African Society,* XXIII (1924), 110–21; 194–207.

DISSERTATIONS AND PAPERS

Brenner, Louis. "The Shehus of Kukawa: A History of the Al-Kanemi Dynasty of Bornu." Ph.D. dissertation, Columbia University, 1968.

Lavers, John E. "Rabih in Bornu (Bornu and its Neighbors in the Years 1893/1900)." Paper read at the 14th Annual Congress of the Historical Society of Nigeria. 1965. Mimeographed.

INFORMANTS

Names of informants given below are followed by their

a. Age (often approximate)
b. Ethnic classification (as stated by them and their coresidents)
c. Place of birth, and place(s) of residence thereafter
d. Principal occupation, where the informant is not a titled official.

I. GOMBE EMIRATE

IA. *Gombe Town* (September–December, 1964; June–July, 1965)

1. Korofin Gombe Abdullahi Bagudu dan Ajiyan Gombe Hamman
   77; Kanuri; b. Gombe Abba, moved with capital site
2. Barden Gombe Muhammadu Tukur dan Muhammadu
   70; Janafulu; b. Gombe Abba, moved with capital site
3. Maina Bello dan Sarkin Gombe Tukur
   76; Janafulu; b. Gombe Abba, moved with capital site
4. Ciroman Yeriman Gombe Sule dan Maina Abare (Tsofo) dan Sarkin Gombe Muhammadu Kwairanga
   70; Janafulu; b. Gombe Abba, moved with capital site
5. Muhammadu Yuguda dan Sarkin Gombe Umaru
   51; Janafulu; b. Gombe Abba, moved with capital site;
   primary school teacher (30 years)
6. Sarkin Keken Gombe Siddiki dan Girema
   77; Kanuri; b. Gombe Abba, moved with capital site

IB. *Nafada District* (June–July, 1965)

1. Yeriman Bage Muhammadu dan Yeriman Bage Muhammadu Sale
   66; Fulanin Jada; b. Bage, always lived there

2. Jarmain Bage Hammadu dan Jarmain Bage Ahmadu
   72; Fulanin Jada; b. Bage, always lived there
3. Limanin Bodor Muhammadu dan Daibu
   66; Fulanin Jera; b. Bodor, always lived there
4. Wazirin Bodor Buba dan Wazirin Bodor Bello
   56; Fulanin Babir; b. Bodor, always lived there
5. Madakin Jillahi Hamadu dan Hammada
   73; Fellata Bornu; b. Wurojabe, 50 years at Busum
6. Hamma Adama dan Buba
   65; Fulanin Babir; b. Dukul, 60 years at Jillahi; *mallamin al-Kur'ani*
7. Sarkin Kupto Muhammadu dan Sarkin Kupto Usumanu
   74; Bolewa; b. Kupto, always lived there
8. Chiroman Kupto Kallunga dan Chiroman Kupto Mallam
   74; Bolewa; b. Kupto, always lived there
9. Sarkin Ribadu Abubakar dan Sarkin Ribadu Atuman
   83; Bolewa; b. Ribadu, always lived there
10. Dallamin Ribadu Abubakar dan Dallamin Ribadu Mammadi
    82; Bolewa; b. Ribadu, always lived there
11. Ardọ Tilde Sambo dan Ardo Tilde Muhammadu
    67; Fulanin Babir; b. Tilde, always lived there
12. Yeriman Tilde Abba dan Galadiman Tilde Muhammadu
    70; Fulanin Babir; b. Tilde, always lived there
13. Limanin Wakkaltu Muhammadu dan Tinjan Wakkaltu Umaru
    65; Fulanin Jada; b. Ribadu, 63 years at Wakkaltu
14. Adamu dan Hamman Bello
    75; Fulanin Jada; b. Dukul, 49 years at Wakkaltu; courtier
15. Galadiman Ashaka Abare dan Galadiman Ashaka Muhammadu
    60; Tera; b. Ashaka, always lived there
16. Limanin Ashaka Hamma dan Maisirdin Ashaka Muhammadu
    62; Tera; b. Ashaka, always lived there
17. Ali dan Alkalin Bajoga Abubakar
    66; Fellata Bornu; b. Bajoga, always lived there; *mallamin al-Kur'ani*
18. Sherif Muhammadu dan Ma'aji
    76; Kanuri; b. Bajoga, always lived there; *mallamin ilimi*
19. Sarkin Yakin Tongo Usumanu dan Umaru
    87; Fulanin Babir; b. Tongo, always lived there
20. Sambo dan Ubandawakin Tambuwal Muhammadu
    79; Fulanin Sokoto; b. Sokoto, lived at Tongo since 1903; *mallamin al-Kur'ani*
21. Dawakin Ashaka Muhammadu dan Da'u
    70; Fulanin Bolari (Kano); b. Bormi, lived at Ashaka since 1903

22. Galadiman Wurogeidam Abdulkadir dan Sarkin Laleko Muhammadu
    74; Fellata Bornu; b. Laleko, to Bormi at age 2,
    lived since 1903 at Wurogeidam
23. Umaru Pindiga dan Sarkin Pindiga Hassan
    54; Jukun; b. Pindiga, 4 years at Bajoga; district scribe
24. Abubakar dan Yeriman Birin Fulani Aliyu
    63; Jafun; b. Birin Fulani, always lived there; *mallamin al-Kur'ani*
25. Ismaila dan Hammadu
    82; Shuwa Arab; b. Birin Fulani, always lived there; farmer
26. Bauchin Wawa Hammadu dan Bauchin Wawa Umaru
    70; Bolewa; b. Wawa, always lived there
27. Ladanin Wawa Umaru dan Ladanin Wawa Usumanu
    73; Bolewa; b. Wawa, always lived there
28. Usumanu dan Madakin Magaba Muhammadu
    63; Fulanin Sika; b. Magaba, always lived there; farmer
29. Adamu dan Barden Magaba Buba
    76; Fulanin Shira; b. Magaba, always lived there; farmer
30. Madakin Nafada Tinja Aliyu dan Madakin Nafada Tinja Abdu
    70; Bolewa (of Daniski); b. Nafada, always lived there
31. Sarkin Barwo Winde Yakubu dan Sarkin Barwo Winde Abubakar
    62; Bolewa; b. Nafada, 44 years at Barwo Winde
32. Sarkin Kukawari Usumanu dan Sarkin Kukawari Kadr
    62; Fulanin Jada; b. Kukawari, always lived there
33. Sarkin Birin Bolewa Umaru dan Sarkin Birin Bolewa Aliyu
    66; Bolewa; b. Birin Bolewa, always lived there
34. Alhaji Abdu dan Abdullahi
    71; Bolewa; b. Birin Bolewa, always lived there; *mallamin ilimi*
35. Limanin Bajoga Hamma Tukur dan Ardo Giade Muhammadu
    86; b. Giade (Katagum), lived at Bajoga since 1903
36. Jibir Tambaya dan Magajin Dawakin Tofa (Kano) Muhammadu
    80; Fulanin Daneji; b. Dawakin Tofa, lived 10 years at Bormi, at Bajoga since 1903

IC. *Yemaltu District* (June, 1965)

1. Sarkin Deba Habe Usuman Muhammadu dan Sarkin Deba Habe Muhammadu
    31; Tera; b. Deba Habe, always lived there
2. Alhaji Abare dan Dawakin Deba Habe Madi
    76; Tera; b. Deba Habe, always lived there; *mallamin ilimi*
3. Gwazan Deba Habe Byagam dan Dalbudin Deba Habe Nyagam
    52; Tera; b. Deba Habe, always lived there

4. Birman Deba Habe Umaru dan Dan Lukan Deba Habe Kadr
   43; Tera; b. Deba Habe, always lived there
5. Kalan Deba Habe Domi dan Makerin Deba Habe Mama
   65; Tera; b. Deba Habe, always lived there
6. Sarkin Zambuk Aji dan Sarkin Zambuk Madi
   46; Tera; b. Zambuk, 20 intervening years at Bida
7. Dalan Zambuk Mama dan Kwariangam Nyagam
   68; Tera; b. Zambuk, always lived there
8. Atuman dan Galadiman Zambuk Ali
   63; Tera; b. Zambuk, always lived there
9. Burungusan Zambuk Madi dan Dalan Zambuk Mele
   57; Tera; b. Zambuk, always lived there
10. Sarkin Shinga Muhammadu dan Sarkin Shinga Ali
    28; Tera; b. Shinga, always lived there
11. Birman Shinga Maikanda dan Zarman Shinga Bukar
    60; Tera; b. Shinga, always lived there
12. Dawakin Hina Leka dan Yeriman Hina Madi
    74; Tera; b. Gwani, lived since age 20 at Hina
13. Galadiman Hina Mama dan Jonga
    70; Tera; b. Hina, always lived there
14. Madakin Hina Madi dan Madakin Hina Kadal
    77; Tera; b. Hina, always lived there
15. Sarkin Lubo Atuman dan Sarkin Lubo Aji
    55; Tera; b. Kulam, lived 11 years at Lubo
16. Barkuman Lubo Melli dan Magaji
    77; Tera; b. Lubo, always lived there
17. Tashilman Lubo Jonga dan Zarman Lubo Bukar
    60; Tera; b. Lubo, always lived there
18. Chiroman Lubo Melle dan Kosuman Lubo Joju
    64; Tera; b. Lubo, always lived there
19. Sarkin Kinafa Aliyu dan Sarkin Kinafa Galaya
    49; Tera; b. Kinafa, always lived there
20. Galadiman Kinafa Buba dan Yeriman Kinafa Badima
    76; Tera; b. Kinafa, always lived there
21. Dalan Kinafa Bature dan Ngurkuman Kinafa Umar
    62; Tera; b. Kinafa, always lived there
22. Sarkin Kohal Abdulkadiri dan Sarkin Kohal Aliyu
    37; Tera; b. Kohal, always lived there
23. Galadiman Kohal Kudi dan Maisoron Kohal Mamma
    64; Tera; b. Difa, 10 years at Kohal

24. Fukuman Kohal Mamma dan Madi Kubli
    85; Tera; b. Kohal, always lived there
25. Dalan Kohal Adamu dan Kelman Kohal Musa
    66; Tera; b. Difa, to Kohal at age 4
26. Galadiman Difa Ardo dan Galadiman Difa Kwona
    58; Tera; b. Difa, always lived there
27. Batarin Difa Kinam dan Batarin Difa Dolaki
    78; Tera; b. Difa, always lived there
28. Zarman Difa Suburnum dan Melle
    68; Tera; b. Difa, always lived there
29. Sarkin Gwani Adamu dan Sarkin Kudun Gombe Muhammadu Bello
    48; Tera; b. Jos, lived 44 years at Gwani
30. Yeriman Gwani Kaito dan Limanin Gwani Minayel
    86; Tera; b. Gwani, always lived there
31. Kala dan Magamdoloki
    66; Tera; b. Gwani, always lived there; farmer
32. Danyaya dan Atuman
    75; Tera; b. Gwani, always lived there; farmer
33. Tafidan Gwani Madi dan Mishelkalan Hina Ahmadu
    54; Tera; b. Hina, 15 years at Dadin Kowa, 36 at Gwani
34. Sarkin Wade Nyagam dan Sarkin Wade Bukar
    57; Tera; b. Wade, always lived there
35. Galadiman Wade Mamman dan Bukar
    77; Tera; b. Wade, always lived there
36. Shettiman Wade Gabdan dan Shettiman Wade Gabdan
    55; Tera; b. Wade, always lived there
37. Sarkin Kidan Wade Kinam dan Shettiman Wade Gabdan
    47; Tera; b. Wade, always lived there
38. Sarkin Jagali Magaji dan Sarkin Jagali Dagama
    74; Jera; b. Jagali, always lived there
39. Zarman Jagali Madi dan Gurkuman Jagali Ali
    66; Jera; b. Jagali, always lived there
40. Kosuman Jagali Madi dan Zarman Jagali Mallam
    65; Jera; b. Jagali, always lived there
41. Alkalin Dadin Kowa Usumanu dan Mukaddamin Alkalin Akko Umaru
    40; Fulanin Gona; b. (new) Gombe, 4 years at Dadin Kowa
42. Keldiman Kodon Hamagam dan Batarin Kodon Mele
    67; Tera; b. Kodon, always lived there
43. Sarkin Kodon Abubakar dan Mele
    33; Tera; b. Kodon, always lived there

44. Fukuman Kodon Aji dan Ibrahim
    61; Kanuri; b. Kodon, always lived there

ID. *Kumo District* (June–July, 1965)

1. Tafidan Akko Ibrahim dan Galadiman Akko Hamma Nina
   72; Fulanin Gona; b. Akko, to Gombe at age 18, 10 years at Garko, 1 year at Tula, 3 years at Kalshingi, and 14 years at Kumo
2. Mukkadamin Alkalin Akko Umaru dan Ajiyan Akko Adamu
   65; Fulanin Gona; b. Akko, to Lafiya Akko at age 14, 7 years at Birndaka, 9 years at Gombe, 17 years at Kumo
3. Ajiyan Akko Abubakar dan Ajiyan Akko Abba
   76; Fulanin Gona; b. Akko, to Gombe at age 15, 19 years at Deba Habe, 37 years at Kumo
4. Ubandoman Akko Buba dan Mainan Akko Baba
   65; Fulanin Gona; b. Akko, to Lafiya at age 20, 25 years at Kumo
5. Limanin Kumo Muhammadu Tukur dan Muhammadu
   63; Fellata Bornu; b. Jada Myam (Bauchi), 40 years at Kumo
6. Sarkin Kalshingi Abubakar dan Sarkin Kalshingi Magaji
   35; Tera; b. Kalshingi, 12 years at Kodon
7. Sarkin Kalshingi (ret.) Madi dan Sarkin Kalshingi Ali
   70; Tera; b. Kalshingi, always lived there
8. Kallan Panda Malla dan Gireman Panda Garaguma
   65; Kanuri; b. Panda, always lived there
9. Ahmadu dan Alkalin Akko Bello
   49; Fulanin Gona; b. Akko, 28 years at Kalshingi; village area scribe
10. Batarin Panda Ali dan Batarin Panda Madi
    40; Kanuri; b. Panda, always lived there
11. Wombain Galadiman Akko Ahmadu dan Sambo
    83; Fulanin Gona; b. Akko, 37 years at Kanawa
12. Chiroman Akko Hassan dan Chiroman Akko Subande
    50; Fulanin Gona; b. Akko, 37 years at Kumo
13. Kaiman Panda Manga dan Paku
    65; Jukun; b. Panda, always lived there
14. Hamma dan Jauro Umaru
    73; Fulanin Gona; b. Tukulma, always lived there; farmer
15. Ubandoman Tukulma Kawu dan Muhammadu
    50; Fellata Bornu; b. Tukulma, always lived there
16. Galadiman Kaltanga Gona Buba dan Ardo Tar
    79; Kanuri; b. Jada Nyewa (Bauchi), 54 years at Kulum Beriberi, then to Kaltanga Gona
17. Sarkin Pindiga (ret.) Ibrahim dan Sarkin Pindiga Hassan
    67; Jukun; b. Pindiga, 23 years at Kumo

18. Magajin Tukulma Buba dan Umaru
    58; Fulanin Gona; b. Tukulma, always lived there
19. Sarkin Kaltanga Gona Muhammadu dan Yeriman Tukulma Abdu
    51; Fulanin Gona; b. Tukulma, 3 months at Kaltanga Gona
20. Sarkin Panda Abubakar dan Sarkin Panda Melle
    29; Jukun; b. Panda, always lived there
21. Sarkin Tukulma Muhammadu Basharu dan Sarkin Tukulma Umaru
    34; Fulanin Gona; b. Tukulma, 10 years at Nafada
22. Tafidan Akko Muhammadu dan Galadiman Akko Umaru
    37; Fulanin Gona; b. Gombe, lived at Tukulma and Kumo

IE. *Kwami District* (June, 1965)

1. Galadiman Kafarati Kari dan Galadiman Kafarati Moi Mala
   67; Bolewa; b. Kafarati, always lived there
2. Chiroman Kafarati Suleimanu dan Sarkin Kafarati Musa
   31; Bolewa; b. Gerikom, 15 years at Kararati
3. Sarkin Kwom Fellata Bello dan Sarkin Yakin Kwom Fellata Buba
   50; Fulanin Kitaku; b. Kwom Fellata, always lived there
4. Sarkin Dami'ya Ali dan Sarkin Dami'ya Umaru
   57; Fulanin Kitaku; b. Kwom Fellata, 20 years at Dami'ya
5. Sarkin Doho Usumanu dan Sarkin Doho Alhaji
   54; Tera; b. Doho, always lived there
6. Sarkin Gadam Usumanu dan Sarkin Gadam Musa
   70; Bolewa; b. Gadam, always lived there
7. Chiroman Bojude Muhammadu dan Sarkin Bojude Mamma
   33; Bolewa; b. Bojude, always lived there
8. Sarkin Dukul Musa dan Sarkin Dukul Abdulkadir
   69; Fulanin Jera; b. Dukul, always lived there
9. Chiroman Dukul Muhammadu Bello dan Dauda
   50; Fulanin Walama; b. Dukul, always lived there
10. Sarkin Deba Fulani Buba dan Madakin Deba Fulani Sule
    72; Fulanin Tara; b. Deba Fulani, always lived there
11. Wazirin Deba Fulani Usumanu dan Madakin Deba Fulani Sule
    60; Fulanin Tara; b. Deba Fulani, always lived there
12. Sarkin Malleri Haruna dan Madakin Malleri Isa
    53; Fulanin Jada; b. Malleri, always lived there
13. Sarkin Jurara Usumanu dan Yeriman Tilde Adamu
    40; Fulanin Babir; b. Tilde, 6 years at Jurara

IF. *Dukku District* (June, 1965)

1. Ajiyan Dukku Muhammadu dan Ajiyan Dukku Muhammadu
   60; Jukun; b. Dukku, always lived there

2. Muhammadu Manga dan Ardo Ahmadu
   49; Fulanin Shira; b. Dukku, always lived there; *mallamin al-Kur'ani*
3. Jarman Dukku Abba dan Madakin Dukku Abubakar
   68; Fulanin Shira; b. Dukku, always lived there
4. Ahmadu dan Wazirin Dukku Muhammadu
   38; Fulanin Shira; b. Dukku, always lived there; district scribe
5. Bappa dan Abubakar
   38; Fulanin Shira; b. Dukku, always lived there; farmer
6. Lamidon Birko (Sengobani) Hamma Bose dan Ardo Usumanu
   78; Fulanin Shira; b. Dukku, always lived there; farmer

IG. *Gombe Abba* (June, 1965)

1. Buba dan Ladanin Ung. Daulewol Salihi
   70; Kanuri; b. Ung. Daulewol, always lived there; farmer
2. Isa dan Ibrahim
   86; Bolewa; b. Ung. Daulewol, always lived there; farmer
3. Audu dan Adamu
   56; Haben Kano; b. Ung. Bardofitti, always lived there; farmer and fisherman
4. Sarkin Yakin Ung. Bardofitti Umaru dan Sarkin Yaki Bagara Abubakar
   57; Janafulu; b. Bardofitti Gada, always lived there
5. Galadiman Wurojada Kadr dan Galadiman Wurojada Tukur
   92; Fulanin Jada; b. Wurojada, always lived there
6. Adamu Gugulin dan Sarkin Gugulin (Misau) Muhammadu
   70; Haben Shira; b. Gugulin, to Ung. Puya at age 3; farmer
7. Bubari dan Suleimanu
   78; Janafulu; b. Ung. Shangale, always lived there; *mallamin ilimi*
8. Kwassu dan Shamakin Ajiyan Gombe Ibrahim Ahmadu
   90; Jukun; b. Ung. Kanoma, always lived there; long-distance trader

II. KATAGUM EMIRATE

IIA. *Azare Town* (June–August, 1964; February–March, August, 1965)

1. Makaman Katagum Ahmadu dan Makaman Katagum Abare
   85; Kerikeri; b. Katagum, to Azare at age 35
2. Wombain Katagum Alhaji Salihu dan Muhammadu
   71; Kanuri; b. Walai (Gadau), 10 years at Katagum Town, 50 years at Azare
3. Ali Gadanga dan Sarkin Katagum Muhammadu
   60; Lawanawa; b. Katagum, to Azare at age 10; messenger

4. Wakilin Makaman Katagum Muhammadu dan Wombain Katagum Muhammadu
   80; Kerikeri; b. Katagum, to Azare at age 30
5. Tafidan Katagum Ali dan Abubakar
   79; Fulanin Kano (Gaya); b. Gaya, to Katagum Town at age 7, to Azare at age 29

IIB. *Katagum Town* (February–March, 1965)

1. Ahmadu dan Muhammadu
   82; Kanuri; b. Teshena, to Katagum at age 7 (Ung. Marma); farmer
2. Maiunguwar Kukadi (Katagum) Shehu dan Magajin Gwanin Katagum Ahmadu
   64; Haben Teshena; b. Ung. Kukadi, always lived there; petty trader
3. Bappa Minna dan Audu
   75; Fulanin Teshena; b. Ung. Rakumanani, always lived there; long-distance trader
4. Ahmadu dan Usumanu
   74; *dengin* Abunoboji; b. Ung. Kukadi, 21 years at Azare; builder and *mallamin ilimi*
5. Muhammadu Dagula dan Muhammadu
   80; Fulanin Teshena; b. Ung. Rimindi, always lived there; long-distance trader and broker
6. Limanin Katagum Ahmadu dan Bappa
   70; Fellata Bornu; b. Ung. Rimindi, always lived there
7. Alkalin Katagum (town) Alhaji Garba Affa dan Sarkin Shira Alu
   52; Lawanawa; b. Udubo, to Shira at age 2, to Azare at age 6; 30 years a primary school teacher
8. Sarkin Koren Mabbi Umaru dan Sarkin Yakin Katagum Mamman dan Maudu
   75; Fulanin Teshena; b. Katagum town, 40 years at Kore Mabbi
9. Alu Dan Koli dan Abdulkadir
   68; Auyakawa (mother a daughter of Waziri Hamji); b. Katagum town, always lived there; petty trader

IIC. *Madara District* (July–August, 1965)

1. Sarkin Dawakin Katagum Shehu dan Sarkin Shira Muhammadu
   60; Lawanawa; b. Shira, 13 years at Madara
2. Sarkin Madara Bello dan Sarkin Madara Abdu
   50; Fulanin Shira; b. Madara, always lived there
3. Wazirin Madara Adamu dan Wazirin Madara Bura
   55; Fulanin Shira; b. Madara, always lived there

4. Sarkin Madara (ret.) Ali dan Sarkin Lariski Muhammadu
   60; Lawanawa; b. Lariski, 8 years at Madara
5. Sarkin Gambaki Muhammadu dan Sarkin Gambaki Ahmadu
   40; Haben Shira; b. Gambaki, always lived there
6. Ibrahim dan Shu'aibu
   55; Haben Shira; b. Gambaki, always lived there; *mallamin ilimi*
7. Muhammadu dan Abdu
   70; Haben Shira; b. Gambaki, always lived there; dyer
8. Suleimanu dan Ismaila
   70; Haben Shira; b. Gambaki, always lived there; *mallamin al-Kur'ani*
9. Sale dan Mamman
   75; Haben Shira; b. Gambaki, always lived there; kola-nut seller
10. Sarkin Buskuri Muhammadu dan Sarkin Buskuri Muhammadu
    70; Fulanin Shira; b. Buskuri, always lived there
11. Wakilin Buskuri Abubakar dan Muhammadu
    55; Haben Gobir; b. Jugga, 17 years at Buskuri
12. Abdullah dan Muhammadu
    65; Kwayamawa; b. Jugga, 40 years at Buskuri; *mallamin al-Kur'ani*
13. Jauron Jugga Manu dan Jauron Jugga Jibir
    70; Fulanin Shira; b. Jugga, always lived there; cattle dealer
14. Wakilin Magonshi Adamu dan Muhammadu
    65; Haben Shira; b. Magonshi, always lived there
15. Wazirin Magonshi Abubakar dan Sarkin Magonshi Jibir
    65; Haben Shira; b. Magonshi, always lived there
16. Sarkin Magonshi Abdu dan Muhammadu
    75; Haben Shira; b. Magonshi, always lived there
17. Alhaji Abubakar dan Muhammadu
    90; Haben Shira; b. Magonshi, always lived there; *mallamin ilimi*
18. Magajin Belin Shirawa Abdulmumin dan Sarkin Belin Shirawa Muhammadu
    63; Fulanin Shira; b. Bidir, to Belin Shirawa at age 40
19. Sarkin Kilemu Adamu dan Sarkin Bidir Muhammadu
    70; Fulanin Shira; b. Bidir, to Kilemu at age 52

IID. *Sokwa District* (July–August, 1965)

1. Sarkin Wanzamin Katagum Muhammadu (Arabo) dan Sarkin Wanzamin Katagum Abubakar
   70; Arab; b. Sokwa, to Azare at age 37
2. Wakilin Sokwa Muhammadu dan Wazirin Sokwa Mu'azu
   49; Arab; b. Sokwa, always lived there
3. Limanin Murmur Ibrahim dan Sarkin Charcharam Muhammadu
   53; Kanuri; b. Murmur, always lived there

4. Ladanin Murmur Muhammadu dan Mamman
   59; Kanuri; b. Murmur, always lived there
5. Muhammadu Kefime dan Lawan Gana
   76; Arab; b. Keffin Larabawa, always lived there; *fari*-cloth sewer
6. Mamman dan Yerima
   60; Arab; b. Keffin Larabawa, always lived there; *fari*-cloth sewer
7. Sa'idu dan Jatau
   65; Arab; b. Sokwa, to Guma'i at age 5; leatherworker
8. Limanin Guma'i Bello dan Haji
   65; Fulanin Sika; b. Guma'i, always lived there

IIE. *Udubo District* (July, 1965)

1. Muhammadu Diri dan Muhammadu Chiromarima
   65; Lerewa; b. Udubo, always lived there; weaver
2. Sarkin Pawan Udubo Ali dan Sarkin Pawan Udubo Shehu Usuman
   59; Haben Kano; b. Udubo, always lived there; butcher
3. Muhammadu Babba dan Jafaru
   64; Gerawa (Bauchi); b. Udubo, always lived there; *mallamin al-Kur'ani*
4. Isa dan Ibrahim
   68; Fellata Bornu; b. Udubo, always lived there; *mallamin al-Kur'ani* and courtier
5. Muhammadu dan Sale
   85; Gerawa (Bauchi); b. Nassarawa, to Udubo at age 25; professional beggar
6. Sarkin Udubo Alhaji Abubakar Garba dan Sarkin Udubo Muhammadu
   62; Lawanawa; b. Azare, to Udubo at age 7
7. Ibrahima dan Sarkin Udubo Muhammadu
   35; Lawanawa; b. Udubo, always lived there; farmer
8. Adamu Jumba dan Adamu
   22; Fulanin Udubo; b. Jarwa, 5 years at Udubo; district scribe
9. Muhammadu Kosa dan Sarkin Bagalu Muhammadu
   76; Fulanin Udubo; b. Kafin Romi, to Gadiya at age 16; dealer in cattle
10. Baba Jauro dan Wazirin Gadiya Bello
    66; Fulanin Sika; b. Gadiya, always lived there; dealer in cattle
11. Bulaman Gajjel Isa dan Bulaman Gajjel Muhammadu
    70; Kwayamawa; b. Gajjel, always lived there; dealer in cattle
12. Tambarin Tarmasuwa Gesum dan Tambarin Tarmasuwa Laboje
    73; Kerikeri; b. Jarmari, to Tarmasuwa at age 29
13. Ladanin Zindiwa Isa dan Umaru
    63; Lerewa; b. Jarmari, to Zindiwa at age 13

14. Idi dan Muhammadu
    61; Lerewa; b. Jarmari, to Zindiwa at age 3; cloth beater
15. Adamu dan Gambo
    72; Kwayamawa; b. Mallam Fateri, to Gayawa at age 34; cattle-rearer
16. Mamman Daudu dan Galadiman Gayawa Muhammadu
    66; Kanembu; b. Gayawa, always lived there; courtier
17. Hassan dan Adamu
    60; Lawanawa; b. Udubo, to Magajiri at age 40; leatherworker
18. Yusufu dan Wakilin Raga
    74; Lerewa; b. Raga, always lived there; *mallamin al-Kur'ani*

IIF. *Chinade District* (July, August, 1965)

1. Dadumi dan Wakilin Yelwa Ali
   77; Haben Shira; b. Yelwa, always lived there; broker
2. Yakuba dan Sa'idu
   85; Haben Shira; b. Gambaki, to Madaci at age 18; farmer
3. Jauro Musa dan Ali
   72; Haben Shira; b. Gangai, always lived there; cattle-rearer
4. Wakilin Janbure Umaru dan Sa'idu
   80; Fulanin Shira; b. Chinade, to Janbure at age 13
5. Sarkin Gadau Muhammadu Bashar dan Yeriman Chinade Muhammadu Bappa
   70; Lawanawa; b. Chinade, to Gadau at age 25
6. Makaman Chinade Muhammadu dan Makaman Chinade Abdu
   70; Haben Shira; b. Chinade, always lived there
7. Huseini dan Ishiaku
   75; Kanuri; b. Dagaro, to Chinade at age 12; salt seller
8. Ahmadu dan Mamudu
   78; Haben Shira; b. Gadau, to Chinade at age 12; broker
9. Muhammadu Maina Abba dan Sarkin Kari Ali
   71; Shuwa Arab; b. Kari, to Chinade at age 2; farmer
10. Adama dan Ibrahim
    82; Haben Kano; b. Yaiyu, always lived there; salt seller
11. Sarkin Ruwan Yaiyu Adamu dan Adamu
    75; Jafun; b. Hardawa, to Yaiyu at age 10
12. Sarkin Ruwan Bursuri Audu dan Hassan
    83; Haben Shira; b. Gambaki, to Bursuri at age 9
13. Ali dan Manu
    70; Haben Shira; b. Charachara (Azare), to Dagaro at age 30; cloth beater

14. Musa dan Muhammadu
    82; Lerewa; b. Gangai, to Magariya at age 17; *fari*-cloth weaver

IIG. *Gamawa District* (July, 1965)

1. Muhammadu Barde dan Muhammadu Dingazo
   62; b. Kafin Romi, always lived there; broker
2. Muhammadu Sambo dan Hardon Kafin Romi Adamu
   66; b. Kafin Romi; always lived there; farmer
3. Sarkin Kafin Romi Ahmadu dan Sarkin Kafin Romi Abubakar
   63; b. Kafin Romi, always lived there
4. Muhammadu Haji dan Sarkin Alagarno Barde
   60; Kanuri; b. Bornu, to Sabon Gari at age 10; farmer
5. Aliyu Babbaji dan Muhammadu Gabdo
   55; Lerewa; b. Sabon Gari, always lived there; farmer
6. Usuman wa dan Muhammadu
   88; Lerewa; b. Gamawa, always lived there; courtier
7. Usuman dan Mustapha
   85; Lerewa; b. Gamawa, always lived there; courtier
8. Abubakar Dodo dan Abdu
   72; Fellata Bornu; b. Gamawa, always lived there; courtier
9. Haji dan Abubakar
   57; Kanuri; b. Kubdiya, always lived there; farmer
10. Wakilin Kore Mustapha dan Adamu
    67; Haben Kano; b. Koren Katagum, always lived there
11. Musa dan Muhammadu
    70; Kanuri; b. Koren Katagum, always lived there; fisherman
12. Ahmadu dan Madu
    80; Lerewa; b. Gatatara, always lived there; barber
13. Ibrahim dan Muhammadu
    60; Lerewa; b. Gatatara, always lived there; *mallamin al-Kur'ani*
14. Ibrahim dan Umaru
    56; Auyakawa; b. Tamazza, to Biriri at age 6; farmer

IIH. *Itas District* (July, 1965)

1. Bulama Yusufu dan Muhammadu
   63; Kanuri; b. Gadau, to Kashumri at age 1; salt seller
2. Ali dan Muhammadu
   80; Fulanin Sika; b. Lizai, to Kashumri at age 27; *fari*-cloth weaver
3. Inusa dan Alkalin Gadau Muhammadu
   55; Kanuri; b. Hausawa (Gadau), to Itas at age 2; farmer

4. Iro dan Sarkin Itas Abdu
   50; Haben Teshena; b. Itas, always lived there; *mallamin ilimi*
5. Garba dan Umaru
   68; Shuwa Arab; b. Itas, always lived there; *mallamin ilimi*
6. Musa dan Kaina
   80; Auyakawa; b. Yayari, to Mashema at age 17; drummer
7. Musa dan Muhammadu
   50; Fulanin Sambo; b. Yarda (Bulangu), to Mashema at age 25
8. Galadiman Gwarai Shehu dan Adamu
   64; Jafun; b. Gwarai, always lived there
9. Barden Gwarai Muhammadu dan Audu
   64; Jafun; b. Gwarai, always lived there
10. Sarkin Zazai Sule dan Sarkin Zazai Abdu
    69; Lawanawa; b. Zazai, always lived there
11. Sarkin Sherifuri Idirisu dan Sarkin Sherifuri Alhaji Bukr
    64; Kanuri; b. Sherifuri, always lived there
12. Wakilin Banbal Musa dan Adamu
    65; Kwayamawa; b. Chamu (Kano), to Banbal at age 11
13. Sarkin Ruwan Abdalawa Adamu dan Sarkin Ruwan Abdalawa Abdu
    40; Haben Kano; b. Abdalawa, always lived there
14. Wakilin Abdalawa Alhassan dan Ibrahim
    50; Haben Kano; b. Wudil area (Kano), to Abdalawa at age 12

II I *Shira District* (February, July, 1965)

1. Sarkin Tsafi Muhammadu dan Ahmadu dan Muhammadu Auta
   75; Lawanawa; b. Tsafi, always lived there
2. Ladanin Tsafi Abubakar dan Jibir
   75; Fulanin Sambo; b. Darajiya, to Tsafi at age 11
3. Sarkin Faggo Dahiru dan Sarki Faggo Shehu
   63; Auyakawa; b. Faggo, always lived there
4. Sarkin Gadama Ibrahim dan Abdulkadir
   75; Auyakawa; b. Faggo, to Gadama at age 13
5. Abubakar dan Limanin Disina Alhassan
   75; Arab; b. Disina, always lived there; *mallamin al-Kur'ani*
6. Muhammadu dan Sarkin Disina Muhammadu Tukur
   65; Lawanawa; b. Disina, always lived there; *mallamin al-Kur'ani*
7. Isa dan Abubakar
   83; Haben Kano; b. Miga (Kano), to Dango at age 11; *mallamin al-Kur'ani*
8. Ahmadu dan Musa
   80; Kanuri; b. Gwadayi (Kano), to Belin Shirawa at age 8; *mallamin al-Kur'ani*

9. Wakilin Dango Ahmadu dan Sarkin Dango Abdulkadir
   45; Lawanawa; b. Dango, always lived there
10. Alhaji Usuman dan Shu'aibu
    77; Kutumbawa; b. Indabo (Kano), to Gagidiba at age 5; long-distance trader
11. Abdu dan Usuman
    65; Kwayamawa; b. Gagidiba, always lived there; builder
12. Sarkin Gwadal Bello dan Sarkin Gwadal Musa
    65; Fulanin Shira; b. Gwadal, always lived there
13. Sarkin Katangari Muhammadu dan Sarkin Katangari Umaru
    70; Fulanin Shira; b. Katangari, always lived there
14. Ibrahim dan Adamu
    55; Auyakawa; b. Bangire, always lived there; hunter
15. Adamu dan Idirisu
    55; Auyakawa; b. Bangire, always lived there; *mallamin al-Kur'ani*
16. Sarkin Ibbawo Muhammadu dan Sarkin Ibbawo Suleiman
    70; Fulanin Shira; b. Daramushe, to Ibbawo at age 25
17. Magaji dan Jauron Yelwa Muhammadu
    65; Fellata Bornu; b. Katabarwa, always lived there; wardhead
18. Chiroman Isore Umaru dan Sarkin Isore Ahmadu
    63; Fellata Bornu; b. Isore, always lived there
19. Wakilin Kilbori Abdulkadir dan Ishiaku
    70; Lawanawa; b. Kilbori, always lived there
20. Majidadin Kilbori Umaru dan Wazirin Kilbori Tukur
    70; Lawanawa; b. Kilbori, always lived there
21. Limanin Sambawal Kafi dan Sarkin Isawa Ibrahim
    49; Yelagawa; b. Jalkatari, to Sambawal at age 32
22. Ibrahim dan Muhammadu
    72; Haben Shira; b. Bukul, always lived there; fisherman
23. Maina Abubakar dan Jatau
    80; Arab; b. Darajiya, always lived there; tailor
24. Wazirin Darajiya Muhammadu dan Sarkin Darajiya Adamu
    70; Fulanin Shira; b. Darajiya, always lived there
25. Ibrahima Gambo dan Shu'aibu
    80; Fulanin Sambo; b. Shira, always lived there; *mallamin ilimi*
26. Sa'idu dan Muhammadu
    70; Fulanin Sambo; b. Shira, always lived there; *mallamin al-Kur'ani*
27. Abdulhamid dan Musa
    82; Kanuri; b. Shira, always lived there; *mallamin al-Kur'ani*
28. Abubakar dan Sarkin Barandamau Ahmadu dan Sarkin Shira Usuman
    82; Lawanawa; b. Azare, to Shira at age 11; tailor

IIJ. *Giade District* (July–August, 1965)

1. Shehu dan Jibir
   80; Fulanin Shira; b. Belin Barnawa, to Isawa at age 36; farmer
2. Adamu dan Ibrahim
   80; Fellata Bornu; b. Isawa, always lived there; barber
3. Mamman dan Abubakar
   70; Kanuri; b. Uzum Beriberi, always lived there; farmer
4. Adamu dan Fuguma
   75; Fellata Bornu; b. Sorodo, to Uzum Beriberi at age 12; tailor
5. Ladanin Yaya dan Sarkin Abornari Adamu
   80; Fellata Bornu; b. Zabi, always lived there
6. Idirisu dan Muhammadu
   80; Fulanin Shira; b. Giade, always lived there; farmer
7. Muhammadu dan Audu
   75; Kerikeri; b. Giade, always lived there; farmer
8. Wazirin Tsagi (Kano) Abdulkadir dan Abubakar
   70; Fulanin Shira; b. Doguwa, to Tsagi at age 30
9. Ahmadu dan Abdullahi
   82; Jafun; b. Doguwa, always lived there; *mallamin al-Kur'ani*
10. Sarkin Banbiyo Adamu dan Sarkin Banbiyo Abdulkadir
    50; Fulanin Shira; b. Banbiyo, always lived there
11. Alhaji Bello dan Galadiman Banbiyo Ibrahim
    66; Fulanin Shira; b. Banbiyo, always lived there; cattle-rearer
12. Galadiman Kurba Abdulkadir dan Galadiman Kurba Adamu
    80; Fulanin Shira; b. Kurba, always lived there
13. Sarkin Zirami Suleimanu dan Sarkin Bidir Muhammadu
    73; Jafun; b. Bidir, to Zirami at age 20
14. Usuman dan Hassan
    74; Lerewa; b. Zirami, always lived there; *fari*-cloth weaver
15. Zakar dan Mamman
    78; Lerewa; b. Jugga, to Zirami at age 16; farmer

IIK. *Azare District* (August, 1965)

1. Muhammadu Jarmai dan Abdurrahman dan Galadiman Azare Yusufu
   70; Haben Shira; b. Azare, always lived there; farmer
2. Muhammadu Lele dan Sarkin Fatara Musa
   65; Haben Shira; b. Azare, always lived there; *mallamin al-Kur'ani*
3. Almadu dan Umaru
   68; Fellata Bornu; b. Azare, always lived there; animal-rearer

4. Limanin Madangala Abubakar dan Limanin Madangala Aliyu
   60; Lerewa; b. Madangala, always lived there
5. Adamu dan Limanin Madangala Aliyu
   58; Lerewa; b. Madangala, always lived there; *mallamin al-Kur'ani*

III. HADEJIA EMIRATE

IIIA. *Hadejia Town* (April–May, 1965)

1. Alhaju Muhammadu Dani dan Usuman
   78; Fulanin Sambo; b. Hadejia, always lived there; kola-nut seller
2. Yahaya dan Muhammadu
   80; Fun Sha'iya; b. Hadejia, always lived there; seller of goats
3. Adamu dan Huseini
   80; Auyakawa; b. Hadejia, always lived there; farmer
4. Muhammadu dan Ibrahima
   83; Katumbawa; b. Hadejia, always lived there; dyer
5. Abdurnasur dan Alhaji Hudu
   72; Fulanin Shira; b. Hadejia, always lived there; *mallamin al-Kur'ani*
6. Idirisu dan Muhammadu Mustapha
   78; Konubordu (Arab); b. Hadejia, always lived there; long-distance trader
7. Ahmadu dan Musa
   90; Auyakawa; b. Hadejia, always lived there; sweets seller
8. Suleimanu dan Adamu
   76; Kolumpardu; b. Hadejia, always lived there; *mallamin al-Kur'ani*
9. Sidi dan Mamman Gula
   86; Auyakawa; b. Hadejia, always lived there; drummer
10. Abdullahi dan Mamman
    85; Auyakawa; b. Hadejia, always lived there; farmer
11. Alhaji Abubakar dan Alhaji Ali
    78; Fulanin Sambo (*dengi*); b. Hadejia, always lived there; farmer
12. Dodo Kasa dan Adamu
    82; Auyakawa; b. Hadejia, always lived there; builder
13. Ibrahim dan Salihu dan Madakin Hadejia Abdullahi
    70; Auyakawa; b. Hadejia, always lived there; farmer
14. Ibrahim dan Ahmadu
    70; Auyakawa; b. Hadejia, always lived there; farmer

15. Sankile dan Sarkin Dawakin Hadejia Umaru
    76; Auyakawa; b. Hadejia, always lived there; courtier
16. Turakin Hadejia Adamu Sadi dan Galadiman Hadejia Usuman
    75; Auyakawa; b. Hadejia, always lived there
17. Sarkin Hatsin Keffin Hausa Haruna dan Sarkin Hatsin Keffin Hausa Sule
    70; Auyakawa; b. Keffin Hausa, always lived there; long-distance trader
18. Fatsuma 'yar Kyallu 'yar Sarkin Hadejia Muhammadu
    80; Fulanin Sambo; b. Hadejia, always lived there
19. Hannatu Babba 'yar Maina Yero dan Sambo Digimsa
    64; Fulanin Sambo; b. Hadejia, always lived there
20. Furera 'yar Ali
    69; Auyakawa; b. Hadejia, always lived there; palace messenger

IIIB. *Bulangu District* (May, 1965)

1. Alhaji Sambo Rakumi dan Shamakin Hadejia Mamman
   67; Fulanin Sambo; b. Hadejia, 53 years at Shakato and Bulangu; courtier
2. Dadalu dan Alkalin Shira Yahaya
   83; Fulanin Sambo; b. Shira, 58 years at Jabo and Bulangu; courtier
3. Babanmande dan Idi
   68; Auyakawa; b. Hadejia, 52 years at Shakato and Bulangu; courtier
4. Audu dan Sale
   73; Kanuri; b. Azare, to Bulangu at age 18; farmer
5. Muhammadu Jauro dan Jatau
   80; Kanuri; b. Azare, to Bulangu at age 25; farmer
6. Maiunguwa Adamu dan Maiunguwa Isiaku
   73; Kanuri; b. Bulangu, always lived there; tailor
7. Usuman Suleiman dan Wombain Hadejia Suleiman
   24; Kanuri; b. Bulangu, always lived there; district scribe

IIIC. *Keffin Hausa District* (April–May, 1965)

1. Zubeiru dan Chiroman Hadejia Ali
   40; Fulanin Sambo; b. Hadejia, 30 years at Auyo and Keffin Hausa; district scribe
2. Babba dan Abubakar
   58; Haben Daura; b. Hadejia, to Keffin Hausa at age 7; courtier
3. Tafidan Auyo Alhaji Suleimanu dan Sarkin Auyo Suleimanu
   58; Fulanin Sambo; b. Auyo, to Keffin Hausa at age 43
4. Muhammadu dan Kacella Mallami
   45; Auyakawa; b. Hadejia, 30 years at Auyo and Keffin Hausa; courtier
5. Ibrahim dan Muhammadu
   74; Auyakawa; b. Aushura, to Keffin Hausa at age 2; barber

6. Also dan Barde Mallam
   69; Auyakawa; b. Keffin Hausa, always lived there; groundnut seller
7. Turakin Keffin Hausa Salihu dan Ibrahim
   69; Auyakawa; b. Keffin Hausa, always lived there

IIID. *Birniwa District* (April–May, 1965)

1. Muhȧmmadu Maishahada dan Chukurami Mela
   52; Mangawa; b. Hadejia, to Birniwa at age 30; district scribe
2. Usuman dan Abba
   74; Mangawa; b. Hadejia, to Birniwa at age 17; farmer
3. Alhaji Haliru dan Sarkin Arewan Hadejia Idirisu
   69; Haben Teshena; b. Hadejia, to Birniwa at age 33; courtier
4. Bulaman Birniwa Muhammadu dan Muhammadu
   56; Mangawa; b. Birniwa, always lived there; long-distance trader
5. Yamusa dan Chiroman Hadejia Sambo
   68; Fulanin Sambo (*dengi*); b. Hadejia, to Birniwa at age 32; courtier
6. Wakilin Sarkin Arewan Hadejia Usuman na Gado dan Sarkin Arewan Hadejia Abubakar
   34; Haben Teshena; b. Hadejia, to Birniwa at age 13; courtier
7. Hamza dan Zakar
   68; Haben Kano; b. Kano, to Birniwa at age 33; courtier

IIIE. *Guri District* (April–May, 1965)

1. Baba Bura dan Barden Hadejia Zangwari
   77; Kerikeri; b. Hadejia, to Guri at age 33; courtier
2. Dandada dan Ahmadu
   65; Mangawa; b. Maje, to Guri at age 15; courtier
3. Bulaman Guri Abdu dan Bulaman Guri Badema
   56; Gizimawa; b. Guri, always lived there
4. Gambo Dabu dan Bulaman Guri Malla
   59; Gizimawa; b. Guri, always lived there; farmer
5. Galima dan Nasser
   69; Gizimawa; b. Guri, always lived there; farmer
6. Aji dan Dubu
   59; Gizimawa; b. Guri, always lived there
7. Jarma dan Duku
   61; Gizimawa; b. Guri, always lived there; farmer
8. Maina Garba dan Sarkin Hadejia Abdulkadir
   50; Fulanin Sambo (*dengi*); b. Hadejia, to Guri at age 38; district scribe
9. Wakilin Sarkin Ba'i Jibiri na Garki dan Salihu
   75; Auyakawa; b. Hadejia, 54 years at Guri

10. Mamman Yari dan Garanda
    70; Mangawa; b. Guri, always lived there; courtier

IIIF. *Kirikasama District* (April–May, 1965)

1. Alhaji Nabayi dan Shamakin Hadejia Muhammadu
   69; Mangawa; b. Hadejia, to Kirikasama at age 29; courtier
2. Abubakar dan Musa
   56; Fulanin Sambo; b. Hadejia, to Kirikasama at age 16; district scribe
3. Bulaman Kirikasama Kambar dan Muhammadu
   69; Mangawa; b. Kirikasama, always lived there; farmer
4. Maimalla dan Bulaman Kirikasama Fukara
   89; Mangawa; b. Dagilbani; to Kirikasama at age 4; farmer
5. Abba dan Mai
   70; Mangawa; b. Madduri, to Kirikasama at age 10; farmer
6. Galadiman Kirikasama Ibrahim dan Zulu
   73; Mangawa; b. Kichidune, at age 28 to Kirikasama; courtier
7. Koli dan Bukr
   70; Mangawa; b. Kasabur, to Mabua at age 5; farmer

IIIG. *Auyo District* (April–May, 1965)

1. Limanin Auyo Ibrahim dan Limanin Auyo Musa
   66; Auyakawa; b. Auyo, always lived there
2. Ahmadu dan Audu
   98; Auyakawa; b. Auyo, always lived there; farmer
3. Ahmadu dan Limanin Auyo Ali
   64; Kanuri; b. Auyo, always lived there; *mallamin ilimi*
4. Audu dan Sarkin Ruwan Auyo Sale
   80; Auyakawa; b. Auyo, always lived there; fisherman
5. Haruna dan Zakar
   89; Auyakawa; b. Auyo, always lived there; *mallamin ilimi*
6. Hassan dan Lamman
   96; Kanuri; b. Auyo, always lived there; *mallamin al-Kur'ani* and long-distance trader
7. Alhaji dan Huseini
   30; Auyakawa; b. Auyo, always lived there; district scribe
8. Garba dan Muhammadu
   77; Auyakawa; b. Auyo, always lived there; courtier
9. Abdu Babanchichi dan Ibrahim
   69; Auyakawa; b. Auyo, always lived there; courtier

10. Babale dan Sarkin Fulanin Hadejia Abubakar dan Sarkin Arewan Hadejia Usuman
    74; Haben Teshena; b. Hadejia, at age 29 to Auyo; courtier
11. Audu dan Sarkin Bayin Auyo Audu
    66; Auyakawa; b. Auyo, always lived there; courtier
12. Wakilin Chiroman Hadejia Ismailu dan Madakin Hadejia Abdu
    51; Fulanin Sambo; b. Hadejia, to Kaugama at age 10; age 30 to Auyo
13. Abubakar dan Sarkin Hadejia Usuman
    40; Fulanin Sambo (*dengi*); b. Hadejia, 5 years at Auyo; district scribe
14. Gizigi dan Jibir dan Sarkin Auyo Mamman dan Sarkin Auyo Gizigi
    61; b. Auyo, to Keffin Hausa at age 6; farmer

IIIH. *Mallammaduri District* (July, 1965)

1. Baba Sabo dan Muhammadu
   93; Fulanin Ardo Lernima; b. Hadejia, to Mallammaduri at age 73; courtier
2. Yusufu dan Sarkin Dawakin Hadejia Umaru
   59; Buzu (Asbenawa); b. Hadejia, 8 years at Dakkido, 32 at Mallammaduri; courtier
3. Alhaji Dalla dan Bulaman Mallammaduri Rafa
   56; Mangawa; b. Mallammadurin Beriberi, always lived there; farmer
4. Maiunguwa Fajuni dan Abubakar
   88; Mangawa; b. Mallammadurin Beriberi, always lived there; farmer
5. Aluwa dan Abba
   78; Mangawa; b. Dunari, always lived there; farmer
6. Magajin Dunari Inusa dan Bulaman Dunari Bulai
   74; Mangawa; b. Dunari, always lived there
7. Barde Abba dan Muhammadu
   68; Fulanin Gombe; b. Nafada, to Hadejia at age 6, 12 years at Sakkidom, 32 at Mallammaduri; courtier

III I. *Kaugama District* (July, 1965)

1. Bulaman Kaugama Abubakar dan Bulaman Kaugama Hamido
   50; Mangawa; b. Zaburam, at age 37 to Kaugama
2. Alhaji Idi dan Bulaman Kaugama Jibir
   63; Mangawa; b. Kaugama, always lived there; farmer
3. Hassan Gana dan Adam
   59; Mangawa; b. Mallamawa, at age 39 to Kaugama; farmer
4. Sarkin Kidan Kaugama Abdu dan Sarkin Kidan Kaugama Abdu
   58; Mangawa; b. Kaugama, always lived there; drummer

5. Chiroman Kaugama Idi dan Chiroman Kaugama Bukr
58; Mangawa; b. Kaugama, always lived there
6. Baba Sarki dan Jibir
81; Damagari; b. Hadejia, to Kaugama at age 25; courtier
7. Sintalin Madakin Hadejia Andu dan Abubakar
66; Mangawa; b. Hadejia, to Kaugama at age 10; courtier
8. Adamu na Gona dan Shamakin Hadejia Muhammadu
47; Kanuri (Damaturu); b. Hadejia, to Mallammaduri at age 29; district scribe

INDEX

'Abd al-Qadīr b. al-Mustafa, 106, 111 n. 30
Abdu dan Nana, Wazirin Sokoto, 185
Abdulkadir, Sarkin Hadejia (ca. 1847–48), 135
Abdulkadir, Sarkin Katagum (1896–1905): Rabeh sends emissaries through, 173; *'yan sarki* appointments by, 186, 194; denied wish to marry, 191; expels Misau agents, 192; personality of, 193 and n. 48; and the Katagum Civil War, 196–98; deposition of, 196–98
Abdulkadir Zailani, Sarkin Gombe. *See* Zailani, Sarkin Gombe Abdulkadir
Abdulla Shiramami, Sarkin Dambam: escapes from Shira, 123–24; kills Sarkin Azare Wesu, 124–25; relations with Bornu and Sokoto, 125; founds Dambam Emirate, 125; expands authority among Kerikeri, 125
Abdullah b. Muhammad, Khalifa (1885–98), 168, 172
Abdullahi, Sarkin Gumel (ca. 1861–72), 205–6
Abdullahi, Sarkin Kano (ca. 1499–1509), 84
Abdullahi, Sarkin Kano (ca. 1855–83): commands Kano force against Buhari, 141; and appointment of Sarkin Katagum Haji, 185; and Muhammadu of Hadejia, 207
Abdullahi Burja, Sarkin Kano (ca. 1438–52), 104, 106
Abdullahi dan Fodio, 91 n. 33
Abdurrahman, Sarkin Katagum (ca. 1846–51): appointed to Azare fief, 117; escapes from Shira, 122; restored to Shira, 123; prevents Habe revolt, 125; appointed to Shira fief, 126; appointed emir, 179; expeditions of, 180, 182; and Buhari, 182
Abdurrahman, Sultan of Sokoto (1891–1902): emissaries from Rabeh to, 173; and appointment of Sarkin Katagum Abdulkadir, 194 and n. 50; character and unpopularity of, 194 n. 50; and the Kano Civil War, 208–10
Abraham, R. C., 82
Abubakar, Sarkin Azare: candidate for Katagum throne, 185, 193–94; appointed to Azare fief, 194; death of, 198
Abubakar Atiku, Sultan of Sokoto (1837–42), 169

Abubakar Atiku na Rabah, Sultan of Sokoto (1873–77), 186–87, 206–7
Abubakar dan Haru: seeks Hadejia throne, 206–7; impoverished and exiled, 208 and n. 28
Abunoboji, Galadiman Katagum, 130
Adama, Modibbo (Lamido Adamawa) (ca. 1806–48): awarded Adamawa region by Shaikh Usuman, 94; campaigns with Buba Yero, 94 n. 42; studies in Birni Gazargamu, 115 n. 50
Adamawa Emirate, 74, 94, 115 n. 50
Adamu, Alkali Katagum, 184
Agades. *See* Asben (Air)
Ahmad, Mai Bornu (ca. 1793–1810): and epidemic, 62–63; and the Bornu jihad, 108–11; flees Birni Gazargamu and abdicates, 111
Ahmadu, Sarkin Misau (ca. 1833–50): resides in Shira district, 120; rebuilds Misau Town, 124; raids western Bornu, 124
Ahmadu Atiku, Sultan of Sokoto (1859–66): approves Umaru as Sarkin Hadejia, 144–45; turbans Haru as Sarkin Hadejia, 204 and n. 15; prefers Muhammadu as Haru's successor, 204, 206–7
Ahmadu dan Sambo Digimsa: preferred by Sambo as successor, 135; sultan tries to reconcile Buhari with, 138; installed by Wazirin Sokoto as emir, 139, 182; executed by Sarkin Arewan Hadejia, 140
Ahmadu Gona, Galadiman Gombe (Akko), 89
Ahmadu Jatau dan Mallam Zaki: candidate for Katagum throne, 182–83, 185, 193–94; moved from Yaiyu to Gadau fief, 183; moved to Udubo fief, 186; martial experience and prowess of, 186; and Katagum-Misau hostilities, 192; becomes blind, 193
Ahmadu Rafa'i, Sultan of Sokoto (1867–73), 187
Akko, Galadiman. *See* Gombe, titled offices
Alhaji Adamu, 108–9
Al-Hajj Sa'id, 136, 139–40
Alhassan, Sarkin Guma'i, 185
Ali, Mai Bornu (ca. 1645–84), 84 and n. 13
Ali b. Hajj Dunama, Mai Bornu (ca. 1753–93), 62 n. 16
Aliyu, Sarkin Kano (1894–1903): helps destroy Isawa, 193; discourages long-distance trade with Rabeh, 195–96; pardoned and appointed emir by Sokoto, 210; territorial conflict with Hadejia, 210
Aliyu Babba, Sultan of Sokoto (1842–59): approves Garko as Sarkin Hadejia, 135; approves Buhari as Sarkin Hadejia, 136; as a mediator, 138; sends Wazirin Sokoto to Hadejia, 139; organizes campaign against Buhari, 140; deposes Sarkin Gombe Suleimanu, 153
Alkali Aliyu, Sarkin Yakin Gombe: appointed by Buba Yero, 87; fiefs held by, and his descendants, 87; kinship with Buba Yero, 88
Al-Kanemi, Shaikh (Shehu) (d. 1835): background of, 112;

responds to Mai's appeal, 112; conflicts of, with eastern Fulanin Mare, 112 and n. 33, 120; aids in first and second reoccupations of Birni Gazargamu, 112–13; pursues Mallam Zaki, 113; founds N'gurno, 114; offers frontier delimitation with Sokoto, 119; founds Kukawa and exercises imperial power, 119 n. 63; constraints on, before 1824, 119, 121; military strength of, 121; intentions toward Sokoto Caliphate, 121 and n. 68; invades eastern emirates, 121–23; invades Gumel and captures sarki, 122; defeats Sarkin Bauchi Yakubu, 122; battles with Kano and Bauchi armies, 122–23; withdraws from Sokoto Caliphate, 123; strengthens western Bornu defenses, 123 n. 77; burns Misau Town, 124; and Abdulla Shiramami, 125; defeats Hadejia and Jafun forces, 135 n. 9

Al-Makrizi, 59 n. 3, 67

Amina, Queen, 84

Arabs. *See* Shuwa Arabs

Ardo Bayo, Galadiman Gombe (Akko), 177–78

Ardo Abdua: and the Bornu jihad, 108–10; and the Hadejia jihad, 115; before the jihad, 133

Ardo Lernima, Sarkin Marma: collects cattle tithe, 108 and n. 21; and the Bornu jihad, 108–10; helps quell revolt at Katagum, 118; Sambo Digimsa relieves, 121

Ardo Sale, 120

Arewa, 138 n. 22

Argungu, 186–87

Asben (Air), pacified by Idris Alooma, 61

Ashaka, 101, 165, 170

Ata-Gara Rock, 84

Auyo, City: walls of, 104; campaigns of Sarkin Kano to, 104; attributes of, before 1800, 106; Fulani subjection of, 115, 134

Auyo, Kingdom: pays tribute to mai through Galadiman Bornu, 60, 62, 107; etymology of name of, 103; history of, 103, 104 and n. 4, 106–7; Islam in, 106

Auyo, Sarkin, 104, 133–34, 144, 165, 205 n. 21

Azare: Lawanawa fiefholders of, 117, 126, 194; Sarki Wesu of, assassinated, 125; Sarkin, 124–25, 192–93; Buhari fails in attack on, 143

Babba Zaki, Sarkin Kano (ca. 1768–76), 104

Babir: Gombe fiefholder of, 101, 152; detachment of western part from Gombe, 155

Babuje, Mai Bedde, 188–89

Bage: Kalam conquers, 85; Buba Yero conquers, 95; Gombe fiefholder of, 101; fieftowns of, 157

Bage, Sarkin: *uban daki* of, 158; Rabeh and, 162–63; appeals to Zailani, 163; and death of Zailani, 164; writes Wazirin Sokoto, 165

Baghirmi: early Fulani settlement in, 67; rebels against Bornu, 119, 121; Rabeh occupies, 172; French treaty with sultan of, 174; Rabeh destroys capital of, 174

Bajoga, 165 and n. 45

Balda, 170

Bappa Isa dan Buba Yero, 154 n. 16
Bappa Usuman dan Buba Yero, 154 n. 16
Bara, 85
Barbari, Sarkin Gobir (ca. 1742–70), 106
Barebari: demographic data on, 7–8, 76; definition and socio-political status of, 8; conversion to Islam, 8, 31; village-head title, 11 n. 17; slavery among, 33; in pre-1800 Border States region, 75–77; migration into Border States region, 76–77. *See also* Beddeland; Kanuri; Lerewa; Mangawa; N'gizim; Shuwa Arabs
Barth, Heinrich, 3, 77, 137 and n. 19
Barwo Winde, 85
Bashema, 93
Bata, 94 n. 42
Bauchi Bula. *See* Bula, Bauchi
Bauchi Emirate, 97–98, 100
Bauchi Gordi. *See* Gordi, Bauchi
Bauchi Province Historical Project, 41
Beddeland: interferes with north-east Nigerian travelers, 61; Galadiman Bornu's authority over, 62; punitive raids by Mai Bornu on, 62 n. 16; Bornu and Sokoto levy tribute on, 119; raids from on Udubo area, 126; Buhari raids, 142, 144; Rabeh and, 173; Haru of Hadejia invades, 188, 204–5; sources for nineteenth-century history of, 188 n. 26; people of in early nineteenth century, 188 n. 26; emergence of federation in, 188–89; geography of, 189 and n. 27; nineteenth-century relations with Muslim neighbors, 189, 204–5; tolls imposed on long-distance traders in, 205
Belle, 85
Bello, Sarkin Dutsi, 139 and n. 27
Bello, Yeriman Gombe, 159–60
Berinde, Sarkin Shira: appointed to Udubo fief, 183 n. 9; dereliction and unpopularity of, 183 n. 9, 186; appointed to Shira fief, 186; death of, 186
Bidir, 143
Billiri, 150, 155
Bilma, 61
Binawa. *See* N'gizim, Western
Biram. *See* Garun Gabas
Biri(n Bolewa): founded, 82; Kano role at, 84; moi of converts to Islam, 96; Buba Yero resides at, 96; ethnic character of, ca. 1800, 96; Mohamman dan Buba Yero stationed at, 99 n. 63; Gombe fiefholder of, 101
Biri(n Fulani), 157
Birni Gazargamu: founded, 60; Western N'gizim pillage around, 61; emerges as entrepôt, 63; Jukun Kwararafa besiege, 84 and n. 13; first campaign of Mallam Zaki to, 110–11; first Fulani occupation of, 111 and nn. 30, 31, 112 n. 40; Mai Dunama recaptures, 112; second Fulani occupation of, 113 and n. 42, 116; Mai Dunama again recaptures, 113 and n. 42; Muhammad Manga raids, 113–14, 119; abandoned as Bornu capital, 114
Birni Kafela, 114, 119 n. 63
Birni N'guru: founded, 62 n. 13; as headquarters of Galadiman

Bornu, 60, 62; Sarkin Kano occupies, 60, 62 n. 13; pastoral Fulani in region of, 67, 73; Fulani drive Galadiman Bornu from, 108
Biu: Kaigaman Bornu exploits, 61; Kwararafa control, 85; Pindiga Jukun role in, 86; Fulani-Babir conflict in, 92; Fulani campaigns in, 93; Gombe boundary with, 94 and n. 43
Biu, Emirate, 92
Bodor, 156, 166
Bojude: founded, 85; Geri Kom colonists in, 85; Yerima Suleimanu conquers and suppresses revolt at, 98; Gombe fiefholder of, 158
Bolewa: community head titles, 10 n. 15; recorded traditions of, 82 and nn. 4, 5; Fika traditions, 82 n. 5; wards at Ribadu and Nafada, 94–95; Gombe fiefholders of, 101
Bolewa, Kingdoms of, role in the Nigerian Sudan before 1500, 81; founded, 82–83; Hausa and Bornu conflicts with, 84–85 and nn. 13, 14, 16
Bomala, 85
Border States: definition of, 3; location of, 3–4; common historical features, 4; physical geography of, 5–6; rural and urban features, 10–11; provincial government in, 15–17, 43, 45; foundation and ethnicity of settlements in, 45, 47–48; non-Fulani states and peoples of, before 1800, 75–76; comparison of, ca. 1850, 199
Bormi: Mallam Jibril builds, 161, 163; joint expedition by eastern emirates against, 165, 166 and n. 47
Bornu, Empire: titled offices in, 12, 60–61; territorial administration of, 12, 60–62; occupational structure of, 20–21; founded, 59–60; expansion of, 59–61; Mai Idris unifies, 60–61; western and southern vassals of, 61–62; history of, ca. 1617–1808, 62–63; pastoral Fulani reach, 66–68; Fulani devastate parts of, 95–96; and Sokoto, 114, 119, 121 and n. 63, 123, 135 n. 9, 182 and n. 3; Kanem and Baghirmi rebel against, 119, 121; military strength of, under al-Kanemi, 121; Rabeh conquers, 172–73; nineteenth-century relations with Beddeland and Southern N'gizim, 189, 190 and n. 29, 205. *See also* al-Kanemi
Bornu jihad: historical sources for, 107 n. 19; causes of, 107, 109 and n. 24; course of, 108–14; accounts of by Shaikh Usuman and Sultan Bello, 109 and n. 24
Bornu, titled offices:
Galadiman: headquarters of, 60, 62; fiefs, power, and wealth of, 60, 62, 107; and the Bornu jihad, 107–9; death of, 109
Kaigaman: territorial fiefs of, 60–62; power and wealth of, 62; killed, 62 n. 16, 109
Buba dan Buba Yero. *See* Mallam Buba dan Buba Yero
Buba Kari Banto, Sarkin Magi, Alkalin Gombe: leads Fulanin Magi across the Gongola, 88; appointed by Buba Yero, 88, 102

Buba Yele, Madakin Gombe: appointed by Buba Yero, 87; fiefs held by, and his descendants, 87; kinship with Buba Yero, 88; Islamic learning of, 102

Buba Yero, Modibbo Gombe (?–ca. 1841): sources for life of, 90 n. 29; early life of, 90–91, 115 n. 50; early campaigns of, 91–94, 107; and the Gombe jihad, 94–97; as Sarkin Nafada, 95; founds Gombe Abba, 97; conflict with Sarkin Bauchi Yakubu, 97–98; delegates authority to sons, 98; encourages residence of Fulanin Kitaku in Gombe, 99; executes Hamma Ruwa, 100; appointed sarkin yaki by Shaikh Usuman, 100 n. 69; allocates flags, titles, and fiefs, 100–2, 157; and the Bornu jihad, 110; abdication and death of, 149 and n. 1

Bubawa, Galadiman Gombe (Akko), 176–78

Budumma, 61

Buhari, Sarkin Hadejia (ca. 1848–63): appointed chiroma, 135; deceives Sambo Digimsa, 136 and n. 12; appointed emir, 136; sources for life of, 136; Qur'anic learning of, 136 and n. 14; early campaigns of, 136–37; Sarkin Kano cedes towns to, 138; executes Sarkin Auyo Nalara, 138; given sanctuary in Machina, 139; defeats Sokoto army at Kaffur, 141–42; raids western Bornu Habe, 142; makes treaty with Sokoto and Kano, 142; invades eastern Kano again, 142; incorporates Marma into Hadejia, 142, 204 n. 17; attempts conquest of Katagum Emirate, 143; high appointments made and proposed by, 143–44; central government under, 143–44, 199–200; desertion and death of, 144–45; Hadejia City under, 200; trade in slaves by, 200 n. 4

Bukar, Shehu Bornu (1880–84), 170, 189, 205 n. 21

Bukhari, Wazirin Sokoto, 208–10

Bula, Bauchi: and the Gombe jihad, 87; conflict with Buba Yero, 87, 99, 101; fiefdoms of, 99

Bulala, 61

Bulangu, 120

Buriburi, 98 n. 61, 121

Buzawa, 106

Carlyle, T. F., 82

Cattle Fulani. *See* Fellata Bornu

Chinade, 117. *See also* Chinade, Yeriman

Chinade, Yeriman: leads Katagum force to Bormi, 165; occupants of office of, 180, 194; Emir Haji rescued by, 188. *See also* Muhammadu Baffa

Clapperton, Hugh: on Kano-Katsina fear of al-Kanemi, 121; and messages from Wazirin Sokoto, 123 n. 76; on Dan Kauwa and Katagum City, 128 n. 89; on Beddeland, 188 n. 26

Clapperton-Denham-Oudney Expedition, 121

Clientage relationships, 14–15, 19 and n. 39, 20. *See also Uban daki*

Cohen, Ronald, 9, 12, 20–21

Comité de l'Afrique Française, Le, 174

Corvée labor, 63

Currencies, 107 and n. 17

Dabema, 88
Dakayawa, 137–38
Damagaram (Zinder): as vassal of Galadiman Bornu, 62, 119; Umaru II of Hadejia flees to, 203; Yusufu of Kano seeks aid of, 209. *See also* Tenemu
Damaturu: pre-1800 pastoral Fulani presence near, 67, 73–74; Muhammad Manga based at, 119. *See also* Fulanin Mare
Dambam Emirate: Abdulla Shiramami founds, 125; submits to Rabeh, 173; Sarkin Misau Sale raids, 190. *See also* Abdulla Shiramami
Dan Babuje, Mai Bedde (ca. 1842–93): Kalilua allies with, 185, 189; and neighboring rulers, 189; denied marriage to Emir Haji's daughter, 189; attacks Katagum City environs, 189; defeats Hadejia army, 205
Dan Fatima, 139, 141
Dan Kauwa, Sarkin Katagum Muhammadu (ca. 1816–46): missionary work of, 115; appointed to Shira fief, 117; raids southwest Bornu Habe, 120; warns Sultan Bello, 120; evacuates Katagum City, 122; appointments by, 126, 130; administration of Katagum under, 126–32; description of, 128 n. 89
Daniski: founded, 82; Buba Yero raids, 95
Dar Runga, 172
Daura (Bornu): Fulanin Jada in, 87, 100; Buba Yero campaigns to, 95; Suleimanu campaigns to, 100; refuses to pay tax to Gombe, 154
Daura, Kingdom and Emirate: and the Sokoto jihad, 107–8; Bornu authority over, 119
Dawa, 133 n. 3
Daya: pastoral Fulani presence at, ca. 1800, 73–74; relations of Fulanin Mare and Mai Bornu with chief of, 110 n. 26; and the Bornu jihad, 110 and n. 26, 111–12; defeats Gombe force, 161
Deba Habe: revolt suppressed at, 98; Gombe fiefholder of, 101; Kwairanga chastises, 152
Demography: of nineteenth-century Gombe, 88–89, 100, 150, 155–57; of nineteenth-century eastern Katagum, 186, 197; of late nineteenth-century Hadejia, 214. *See also* Population data
Dendi, 138 n. 22
Denham, Dixon, 121
Dibana River, 94 n. 43
Digimsa, 133
Dikwa: Fellata Bornu in region of, 62 n. 16; Rabeh establishes himself at, 173; Mallam Hayatu at, 174; trade with Sokoto Caliphate, 195
Dirri, 86
Doho, 85, 158
Dukku: formed by Buba Yero, 97; dissident elements at, 97; defensive position of, 99; Gombe fiefholder of, 101; Fulanin Shira emigrate from, 156; Alkalin, 156; Lamido, 101, 156–58, 164 n. 41
Dukul, 156, 166
Duna, Mai Bedde, 211
Dunama Dabalemi, Mai Kanem (ca. 1200), 59 n. 1
Dunama Lafiami, Mai Bornu (ca. 1808–11, 1814–17): succession

of, 111; appeals to al-Kanemi, 112; recaptures Birni Gazargamu, 112; flees, then recaptures Birni Gazargamu, 113; transfers capital to Birni Kafela, 114, 119 n. 63
Dutsi, 106, 123, 142
Dutsi Gadawur, 169

Emirate administration: in the Border States, 11–19, 43; in Bornu and Hausaland, 12; role of Wazirin Sokoto in, 13; role of the *uban daki* system in, 13–14. *See also* Gombe, Emirate; Katagum, Emirate; Hadejia, Emirate
Ethnic differentiation, 6–9; determination of, 7, 45, 47; proportions, 7–8, 45–46, 199
Ethnic group, 7 n. 7
Eunuchs, position of, 15 n. 30
Europeans: Muslim response in caliphate to approach of, 171 n. 68; Rabeh and, 174; advance into northern Nigeria, 178

Fadlallah b. Rabeh, 175
Fagi, 133 n. 3
Fali, Land of, 61 and n. 9
Fanda, 84
Fellata Bornu (Fulanin Bornu): Southern N'gizim raid, 60–61; presence in Mandara, 62 n. 16; arrival in Bornu, 66, 67 and n. 28, 68; traditional socioeconomic life, 68–72; defined, 75; and the Bornu jihad, 108–14. *See also* Fulanin Mare
Fiefholding, 16–17, 45, 47–48, 54. *See also* Territorial organization; Titled office
Fika Town: Nafada threatened by, 95; raided by Buba Yero, 95; Gombe struggle with, 154–55
Fitila, 88
Fort Archambault, 174
Fulani: common heritage of, 4, 8; defined, 7; demographic data on, 7–8, 199; transition to sedentary life, 8, 68, 74; settlement and sociopolitical dominance in Border States, 8, 98–99, 214; community head titles, 10 n. 15, 11 n. 17; and Islam, 64 and n. 20, 68, 71–72, 99; Shaikh Usuman preaches among, 65; preparations for Bornu jihad, 65; community designations of, 66 and n. 26; movements across West Africa, 66, 67 and nn. 28 and 33, 68; pastoral sociopolitical life of, 67 n. 33, 68–73; relations with eighteenth-century neighbors, 70, 71 and n. 38; classification of, 73–75; friction with non-Fulani before 1800, 92–93
Fulanin Babir: situation, ca. 1800, 87; campaigns in Mubi and Marghiland, 87–88; and the Gombe jihad, 94; Gombe fiefholder of, 99, 156; found Jillahi and Jurara, 156
Fulanin Bornu. *See* Fellata Bornu
Fulanin Dabe: situation, ca. 1800, 88; settlements in Gombe, 88; Gombe fiefholder of, 88, 99, 156; and the Gombe jihad, 94; found Dukul and Tongo, 156
Fulanin Dukku. *See* Fulanin Shira
Fulanin Gona: situation, ca. 1800, 89; Gombe fiefholder of, 89, 99, 156; found Tukulma and Sheddo, 156; rival houses of, 177

Fulanin Gori, 73 n. 44, 130
Fulanin Hadejia (Fulanin Sambo): defined, 73; found Hadejia Emirate, 73; Gombe fiefholders of, 101; and the Bornu jihad, 107–10; eighteenth-century position of, 133 and n. 1; nineteenth-century life style of, 135, 199–200, 214; demographic data on, 199, 214; year-round settlement of, 214
Fulanin Hina: situation, ca. 1800, 88; ward in Gombe Abba, 88; and the Gombe jihad, 92; Gombe fiefholder of, 99
Fulanin Jada: situation, ca. 1800, 87; Gombe fiefholders of, 87, 99–100, 157; found Nafada, 95; component at Biri, 96; Buba Yero resides among, 96; settlements in Bauchi, 100; return to Daura, 100; new settlements in nineteenth-century Gombe, 157
Fulanin Jafun (Jafunawa), 75, 184
Fulanin Janafulu: defined, 88 and n. 26; situation, ca. 1800, 88; and the Gombe jihad, 91; fiefdoms of, 101; political authority of, 153
Fulanin Jera: situation, ca. 1800, 87; Gombe fiefholder of, 87, 99, 156; kinship with other Fulanin Kitaku, 88 n. 26; and the Gombe jihad, 93; position in Wajaland, 150; found Bodor, 156
Fulanin Kiri: kinship with other Fulanin Kitaku, 88 n. 26; situation, ca. 1800, 89; found Muri Emirate, 89, 99–100, 212; and the Gombe jihad, 91–92. *See also* Hamma Ruwa
Fulanin Kitaku (Kitiyen): etymology of name, 74 and n. 47; governing elite of Gombe and Muri, 74, 100–2, 154; life style of, ca. 1800, 86; classification of, 87–89; proportions of, 89 n. 28; early role in Gombe jihad, 91–94; Islam and settlement among, 98–99; migrations into Gongola Basin, 98–99, 150; found Mbilla, 99; ardos given flags, titles, fiefs, 100–2, 150, 157; ardos and Islam, 102; and the Bornu jihad, 110–11; demographic changes under Kwairanga, 155–57; leaders and Zailani, 160–61; towns and Mallam Jibril, 166
Fulanin Magi: situation, ca. 1800, 88; and the Gombe jihad, 91; Gombe fiefholder of, 99, 156; found Tilde, Dukul, and Tongo, 156
Fulanin Mare: origin of, 73–74, 124 n. 80; found Misau, Jema'are, and Adamawa, 74, 120, 125; occupy Birni Gazargamu, 95, 111 and nn. 30, 32, 112 n. 40; devastate parts of Bornu, 95–96, 112 n. 36; and the Bornu jihad, 108–14, 119; lose Birni Gazargamu, 112; raids to southwest Bornu Habe, 119–20, 122, 123 n. 77, 124; Misau awarded Damaturu branch of, 124; Sarkin Misau and, 124, 190–91; settlements outside Misau, 190 and n. 32
Fulanin Sambo. *See* Fulanin Hadejia
Fulanin Shira: locations of, 74; exclusion from Gombe central government, 74; settlement at Nafada, 95; settlement near Kalam, 96; Buba Yero resides

among, 97; Gombe fiefholders of, 101, 156; emigration from Dukku, 156
Fulanin Sika, 75 and n. 52, 95
Fulanin Tara: etymology of name, 87; situation, ca. 1800, 87; Gombe fiefholders of, 87, 99, 156; kinship with other Fulanin Kitaku, 88 n. 26; and the Gombe jihad, 93; found Tilde, Dukul, and Tongo, 156
Fulanin Teshena, 116, 118 and n. 61
Fulanin Udubo, 75, 115
Fulanin Walama: situation, ca. 1800, 88; settlements in Gombe, 88; and the Gombe jihad, 91; Gombe fiefholder of, 99, 156; found Dukul and Tongo, 156

Gabukka, 85
Gadam: founded, 85; Geri Kom colonists in, 85; Yerima Suleimanu conquers, 98; Geri Kom attempts subversion of, 155
Gadau, 126, 182–83, 186
Gadiya, 197–98
Gamawa: incorporated into Katagum, 116; fiefholders of, 126, 196; as entrepôt of long-distance trade, 195–96, 210–11; and the Katagum Civil War, 195–98; demographic change in fiefdom of, 197 and n. 58
Gambaki, 143
Garga Kopchi, Mai Biu (d. ca. 1793), 92
Garga Moda, Mai Biu (d. ca. 1760), 92
Garko, 123 and n. 76, 142
Garko, Sarkin Hadejia (ca. 1845–47): appointed chiroma, 134; appointed emir, 135; death of, 135
Garun Gabas (Biram), 133 n. 3, 134
Gasi, 101
Gatarwa, 133 n. 3, 134
Gaya, 106, 142
Geidam, 135
Gentil, Lieutenant, 174
Geri Kom: founded, 84; competes with Kalam and Pindiga, 85; subjects and colonizes Bolewa towns, 85–86; remains independent of Gombe, 150, 154–55; Kwairanga subjects, 154–55
Gidado, Wazirin Sokoto: collects Bornu imperial treasure, 111; helps quell Habe revolt at Katagum, 118; messages to Sokoto from, 123 n. 76
Gijip, 120 n. 66
Gizimawa. *See* N'gizim, Western (Binawa); N'gizim, Southern
Gobir, Kingdom: defeat of, 65; king of abrogates agreement, 65; attacks Shira, 106; Emir Haji commands Sokoto army against, 187
Gombe, Emirate: boundaries of, 5, 94 and n. 43, 97–98, 155; physiography of, 5–6; significance of the Gongola on, 5–6; ethnic proportions in, 7–8; slave-to-free ratios in, 36; Fulanin Kitaku proportions in, 89 n. 28; early central government in, 99–102, 149–52, 157; demographic change under Kwairanga in, 155–57; central government in, under Kwairanga, 157–59; royal succession process in, 159–60, 175–77; Mallam Jibril and, 162–67, 176; civil war in, 177–78
Gombe, jihad: origins of, 91–94; Buba Yero and, 94–97; signifi-

cance of flags distributed in, 101–2
Gombe, titled offices:
Ajiyan: fiefdoms of, 101, 156; as *uban daki,* 158–59; wealth and power of, 158–59; and Zailani's death, 164; and choice of Umaru as emir, 176
Ardo Maitutan: fiefdoms of, 88, 99, 101, 152, 155; *uban daki* of, 158
Ardo Na'in: function of, 157–58; occupants of office of, 157, 159–60
Ardo Walaman: fiefdoms of, 99, 101, 152, 155; *uban daki* of, 158
Chiroman: fiefdoms of, 101; deposition and exile of, 160 n. 30
Dan Buramin, occupants of office of, 160
Galadiman (Akko): residence of, 89, 101; fiefdoms of, 99, 101, 150, 154–57; *uban daki* of, 158; deposition of, 160, 177. *See also* Bubawa; Ardo Bayo
Madakin: fiefdoms of, 99; *uban daki of,* 158; deposition of, 160
Magajin Garin, first appointee as, 157
Santurakin, occupants of office of, 159–60
Sarkin Daben: fiefdoms of, 88, 99; *uban daki* of, 158
Sarkin Magin: fiefdoms of, 99, 101, 155; *uban daki* of, 158; deposition of, 160
Sarkin Yakin: residence of, 98, 101; fiefdoms of, 99, 101, 150; *uban daki* of, 158; deposition of, 160
Tafidan, occupants of office of, 159–60, 176
Turakin: as *uban daki*, 158; wealth and power of, 158–59; and Zailani's death, 164 and n. 41; and choice of Umaru as emir, 176
Wazirin: Islamic learning of, 102; occupants of office of, 157
Yeriman: occupants of office of, 98, 157, 159–60, 175; fiefdoms of, 157
Gombe Abba: precolonial development and features of, 10; Fulanin Hina settlement in, 88; founded, 97; locational advantages of, 97; Rabeh burns central market, 176
Gongola River: as political boundary, 5; as locus of settlement in Gombe, 5; pastoral Fulani presence in basin of, 67, 74
Gongon, Ardidon Shellen, 90–91
Gordi, Bauchi: campaigns in Mubi-Marghi country, 87–88, 92; fiefdoms of, 88, 99, 101, 152, 155
Gorgoram: desertion of, 173, 211; foundation and geography of, 188, 189, and n. 27; failed attack by Hadejia and Katagum on, 188, 205
Government. *See* Territorial organization; Titled office; Emirate administration
Gube, 95, 101
Gujba, 74, 173
Gulani, 91, 93, 152–53
Guma'i: Fulanin Sika and, 75 and n. 52; incorporated into Katagum, 116; Lawanawa fiefholders of, 185
Gumel, Kingdom: Galadiman Bornu authority over, 62; al-Kanemi captures chief of, 122; Bornu as patron of, 205;

Hadejia invaded by, 205–6; Yusufu of Kano seeks aid of, 209
Gunduawa, 209
Guri, 202
Gwadayi, 169
Gwani, 87
Gwanja (Gonja), 60 n. 4
Gwoni Mukhtar: family and youth of, 110; occupies Birni Gazargamu, 111; death of, 112; perpetual grant by Sulton Bello to house of, 124, 190–91

Habe: numbers and proportion of, 7–8, 9; definition of, 8; socio-political status of, 8, 31; community head titles, 11 n. 17; slavery among, 33; conversion to Islam, 98–99; Gombe fiefholders of, 101
Haben Shira (Shirawa): origins of, 103; languages of, 103 n. 2; defection of to al-Kanemi, 122
Hadejia, City: urban development and features of, 10, 199–200; pre-1800 settlement, 133 and n. 3; early nineteenth-century attributes, 134, 199–200; Tenemu of Damagaram besieges, 201–2, 205; as a main entrepôt, 205
Hadejia, Emirate: physiography of, 6; ethnic proportions in, 7–8; reverse by al-Kanemi in, 122; boundaries, 134, 138, 210; early state government, 134 and n. 8, 200, 211, 213 n. 47; royal succession process in, 135–36, 200–1, 203–4, 207–8; state government under Buhari, 143–44, 200, 211, 213; reintegrated into Sokoto Caliphate, 145, 200–1; Haruna of Ningi defeats columns from, 188; situation, ca. 1850, 199–200; invasion and siege of capital of by Tenemu, 201–2; Sarkin Gumel invades, 205–6; and the Kano Civil War, 209–10; border conflict with Kano, 210–11; enrichment of officials in, 211; *uban daki* system in, 212–13; central government under Haru and Muhammadu, 212–14; titled slaves in, 212, 213 and n. 47; growth of Fulani settlement in, 214
Hadejia, titled offices: Alkalin, 21, 134; Barden, 144 n. 50; Baruan, 144 n. 50; Chiroman, 134–35, 143, 206; Galadiman, 134 n. 8, 143–44, 197, 203, 206–7, 214; Jarman, 137, 144 n. 50; Limanin, 134; Mabudin, 137; Madakin, 134 n. 8, 144; Maidalan, 134 n. 8; Piriyan, 134 n. 8; Sarkin Arewan, 144, 202, 206; Sarkin Dawakin, 144 n. 50; Sarkin Lifidan, 144 n. 50; Sarkin Wanzamin, 134 n. 8; Sarkin Yakin, 144, 202; Sarkin Yaran, 134 n. 8; Shamakin, 144 n. 50, 205 n. 21; Wazirin, 144 n. 50, 206, 213
Hadufia, 122
Haji, Sarkin Katagum (ca. 1868–96): appointed to Azare fief, 126; campaigns of, to Kerikeriland, 161; and Mallam Jibril, 161–62; appointed to Shira fief, 182; appointed emir, 185; renews local jihad, 185–86; appoints and transfers *'yan sarki* fiefholders, 186; services in Sokoto campaigns, 186–87; defeated by Haruna of Ningi, 188; campaigns to Gorgoram, 188–89; refuses daughter to Mai

Bedde, 189; conflict with Sarkin Misau Sale, 190–93; shifts Katagum market to Gamawa, 195; tries to restore Mai Duna to Gorgoram, 211
Hamji, Wazirin Katagum Muhammadu: family background of, 130; function and powers of, 130, 131; and nomination of new emir, 180, 183, 185; wounded in battle against Ningi, 188
Hamma Bano, Ardo Walama, 88
Hamma Ruwa: kinship with Buba Yero, 88; executed by Buba Yero, 89, 99–100; fiefdoms of, 99; Islamic learning of, 187
Hamza, Sarkin Ningi, 187
Hardawa: Fulanin Jafun settled at, 75; revolt of, 184
Haru, Sarkin Hadejia (ca. 1865–85): and Buhari's death, 144; deals with Liman Yamusa, 169; raids Lerewa, 185–86, 204; attacks Gorgoram, 188, 204–5; tries to unseat Umaru II, 201; appointed chiroma, 202; appointed emir, 204 and n. 15; raids and campaigns of, 204–6; retires from jihad, 206; death of, 207; central government under, 212–14; Islam and, 213 n. 46
Haruna, Sarkin Ningi, 187–88
Hashim, Shehu Bornu (1885–93), 172, 191 n. 36
Hassan, Sarkin Gombe (ca. 1888–95): appointed santuraki, tafida, and yerima, 159–60; joins Sarkin Misau against Bormi, 164; turbanned emir, 164; personality of, 164, 165 and n. 44, 175; and allied expedition to Bormi, 165, 166 and n. 47; Mallam Jibril's success against, 166–67; reasons for choice of as emir, 175; '*yan sarki* appointments by, 175
Hausa, Kingdoms of: tribute to Bornu, 59–60, 62–63; trade with Bornu, 60 n. 4; Islam in, 63, 64 and nn. 19, 20; political development of by 1500, 63, 103
Hausa-Fulani emirates: compared with Border States, 3–4; titled offices in, 12; occupational structure in, 20–21
Hausa-speakers: in the Border States, 6 and n. 6; missionary work by Shaikh Usuman among, 65; Gombe fiefholder of, 101; in Shira, 103 n. 2
Hayatu bn. Sa'idu, Mallam: activities of, from Balda, 170; personality of, 170 n. 62; commissioned West African Mahdist deputy, 170–71; relations with Mallam Jibril and eastern emirates, 171 and n. 66; declares a jihad, 171; and Rabeh, 173–74; conquers Marua-Mandara region, 173; death of, 174, 175 and n. 90
Heussler, Robert, 52–53
Hinna, 87, 94
Hona, 94 n. 42

Ibrahim, Mai Bornu (ca. 1818–46), 119 n. 63
Ibrahim Dabo, Sarkin Kano (ca. 1819–46), 119 n. 63
Ibrahim Zaki. *See* Mallam Zaki
Idah, 84 n. 10
Idirisa, Sarkin Dabe, 88
Idris Alooma, Mai Bornu (ca. 1580–1617): campaigns of, 60–61; unifies new Bornu Empire, 61; imperial administration under, 61–62

Imams, in Border States, 32–33
Irin Lawan. See Lawanawa
Iron-working, 106, 107 and n. 17
Isawa, 192–93
Islam
conversion to, 8, 31, 98–99; requirements of, on Islamic ruler, 14; state and society in, 25–34; slavery in, 34; introduced into Border States region, 106; Gombe Emirate and, 98–99, 102, 129, 153, 156, 199–200, 213 n. 46; Hadejia Emirate and, 134, 199–200, 213 and n. 46; Katagum Emirate and, 180, 189–90, 193 n. 48, 199–200, 213 n. 46; Mahdism in, 167, 169. *See also* Muslim state
Islamic law (*Sharī'a*): in classical Muslim state, 26–27; definition of a Muslim, 28; schools ("ways") of, 30 n. 12; and division of spoil, 29–31; Fulani conquests and, 30 and n. 13, 31; the Imam and, 31, 32 n. 16, 33; Border States emirs and, 32–33; chief judges and, 32–33; execution of, in Border States, 43
Ismaila dan Mallam Zaki: appointed Yeriman Chinade, 117; appointed to Shira fief, 180; nominated as emir, 182; deposed, 183 and n. 8

Jabdo, 161
Jafun, 135 n. 9, 137, 142
Jafunawa. *See* Fulanin Jafun
Jaji, Sarkin Yakin Hadejia: background and status of, 144; declares Umaru emir, 144; and defense of Hadejia from Tenemu, 201; murders Tatagana, 202; murdered, 202
Jalo dan Muhammadu Kwairanga, 176
Jalori, 192
Jangefe, 125
Jaragwol, 87
Jatau dan Mallam Zaki. *See* Ahmadu Jatau
Jellum, 125 and n. 86, 161
Jema'are, Emirate: founded, 74, 120 and n. 66; Haruna of Ningi defeats, 188; and the Katagum Civil War, 197
Jema'are, Sarkin: and Katagum-Misau hostilities, 192; aids Haru of Hadejia, 203
Jema'are, Town: founded, 120; sacked by Buhari, 143
Jera: Pindiga Jukun authority over, 86; Fulanin Jera communities among, 87; Gombe fiefholders of, 87, 101; Fulani campaigns among, 93; local administration among, 150
Jere, 85
Jibril, Mallam. *See* Mallam Jibril
Jibrim, Sarkin Auyo, and Fulanin Hadejia, 133–34
Jihād: in the Border States, 4, 14; Muslim obligation to conduct, 26, 28–29; purposes of, 26–29; proper objects of, 28–29, 31; rewards of, 29–30; non-Muslims and, 31
Jillahi: founded, 156; fiefholder of, 156; Mallam Jibril controls, 166
Jizya: paid by Haben Shira, 116; paid by Gombe Habe, 154
Jombo, 85
Judges, in Border States, 32, 43
Jukun: defined, 75, 81, 82 and n. 3; defeated by and tributary to Bornu, 85 nn. 13, 14; occupation of Kano by Pindiga, 85

n. 16; Gombe fiefholder of, 101, 154. *See also* Pindiga; Kwararafa
Jurara, 156, 166
Justice, administration of: in Islam, 31–33; in Katagum, 129–30; Mallam Jibril denounces, in Gombe, 163; Liman Yamusa denounces, in Kano, 169; in Hadejia, 213

Kabadai, 129–30
Kadr, Sarkin Katagum (ca. 1851–68): appointed to Gadau fief, 126; gives land to Marma refugees, 142 and n. 41; appointed emir, 183; appointments made by, 183; relations with Buhari, Hardawa and Bornu, 184; death of, 184; gives refuge to Tukur of Hadejia, 204 n. 15
Kafarati: founded, 155; fiefholder of, 158; Sarkin Gombe Tukur besieges, 176
Kaffur, Battle of, 141–42
Kaiuri (Kaweri), 182
Kalam, City: Buba Yero conquers, 97; Gombe fiefholder of, 101
Kalam, Kingdom: authority over Fulanin Shira, 74; founded, 84; Kano raids, 84; and Kwararafa campaigns to Hausaland, 85 n. 16; competes with Geri Kom and Pindiga, 85–86; position of, ca. 1820, 96
Kalilua, 185, 189, 204
Kalshingi, chastised by Kwairanga, 152
Kanakuru: of Shellen, 90–91; Fulani campaigns among, 93; Buba Yero relinquishes control of, 94; Gombe fiefholders of, 101, 152; detached from Gombe, 155
Kanem, Kingdom: Maghumi (Saifawa) rulers of, 59, 103; influence west of Lake Chad, 59 and nn. 1, 3; dynasties moves to Bornu, 59; Fulani arrival in, 66–67
Kanem-Bornu, Empire. *See* Bornu, Empire; Kanem, Kingdom
Kanembu, 112, 121
Kano, City: as long-distance trade center, 63; Kwararafa occupy, 84–85
Kano, Emirate: Buhari devastates eastern part, 136–38, 142–43; Ningi raids on, 187; long-distance trade with Rabeh of, 195–96; civil war, 208–10; border conflict with Hadejia, 210–11
Kano, Kingdom: pays tribute to Bornu, 59–60, 104; occupies Birni N'guru, 60; conflict with Mai Idris Alooma, 60; wars and raids between Kwararafa and, 84–85; campaigns to Shira and Auyo from, 104; and the Sokoto jihad, 107–8
Kano, titled offices:
Sarkin: and Katagum-Misau hostilities, 191–92; gives refuge to Umaru II of Hadejia, 203
Wazirin, 123 n. 75
Kanuri: demographic proportion in Gombe, 76; ward at Nafada, 95; Gombe fiefholders of, 101, 157; new nineteenth-century settlements in Gombe, 157; migrate into eastern Katagum, 197
Kasar amana, 152, 154
Katagum, City: urban development and features of, 10; Mallam Zaki

founds, 116; Dan Kauwa evacuates, 122; al-Kanemi plunders, 122; Clapperton describes, 128 n. 89; Buhari besieges, 143; Dan Babuje attacks environs of, 189
Katagum, Emirate: physiography of, 4–6; ethnic proportions in, 7–8; slave-to-free proportions in, 36; languages of, 103 n. 2; founded, 116; earliest state office in, 117; titled office in, 117, 126–28, 131, 132 n. 93, 212; provincial administration of, 117, 126–30, 213; royal succession process in, 117, 179 and n. 1, 182–85, 193–94; internal dissension in, 117–18, 184, 195–98; slave-raids to Kerikeriland from, 125; central government under Dan Kauwa in, 126–32; taxation in, 127, 129; military in, 128 n. 89; trade in, 128 n. 89; Buhari invades, 143, 184; at Dan Kauwa's death, 179; boundaries of, 182, 185–86, 190 and n. 29; demographic displacement in, 184, 186; hostilities with Misau, 190–93; civil war in, 195–98
Katagum, titled offices:
Alkalin: functions of, 131, 184; and royal electoral council, 180 and n. 1, 195; and Katagum Civil War, 196
Ardon, 117
Chiroman, 117, 126
Dandelman, 188
Galadiman: Fulanin Gori fill office, 73 n. 44, 131; functions of, 117; Abunoboji as, 131; status of, 131; and royal electoral council, 179 n. 1, 180, 194; dies in battle with Ningi, 188; deposed, 196; and Katagum Civil War, 196
Jarman, 117
Jekadan, 117
Kilishin, 132
Limanin: functions of, 130, 132; and royal electoral council, 179 n. 1, 194; deposed, 195; and Katagum Civil War, 196
Madakin: functions of, 130; and royal electoral council, 179 n. 1, 194; dies in battle with Ningi, 188; and Katagum Civil War, 196
Magatakardan, 117
Maidalan: functions of, 117, 132; and royal electoral council, 179 n. 1, 194
Majidadin, 130
Makaman: functions of, 117; and royal electoral council, 179 n. 1, 194; flees emirate, 180; Abdurrahman appoints new, 180 n. 2; and Katagum Civil War, 196–97
Sarkin Dawakin, 130
Sarkin Yakin, 130, 188
Tambarin, 132
Wombain: status and functions of, 130; and royal electoral council, 179 n. 1, 194; and Katagum Civil War, 196
Wazirin: status and functions of, 130–32; occupants of office of, 130, 193; conditions of appointment as, 131 n. 92; and royal electoral council, 179 n. 1, 194. *See also* Hamji, Wazirin Katagum; Sa'idu, Wazirin Katagum
Yeriman. *See* Yeriman Chinade
Katsina, City: as long-distance trade center, 63; Kwararafa wars with, 84
Katsina, Kingdom, 107–8, 119

Kaweri. *See* Kaiuri
Kazura, 133 n. 3, 134
Kebbi, Kingdom, 68 n. 35, 138 n. 22
Keffin Alkali (Keffin Romi), 184
Keffin Hausa, 137
Keffin Romi. *See* Keffin Alkali
Kerikeri: enslave Buba Yero, 90; threaten Nafada, 95; Buba Yero campaigns among, 95; raids by Fulanin Mare on, 119–20; raids by Abdulla Shiramami on, 125; raids by eastern emirates on, 125 and n. 86, 142, 162, 182, 206, 208; raids on Udubo region, 126, 186; Mallam Jibril settles and raids among, 161–63; raid on Bage area, 163
Kharāj, 30
Kibba, 94 n. 42
Kiri, 89
Kirifi: founded, 84; under Geri Kom, 85; Buba Yero subjects, 97
Kitiyen Fulani. *See* Fulanin Kitaku
Kodon, 152
Kom Fellata: founded, 156; Gombe fiefholder of, 158–59, 176
Kordofan, 93
Korori, 197, 198 n. 60
Kubegasi, 87
Kukawa: founded, 119 n. 63; Rabeh destroys, 172
Kuladeni, 87
Kunde, defensive position of, 99
Kusseri, 175, 197
Kwairanga, Sarkin Gombe. *See* Muhammadu Kwairanga, Sarkin Gombe
Kwamu, 9 n. 12
Kwanda, 210
Kwararafa peoples: cultural and political influence of, 81; description, 81, 82 and n. 3; movements into Gongola-Benue region, 82–83; towns founded by, 82–83
Kwararafa States: sources for history of, 82 and n. 4; wars with Hausa kingdoms and Bornu, 84–86; Zaria, Bornu, Teshena, and Misau pay tribute to, 85 and n. 14; occupy Teshena, 104; invaded by Shira Kingdom, 106 n. 11
Kwaya, 94 n. 43

Lakumna, 90 and n. 30
Lala, 93, 94 and n. 42
Lander, Richard, 122
Lavers, John E., 82 n. 5
Lawanawa (*irin Lawan*): defined, 114; fiefdoms allocated, 117, 126–28; childhood and youth of male, 127; sources of income, 127–28; common interests of, 183. *See* Katagum Emirate, royal selection process
Lerewa: proportion of, in Katagum, 76; antiquity of Katagum settlements, 76; early support of Katagum jihad, 115; incorporated into Katagum, 116; seek aid from Bornu, 184–85; Haji chastises, 185–86; emigrate to west Bornu, 186
Liman Adandaya. *See* Suleimanu (Liman Adandaya)
Liman Yamusa, 169 and n. 61, 171 and n. 68
Linguistic groupings in Border States, 9 n. 12
Longuda, 93

Machina: Fulanin Hadejia from, 133 n. 1; Buhari given sanctuary in, 139; Buhari falls out with sarki of, 140

Maga: Gombe fiefholder of, 101, 153; detachment from Gombe of, 155
Magaba, Mallam Jibril and, 162–63, 165
Magaji, Sarkin Gamawa, 196–98
Maghrib, 64 and n. 19
Maghumi (Saifawa). *See* Kanem, Kingdom
Mahdi: traditions of, 167 and n. 54, 168; Muhammad Ahmad as, 168, 170; Shaikh Usuman denies being, 168–69; expected arrival in West Africa, 168–70; Liman Yamusa and, 169; Mallam Hayatu and, 170, 173; Mallam Jibril and, 171
Mahdiya, Sudanese, 168–69
Maina Adamu dan Sambo Digimsa, 206
Mainarin Yamma, 142 n. 41
Mairakumi, 135
Majiya, 210
Malala, 156
Mallam Buba dan Buba Yero: resides at Ribadu, 99, 153; lacks titled office, 153–54; death of, 154 n. 16; gives towns to sister, 157
Mallam Buhari, 110
Mallam Hayatu. *See* Hayatu bn. Sa'idu
Mallam Jibril: inroads into Gombe of, 31, 166, 176; background of, 161; moves to Kerikeriland, 161; prepares campaign to Bauchi, 161; builds Bormi, 161, 163; conducts jihad in Kerikeriland, 161, 163; moves to Gombe Emirate, 162; quasi-Islamic conduct of, 162 and n. 37; Zailani's reception of, 162–63; pledges to correct misrule, 163; joint expedition against, by eastern emirates, 165, 166 and n. 47; political-military tactics of, 166 and n. 50, 167 and n. 51; Mahdism and, 171; and Mallam Hayatu, 171 and n. 66, 174–75; burns Gombe Abba central market, 176
Mallam Kiari, 115 n. 50
Mallam Mango, Ardo Maituta, Ardo Hina, 88
Mallam Zaki, Sarkin Katagum (ca. 1808–14): first campaign to Birni Gazargamu of, 110–11; occupation and evacuation of Birni Gazargamu by, 113 and n. 42, 116; background of, 114 and n. 47, 115; and the Katagum jihad, 115–16; appointments by, 117; death of, 117
Mallam Zare, 116
Mamman Haji. *See* Haji, Sarkin Katagum
Mamman Kuso, Sarkin Yakin Bauchi, 98 n. 61
Mandara: pacified by Idris Alooma, 61; punitive raids to, by Mai Bornu, 62 n. 16; Fulani presence grows in, 62 n. 16; early Fulani presence in, 67
Mangawa: proportion in Hadejia, 76; identity of, 77; economic activity of, 77
Maradi, 120 n. 66, 186–87, 206–7
Mare (Dilara) Plain, 73
Marghiland: Idris Alooma pacifies, 61; and Bauchi Gordi, 87–88, 92; Fulani-Marghi conflict in, 92; migration from, of Shira-Teshena-Auyo kingdom founders, 103
Markets, 45, 50, 53; in pre-1800 Auyo City, 106; and 1903 famine in Katagum, 195

Marma, Emirate: incorporated into Hadejia, 66 n. 25, 142, 204 n. 17; founded, 73; al-Kanemi campaigns against, 121; reduced condition of, 142 n. 40
Marma, Town, 142 n. 40
Marua, 87, 170
Mayofaro, 90
Mbilla, 99, 156
Mbulla, 93
Miga: Buhari devastates region of, 137, 142; role of Sarkin, in advance to Kaffur, 141; plundered by Umaru II of Hadejia and Tenemu of Damagaram, 203; Hadejia and Kano dispute claim to, 210
Miriya, 112 n. 37
Misau, Emirate: founded, 74; conflict with Katagum, 190–93
Misau, Town, 124
Mohamma Kisoka, Sarkin Kano (ca. 1505–65), 62 n. 13
Mohamman dan Buba Yero, 99 n. 63
Mu'azu dan Muhammadu Kwairanga, 160
Mu'azu, Sultan of Sokoto (1887–91), 187
Mubi, 92
Muhammad Ahmad, Mahdi: declares himself Mahdi, 168; writes Sokoto and Kukawa, 170 and n. 64; commissions Mallam Hayatu his West African deputy, 170–71
Muhammad Bello, Sarkin Kano (1883–93), 208 and n. 29
Muhammad Bello, Sultan of Sokoto (ca. 1817–37): determines Gombe-Bauchi frontier, 98; grants Fulanin Kiri a separate emirate, 100; state offices created by, 100; on causes of the Bornu jihad, 109; accepts al-Kanemi's boundary proposal, 119; gives land to Sambolei, 120 n. 66; gives Misau to Muhammad Manga, 124; orders attack on Abdulla Shiramami, 125
Muhammad Manga, Sarkin Misau (ca. 1808–33): conveys spoil to Sokoto, 111; succeeds as head of Daya Fulani, 112–13; raids Birni Gazargamu, 113–14, 119; difficulties of, at Damaturu, 120; emigrates from Bornu, 120; al-Kanemi cites raids in Bornu of, 122; awarded Misau by Sokoto, 124; awarded administrative rights over Fulanin Mare, 124
Muhammad(u) Manga II, Sarkin Misau (ca. 1886–1900): battles with Mallam Jibril's allies, 164; and allied expedition to Bormi, 165; corresponds with Sokoto about Hayatu, 171 n. 66; and the Gombe Civil War, 177; and Katagum-Misau hostilities, 191–93
Muhammad Ngileruma, Mai Bornu (ca. 1811–14), 119 n. 63
Muhammad Rimfa, Sarkin Bornu (ca. 1463–99), 86
Muhammad Wabi, 120
Muhammadu, Barden Rinde, 141 and n. 36
Muhammadu, Sarkin Hadejia (ca. 1885–1906): warns Kano of Rabeh's intentions, 173; and the Katagum Civil War, 197–98, 211; appointed Sarkin Marma, 204; preferred by sultan to succeed Haru, 204, 206; appointed waziri, 206, 213; competes with Abubakar for throne, 206–8; victorious

against Maradi, proclaimed emir, 207; raids Kerikeriland, 208; appoints Sambo and impoverishes Abubakar, 208; and the Kano Civil War, 209–10; disputed claim of, to Kano provinces, 210–11; tries to restore Mai Duna to Gorgoram, 211; central government under, 212–14

Muhammadu, Sarkin Sokwa: appointed to Sokwa fief, 194; charged with oppression, 196 and n. 57; and the Katagum Civil War, 196

Muhammadu Baffa, Yeriman Chinade: as candidate for Katagum throne, 194; and the Katagum Civil War, 196–97; appointed sultan's deputy in Katagum, 196–97

Muhammadu Bunni, 115

Muhammadu Dan Kauwa. *See* Dan Kauwa, Sarkin Katagum Muhammadu

Muhammadu Fema, Sarkin Marma, 142 n. 40

Muhammadu Hamji, Wazirin Katagum. *See* Hamji, Wazirin Katagum

Muhammadu Lawan, 114–15

Muhammadu Kwairanga, Sarkin Gombe (ca. 1844–82): Buba Yero entrusts Gombe jihad to, 98; campaigns from Akko by, 98; campaigns as yerima by, 152, 154; as emir, 153–55; conquers Pindiga Town, 154 and n. 17; demographic changes in Gombe under, 155–57; central government in Gombe under, 157–59; death of, 159

Muniyo, 119

Muri, Emirate, 89, 100, 212 n. 44

Muslim State: religion and the body politic in, 25–26; relation to citizenry of, 25–27; classical definition of, 26–28; non-Muslims in, 26–28; leaders of, 27 and n. 6, 29; non-Muslim lands and peoples and, 28–29

Mutwe, 95

Nachtigal, Gustave, 77

Nafada: founded, 94–95; ethnic character of, 94–95, 114–15; Buba Yero and, 95–96; Gombe fiefholder of, 101, 158; Muhammadu Lawal resides at, 114–15; struggle with Fika of, 155; and Mallam Jibril, 162–63, 166; role of Sarkin, in Zailani's death, 164; letter of Sarkin, to Wazirin Sokoto, 165

Nafata, Sarkin Gobir, 91 n. 33

Nalara, Sarkin Auyo, 138, 144

N'gasar, 87, 95

N'gizim, Southern: location of, ca. 1600, 60; raid "Fellata" of west Bornu, 60–61; Bornu relations with, 60–61, 189–90; Idris Alooma punishes, 61; Galadiman Bornu's authority over, 62; enslave Buba Yero, 90; Buba Yero campaigns to, 95; Fulanin Mare raids on, 119–20; Katagum relations with, 189–90

N'gizim, Western (Binawa): Idris Alooma punishes, 60–61; location of, ca. 1600, 60, 61 n. 9, 76 n. 57; military activities in west Bornu, 61; Galadiman Bornu's authority over, 62; in northeast Hadejia before 1800, 76; Ardo Lernima collects tax among, 108 n. 21

N'gurno, 114, 119 n. 63
N'guru. *See* Birni N'guru
Nigeria, northern. *See* Nigerian Sudan
Nigerian Sudan: geographical features, 4–5; legal abolition of slavery in, 48–49; famines in early twentieth century, 49 n. 11; influence of Kanem in, 59 and nn. 1, 3; involvement in long-distance trade, 60 n. 4, 63; Maghribi influence on, 63, 64 and n. 19; Kwararafa influence on, 81, 84 and n. 13, 85 and nn. 14, 15
Ningi, State: founded, 187; sources for history of, 187 n. 22; raids into neighboring states, 187 and n. 22, 188; invades Shira and defeats Haji, 187–88; Yusufu of Kano seeks aid of, 209
Nupe, 84, 121

Occupational titles, 15
Occupations, 20–22; criteria for popular ranking of, 21–22; rank status by emirate of, 22; office-holding, 41, 43; nonofficeholding, 43, 53
Oral data: sources of, 41–42, 45, 54; verification of, 42, 45, 46 and n. 9, 47–51, 54–56; recording of, 42–43; validation (value) of, 44, 46 and n. 9, 51–56, 177 n. 94; future possibilities of, 51–52; presentation of, 53–54

Palaces, in Border States, 53
Petembere, 90 and n. 30
Pindiga, Kingdom: competes with Kalam and Geri Kom, 85; founded, 86; political-religious influence of, 86; campaign to Kano, 86; conquers much of Geri Kom and Kalam, 86, 96 and n. 55; Gombe fiefholder of towns within, 89, 154; Buba Yero's inroads on, 97
Pindiga, Town: Muhammadu Kwairanga exerts pressure on, 98; remains independent of Gombe, 150; conquered by Kwairanga, 154 and n. 17
Population data, 4, 6, 45, 48, 49 and n. 10, 54. *See also* Demography
Potiskum, 90, 106

Qadiriyya Brotherhood, 43

Rabeh (Rabīh ibn Fadl Allāh): early career of, 172; sources for life of, 172 n. 69; conquers Baghirmi and Bornu, 172–73; and Mallam Hayatu, 173–74; menaces eastern emirates, 173 and n. 79, 195 and n. 56, 196, 211; French expeditions and, 174; and long-distance trade with Sokoto Caliphate, 195 and n. 56, 196, 210–11; death of, 197
Rai Buba, 90
Rakumanani Ward (Katagum), 118
Rank orders, 14
Rauda, Sarkin Maradi, 120 n. 66
Religion: religious differentiation, 45, 48; mosques in Border States, 45, 50
Ribadu: founded, 82–83; Kalam conquers, 85; as base of Gombe jihad, 94–95; ethnic character of, 94
Rinde, 133
Royal succession, in Border States, 17–18

Sa'idu, Wazirin Katagum, 131 n. 92, 193–94, 196
Sale, Sarkin Misau (ca. 1862–86): defeats Buhari, 143 n. 46; deals with Liman Yamusa, 169; conflict of, with Sarkin Katagum Haji, 190–91; killed in Tangale-Waja, 191
Sambo, Chiroman Hadejia, 208
Sambo Digimsa, Sarkin Hadejia (ca. 1805–48): and the Bornu jihad, 108; and revolts at Katagum, 118 and n. 61; raids southwest Bornu Habe, 120, 135; discourages Bornu attack on Marma, 121; Shaikh Usuman gives flag to, 133–34, 213 n. 47; and the Hadejia jihad, 134; Islam and, 134; abdicates and resumes throne, 135; age of, 135 n. 10; expeditions to west Bornu, 135 and n. 9; deceived by Buhari, 136 and n. 12
Sambolei, Sarkin Jema'are (ca. 1824–54): raids southwest Bornu Habe, 120; founds Jema'are town and emirate, 120 and n. 66; kills Sarkin Maradi, 120 n. 66; kills last Habe king of Shira, 124 n. 78; leads joint attack on Buhari, 140
Sangaru, 163
Serkio, Chiroman Hadejia: position under Buhari, 143; wounded by Alkalin Katagum, 184; tries to unseat Emir Umaru II, 201; deposed, impoverished, and exiled by Umaru, 202 and n. 10
Shaikh Laminu. *See* al-Kanemi, Shaikh (Shehu)
Shani, 90 and n. 30
Sharī'a. *See* Islamic law
Sheddo, 156
Shellen: Fulanin Kitaku near, 88; Buba Yero and, 90–91; ardidon, 152; refuses to pay Gombe taxes, 154
Shellim, 115, 126
Shira, Fiefdom: annual crop and other production, 53; Habe of, rally to al-Kanemi, 122; Haruna of Ningi invades and raids, 187–88; towns transferred to Sokwa, 194
Shira, Kingdom: pays tribute to Mai Bornu, 60, 107; languages of, 103 n. 2; foundation and history of, 103–7; Islam in, 106; size of, 106; iron ore and manufactures in, 106–7; Mallam Zaki subjects, 116; Habe dynasty restored by al-Kanemi, 122; last Habe king killed, 123, 124 n. 78
Shira, Sarkin: Mallam Zaki negotiates with, 116; Dan Kauwa appointed, 117; special prerogatives in nineteenth century, 130; as heir to Katagum throne, 179; and the Katagum Civil War, 196–97
Shira, Town: as capital, 103; Mallam Zaki subjects, 116; Lawanawa fiefholders of, 117, 126, 186, 193–94
Shiraka, 103
Shirawa. *See* Haben Shira
Shirenci, 103 n. 2
Shuwa Arabs, 101, 112
Slave-raiding: Hausa, by 1500, 63; Buhari and, 200 and n. 4
Slaves: manumission of, 14, 34–35; Islamic law and, 29, 33–34; Border States and, 33–37, 49–50; Maliki code and, 34; children of, by free masters, 35; slaves of, 35; titled, 35–36, 212, 213 and

n. 47; socioeconomic position of *dimajai*, 35–36; ratio to free persons, 36; in trade, 36; settlements of, 36–37; agricultural and domestic, 36–37; descent from, 47; Kerikeri as a main source of, 125, 163; capture of, at Battle of Kaffur, 141; traffic in, under Buhari, 200 and n. 4, 211
Smith, Michael G., 9, 12, 21, 40–41, 44, 63
Social status, 14, 20; of freemen, 14; of clerics, 14–15; of clients, 14–15; of royals, 14–15, 16 n. 33, 17, 43; of messengers, 17, 19
Sokoto, Caliphate: corporate and emirate boundaries of, 53; Bornu relations with, 114, 119, 121 and n. 68, 123, 182 and n. 3; revolts against by western states, 138 n. 22; all major states of join against Buhari, 141–42; unity of, 145 n. 51, 183; Hadejia reintegrated into, 145, 200–1; the Sudanese Mahdiya and, 170 and n. 64, 171; Mallam Hayatu and, 170, 171 and n. 66; Muslim response in to European encroachment, 171 n. 68; Rabeh and, 195
Sokoto, jihad: origins of, 65, 91 n. 33; motivations of, 72 n. 42; nineteenth-century episodes in, 186–87
Sokoto, titled offices:
Dangaladiman, 140
Magajin Rafin, 138
Magajin Wazirin, 165, 185, 194
Walin, 149
Wazirin: and the Border States, 13, 136, 139–42, 185, 192, 194, 196, 203, 204 and n. 15, 208, 209 and n. 31; and Buhari, 136, 139–42; and the Kano Civil War, 208–10; confers with Muhammadu of Hadejia, 209–10
Sokoto, Sultan of, relations with Border States, 3, 12–13, 43, 131 n. 92, 160, 195–98, 203–4
Sokwa: Lawanawa fiefholders of, 185, 193–94; Katagum-Misau hostilities and Sarkin, 192; towns transferred from Shira to, 194. *See also* Muhammadu, Sarkin Sokwa
Song, 92
Songhay, 60, 63
Sosebaki States, 62, 112 n. 37
Sudan Savanna: definition of, 4–5; long-distance trade across, 63
Suleimanu, Sarkin Gombe (ca. 1841–44): and Fulani occupations of Birni Gazargamu, 95, 98; and Sarkin Bauchi Yakubu, 98 and n. 61; entrusted by Buba Yero with Gombe jihad, 98; stationed as yerima at Wawa, 98; and Gombe jihad, 98–100; moves as emir to Gombe Abba, 149; reign and death of, 152–53
Suleimanu (Liman Adandaya), Sarkin Katagum (ca. 1814–16): appointed emir, 117; deposed, 118; appointments made by, 126
Sumbe, 89

Takoko, Battle of, 140
Tangale: survival of, 82; Pindiga Jukun dominion over, 86; local administration among western, 150; position of eastern, 150; Kwairanga chastises western, 155
Tangale-Waja: Kwararafa control of, 85–86; Buba Yero raids, 95

Tappi, 85
Tarangara, 87
Tatagana, Sarkin Arewan Hadejia: kills Ahmadu dan Sambo Digimsa, 140; background and status of, 144; declares Umaru emir, 144; and invasion by Tenemu, 201–2; murdered, 202
Taxation and tribute: assessment and collection of, 19, 30–31, 43, 187; annual proceeds of, 53; collection in Gombe, 150, 152, 157–58; and Mallam Jibril, 163; and founders of Ningi State, 187; and Fulanin Mare, 190–91; and the Katagum Civil War, 196
Tebu (Teda), 61
Tenemu, Sarkin Damagaram: annexes Fulani and Tuareg territory, 201; invades Hadejia, 201–2; destroys Guri, 202; plunders Miga, 203
Tera: of Kafarati, 7 n. 7, 9 n. 12; Pindiga Jukun dominion over, 86; Fulanin Tara communities among, 87; Gombe fiefholders of, 87, 89, 101; Fulani campaigns among, 93; local administration among, 150; Kwairanga chastises towns of, 152
Territorial organization: patterns of, in Border States, 9–11; in Gombe Emirate, 99–102, 150, 152; in Katagum Emirate, 117, 126–31; in Hadejia Emirate, 199–200, 211–14
Teshena, Kingdom: pays tribute to mai, through Galadiman Bornu, 60–62, 107; etymology of name of, 103; history of, 103–4, 106–7; Islam in, 106
Teshena, Town: recovery of Bornu spoil at, 113; Mallam Zaki conquers, 116; Buhari occupies, 143
Tijaniyya Brotherhood, 43, 177
Titled office (*sarauta*):
in Border States: qualifications for, 14, 17–18; rank ordering of, 14; succession to, 15–17; competition for, 18; functions and perquisites of, 18–19; significance of, 41, 44
in Gombe: appointment to and removal from, 152; ranking of, 159; growth of slaves in, at Hadejia, 212, 213 and n. 47
in Katagum: *'yan sarki*, 117, 126–28, 212; ranking of, 131; competition for, 131; installation into, 132 and n. 93
Tilde, 156, 166
Timbuktu, 64 n. 19
Tinda, 97
Tirwun, 84
Tongo, 156, 166
Torodbe Clan, 65
Trade, local: slaves as article and medium of exchange in, 36, 128 n. 89; in Katagum, 128 n. 89
Trade, long-distance: slaves as medium of exchange in, 36; slaves as article of, 36, 128 n. 89, 200 n. 4; and Western N'gizim, Bedde, and Tuareg, 61; in Auyo City before 1800, 106; in early nineteenth-century Katagum, 128 n. 89; Gambaki as a center of, 143; Rabeh and, 195 and n. 56, 196; in late nineteenth-century Katagum, 195, 210–11; in late nineteenth-century Hadejia, 205, 210–11; and Gumel, 205
Tuareg: interfere with northeast Nigeria travelers, 61; devastate northern Bornu, 62; Shaikh Usuman preaches among, 65
Tubule, 97

Tukulma: founded, 156, 177; besieged, 177; Emir Umaru moves court to, 177
Tukur, Sarkin Gombe (ca. 1895–98): appointed santuraki and dan buram, 160; aborted appointment as emir, 160; raids Kerikeri with Mallam Jibril, 163; grievances of, against Zailani, 175; appointed yerima, then emir, 175–76; reign of, 176
Tukur, Sarkin Kano (1893–94): appointed emir, 209; attitude of fellow emirs to, 209 and n. 35; and the Kano Civil War, 209–10; death of, 210
Tukur dan Sambo Digimsa: appointed emir, 140 n. 33, 203 and n. 14; exiled to Kano and Katagum, 140 n. 33, 203 n. 14; sultan refuses to recognize, 203, 204 and n. 15
Tumfafi, 187–88, 192
Tumfafi, Battle of, 188
Tushim, 118

Uban daki: administrative role of, in Border States, 13–14; in Katagum, 128–30; in Gombe, 158–59; in Hadejia, 212–13
Udubo, Town: Mallam Zaki fails in attack on, 115; incorporated into Katagum, 116; Lawanawa fiefholders of, 126, 182, 183 n. 9, 186; Kerikeri raids on fief-area of, 126, 186; relative importance of, as fief-area, 183 n. 9; Sarkin, 196–97
Umar, Shehu Bornu (ca. 1837–80): relations with Sokoto of, 135 n. 9; supports Buhari, 137
Umaru, Sarkin Bauchi (ca. 1883–1902): and allied expedition to Bormi, 165, 166 and n. 47; mediates Gombe Civil War, 177 and n. 94
Umaru, Sarkin Gombe (1898–1905): appointed tafida, 161, 175; embitterment of, 175; appointed and deposed as yerima, revolts, 176; recognition of, as emir, 177; and the Gombe Civil War, 177–78
Umaru, Sarkin Hadejia (ca. 1863–65): appointed Sarkin Auyo, 143–44; proclamation and approval of, as emir, 144–45, 200–1; and Tenemu of Damagaram, 201–2; depositions and murders by, 202; mental derangement of, 202 and n. 11; end of reign of, 202–3
Umaru dan Ali, Sultan of Sokoto (1881–91), 13 n. 24, 170
Umaru dan Ardo Abdua: and the Bornu jihad, 108; sends Sambo Digimsa to Shaikh Usuman, 133; and the Hadejia jihad, 134; death of, 134
Unuk, 139
Usuman, Sarkin Shira, 194
Usuman dan Fodio, Shaikh: and the Bornu jihad, 64, 107–13; life and work, before 1804, 65, 91; emigrates from Degel, 65; Buba Yero disobeys, 91; recalls Buba Yero, 93–94; authorizes Gombe jihad, 94; state offices authorized by, 100, 117, 214; appoints Buba Yero sarkin yaki, 100 n. 69; and Mallam Zaki, 115; gives Sambo Digimsa a flag, 133–34, 213 n. 47; Mahdism and, 168
Usuman Subande, 90

Vansina, Jan, 40, 49 n. 10, 56 n. 16
Village area, boundaries of, 11

Wacha, 112 n. 37
Wade, 87
Waja: Pindiga Jukun dominion over, 86; Gombe fiefholders of, 86, 101, 154; Fulanin Jera communities among, 87, 154; Yerima Suleimanu raids, 98; nineteenth-century position of, 150; Kwairanga chastises the Plain, 152, 155
Wakkaltu, 166
Walama, 88, 90 n. 30
Walls and stockades, in Border States, 45, 50
Wawa: Buba Yero captures, 96; Yeriman Suleimanu based at, 98; Gombe fiefholder of, 101; Mallam Jibril controls, 166
Weaponry: Bornuese, under al-Kanemi, 121; in early nineteenth-century Katagum, 128 n. 89; used by Mallam Jibril and Gombe, 167; Tenemu of Damagaram imports and manufactures own, 201
Wesu, Sarkin Azare: appointments of, 117, 126; assassinated, 124–25
Wodaabe Fulani, 68
Written sources: for the Border States, 39–40, 56–57; for the Sokoto Caliphate, 53; verification and value of, 55–57

Yaiyu, Lawanawa fiefholders of, 182–83
Yaji, Sarkin Kano (ca. 1349–85), 84
Yakin Gamawa. *See* Katagum Emirate, civil war in
Yakin Yusubenchi. *See* Kano, Emirate, civil war
Yakubu, Sarkin Bauchi (ca. 1805–45): campaigns with Buba Yero, 97; conflict with Buba Yero, 97–98; and Buriburi Fulanin Mare, 120–21; and al-Kanemi, 122–23; besieges Misau Town, 124
Yakubu, Sarkin Gobir (ca. 1795–1801), 106
Yayari, 203 n. 14
Yola, 170 and n. 62
Yorubaland, 59 n. 1
Yungur, 93, 94 n. 42
Yusufa, Sarkin Shira: appointed to Azare, Udubo, and Shira fiefs, 126, 183; nominated for the throne, 182; deposed and exiled, 183
Yusufu dan Sarkin Kano Abdullahi: attitude of fellow emirs to, 209 and n. 35, 210; and the Kano Civil War, 209–10; seeks allies, 209–10; death of, 210
Yusufu, Sarkin Auyo, 134

Zaberma, 138 n. 22
Zabi, 192
Zaburam, 201, 206
Zai, 161
Zailani, Sarkin Gombe Abdulkadir (ca. 1882–88): appointed tafida and yerima, 159–60; appointed emir, 160 and n. 29; executes and deposes Gombe officials, 160 and n. 30; appointments made and planned by, 160–62; and Mallam Jibril, 162–63; personality of, 164; desertion and death of, 164
Zamfara, 65, 140
Zaria, City, 85 n. 14, 131 n. 91, 187
Zaria, Emirate, 187
Zaune, 156
Zinder. *See* Damagaram
Zubeir Pasha, 172
Zubuki, 196 n. 57